The Confusions of Pleasure

D0916438

The Confusions
of Pleasure

*Commerce and Culture
in Ming China*

Timothy Brook

UNIVERSITY OF CALIFORNIA PRESS
Berkeley   Los Angeles   London

University of California Press
Berkeley and Los Angeles, California

University of California Press, Ltd.
London, England

First Paperback Printing 1999

Library of Congress Cataloging-in-
Publication Data

Brook, Timothy, 1951–
    The confusions of pleasure : commerce and
culture in Ming China / Timothy Brook.
        p.   cm.
    Includes bibliographical references and
index.
    ISBN 978-0-520-22154-3 (pbk. : alk. paper)
    1. China—History—Ming dynasty, 1368–
1644. 2. China—Commerce—History.
I. Title.
DS753.B76   1998
951'.026—dc21
                                    97-8838
                                    CIP

Manufactured in the United States of America

12   11   10   09   08   07   06
12   11   10   9   8   7   6   5

For Jonah, Taylor, Katie, and Vanessa,
each in a different time
and a different way

Let the state be small and the people few:
So that the people . . .
   fearing death, will be reluctant to move great distances
   and, even if they have boats and carts, will not use them.
So that the people . . .
   will find their food sweet and their clothes beautiful,
   will be content with where they live and happy in their
      customs.
Though adjoining states be within sight of one another
   and cocks crowing and dogs barking in one be heard in
      the next,
yet the people of one state will grow old and die
   without having had any dealings with those of another.

*Daode jing (The Way and Its Power): a
favorite passage of the founder of the Ming,
the Hongwu emperor (reigned 1368–98)*

How important to people are wealth and profit!

Human disposition is such that people pursue what is
profitable to them, and with profit in mind they will go up
against disaster. They gallop in pursuit of it day and night,
never satisfied with what they have, though it wears down
their spirits and exhausts them physically.

Since profit is what all people covet, they rush after it
like torrents pouring into a valley: coming and going without end, never resting day or night, never reaching the
point at which the raging floods within them subside.

Zhang Han (1511–93)

One man in a hundred is rich, while nine out of ten are
impoverished. The poor cannot stand up to the rich who,
though few in number, are able to control the majority.
The lord of silver rules heaven and the god of copper cash
reigns over the earth.   *Zhang Tao (1609)*

Contents

Illustrations

FIGURES

Aside from three Ming paintings, one statue, and a photograph, the illustrations in this book have been taken from nine Ming and Qing books, which are coded to their sources as follows:

1592   *Bianmin tuzuan* [Annotated Illustrations for the Convenience of the People]

1599   *Wanyong zhengzong* [The Correct Source for a Myriad Practical Uses], an almanac published in Fujian

1609   *Hainei qiguan* [Marvelous Sights of the Realm], an armchair tourist's pictorial guide to famous sights

1610   *Shuihu zhuan* [Water Margins], the famous Ming novel in a newly illustrated edition published in Hangzhou

1637   *Tiangong kaiwu* [The Exploitation of the Works of Nature], Song Yingxing's survey of technology published in Nanchang

HH   *Gu hanghai tu* [Ancient Navigation Map], a Qing copy of a Ming coastal mariner's route map

NK   *Nanke meng* [The Dream of Governor Nanke], an opera by Tang Xianzu (1550–1616)

ZX   *Zixiao ji* [The Purple Flute], another Tang Xianzu opera, published in Nanjing by Fuchun Hall as "the newly carved illustrated edition with punctuation and pronunciations"

YL   *Yuli chao* [Documents of the Jade Calendar], an undated popular religious text printed in the Qing dynasty

The woodcuts adorning the title page and chapter headings come from the almanac of 1599 and date each stage of the book. The Ming dynasty began and ended with years of the monkey (Winter, Fall); Jean Nicolet set out in search of China in 1634, which was a year of the dog, as was 1550 (preface, Summer); Zhang Tao published the Sheh county gazetteer in 1609, a year of the chicken (introduction); 1450 was a year of the horse (Spring).

MAPS

Preface

In the summer of 1634, Jean Nicolet (1598–1642) set out from the French colony in Québec to sort out tribal conflicts on the Great Lakes that were threatening the fur trade, Canada's small part in the world economy. Nicolet was also instructed to make his way, if he could, to the Mer de l'Ouest. Natives directed him to Lake Michigan, and over this Western Ocean, he was sure, lay China. Determined to make a good impression, he packed what he thought would be suitable for meeting Chinese. How he got his hands on a Chinese damask robe woven with flowers and multicolored birds we do not know, but by 1634 silks had been flowing from China to Europe for a century. He crossed Lake Michigan and put on his robe, only to find Green Bay.

The error strikes us as humorous because it is all out of proportion to our knowledge. Not to his. We are so far from the Ming dynasty (Nicolet drowned two years before it ended) that we forget the acquisitive passion China inspired. Stimulated by Marco Polo's eagerly read *Travels*, European adventurers like Christopher Columbus and explorers like Nicolet dreamed that the China they would find at the other end of the world would be Marco's world of stately pleasure domes and unsurpassed wealth. They were looking as well for things a little harder to the touch: porcelains, the silks in which

Nicolet robed himself, rhubarb, and other such curiosities that the
Ming economy was producing. These artifacts fetched extraordinary prices in Europe, and Europeans charted routes across the
world in the hope of cutting import costs. Canada is one of the historical accidents that resulted from this geographical miscalculation,
and Ming China the lure for miscalculating so greatly.

Nicolet's venture was not a complete failure. He explains that
when he appeared before the natives in his multicolored robe, they
mistook him for a god and devoutly agreed not to block the flow of
furs back east. We cannot know whether the Amerindians saw their
cooperation with French commerce in these religious terms, nor
whether they thought Nicolet was out of his mind for wanting to
canoe the upper tributaries of the Mississippi looking for the Western
Ocean. Eventually he had to give up his search for a northwest passage to China, returning in disappointment to Québec.

Consider Nicolet's error carefully. Perhaps we, like he, look at the
world through the wrong end of the telescope. We are used to
thinking of Europe as the center of the world in Nicolet's time
because that is what Europeans thought then and what it became
later on. But it wasn't so in Nicolet's time. Europeans may have developed a technical capacity to circumnavigate the globe, but their
"trade" was not based on markets or on efficient production at
home. It depended on plundering and enslaving others, disrupting
preexisting exchange networks, taking out precious metals, furs, and
spices at bargain prices and selling them for fortunes in Europe.
Nicolet wanted to buy from China, but he had nothing to sell. All he
had to offer was silver—pure money in Chinese eyes, and therefore
worth the trade. His search for a route to the Chinese market
reminds us that China, not Europe, was the center of the world in
Ming times. This book is a portrait of that center: not an economic
history of the Ming dynasty (that is not yet possible), but a cultural
history of a place that commerce was remaking. It is about the role
of commerce in Ming society—the pleasures its wealth brought and
the confusions that it fueled—during one *longue durée* of Chinese
time.

My interest in the Ming dynasty goes back to my student days
at Fudan University in Shanghai, when Professor Li Qingjia first
introduced me to the writings of late-Ming philosophers. That was
in the heady spring of 1976, when Shanghai was caught in the final
year of the Cultural Revolution, suspended between the high-court

politics and anticommercialism of the "Gang of Four" (all of them natives or one-time residents of Shanghai) and the world of what then passed for fashion down on Huaihai Road, where muted commercial instincts sought to inch past the political cordon. With the death of Chairman Mao Zedong later that year, China slipped from socialism to the market with a rapidity most Chinese found shocking, provoking anxieties about what in the late 1970s was called a "poverty of philosophy," then moving on to a more general sense of cultural crisis in the 1980s. Struggling with the conundrum of how to blend desire for profit with desire for moral good, Chinese in the post-Mao age found themselves reliving a contradiction that Chinese of the late-Ming dynasty knew well. From the perspective of the 1990s, when silver has become the undisputed lord of the land and the urban sex and luxury trades assume almost late-Ming-like proportions, even that debate now seems antique, a quick backward glance to a moral vision that disintegrates as China finds its place in the international division of labor.

In presenting the Ming dynasty as a coherent arc of change from ordered rural self-sufficiency in the early Ming to the decadence of urban-based commerce in the late, I am conscious of parallels with my own time. Had I not experienced the compressed journey China has taken from rural state-socialism to urban state-capitalism since the 1970s, I might not have conceived of writing this history, nor of writing it in this way. This is not to say that the narrative arises from other than Ming sources, only to acknowledge that every historian writes the past from the present.

I must thank Frederick Mote and Denis Twitchett for prompting me to write this book when they asked me to contribute a chapter on Ming communications and commerce for volume 8 of the *Cambridge History of China*. Finding myself unable to shoehorn all that I wanted to say about the dynasty into the generous format of that chapter, I ended up writing *The Confusions of Pleasure*. I am grateful to Denis for giving me the freedom to meet his commission in my own way and encouraging me to proceed with this book.

Zhenping Wang, Jun Fang, and Yunqiu Zhang, one a colleague and the others my graduate students at the University of Toronto, contributed research in an early phase of this project. For their help toward the end, I am grateful to Paul Eprile for reading the first draft and getting me on the right track for the second; Roger Des Forges for scrutinizing the second draft and reminding me to keep my paean to commerce down to two cheers; Richard von Glahn for warning me away from some of the simplifications I was making about the late-Ming economy in the third; and André Gunder Frank for pushing me always to think of Ming China in a global context. My literary agent Beverley Slopen helped to steer this book in the direction it wanted to go, and I am once again in her debt for the confidence she has shown in my writing. I am also delighted to have been able to work with Sheila Levine, Laura Driussi, and Rachel Berchten at the University of California Press, who provided warm encouragement at every step from manuscript to book. Lynne Russell compiled the index.

To the end I reserve two special debts of thanks: to Bin Wong, who critiqued the entire manuscript with the erudition of a scholar and the care of a friend; and Fay Sims, who helped me find the time and place from which I could complete the manuscript while gazing out over the blue waters of Lake Huron. I wonder if Nicolet ever saw it like this?

A Ming Chronology

THE EARLY MING (1368–1450)

1368   Zhu Yuanzhang founds the Ming dynasty and enthrones himself as the Hongwu emperor; orders every county magistrate to set up four granaries; cancels the book tax

1369   Hongwu orders every county magistrate to open a Confucian school

1380   Hongwu purges Chancellor Hu Weiyong and imposes direct imperial rule

1381   the *lijia* village registration system is universally imposed

1398   death of the Hongwu emperor

1400   date of the earliest surviving land-sale contract in the Ming

1402   Zhu Di ascends the throne after overthrowing his nephew, the Jianwen emperor, and declares the inauguration of the Yongle reign the following year

1405   Zheng He launches the first of his six expeditions into the waters around Southeast and South Asia

1415   the Grand Canal is fully restored to use

1420   the Yongle emperor confers the name Beijing on his new capital

1429   a series of seven customs barriers is installed along the Grand Canal

1433   the seventh and last of the great maritime expeditions
        reaches Africa; cotton appears as a permanent item on the
        tax registers in Songjiang prefecture

1436   a portion of the southern grain tax is commuted to silver;
        inauguration of the reign of the Zhengtong emperor

1449   the rebellion of Deng Maoqi's "silver bandits" in Fujian is
        suppressed; Beijing officials depose the Zhengtong emperor
        after he is captured by the Mongols in favor of his brother,
        who ascends as the Jingtai emperor in 1450

THE MID-MING (1450–1550)

1457   restoration of the Zhengtong emperor as the Tianshun
        emperor

1464   marginal people in the hills of the interior province of
        Huguang rebel

1465   massive flooding in central and south China sets off a
        spate of bridge building

1492   the commercial transportation of grain to the northern
        border in exchange for salt certificates is monetarized

1506–21 troubled reign of the Zhengde emperor

1506   the local costs of the courier system are met by a tax in
        silver assessed on landholdings rather than by corvée

1525   Ministry of War orders ships of more than one mast on
        the southeast coast seized, investigated, and destroyed

1527   granary quotas are severely reduced, diminishing the
        state's capacity to relieve famines

1538   first in a decade-long wave of severe famines and
        epidemics sweeps central and southeast China

1548   closure of the coast against all foreign trade

1549   Portuguese and Chinese begin regular seasonal trading
        at Sao João Island near Macao

THE LATE MING (1550–1644)

1557   Portuguese gain permission to establish a permanent
        settlement on the Macao peninsula (retroceded in 1999)

1567	the ban is lifted on maritime trade to all but Japan
1570	the first commercial route book is published in Suzhou
1573–1620	reign of the Wanli emperor
1581	Chief Grand Secretary Zhang Juzheng imposes the Single Whip Reform, by which taxes are assessed on land and paid in silver
1582	earliest reference to the publishing of private newssheets in Beijing
1587	severe nationwide famine
1602	the iconoclastic Confucian philosopher Li Zhi commits suicide in prison
1629	the Chongzhen emperor reiterates the state prohibition against female infanticide; a third of courier stations are closed for lack of funds
1638	the Beijing Gazette switches to movable type
1641	massive epidemic throughout north and central China
1642	Manchus raid into Shandong province
1644	rebels capture Beijing and the Chongzhen emperor commits suicide; the Manchus invade and declare the founding of the Qing dynasty

A Genealogy of Ming Emperors

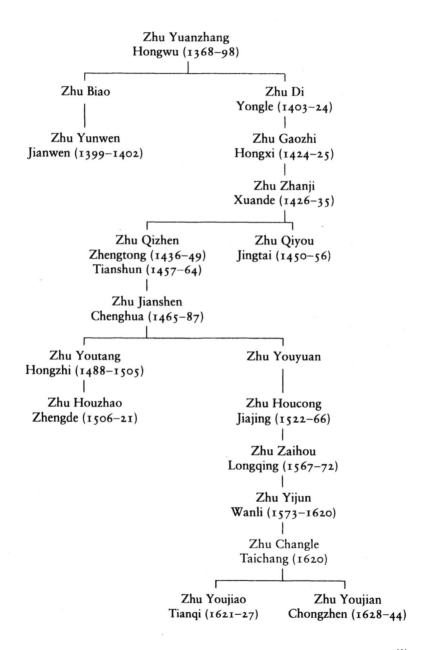

Zhu Yuanzhang
Hongwu (1368–98)

Zhu Biao

Zhu Yunwen
Jianwen (1399–1402)

Zhu Di
Yongle (1403–24)

Zhu Gaozhi
Hongxi (1424–25)

Zhu Zhanji
Xuande (1426–35)

Zhu Qizhen
Zhengtong (1436–49)
Tianshun (1457–64)

Zhu Qiyou
Jingtai (1450–56)

Zhu Jianshen
Chenghua (1465–87)

Zhu Youtang
Hongzhi (1488–1505)

Zhu Houzhao
Zhengde (1506–21)

Zhu Youyuan

Zhu Houcong
Jiajing (1522–66)

Zhu Zaihou
Longqing (1567–72)

Zhu Yijun
Wanli (1573–1620)

Zhu Changle
Taichang (1620)

Zhu Youjiao
Tianqi (1621–27)

Zhu Youjian
Chongzhen (1628–44)

Abbreviations

b.   born

d.   died

fl.   flourished

gs.   *gongsheng*, "tribute student" (university licenciate)

jr.   *juren*, "recommended man" (provincial graduate)

js.   *jinshi*, "presented scholar" (metropolitan graduate)

Introduction

Seasons of the Ming
(1609)

The Ming dynasty began with the peace of the winter season. Or so our late-Ming author (we'll leave him nameless for the moment) thought as he stood in the opening decade of the seventeenth century and looked all the way back to the fourteenth. The first half of the dynasty seemed to him the very picture of sensible order and settled life. "Every family was self-sufficient," he was sure, "with a house to live in, land to cultivate, hills from which to cut firewood, gardens in which to grow vegetables. Taxes were collected without harassment and bandits did not appear. Marriages were arranged at the proper times and the villages were secure." Men and women followed the time-honored division of household tasks, men in the fields and women at home weaving. (See figures 1 and 2.) "Deception did not sprout, and litigation did not arise." All as it should be.

A century before his own time, our author declared, the dynasty's winter of repose gave way to the bustle of spring. The sedate certainty of agriculture was edged out by the hotter speculative world of commerce: "Those who went out as merchants became numerous

Figure 1.   This mid-Ming image of the classical subsistence ideal of men harvesting rice is contradicted by the presence of a managerial landlord holding a parasol, from whose perspective the picture is composed. The harvesters are not owner-cultivators but tenants or hired laborers (*Bianmin tuzuan*, 1592).

and the ownership of land was no longer esteemed. Men matched wits using their assets, and fortunes rose and fell unpredictably." Polarizations of capability and class followed, with some families becoming rich and others impoverished. "The balance between the mighty and the lowly was lost as both competed for trifling amounts." As the prospect of wealth fueled avarice, the moral order that had held society together gave way. "Each exploited the other and every-

Figure 2. A matching image pictures the ideal of women working at textile production within the home. It too is rendered unreal by the elegant setting in which the weaver and her assistant are placed. The ideal of unity of labor within the household largely disappeared in the Ming as textile production became commoditized (*Bianmin tuzuan,* 1592).

one publicized himself." In this evil climate, "deception sprouted and litigation arose; purity was sullied and excess overflowed."

The chaotic growth of the spring season of the Ming proved mild compared to what came after. In the frantic press of the dynasty's summer starting in the latter half of the sixteenth century, "those who enriched themselves through trade became the majority, and those who enriched themselves through agriculture were few. The rich became richer and the poor, poorer. Those who rose took over, and those who fell were forced to flee. It was capital that brought power; land was not a permanent prospect." The agricultural base of society was abandoned. In its place "trade proliferated and the tiniest scrap of profit was counted up. Corrupt magnates sowed disorder and wealthy racketeers preyed." As moral rot crept in, "deception reached the level of treachery and litigation led to open fights; purity was completely swept away and excess inundated the world."

Our author completed his narrative of the seasons of the Ming with the world of his own adulthood since the 1570s. The face of Ming society was ravaged in the fall. "One man in a hundred is rich, while nine out of ten are impoverished. The poor cannot stand up to the rich who, though few in number, are able to control the majority. The lord of silver rules heaven and the god of copper cash reigns over the earth," he declared. "Avarice is without limit, flesh injures bone, everything is for personal pleasure, and nothing can be let slip. In dealings with others, everything is recompensed down to the last hair." His vision of descent into actuarial frenzy was apocalyptic. "The demons of treachery stalk," he warned. "Fights have turned to pitched battles; pounding waves wash over the hills; torrents flood the land." The sole remedy for this grim state of affairs was to "establish policies to close the gates and prevent the merchants from traveling about." But our author sensed that this remedy was impossible. All he could do was lapse into despair and offer up the standard sigh of vexation in classical Chinese when everything is going wrong: "*Juefu!*"[1]

This account of Ming time comes from the 1609 gazetteer of Sheh county.[2] Sheh was an inland county perched in the picturesque, hilly region south of Nanjing. Its gazetteer of 1609, a locally produced publication that recorded information concerning the official life and history of the county, was its first. Sheh was slow off the mark to produce a gazetteer. Most Ming counties already had one edition, if not several, by this time. Sheh's backwardness here is striking in light of its enormous reputation as the home of some of the wealthiest merchants of the age; but then, merchants were beyond the social pale of many of the gentry who wrote the gazetteers.

The man wielding the pen was the centrally appointed county magistrate, Zhang Tao. Shortly after arriving in 1607, Zhang opened discussions with the local gentry about compiling a gazetteer.

Figure 3.   This six-oared river boat is of the type Zhang Tao might have taken down the Yangzi River to reach his post in Sheh county (*Tiangong kaiwu*, 1637).

An editorial board was set up, compilers were commissioned the following year, and by 1609 the manuscript was finished and the woodblocks cut. Although it was conventional to name the magistrate as editor-in-chief, even when he did nothing, the Sheh gazetteer was very much Zhang's book and a record of his personal views. Lest there be any doubt, he marked his editorial comments dotted throughout the gazetteer with the slightly immodest byline, "Master Zhang Tao says." One of these is the essay we have just perused on the seasons of the Ming, which appears as a commentary closing the chapter on "local customs."[3] This section was where the compiler could comment on local attitudes and practices and note "whether the people are hard or pliant, lethargic or agitated,... what they like and dislike, what they take and discard, whether they move or stay in one place."[4] Since locals wanted to put the best face on their home county, in this section matters might be raised that were potentially controversial, as we shall see.

Zhang Tao is a minor figure in Ming history. In the bulky official history of the dynasty his name comes up only once.[5] But we can piece together something of his story from the gazetteers of Sheh and his home county of Huangpi, some 500 kilometers up the Yangzi River. Huangpi was in the hinterland of Wuchang, the great interior marketing center where the Han River flowed into the Yangzi, yet it was slow to be swept into the commercial stream. Huangpi in the mid-Ming was known as a quiet backwater where "the people all devote themselves to agriculture and sericulture and few go off on commercial travel." Women were almost never seen outside the home but stayed indoors from morning till evening spinning and weaving. In Zhang's youth, however, the county was coming under influences that the local gentry regarded with suspicion. "In recent years," according to the 1591 county gazetteer, "local customs are gradually weakening. A family without as much as an old broom go about in carriages and on oramented mounts and dress themselves up in the hats and clothing of the rich and eminent." Despite the poverty of the region, "in all things style now substitutes for substance."[6]

We cannot say when Zhang Tao was born into this slowly changing world. All we know of his origins is that his father, regarded as a paragon of filial piety, studied medicine to help the local people and provided the poor with free coffins. The first sure date in Zhang's biography is 1586, the year he passed the highest examination in Beijing and gained the title of *jinshi*. Unless he was exceptionally brilliant or lucky, he was probably not much under thirty when he passed his *jinshi*. This would put his birth about 1560 or slightly earlier.

His first posting was a three-year magistracy far up the Yangzi River in Sichuan province. His work there won him a strong promotion to Beijing as a supervising secretary in the Office of Scrutiny for Works. This post invested in him the power to investigate official corruption. Zhang was too outspoken. According to his one appearance in the official history, he joined the chorus of critics who attacked the mild-mannered Chief Grand Secretary Zhao Zhigao (1524–1601). Zhao Zhigao was already in his seventies when he became chief grand secretary and struggled feebly to hold to the power that his great predecessors, like the fiscal reformer Zhang Juzheng (1525–82), had concentrated in the post. Junior officials such as Zhang Tao were dead set on preventing Zhao from wielding the sort of autocratic power his predecessor had so conspicuously enjoyed in the 1570s. The official history does not give the date or substance of his attack; Zhang Tao is simply a name mentioned in passing. Falling afoul of the power brokers who dominated Beijing politics, Zhang had no choice but to retire to Huangpi. He spent the next fifteen years at home writing and staying out of politics.

When the court reversed the verdicts on the young activists who had spoken out in the 1580s, Zhang was called back to public life. His first assignment in 1607 was the magistracy of Sheh county. The county was in famine when he arrived. Punishing spring rains had washed away crops earlier in the year. Zhang watched the price of rice as a barometer of the disaster, and when it rose to .13 tael (a tael is roughly equivalent to an ounce of silver) per *dou* (10.74 liters), he released grain stocks in the county granary to moderate that price and ordered the wealthy of Sheh to buy grain from elsewhere and sell it below the market rate. As a result of his efforts, no one starved to death. Once the immediate crisis passed, he turned to dike-building to prevent further flooding. The investment proved wise, for rain would inundate the region in the following years without causing major distress in Sheh.[7]

Zhang Tao also invested in symbolic resources. That same year he restored the county's leading academy honoring the great Song philosopher and native son Zhu Xi (1130–1200); he built a pagoda on a hill deemed to have geomantic influence on the success of local sons in the civil examinations; and he restored two shrines, one to virtuous former officials and another to a local paragon of filial devotion. Shrines, academies, and pagodas symbolized the values of self-cultivation, reverence, and virtuous action that Zhang was committed to nurturing in his program of renovating local customs. Zhang also recognized the need for building practical incentives into his moral program and reformed the service levy that furnished the county office with corvée labor for maintaining local infrastructure, particularly the state courier service. His appreciative biography in the 1771 county gazetteer closes with the observation that "over his two years' residence, styles shifted and customs changed"[8]— precisely what Zhang aspired to achieve. He would have been pleased by this judgment.

As soon as Zhang's work began to take effect in Sheh, he was promoted out of the county and back to Beijing. His career went upward through a succession of posts in the capital and culminated with his appointment as governor of Liaodong, the Ming bridgehead in the northeast that would fall to the Manchus in 1644.[9] Zhang held this appointment in the second decade of the seventeenth century, prior to the Manchu annexation of the region in 1621.[10] He then retired from service and spent the remainder of his life at home in Huangpi county, where he enjoyed a local reputation for his wide experience and erudition. He lived at least until the late 1620s.

Zhang Tao was critical of his time, but he was also of his time. When he attacked the chief grand secretary, he acted not as a lone crusader but as someone who shared the commitments of his contemporaries to limit the power of that post. So too, when he attacked commerce in the Sheh county gazetteer, he voiced anxieties that disturbed others in the reform-minded but conservative wing of his generation. What sets Zhang Tao's diatribe against commerce apart from similar texts by his contemporaries is its extreme tone—which is why it caught my attention. I have ended up writing this history of the Ming dynasty in order to understand *his* history of the dynasty and why it made sense to him. By engaging in a dialogue with someone four centuries in the past, I have sought to write in some small part from inside the Ming world, using Zhang Tao as my guide.

Zhang read the history of the Ming as an inexorable fall. The dynasty had descended from the fixed moral order imposed by the dynastic founder, Emperor Taizu of the Hongwu era (r. 1368–98; also called the Hongwu emperor), toward a thoroughly commercial, and, in his eyes, morally debased, society. Commerce—personified in the evil figure of the lord of silver—is fingered as the culprit that reduced a once settled China to a world of anarchic motion where commerce set people traveling, imaginations soaring, and taboos tumbling. By allowing consumption to drive production, commerce disrupted the moral solidarity that Zhang believed obtained in pure agrarian social relations and fueled a competition that dissolved communal norms.

Zhang Tao's interpretation accepted the Hongwu emperor's claim that, by intervening in the lives of his people in thorough and often harsh ways, he was resurrecting the ancient Daoist ideal expressed in the passage from the *Daode jing* quoted on the opening page of this book. The Hongwu emperor believed that closed rural communities ruled by a little elite would restore order to a troubled realm and bring a lasting stability to his dynasty. Having lived through a childhood of intense poverty—he lost his parents in a famine, survived in a monastery until the monks were too poor to feed him, and then went begging—the Hongwu emperor regarded the idea of living and growing old in one's home village without ever going to the next, only a dog's bark away, as a heaven he had never known. As emperor he would do anything to bring that heaven down to earth. No matter that this ideal was, as we shall see, a nostalgic fiction written onto a reality more mobile and commercialized than either the Hongwu emperor or Zhang Tao was willing to admit. The emperor enjoyed enormous coercive and communicative means to impose his vision of order, and was moderately successful in doing so. His descendants were less energetic in their efforts and ultimately less committed to his goals. By Zhang Tao's time, the Hongwu vision—one part arcadian and two parts draconian—had attenuated to nothing more than a textual memory with little purchase on daily life. For Zhang to reimagine this vision was only to compound his and the emperor's nostalgia.

In terms of Zhang's understanding of what was at stake for Chinese culture, the vision's fictionality doesn't matter. Nor does it matter that he may not have grasped the larger trends that we now see and emphasize in our analysis: that China's population more than doubled through the dynasty; that merchants were drawing producers and consumers into regional and national commercial networks that neither could do without; that exports were luring Japanese and Spanish silver into the Chinese market and helping to lubricate the economy; and that the new wealth was affecting the ways in which information was circulating and knowledge being recorded. Zhang saw only a harrowing contest of rich against poor, traders against plowmen, profit against virtue. The analysis left him powerless, and feeling so. All he could do was lament, and in lamenting give us clues for tracing the contours of his world.

Not everyone at the time agreed with Zhang's grim evaluation of the changes overtaking the Ming. Zhang acknowledges the local unpopularity of his views in a dedicatory text to the City God of Sheh, in which he declares that he wrote the gazetteer with "an upright pen" and carried out the work with "an icy heart and an iron face."[11] He implies that he had been pressured to change his text and had refused. What had people objected to? His report to the deity is too tactful to say, though most likely it was his condemnation of the commercial environment of the county. Local unhappiness with Zhang Tao's pronouncements in the 1609 gazetteer meant that a replacement edition appeared in 1624, just fifteen years later (the customary interval was sixty). The magistrate who edited the 1771 edition of the Sheh gazetteer called the 1624 version "a work of reconciliation." He conceded that Zhang's 1609 gazetteer was "in form closest to true history and extremely informative." But he found the "pronouncements on public affairs strident and discordant." Zhang's comments about the lord of silver he regarded as "verging on impropriety and lacking in restraint."[12] The good merchants of Sheh still rankled from the sting of his words.

Zhang Tao's attack on silver is prescient. Silver may have been only a symbol for Zhang of the money-madness of his time. Yet silver was indeed flowing into China from Japan and the Spanish mines in South America to pay for Chinese exports just at this time. Its impact was mildly inflationary, stimulating the circulation of commodities and contributing to the social effects that so distressed Zhang. But silver no more explains the growth of Ming commerce than does moral decline. It was but one factor feeding and stimulating an economy that was already well commercialized before Zhang was born, if he had only known it. The lord of silver didn't just arrive in China unbidden. He was drawn in and absorbed by an economy that had already developed considerable commercial capacity before the Spanish mined the mountain of Potosí and the French sent Nicolet to find a northwest passage.

The Ming became a commercial world, not only despite the restoration of agrarian order that the Hongwu emperor put in place at the start of the dynasty, but as well because of it. The economic purpose of Hongwu's restrictions on mobility was to increase agricultural production. In this he succeeded. Enhanced production resulted in surplus that went into trade, and the regular circulation of surplus encouraged a move from surplus-production to commodity-production. At the same time, Hongwu's investments in communicative means to supply his armies and move his personnel (Zhang Tao must have covered at least 20,000 kilometers on official service) contributed to improvements in infrastructure that allowed commodities to circulate more easily. Merchants' cargoes flowed along the same canals as tax goods, and commercial agents traveled the same roads as government couriers, even with the same printed route guides in their hands. The Ming state provided a push to movements of people and goods—and as well of ideas and statuses—that market pull accelerated. Commercialization was not a simple U-turn from the state-dominated system of communication and state-sponsored self-sufficiency that Hongwu envisioned, but a consequence of them.

Commerce had distinctive social and cultural effects, for mobility and wealth altered and upset the expectations of most people, especially gentlemen like Zhang Tao. These effects are what interest me, and making sense of them—by following a trail from communication to commerce to culture[13]—is the intention of this book. What you are about to read is therefore a cultural rather than economic history of the Ming. Our knowledge of the economy is still too crude to undertake the latter. We are not yet near deciphering the close shifts and reversals of the sort identified in the economic history of medieval Europe. The broad brushstrokes in this book—tracing what looks like a progressive and unstoppable expansion of commerce from the late fourteenth to the mid-seventeenth century— paint out disruptions, countertrends, and regional variations we have not even learned how to detect. But the larger landscape of relentless commercial intensification and the growing unease it imparted to the people of Ming China is clear enough to let us proceed.

The thoughts that Ming people have left behind in their gazetteers, essays, epitaphs, and letters of the period make possible this account of how the experience of being Chinese changed over the dynasty as the economy excited new desires to consume and to seek pleasure. The excitements and confusions that Ming observers felt may strike us today as merely quaint, as curious cultural footnotes to China's ascent to the natural order of things. But that would be to neglect the claims of history. The reader's task will be to remember that Ming China was another place and time, a world and an era in which our assumptions, whether Chinese or Western, do not obviously apply. Their problems and delights with material civilization may not be ours, and ours may have nothing to do with theirs. We must listen for their fears and expectations, bearing in mind that when men like Zhang Tao complained, they could never have guessed that we would be listening to their despair.

The Ming was not the first time Chinese struggled with the confusions of pleasure. Tension between social stability and economic growth has been for Chinese a recurring anxiety for at least a millennium if not two, and it animates debates within the culture even today. Despite the continuity of concern, some things were different this time around, among them the changes in the world economy. As the Ming economy grew, Europeans were developing both the technical capacity to sail beyond Europe and the bullion stocks necessary to buy their way into that market. But the world economy was not yet centered on Europe in the sixteenth century. It would be centuries before the West reversed this interaction between Chinese production and European consumption with the power of technology and the drug trade. While it has become conventional to declare that "China under the Ming was losing her autonomy and becoming dependent on a world system not of her making,"[14] I would prefer to put the situation the other way round. Rather than saying that "the Chinese economy was ebbing with the tide of the Atlantic," we should think of the tide of the Atlantic as being pulled by the Chinese moon. If Europeans were striving to construct a place for themselves in the world economy, it was toward China that they were building.

Zhang Tao was not concerned with cycles beyond his dynasty or worlds beyond his own. His concern was solely with the Ming dynasty, and he pictured its rise and fall as an arc of four seasons. I have adopted his cyclical metaphor in structuring my narrative so as to capture some sense of how Ming Chinese thought about the temporal dimensions of the world they inhabited. They knew nothing of centuries (their larger unit of time reckoning was the sixty-year cycle), nor of the feudal, imperial, or late imperial periods that jostle for academic priority in China studies today.[15] What they did know is that they lived in a dynasty, that dynasties rose and fell, and that their dynasty was just as subject to the cycle of growth and decline as the rule of every other family on the Chinese throne had ever been. The particular alignment Zhang Tao makes between this cycle and the turning of the seasons from winter through fall was not conventional thinking. It was his own way of capturing the swell of change. Having no good reason to quadrisect the Ming, this book makes do with three phases of approximately equal centuries arranged in three long chapters: a beginning (winter), a middle (spring), and an end (summer), with each season starting or ending arbitrarily at midcentury.[16] To complete Zhang's metaphor, I evoke his final season, autumn, for a brief concluding chapter in which the dynasty is destroyed and the resilience of his claims tested.

In this text, he will fail. Even though Zhang Tao did not survive to witness the collapse of his dynasty, he saw himself at the end of things, trapped in a decadent era with nothing further to do or discover. Many in the late Ming shared Zhang's keen disappointment at having to live in declining times. Yet the social elite that went tragically into the crisis of dynastic collapse will be shown at the end of this book to reemerge, resting on broader bases of social power and solidly in control once again, decadence spent and order re-imposed. In drawing such conclusions, we may have to cut our cranky guide to the Ming adrift in his nostalgia for an order that had to fade and a time that was never quite as he dreamed it. Until then, we will keep him with us. If the things he detected seemed real enough to him, we must find out why.

Dramatis Personae

in order of appearance

ZHANG TAO (js. 1586), native of Huguang; capital official sidelined for attacking the chief grand secretary; magistrate and chronicler of Sheh county, the home of many Huizhou merchants; critic of Sheh's commercial customs; our guide to the fortunes of the dynasty

ZHU YUANZHANG (1328–98), orphan from the poor north end of South Zhili; founder of the dynasty; keen and sometimes desperate emperor for the three decades of the Hongwu reign (1368–98); imperial ancestor to whom Zhang Tao looked back with nostalgic respect

CH'OE PU (1454–1504), Korean official; head of a group shipwrecked on the Zhejiang coast in 1488; diarist of the homeward journey up the Grand Canal and back to Korea; enthusiast of wealthy Jiangnan and disparager of the comfortless north

ZHANG YUE (1492–1553), scholar from coastal Fujian; prominent provincial official and statecraft activist; editor of his native county's gazetteer of 1530

YE CHUNJI (1532–95), native of Guangdong; first-time magistrate in Zhang Yue's home county; first official to draw county maps on the basis of on-site topographical surveys; victim of local political vengeance that sidelined his career for seventeen years

HUANG BIAN (fl. 1570), Huizhou merchant; commercial traveler; resident of Suzhou, the center of commercial China; author of China's first route book

ZHANG HAN (1511–93), native of the other great commercial city, Hangzhou; scion of a wealthy textile family; minister in Beijing; author, painter, Buddhist, and essayist in retirement; close observer of the changes of the age

LI LE (1532–1618), native of Tongxiang county in the flourishing silk region of Jiaxing prefecture; official of long career; in his retirement, compiler of a gazetteer of Tongxiang's main commercial town; canny commentator on life in and out of office

ZHANG DAI (1597–1689), native of Shaoxing, Zhejiang; aficionado of Hangzhou where his extraordinarily wealthy family owned a fine residence; self-proclaimed dilettante; master stylist and eclectic historian; nostalgic recorder of the dynasty's fin de siècle

Winter

The First Century
(1368–1450)

Every family was self-sufficient, with a house to live in,
land to cultivate, hills from which to cut firewood, and
gardens in which to grow vegetables. Taxes were collected
without harassment and bandits did not appear. Marriages
were arranged at the proper times and the villages were
secure. Women spun and wove and men tended the crops.
Servants were obedient and hardworking, neighbors
cordial and friendly.

Zhang Tao

The first Spring Festival of the Ming dynasty ushered in a year of
the monkey. By Western reckoning, the festival was celebrated on
20 January 1368. Then as today, the first day of spring was the most
joyful and noisiest annual holiday. Accounts having been settled
the day before, people went out to greet relatives, meet friends, and
launch each other into the bustle of the coming planting and business

year. In Zhang Tao's home county of Huangpi, the highlight of the day was a procession of musicians who fluted and clanged their way out to the eastern suburb, led by members of the local gentry. There they paraded the ceremonial clay ox and the figurine of Strawgod who drove it into the new growing season. Absolutely everyone went.[1] The clamor and crowds made it the liveliest day of the year.

Zhang Tao may not have cared much for Spring Festival. At least, he certainly disliked spring. To him, the three quiet months of winter that preceded Spring Festival were best. Winter was the season he chose in his gazetteer of Sheh county as the metaphor for the spirit of settled village life in the early Ming, a spirit of self-sufficiency, diligence, and mutual accord. The dream of order was indeed strong in 1368, for China in the decades leading up to 1368 had been anything but orderly. The fourteenth century was one of the most calamitous of the last millennium, not only in China but all over the globe: one of every three winters exceptionally cold; plague flowing east and west from High Asia; famine, depopulation, and agricultural decline.[2] In keeping with the times, the Yangzi and Yellow River floodplains had been awash in armed struggle for seventeen years before 1368 as Chinese rebels contended among themselves for the right to drive the Mongols from China after their century-long occupation. Among them was Zhu Yuanzhang (1328–98). In 1367, all rivals defeated, Zhu declared that the next Spring Festival would mark the beginning of his new dynasty. On that day in 1368 he ascended the throne in Nanjing as the Hongwu ("Vast Martial") emperor. (He would be canonized after his death as Taizu ["Ultimate Ancestor"], a name by which he is also known.) In September 1368, the last forlorn Mongol emperor had been chased in disarray from the throne in Beijing. Hongwu ruled the realm.

The evil times had taken a terrible toll. The emperor knew that he ruled over a realm where "households had disappeared and the land was uncultivated." His first appointees as county magistrates made their way to their offices, or yamens, to find devastation, dearth, and desertion. "All the people have fled and disappeared," one magistrate observed when he arrived at his county on the other side of the Yangzi River from Nanjing in 1369. He set about "calling the people back, returning them to agriculture, setting up schools, and rebuilding the yamen." Gradually former residents were induced to return and reclaim the war-torn landscape. Magistrates were judged on the basis of how many came back.[3]

Once reimposed, stability had to be protected. Emperors of the earlier Song dynasty had sought stability by securing the loyalty of elites and giving them a stake in the new regime. Hongwu, a former Buddhist novice and himself a victim of midcentury famines, had a poor man's distrust of elites. He turned for his allies to the common people and spent the three decades of his reign devising regulations more interventionist than anything a Chinese state had ever imposed, and exceeded only by the Communist Party six centuries later. The emperor's vision of an agrarian order was the Daoist model of a little elite of virtuous elders supervising self-sufficient villages and forwarding modest taxes to a minimalist state. Cultivators were tied to their villages, artisans bound to state service, merchants charged with moving only such necessities as were lacking, and soldiers posted to the frontier. Administration would be placed in the hands of a small educated class on whom the people themselves would keep vigilant watch.

Hongwu's goal was to immobilize the realm. People were to stay put and could move only with the permission of the state. The emperor imagined 20 *li* (12 kilometers) to be the farthest distance anyone should go (exactly the distance that a thirteenth-century English legal treatise used to define "neighboring," as this was the maximum distance a short-hauler could be expected to cover to get to market and back in a single day[4]). Hongwu wrote into law an outer limit of 100 *li* (58 kilometers); one needed a route certificate to go any farther, and to do so without one cost a person a flogging of eighty strokes. Undocumented travel abroad entailed execution upon return. *The Ming Code,* the compendium of the core laws of the dynasty, sought to block social as well as physical mobility. The son of an artisan was an artisan, a soldier's son a soldier, and the penalties for switching occupations just as severe as those for jumping physical barriers.[5] This was Zhang Tao's winter of content.

A BRICK IN THE WALL

THE KILNMASTER

Lu Li made bricks in central China in the first decade of the Hongwu reign. Lu Li is a simple name for a simple man who had no education other than having mastered the technique of firing clay bricks. Brick making was one of the lowliest jobs an artisan could do. Lu

Figure 4.   At a brick kiln, the kilnmaster checks the
temperature as an assistant douses the kiln to induce
superficial glazing (*Tiangong kaiwu*, 1637).

was a step above the ordinary laborer, however, for he operated the
kiln. This could be delicate work, since the kilnmaster had to make
sure that the temperature inside the kiln stayed at a level that caused
the clay to shimmer with the color of molten gold or silver. He also
had to know when to quench the kiln with water so as to produce
the surface glaze.[6] (See figure 4.)

To anonymous laborers fell the less skilled stages of brick production: mixing clay and water, driving oxen over the mixture to
trample it into a thick paste, scooping the paste into standardized

Figure 5.   The brick maker in the foreground fills
the wooden mold with clay, then dresses the brick's
surface with a finishing wire strung on a bow
(*Tiangong kaiwu,* 1637).

wooden frames (to produce a brick roughly 42 centimeters long, 20
centimeters wide, and 10 centimeters thick), smoothing the surfaces
with a wire-strung bow, removing them from the frames, printing
the fronts and backs with stamps that indicated where the bricks
came from and who made them, loading the kilns with fuel (likelier
wood than coal), stacking the bricks in the kiln, removing them to
cool while the kilns were still hot, and bundling them onto pallets
for transportation. It was hot, filthy work. (See figure 5.)

Really, we know nothing about Lu Li. We know only his name. You can find it on one of the bricks cemented vertically in the upper wall of what used to be called the Gate of Assembled Treasures, which was the gate in the south wall of the inner city of Nanjing. Nanjing had been Zhu Yuanzhang's headquarters since 1356, and it became the capital of the dynasty in 1368. Zhu had begun the work of building the massive wall around Nanjing in 1366, though little of it still stands today. The Gate of Assembled Treasures is the only full gate still intact. Allegedly it got the name from a great porcelain dish (a "basin of assembled treasures" or *jubao pen*) buried in its foundations. This dish had been in the possession of the fabulously wealthy Shen Wansan. Zhu Yuanzhang had acquired it in a fit of jealous desire—or as a gesture of righteous leveling, depending on your perspective. He forced Shen to pay for roughly a third of the cost of building the city walls, took over the man's private garden as an internment camp for the Ministry of Justice, and confiscated his household goods to furnish the palace. He completed his expropriations by exiling Shen's entire family to virtual extinction on the frontier as border guards.[7]

Walk around the terrace on top of the Gate of Assembled Treasures and you soon discover that many of the long gray bricks have inscriptions stamped into their surfaces. Among them is at least one of Lu Li's bricks (see figure 6). Its reverse side reads like this:

Ten-Tithing Xi Junweng	Tithing Head Fang Chaozhang
Kilnmaster Lu Li	
Brick makers	Guangfu Monastery

Lu Li's name does not appear out of pride in his work. It was legally required, following a practice that goes back almost two millennia before the Ming, when the state of Qin required weapon makers to inscribe their names on the weapons they made. Signing meant that each individual piece could be traced to its maker should the

Figure 6.   Lu Li's brick is currently embedded in a
Nanjing city gate.

weapon prove substandard. The same logic of responsibility was
what put Lu Li's name on the brick.

The two other names on the brick are the threads by which we
can begin to unravel how Zhu Yuanzhang got the Nanjing city wall
built. The men named are neither officials nor brick makers but
officers of the dynasty's comprehensive system for registering the
population and assessing each household for corvée and other
services. Known as the *lijia* or hundreds-and-tithings system, it was
instituted throughout the Yangzi Valley region in 1371. The *lijia*

system grouped ten households together into a *jia* or "tithing"; ten adjacent tithings were combined into a *li* or "hundred" (*tithing* and *hundred* are rough equivalents used in medieval England). Each tithing had a "tithing head" (*jiashou*), a duty that rotated annually among the member households. The ten wealthiest households in the community were set apart, however, to serve as "hundred captains" (*lizhang*) again on a ten-year rotational basis. Over them were appointed up to half a dozen regional "tax captains" (*liangzhang*).[8]

Fang Chaozhang was a tithing head. His name appears on Lu Li's brick because he was responsible for seeing that anything levied from his tithing (whether grain or bricks) be passed up to his hundred captain, in this case Xi Junweng. Xi's title of "ten-tithing" captain suggests that he was one of the nine captains on an off-duty year, appointed specially to handle the brick levy so as to leave the on-duty hundred captain free for his tax duties. Xi would have been a figure of greater wealth and prestige than Fang, particularly at this early stage in the dynasty before village elites fully realized the scale of the burden that the *lijia* system placed on the rich and did their best to evade service.

Exactly where and when did Lu Li live? We could find out by prying the brick out of the wall, for a stamp on the obverse side records the names of the assistant county magistrate to whom Xi Junweng reported and the assistant prefect to whom the assistant magistrate reported. Before it was cemented into place, the two sides of each brick revealed what prefecture and county it had come from and who held office at the time it was made, and therefore roughly when it was made.[9] Short of removing the brick, however, there is no sure way to determine where it was made and how far it had to travel. There is only one clue, the Buddhist monastery named on Lu Li's side of the brick.

Monasteries were registered in the *lijia* as fiscal households, just like regular households, and were expected to provide the same labor services to the state. Guangfu Monastery must have been one of the ten households under Fang Chaozhang. Its fiscal burden in the brick-making levy was to feed the laborers who made the bricks under Lu Li's supervision. It is unlikely that the laborers were monks. They were probably just men of the local tithing who were levied for their labor. Since the Ming fiscal system did not provide wages for those corvéed into its service but did arrange to feed them, Guangfu Monastery's role was probably to provide them with their

food while they were working. It may also have borne a portion of
the transport costs. This burden was considerable, since one brick
weighed about twenty kilograms and the standard barge load was
no less than forty bricks.[10] The numbers of boats and crews needed
to ship millions of bricks in forty-brick consignments to Nanjing
must have been enormous, but that cost was parceled out to the
tithings from which the bricks originally came. Guangfu Monastery
may have been assessed for some of these costs.

How far did Lu Li's brick have to travel? Short of removing his
particular brick from the wall to read the obverse side, the only way
to find out is to try to track down Guangfu Monastery. Unfortu-
nately, Guangfu ("broad good fortune") was a monastic name widely
used. Map 1 shows eight counties in three provinces within the
watershed upriver from Nanjing for which I have been able to locate
a Guangfu Monastery: two in South Zhili (the metropolitan region
around Nanjing that was equivalent to a province), one in Huguang
province (now divided between Hubei and Hunan), and five in
Jiangxi.[11] The closest Guangfu Monastery was in Dangtu 100 kilometers upriver from Nanjing. The farthest, in Gan county, was
1,500 kilometers from Nanjing, though at that distance it may have
been excused from the brick levy. So let us suppose that Lu Li's
brick came from the Guangfu Monastery next most distant from
Nanjing. (See map 1.)

That monastery sat in Yongfeng county in the hills of eastern
Jiangxi. The river route from Yongfeng to Nanjing, a distance of
1,060 kilometers, was regularly used to ship grain to the capital and
would have handled brick barges just as well. The compiler of the
Yongfeng county gazetteer of 1544 records nothing about brick
making, though he makes a point of saying that he has not bothered
to record ordinary local products, and bricks were hopelessly common. Nor does he reveal anything about how the *lijia* system operated in Yongfeng, noting only that it still survived as of 1544 as a
tax registration system.[12] It is no surprise that someone as common
as Lu Li does not appear in the gazetteer. Thus we have no way of
knowing whether this Guangfu Monastery was the one that fed the
laborers working for Lu Li, nor when Lu Li made this brick, until
such time as the Gate of Assembled Treasures is torn down.

At the time it was installed, the *lijia* system shaped the visible
organization of the countryside. It was almost inevitable, though,
that the system would eventually fall short of realizing the under-

Map 1.   Central China, ca. 1370, showing the counties in Jiangxi and the surrounding provinces along the Yangzi River upstream from Nanjing from which Lu Li's brick could have come.

lying ideal of an undivided community reproduced uniformly and obediently across the Chinese landscape. Hongwu acknowledged as much in a directive issued to the Ministry of Rites in the spring of 1395, in which he observed: "In every hundred there are poor people and there are rich people." The *lijia* hundreds were not the undifferentiated communities of mechanical solidarity of which he dreamed, but natural villages stratified by wealth and kinship. Making the wealthiest responsible for seeing that taxes were paid had not achieved much leveling of wealth, though some captains had indeed found these posts so burdensome as to be ruined by them. Who knows how Xi Junweng had fared? The tithings and hundreds were communities of unequal members, and their inequality worked against the equalizing logic of the system. In 1395, Hongwu could only exhort that, should someone in the community face ruin, "the rich should come to his assistance with their wealth and the poor with their labor." This, he lamely concludes, was his policy for eliminating poverty in the realm.[13]

Hongwu's expectations of *lijia* communities were not entirely unrealistic for the early Ming when he ordered his officials to work to the letter of the law. The gates and walls of Nanjing are proof of the revenue extraction the *lijia* made possible, so long as it was closely supervised. But as closed villages opened and exchange worked its way into the spaces between rich and poor, the mechanical solidarity implicit in the *lijia* model could not be expected to animate daily life, or even tax collection. Hongwu's passion for an obedient social order made him want to bend the reality of villages of all shapes and sizes to his vision of a self-replicating decennial order. Under the reigns of the next four emperors down to 1449, reality slowly bent back. In the mid-Ming the *lijia* would be little more than a nominal tax-registration system, which it was in Yongfeng by 1544.

THE CENSUS

What the *lijia* system did accomplish well, at least under Hongwu, was to provide the mechanism for conducting a reasonably good census, the basis of effective taxation. The first enumeration was in 1381, the year the *lijia* system became fully operational. Historical demographers are confident that the *lijia* system captured most of the people then living in the Ming realm, with the exception of parts of the southwest. The official total was 59,873,305 "mouths" (the Chinese unit of census reckoning). (For comparison's sake, England at the time in the wake of the Black Death had declined from over 6 million to about 2.2 million.) The only problem in using the *lijia* to count mouths was that registration entailed direct fiscal obligations: the more mouths a household had, the higher its tax assessment; and the more households a county had, the higher its tax quota. Inducement was therefore great at all levels to underreport the number of households and the mouths within them.

Underreporting was made a capital crime in 1381, but that didn't
dissuade at least 3 million people from disappearing at the next
decennial census in 1391. Once the central government tallied the
provincial figures, it realized the scale of miscounting and two years
later published a revised total of 60,545,812.[14] The adjustment was
conservative. Actual population was at least 65 million;[15] probably
it was closer to 75 million.[16] Demographic recovery continued, but
enumeration did not, for censuses after 1393 wobbled between 51
and 62 million, losing all contact with actual population.

As population growth was a sign of a well-ordered realm, the
political implications of apparent demographic stagnation were unhappy. The Xuande emperor told his courtiers in 1428: "Growth
occurs basically when the people have a chance to engage in their
livelihoods, whereas decline is due to palace construction and military
adventures."[17] Population was actually rising under Xuande. It was
just that people were wandering from their original places of residence and slipping off the tax rolls: "entrusting themselves as wards
of powerful families" and in the process vanishing from the population registers; "or else posing as artisans and sneaking into the
two capitals" to disappear among the unregistered urban poor; "or
else claiming to hold state monopoly certificates [to trade in salt
or tea] and traveling as merchants to the four quarters, loading
their entire families onto boats and leaving not a trace behind."[18]
Itinerant commerce, urban manufacture, and landlordism were
well enough developed by 1432, when Governor Zhou Chen of
South Zhili reported this state of affairs to the Xuande emperor,
that Hongwu's vision began to seem little more than a legislator's
memory. Where the state had pushed people in one direction, the
need to survive pulled them in the other, and indeed was pulling
them into underpopulated regions in the interior and slowly shifting
the distribution of population away from China's eastern half.[19]

It was clear to the new regime that a lot of land north of the
Yangzi River was lying fallow and generating no tax revenue, and
Hongwu and his son, the Yongle emperor (r. 1403–22), paid much
attention to filling in the spaces rather than allowing natural drift
to take care of the problem. According to Yuan census records for
1290, the population north of the Yellow River amounted to a
meager 6 percent of the Chinese whole, whereas the population
south of the Yangzi accounted for 85 percent.[20] This extreme imbalance projects a statistical distortion since soldiers and unfree

labor were excluded from the census, yet the north did suffer under the Mongols. The rebellion against the Mongols did nothing to alleviate the poverty and depopulation there, and did much to make things worse in the Yangzi Valley. To adjust population to resources, the Ming court imposed a series of relocation schemes between 1364 and 1405, some voluntary, most forced.[21] The earliest forced relocations (between 1364 and 1389) moved people living south of the Yangzi to the emperor's home prefecture of Fengyang, a chronically poor region between the Yangzi and Yellow Rivers that the Yuan-Ming transition had further depopulated. The Hongwu emperor soon gave up his dream of making Fengyang his capital and decided instead to center his regime in the prosperous lower Yangzi region, best known by its casual name of Jiangnan ("south of the Yangzi"). The next wave of relocations was to the region around Nanjing, which did become his capital; wealthy residents of northern Zhejiang were targeted. (At the same time, Hongwu was concerned to get rid of military widows in Nanjing and in 1370 and again in 1373 offered them incentives to go back to their native places.)[22]

Beijing was the third destination for forced migrants, initially (1370–89) to fill in a buffer zone against the Mongols, then later (after 1403) to build up the local population for what was to become the primary capital. The relocated had a knack for taking off as soon as they could, however, and slipped through the holes in the registration system. Other schemes in north China were mounted to get fallow land under the plow, mostly moving peasants from relatively protected areas of Shanxi into northern Henan and southern North Zhili.[23] The effect of all this movement was to reshape the demography of the north. About 1416, however, these schemes were abandoned. Rather than develop poor areas by subsidizing in-migration (if poverty was due to a lack of labor) or out (if poverty was due to lack of enough land to go around), the government shifted to a policy of encouraging local development. Sponsored and forced migrations had been short-term solutions to postwar problems; development in situ would be the state's long-term preference. Thenceforth, people were made to stay where they were—in sight of the state and its tax-collectors. Even mendicant Buddhist monks were to be checked to see that they had legal ordination certificates, lest would-be migrants shave their heads to look like monks and sneak past officers at bridges and fords.[24]

It didn't work. The poor continued to search for land and the destitute for survival.[25] Some had no choice but to flee, leaving the young and elderly to collapse and die on the roads, as an official observed to the Yongle emperor during the massive famine that struck north China in 1421, just as the capital was being moved there from Nanjing.[26] By 1436, when the government ordered every county and prefecture in the country to compile registers of all households that had vanished, the precise relationship between administrative units and village boundaries dreamed of by the Hongwu emperor had become too blurred to track who was missing. The plan in 1436 was to combine these registers into a national register of illegal migrants, which would then be distributed to all county magistrates. It was never realized. There had just been too much spatial reorganization, too many migrants, and no way to trace their movements using the communicative means available to the Ming state, as the emperor noted despondently five years later.[27] Getting bricks to Nanjing was looking more and more like an exceptional moment in a world increasingly indifferent to direction from the center.

THE BURDEN OF COMMUNICATION

Part of the problem was that Ming China was vast. Its population of 75 million grew steadily and was too large not to seep through the holes in the *lijia* basket. Its territory required months to cross (the longest route that a foreign tribute mission could take, from the border of Yunnan to Beijing, was rated for a journey of ninety-six days).[28] To rule all these people and "all under heaven," and to rule them for "ten thousand years," as long-term dynastic survival was expressed with polite exaggeration, were the ideals of every dynasty. Scale along both axes demanded large communicative means. To appreciate the communicative burden of centralized rule, consider the following four notices issued during the Hongwu reign:

In 1370, the Hongwu emperor decided that every person in the realm should wear the so-called four-quarters pacification turban (*sifang pingding jin*). (See figure 7.) He ordered that samples be circulated so that everyone would know what this particular form of headwrap looked like.[29] Hongwu yearned for uniformity, though I have found no record of whether everyone, or anyone, wore it. Hongwu also yearned for differentiation. He had patterns for women's clothes circulated to dictate how wives of officials should

Figure 7.   This ancestral portrait of the Hongwu emperor has idealized the rough features of the real Zhu Yuanzhang. Reproduced courtesy of the National Palace Museum, Taipei.

dress—"to get rid of Mongol customs," he said, but also not to appear like commoners. The attempt must have failed, for in 1390 he repeated the order and backed it up with an offer to provide a subsidy for any official family that could not afford to make clothes in the required style.[30]

Also in 1370, he declared the use of salutations such as "I bow my head" (*dun shou*) or "I prostrate myself a hundred times" (*bai bai*) in private correspondence as "contrary to ritual" and ordered the Ministry of Rites to devise and circulate more suitable models for formal greetings. He followed this directive with another in 1373 banning the use of the parallel-prose (*pianti*) style in laudatory texts, not so much to get people to say what they meant as to get their writing out of the high stylization that favored the well-educated. He ordered the ministry to circulate sample texts by Tang-dynasty authors Liu Zongyuan and Han Yu as models for composition.[31]

In 1375, the emperor received a memorial from Ru Taisu, a bureau secretary in the Ministry of Justice, that was 17,000 characters long. He had the memorial read aloud to him. When the lector got to the 16,370th character, Hongwu took offense at two harsh comments and had the man summoned and beaten at court. The following evening when Hongwu finally had the whole text read to him in bed, he decided that in fact four of Ru's five recommendations in the memorial were quite good, and at court session the next morning ordered that they be carried out. He admitted that he had erred in getting angry, but blamed the victim for having left the substance of the memorial to the last 500 characters. Arguing that a truly loyal official should not trouble an emperor with 16,500 characters' worth of fluff, he extracted the last 500 characters as a model of memorial-writing, added a preface explaining his distaste for florid prose, and ordered it distributed throughout the realm as a model of how officials should write.[32] Clarity of communication mattered in the running of so vast a bureaucratic operation, though who knows whether he was successful in trimming the loquaciousness of his other officials down to precise prose.

For a final example, in 1394 the Hongwu emperor ordered the Ministry of Works to publish a notice to his subjects that they were obliged to cultivate mulberry and jujube trees. Every *lijia* hundred should set aside 2 *mu* (1,390 square meters) for these crops.[33]

These interventions are interesting for what they say about the emperor's vision of the world he wished to rule, as well as his sense of what an emperor should do. But they are equally interesting as evidence of the communicative means he thought the state should control. These instructions required not only producing and distributing directives and models so that all his subjects would know of them, but also collecting and processing written responses. The 1394 order to plant mulberries and jujubes—for which I have found no evidence of compliance—was not designed to go just one way. It stipulated that anyone growing more than his allotted share had to report the amount above quota to the local magistrate, presumably because of tax consequences. Anyone who failed to make this report would be banished to military service (and the prospect of an early death) on the southwest border. Further, the magistrate was required to combine these reports into bound files and submit them in a return memorial to the ministry. The Ministry of Works was expected to receive these reports from over a thousand county magistrates, examine the data for consistency, summarize it, submit a report of that summary to the throne and the appropriate ministries, and, last, file them away in storage so arranged that they could be retrieved and updated whenever new reports of above-quota mulberry cultivation came in from the provinces.

To manage the heavy flow of communication between the capital and the field administration, an Office of Reports Inspection (*Chayan si*) was set up in 1370 to receive officials' written submissions, or memorials to the emperor. In August 1377 this office was expanded and upgraded under the new name of the Office of Transmission (*Tongzheng si*). The emperor had announced the previous month that anyone could submit a memorial to the throne, commoner and official alike, so long as it concerned affairs of importance. (In fact, commoners could memorialize the throne only to impeach their local magistrate—which some did.)[34] The Office of Transmission may have been enlarged in the expectation that this edict would elicit an enlarged flow of communications to the throne.

When a memorial arrived, duplicates were made and the original sent to the emperor. The copies were transmitted to the Office of Supervising Secretaries. The emperor read the document, attached his rescript outlining what the state's response would be, then sent both memorial and rescript to the Office of Supervising Secretaries to route to the appropriate department for action. The Office of Transmission was thus in a critical position in the chain of communication between the emperor and his subjects—and by the beginning of the Yongle era its director had become a powerful court official who could bring issues directly before the emperor.[35] Failure by that office to report to the throne a document it received was regarded as a serious offense. As the Yongle emperor thundered when on one occasion he discovered that a few memorials on minor matters had not reached him, "Stability depends on superior and inferior communicating; there is none when they do not. From ancient times, many a state has fallen because a ruler did not know the affairs of the people."[36]

After a memorial had been seen by the emperor, it and his rescript were edited into a court record (*chaobao*). From this, a summary was prepared for the Beijing Gazette (*dibao*), a regular government bulletin that circulated in handwritten copies. Memorials and edicts constituted the largest part of the gazette, but other topics relative to state affairs were also reported: promotions and demotions, military affairs, foreign relations, and natural disasters. Officials in the field administration were so keen to know what was happening at the center that some provincial administrations set up offices in the capital and hired scribes to copy the gazette and send it down to their provincial capital, where it could be recopied and circulated among local officials. Copies of the gazette were archived in both capitals for the use of those assigned to edit the Veritable Record (*shilu*) of official court acts and pronouncements that was compiled following the death of each emperor.[37]

To handle the enormous volume of information and goods that the state desired to collect and circulate, the Ming state activated three partially integrated services: the courier service (*yichuan*), the postal service (*jidi*), and the transport service (*diyun*). Among them they handled the relaying of messages between the central government and the field administration, the shipping of grain and other tax goods, and the moving of soldiers and corvéed laborers. The courier service was also charged with transporting foreign visitors, several of whom wrote detailed accounts of the experience of traveling through Ming China. Two such accounts follow to bring these services to life: first, the overland conveyance of a Persian embassy from the northwest border to Beijing in 1420; second, the journey to Beijing by river and Grand Canal of a group of Koreans shipwrecked on the southeast coast in 1488.

THE CONVEYANCE OF A PERSIAN EMBASSY, 1420–22

In 1419, the Timurid ruler of Persia, Mirza Shahrukh (r. 1404–47), dispatched a large embassy to the Yongle emperor, Hongwu's usurping son. A member of the embassy, Ghiyasu'd-Din Naqqah, kept the official diary. Although his diary does not survive, portions were excerpted and entered into the court history of Persia by Hafiz Abru, who took care to preserve the observations of the original text.

The party of Persians reached the gate of Jiayu Guan at the western end of the Great Wall on 29 August 1420. After their number was counted and their names written down in an official register, they were allowed to proceed 45 kilometers to Xiaozhou, the first city within China's northwesternmost corner. As they approached Xiaozhou, the great courier station built into the west gate of the city loomed up before them. The station at Xiaozhou was the first of ninety-nine that marked the stages of the courier route between the border and Beijing. For the rest of their journey, they were entirely in the hands of the courier service (*yichuan*).

The courier service was operated under the Ministry of War to provision officials traveling on assignment, foreign envoys, and government couriers carrying communications to and from the capital. The Mongols had expanded this system of communication during the Yuan dynasty to tie together the immense distances of their realm,[38] and the Ming continued and strengthened the system. The courier service operated along a web of official land and water routes that radiated first from the capital in Nanjing and, by the time the Persians arrived, from Beijing as well (see map 2). Its routes amounted to a total distance of 143,700 *li* (84,200 kilometers). Courier stations (*yi*), which provided free accommodation, food, and transport labor to those bearing travel permits, were spaced along routes every 60 to 80 *li* (35 to 45 kilometers). Their spacing marked the stage that an official was expected to cover in a day's travel. China in the Hongwu era was serviced by 1,936 stations, though as we shall note in later chapters, fiscal tightening reduced this number over the next two centuries by close to a half.[39] Most stations were designated as either overland stations ("horse stations") or water stations, or sometimes both, depending on location and the services they were required to supply.

Courier stations tended to be located at centers of population such as county seats, and where they weren't, small towns quickly grew up around them. At most of these settlements, Ghiyasu'd-Din Naqqah was struck by the rich offerings of the markets. He could scarcely believe the first market he saw, the central market of Xiaozhou, which he says was "fifty statute yards in width completely sprinkled with water and swept up in such a manner that if for instance oil were to be spilt there it could again be gathered up." His attention was caught by the shops where butchers mixed mutton

Map 2. China, showing the principal routes of the courier system as of
1587. Xiaozhou, the first courier station to receive the Persian embassy in
1420, is at the upper left corner of the map.

and pork in profane style, and by the booths that artisans set up to
sell their wares. Their fine craftsmanship is a recurring comment in
his diary.

Eight courier stations and one military battalion serviced the Persian embassy between Xiaozhou and Ganzhou, roughly one every
45 *li* (26 kilometers). Each station was required to produce 450
mounts (horses and mules) and 50 to 60 sedan chairs. "The boys
who were in charge of the horses were called *mafu* [horse grooms],
and those who were in charge of the mules were called *luofu* [mule

grooms], while those who pulled the vehicles were called *chefu* [chair bearers]." All three types of laborers were locally conscripted to convey the embassy from station to station. The Persians found the experience of riding in sedan chairs a novelty. The diarist recounts that the chair bearers "fasten ropes to the vehicles and those very boys place them across their shoulders and pull them on. No matter whether it be raining or it be a mountainous region those boys pull the vehicles over their shoulders with force and convey them from one post-house [courier station] to another. Each vehicle is carried by twelve persons. The boys are all handsome with artificial Chinese pearls in their ears and their hair knotted on the crown of their head." The diarist was also impressed with the speed with which the courier service conveyed his party forward. The escorts on horseback who galloped ahead to the next courier station traveled faster than the swiftest couriers in the Persian Empire, he claimed.

Once at the stations, Ghiyasu'd-Din Naqqah was impressed with the resources that the courier service furnished. Via Abru's account, he observed that "whatever requirements the envoys had as regards horses, food, drink, and bedding were all provided from the courier station. Every night as long as they were there, every one of them was given a couch, a suit of silken sleeping dress, together with a servant to attend to their needs." For their sustenance, each member of the party was given, "in the measure that had already been fixed according to the rank, mutton, geese, fowls, rice, flour, honey, beer, wine, garlics and onions preserved in vinegar and different kinds of vegetables which had been pickled in vinegar, in addition to other requisites that had been appointed."[40]

The diarist noted that their route had not only courier stations, but two other types of installations, also operated under the Ministry of War. One, exclusive to border areas, was the beacon tower. Each tower was staffed by ten soldiers who were charged with lighting a signal fire to warn of dangers on the border. Strings of these towers formed crude communication lines between the border and the interior. "In this manner during the course of a night and a day, it comes to be known over the distance of three months' journey that something has happened. In the wake of this fire the matter that has happened is written down in a despatch and conveyed by means of runners from hand to hand."

The runners belonged to a second installation, the post house (*jidipu*), designed to relay urgent communications. The runners were post soldiers who "engage themselves in cultivation and tillage, their only duty being to convey the news as soon as it is received." The postal service was distinct from the courier service and of more recent (Yuan) origin. Designed to move communications quickly within the field administration, its post houses (*pu* or *jidipu*) were spaced only 10 *li* (6 kilometers) apart, unlike the much greater spacing of courier stations. The speed of relay from one post house to the next was set at three-hundredths of a twenty-four-hour period, roughly forty-five minutes. This speed sent messages at a rate of 300 *li* (170 kilometers) per twenty-four hours. The postal service thus constituted a tighter and more extensive communication system than the thinly stretched courier net. In practice, postal and courier routes and their personnel tended to overlap, despite strenuous regulations to the contrary.[41]

From Ganzhou, the embassy traveled to Lanzhou, a distance of 1,060 *li* (610 kilometers), crossing the Yellow River into Lanzhou city on 22 October. The pontoon bridge over the Yellow River was unlike anything the Persians had seen. It was "composed of twenty-three boats, of great excellence and strength attached together by a long chain of iron as thick as a man's thigh, and this was moored on each side to an iron-post as thick as a man's waist extending a distance of ten cubits on the land and planted firmly in the ground, the boats being fastened to this chain by means of big hooks. There were placed big wooden planks over the boats so firmly and evenly that all the animals were made to pass over it without difficulty." Floating bridges like this one, constructed in 1372, were common in Ming China. The best bridges in the early Ming were permanent constructions built of stone, but many crossings made do with cheaper wooden structures, floating pontoon bridges, seasonal earthen causeways, or ferries.

The courier route proceeded down through Shaanxi province (the "a" is doubled to distinguish it from Shanxi province farther east) to the provincial capital at Xi'an—a city about which the diarist is puzzlingly silent, given the Chinese Muslim presence there—then headed east along the trunk route connecting the northwest to Beijing. On 18 November, the embassy crossed the Yellow River for a second time, at Tongguan. They did so this time in boats without realizing that it was the same river they had crossed by floating bridge at Lanzhou. They proceeded eastward across Henan into North Zhili, entering the prefectural capital of Zhending on 3 December.

As the official distance of the courier route between Tongguan and Zhending was 1,540 *li* (890 kilometers), the embassy covered this stretch of the route at the quicker rate of 60 kilometers a day. The final 585 *li* (330 kilometers) route north from Zhending to Beijing, consisting of eleven stages, they completed in eleven days. The embassy "made an early start on 14 December [1420], arriving at the gates of Beijing while it was still dark."[42] Altogether, the Persians had taken three and a half months to cover the ninety-nine stages from Jiayu Guan to Beijing. According to the published distances, the route was 5,042 *li* (2,900 kilometers) in length. The embassy's daily rate of travel, averaged over the journey, was about 30 kilometers a day—roughly the average distance between one overland courier station and the next for most of the route.

After five months in the capital, where they were received and entertained by the Yongle emperor (more on their conversation later), the Persians left Beijing on 18 May 1421 and set off on their return journey. The diarist provides little information about their passage, noting only that on most days the party covered the distance between one courier station and the next. Once they were back up in the northwestern corner of Shaanxi, they were delayed two months in Ganzhou and another two in Xiaozhou because Mongol raids made the roads unsafe. The only way to get through was to leave the main road and cross through the mountains, something a party of this size could not do undetected, and so they waited.

The only other event that the diarist took the trouble of noting was that, at some location prior to reaching Lanzhou, they had their bags searched to check that they were not exporting any contraband goods such as precious metals or tea, the latter being the staple of the government trade for nomad horses.[43] At last, on 13 January 1422, after some 6,000 kilometers of traveling through China, the Persians passed through Jiayu Guan. All members' names were recorded and checked against the register in which they had been written when the embassy had arrived a year and a half previously. When the lists were found to be consistent, the party was permitted to leave.

THE CONVEYANCE OF A KOREAN PARTY, 1488

Sixty years after the Persians' departure, a party of forty-three shipwrecked Koreans was similarly conveyed by the courier service to

Beijing. The Koreans entered China, however, at a completely different point, the southeast coast; traveled by completely different
means, boats; and were conveyed along a completely different route,
the Grand Canal. The head of this party, Ch'oe Pu (1454–1504),
wrote an account of his experiences in China that is particularly at-
tentive to the business of travel. Unlike the Persians who had no
sense of Chinese ways and could communicate only through inter-
preters, the Koreans were steeped in Chinese learning (of a decidedly
conservative stripe) and well versed in Chinese history and letters
(a knowledge with which they could occasionally shame their local
interlocutors for their ignorance). Although they could not speak
Chinese, they knew the classical language and could converse with
the literate by tracing characters on their palms or writing out their
words in what were called "brush conversations." Ch'oe's diary,
which unlike the Persian account was not rewritten by a later author, provides a more intimate and exact portrait of the experience
of travel in fifteenth-century China.[44]

The Koreans' boat washed into a bay on a near-deserted stretch
of the rainy Zhejiang coast in Taizhou prefecture on 28 February
1488. Their boat was immediately surrounded by six other boats.
The Chinese sailors did not attempt to board the Korean vessel until
the following morning. When they approached, Ch'oe Pu asked
them (by writing in Chinese characters) how far it was to the nearest
"official road," which he knew to be the designation for roads used
by the courier and postal services. Immediately he received three
different estimates of the distance to the Taizhou prefectural capital,
ranging from 150 *li* (85 kilometers) to 240 *li* (140 kilometers). He
took this as a sign of deception rather than what it probably was:
the ignorance of people who worked in boats along the coast and
rarely, if ever, went inland to the city. The Chinese proceeded to rob
the Koreans of whatever they could lay their hands on, but when the
rain grew worse they retired to their boats. No one kept surveillance.
Fearing for their lives should the Chinese come aboard again, the
Koreans made a dash for the shore under cover of rain. After several
days trudging overland, they were taken to Taozhu Battalion, from
which the defense of this section of the coast was supervised (see
map 3).

To get a sense of where Taozhu was, Ch'oe Pu again asked for
distances. An elderly man in Taozhu told him it was over 5,800 *li*
(3,340 kilometers) to Beijing. In fact, Beijing was 1,200 *li* (700 kilo-

Map 3.   Jiangnan and the northeast coast of Zhejiang province, showing the first part of the route that Ch'oe Pu took up the Grand Canal to Beijing in 1488.

meters) closer than the man thought. When the man estimated the distance to the Yangzi River as being over 2,000 *li* (1,150 kilometers), he again exaggerated by roughly a quarter. Perhaps these figures were local lore: to someone in a coastal backwater, such faraway places must have seemed so distant that only large numbers did justice. The man did add, however, that "I should not presume to know." These distances, after all, were data controlled by the Ministry of War, not public information.

The battalion commander at Taozhu ordered one of his officers, Zhai Yong, to escort the Korean party to the regional command in Shaoxing, whence they were to be transferred first to the provincial capital in Hangzhou, then up to Beijing for repatriation back to Korea. The party set out on 6 March. Ch'oe and his officers rode in eight sedan chairs and the others walked, though on hilly stretches the men riding in the sedan chairs got out and walked because the road was too difficult for the bearers to manage. Following military communication roads, which were all that were maintained in this border region, the party reached Jiantiao Battalion in two days. The next morning they took boats across Sanmen Bay to the Yuexi Police Station (*xunjiansi*). Here they made contact with the post service, as the Yuexi Post House was just across the river from the police station. The following morning the Koreans set off on the postal route to Baiqiao Station, where they in turn linked up with the courier service, as Baiqiao lay on the courier route between Taizhou and Ningbo prefectures. From this point the travelers could avail themselves of the resources of the courier service, though the keenness of some of the station masters to see the Koreans quickly on their way may indicate that the supplies and labor that courier stations in this part of China could raise were limited; a party of forty-three plus escort was an unusually large group to accommodate.

The Koreans pushed on that day until the second watch of the night in order to get to the next courier station, 60 *li* (35 kilometers) north. High winds and heavy rains on 10 March made further progress impossible, and the party remained at this heavily guarded station. Although the storm continued to blow the following day, Zhai Yong insisted the party go forward regardless of the weather. "The laws of China are strict," he told Ch'oe. "If there is the slightest delay, it will bring punishment upon us. It is raining hard now, but we cannot stay longer."

They covered 60 *li* (35 kilometers) that day. By the time they reached the next station they were soaked to the skin. The station master took pity on them and built them a fire, but as they warmed themselves, a man who thought they were captured pirates barged in and kicked the fire out in anger. Zhai wrote a deposition regarding the assault, as he was obliged to do, and sent it on to the county magistrate's office. The next day, 12 March, they rode in sedan chairs to the Beidu River, then boarded boats and began the river course that eventually linked up to the Grand Canal and would take them all the way to Beijing. Officially the Grand Canal began not there but in Hangzhou, but the network of waterways from the Beidu west to Hangzhou, broken by two short overland transfers before Shaoxing, effectively extended the canal by another 465 *li* (270 kilometers), making Ningbo the real southern terminus. Water was the preferred route for the courier service. Ch'oe explains that "all envoys, tribute, and commerce come and go by water. If either the water in the locks and rivers is too shallow because of drought to let boats pass or there is a very urgent matter, the overland route is taken."

The party passed the maritime trading city of Ningbo that day ("wonderfully beautiful"), Cixi the next ("on both banks of the river, markets and warships were gathered like clouds"), and reached the office of the Supreme Piracy-Defense Commander in Shaoxing the following day ("the profusion of gates and crowds of people were three times as great as those of Ningbo"). The regional commanders closely questioned Ch'oe, as they did his escort Zhai, who was flogged for the fire-kicking incident, taken as evidence that he could not keep order. Zhai would be flogged yet again when they reached Hangzhou two days later on the charge of having taken too many days to get the Koreans from Taozhu Battalion to the provincial capital. The courier system worked by strict deadlines based on distance, and delays were punished as though they were military infractions. One day's delay was worth twenty strokes, with an additional stroke for every three subsequent days to a maximum of sixty, plus an increase by half as much again if the communication related to military matters.[45] Zhai's fear of delay had been well placed.

"It truly seems a different world, as people say," was Ch'oe's reaction to Hangzhou when he arrived in that city. It was a bustling commercial city on a scale he had never before seen. "Houses stand in solid rows, and the gowns of the crowds seem like screens. The markets pile up gold and silver; the people amass beautiful clothes and ornaments. Foreign ships stand as thick as the teeth of a comb, and in the streets wine shops and music halls front directly each on another." Ch'oe is perceptive enough to note that the many boats moored along the river outside Hangzhou were mostly merchant boats from points south, indicating that Hangzhou acted as a central market for trade coming up through Zhejiang province into the

Jiangnan economy. While in Hangzhou, Ch'oe was told of the active smuggling trade that passed through the city, as mariners brought in sandalwood, pepper, and perfumes from Southeast Asia and the Indian Ocean. It was a dangerous trade: he was told that of every ten vessels that set sail, only five returned.

On 23 March, the Hangzhou prefectural government assigned Ch'oe's party a different escort and issued them a document explaining their presence in China and empowering them to travel by the courier service: "Let the stations and transport offices give to the dispatched official food and boats, and to the escorting troops and Ch'oe Pu and his company rations, red [i.e., official] boats, and laborers. It is fitting that all offices on the road ahead comply." Transport offices (*diyunsuo*) were part of yet another state transportation service, distinct from both the courier and postal services though in practice closely linked to the former. Founded in 1376 at a rate of roughly one per prefecture, transport offices were charged with handling large-scale transportation needs beyond the means of the courier service, such as shipping state grain or organizing the transport of corvéed laborers for public works projects.

Ch'oe Pu's party tarried for two days before starting the journey from Hangzhou to Beijing on 25 March. The delay is not explained but had to do with common belief that some days were auspicious for setting out on a journey and some were not. No official or courier would start out without referring to the civil service handbook, *The Bureaucratic System of the Ming Dynasty* (*Da Ming guanzhi*). There he would find a circular chart by which to calculate which days of the month were very auspicious for travel, somewhat auspicious, passable, or disastrous—that is, would end in death by violence, error, or crime.[46] The Portuguese Dominican friar Gaspar da Cruz would later observe that travelers used such a book to "cast lottes when they beginne any iourney" when he was in Fujian in 1575.[47] *The Bureaucratic System of the Ming Dynasty* also included lists of the stations and county seats on the main courier routes and the distances between them.

Ch'oe was told informally that the journey from Hangzhou to Beijing would take about forty days. The official escorting him to the capital was issued with an arrival deadline of 11 May, which entailed punishment should he fail to meet it. Setting out on the morning of 25 March, the party had forty-seven days in which to get from Hangzhou to the capital. As that distance was officially rated at 3,621 *li* (2,090 kilometers), they had to travel at a rate of 77 *li* (45 kilometers) a day. Their actual travel time, deducting delays for a day's stopover to see Suzhou and a day lost because of bad weather, was forty-three days, which meant that the party covered roughly 85 *li* (50 kilometers) a day. They arrived in Beijing on 9 May, two days before their travel permit expired.

Leaving Hangzhou, the party took two days to cover the 195 *li* (110 kilometers) to Jiaxing (Ch'oe found it the equal of Ningbo), and one day to cover the 145 *li* (85 kilometers) to Suzhou. For Ch'oe, this city exceeded every other in China. As his boat sailed up to it on the Grand Canal, he could see that "shops and markets one after another lined both river banks, and merchant junks were crowded together. It was well called an urban center of the southeast." Given little chance to wander about and see things for himself, he has relied on standard literary phrases to describe the city. One of his own observations is that the merchant boats moored at Suzhou came from north (Henan, North Zhili) and south (Fujian), testifying to its national centrality as a point of exchange. Ch'oe was also impressed with the suburban settlements sprawling out around this and every other town on the Yangzi delta. "Often for as much as twenty *li* around them, village gates crowd the ground, markets line the roads, towers look out on other towers, and boats ply stem to stern."

Four days later, Ch'oe's party reached the Yangzi River, which it would cross upstream from the famous island monastery of Jinshan (see figure 8). At the beginning of the century, before the Grand Canal was in operation, lines penned at the Jinshan crossing by the high official Yao Guangxiao (1335–1418) suggest that courier travel in this area was difficult:

> I gaze out over the Yangzi River
> Into the vast murk where it meets the sky:
> Evening fog chokes the trees on the bank,
> Wintering geese settle on the sandbar plots.
> Fragrance from the forest penetrates the monastery,
> Voices on the bank reach the merchant's boat.
> The courier road is bafflingly hard to follow;
> At least another year before I pass this way again.[48]

By 1488, when Ch'oe Pu's party crossed, the Jin Shan crossing was well marked and thoroughly serviced by the numerous transport agents who handled commercial cargo crossing the Yangzi.[49] The

Figure 8. The island monastery Jin Shan was built
at the point the Grand Canal crossed the Yangzi
River (*Shuihu zhuan*, 1610).

only obstacle the Koreans faced was the tide. They crossed the next
morning to Guazhou on the north bank of the Yangzi River and
began their journey up the northern section of the Grand Canal.

This part of the Grand Canal had fallen into disuse in the Yuan
dynasty, when tax goods were transported to Beijing by sea. It remained out of service in the Hongwu era, but the Yongle emperor's
decision in 1403 to relocate the primary capital to Beijing obliged
that the Grand Canal be reopened to handle the annual northward
shipment of some 4 million *shi* (one *shi* has a capacity of 107.4 liters)
of "tribute grain" assessed on the southern provinces, the equivalent

of one-seventh of the national land tax revenue. Initially grain going to the northern border was carried in large river barges (having capacities of 300 *shi* of grain and over) up past the Huai River, then transferred to shallow barges (with capacities of 200 *shi* and over) for conveyance across southwestern Shandong, then transferred back to large barges and taken to the Yellow River. There it was off-loaded and transported by Henanese carters to the Wei River, to be reloaded onto barges and taken up to Beijing. The frequent transfers caused such a strain on manpower that the magistrate of Jining requested in a memorial to the Yongle emperor that the old Grand Canal, which had been allowed to fall into disuse in the Yuan dynasty, be resurrected so as to eliminate the overland bottleneck.[50]

The Grand Canal was not one continuous waterway. North of the Yangzi it was called the Huitong ("linking together") Canal, being a series of short stretches of canal that linked together existing waterways. Canal building was kept to a minimum, though the task of controlling silting so as to maintain the minimum depth of three *chi* (just under a meter) needed for the shallow-draught grain barges to clear the bottom challenged the ingenuity of engineers. The highest section in southwestern Shandong had to be completely redesigned in 1411 as part of the project ordered that year to restore the Grand Canal. A dam was built there to divert the Wen River southwest to feed 60 percent of its water north into the Grand Canal and 40 percent south. Four large reservoirs were also dug in Shandong to regulate water levels without having to pump water out of the local water table. Between 1411 and 1415, 165,000 laborers were mobilized to dredge the canal bed in Shandong and build new channels, embankments, and locks along the lower section of the Grand Canal to bring the waterway into full operation. The designers made brilliant use of the many riverine systems the canal crossed, though the linking of distinct hydraulic environments meant that a flood at one point in the system could disrupt the overall network. The flood-prone Yellow River (which until 1492 flowed south of Shandong as well as north, as it does today) was the weak link in the chain. The point where the canal crossed the Yellow River was the throat of the realm, as one official put it in 1447, and like a throat could be easily strangled.[51] This view would be repeated in the sixteenth century, when officials argued for reopening the old sea route.

The Grand Canal needed vast numbers of people to maintain its facilities, keep levees and banks in repair, operate locks, and handle the boats. According to statistics collected by the early-Qing scholar Gu Yanwu, 47,004 full-time laborers were required to keep the Grand Canal functioning in the Ming. This labor came from the *lijia* corvée. The actual barges ferrying grain to Beijing were supplied by the army, which by the mid-fifteenth century had 121,500 officers and soldiers operating the 11,775 grain barges.[52] The system, being based on corvée, was not centrally funded. As the burden of transportation on the canal increased, however, the principle of corvée came to be subsidized by the more "modern" principle of commercial trading, for the boatmen were given permission to carry a limited volume of goods beyond their personal effects on the government boats they operated. These goods they could trade or carry on consignment for others and use the profit to cover their expenses. Boatmen of course transported far more private goods than their legal entitlement allowed, an open secret that only a tactlessly sanctimonious official would seek to disclose or punish. This "smuggling," along with the operation of purely private cargo barges, made the Grand Canal the main artery for commercial transport between north and south. It was not the state's purpose to facilitate private trade in this way, nor to stimulate the expansion of commercial networks into the Grand Canal hinterlands in northern South Zhili, Henan, and Shandong provinces, yet both results occurred. This outcome was to be expected, for the canal was not restricted to state traffic. The 11,775 government barges were only a fraction of the traffic on the canal. State regulations required only that its boats be given clearance priority over private vessels. Corvée and commerce thus combined to underwrite a portion of the transportation costs of both state and private goods.

The Grand Canal was a courier route as well as a grain tribute route, stations being spaced along it every 35 to 45 kilometers The names of the courier stations were available in government publications, though the nonliterate relied on mnemonic verses. "Song of the Route between the Two Capitals," which probably dates to the fifteenth century, describes the route from Nanjing to Beijing in weakly rhymed verse:

> It's several thousand *li* from Nanjing to Beijing,
> So now, one by one, the courier stages will I sing
> That you may commit to memory this travel information:
> Everyone who leaves Nanjing leaves by *Longjiang* Station,
> Your boat reaches *Longtan* all in the very same day,

After you've passed *Yizhen*, *Guangling* marks your way;
Then start looking for *Shaobo* first and *Mengcheng* second;
Having crossed the border, your way by *Anping* now is reckoned.
Huaiyin is the next station, a name that everyone knows,
Qingkou and *Taoyuan* crossing are where the route then goes....

The song continues on for another twenty-one lines to name the rest of the courier stations on the Grand Canal north of the Yellow River, and then concludes:

By journey's end the courier stations number forty-six
Along the winding waters that swirling and muddied mix;
So now you know the names of all the stations, gentlemen,
And will recall them well when you take this route again.[53]

Ch'oe Pu's party headed up the Grand Canal from Yangzhou and on 13 April reached the Lüliang Rapids, the first of two sets of rapids at the north end of South Zhili that broke the flow of canal traffic. Ten-ox teams pulled their boats through the Lüliang Rapids that day, and over a hundred laborers were needed to get their entourage safely through the Xuzhou Rapids the next. The tow-path of stone slabs fastened with iron bolts and cemented with lime had been constructed in the previous reign. Once past the rapids, Ch'oe was impressed with the complex system of locks and reservoirs that maintained the water level in the canal. The locks were relatively simple barriers of planks wedged at narrow points between stone levees. These were closed to build up enough water, then opened to release a sufficient flow for boats to be pulled over shallow stretches.

Linqing was the main canal port and customs station in northern Shandong, located at the dangerous point where boatmen had to maneuver their barges out of the canal into the turbulent Wei River, the northern channel of the Yellow River.[54] Linqing was "a place to which traveling merchants flocked," according to Ch'oe. "For several tens of *li* inside and outside the wall, the wealth of valuable goods and the fleets of moored boats, though not equal to those of Suzhou or Hangzhou, were still the greatest in Shandong and famous everywhere." Dezhou, the next major canal port four days north on the Shandong border, was almost as vibrant. "It was a big place, crowded with people, and traveling merchants gathered there." For Ch'oe, these were the only bright spots on the north China landscape, a region that struck him as a place of poverty, underdevelopment, and ill humor. At the end of his diary he presents a litany of depressing contrasts: spacious tile-roofed houses south of the Yangzi, thatch-roofed hovels north; sedan chairs south, horses and donkeys north; gold and silver in the markets south, copper cash north; diligence in farming, manufacturing, and commerce south, indolence north; pleasant dispositions south, quarrelsome tempers north; education south, illiteracy north. The only point in common was that, north or south, "everyone does business: even some successful officials and men from powerful families carry balances in their own sleeves and will analyze a profit of pennies."

As he passed from Shandong province into North Zhili, Ch'oe noticed a steady stream of boats ferrying officials from the Ministries of War, Punishment, and Personnel. He asked what was afoot and was told that this was because the newly enthroned Hongzhi emperor (r. 1488–1505) was ridding his court of incompetent bureaucrats. The emperor was allowing them to travel by the courier service, a privilege that a dismissed official did not rightfully enjoy. Their comfortable departure was a gentle but firm message that they were being sent home without loss of face but for good. After eleven days crossing the North China Plain they reached Tongzhou, the warehousing depot east of Beijing, and proceeded by donkey and by foot into the capital. They lodged at the Central Courier Hostel (*Huitong Guan*, or Hostel where All Communications Converge), as the two central nodes in the courier network (the other was in Nanjing) were called.

Adding up the published distances between courier stations, the total length of the inland waterway connecting Ningbo to Beijing was 4,064 *li* (2,340 kilometers). Ch'oe's party covered that distance in forty-nine days of actual traveling. The journey had gone most quickly across the flat plain of North Zhili, where they proceeded at a rate of 61 kilometers a day. Between Hangzhou and Yangzhou, their rate of travel had been 49 kilometers a day. For the rest of the journey, they averaged a daily pace of almost 44 kilometers. Compared with the daily rate at which the Persian embassy's sedan chairs moved (30 kilometers), the boat-borne Koreans enjoyed the advantages of speed and ease of travel. In either case, a day's travel in Ming China was not unlike a day's travel in Augustan Rome, where 45 kilometers was viewed as a reasonable average and 30 kilometers a barely acceptable minimum.[55]

On June 3, the Chinese officer escorting Ch'oe Pu and his party to the Korean border notified the transport office in Beijing that three carriages plus horses and donkeys would be needed for their journey. These were duly assembled the following morning and the Koreans set off. Ch'oe was happy to leave Beijing. He did not care for the local people. "They work at business, not farming," he condescended. "Their clothing is short and tight" following Mongol fashion, "and men and women dress the same. Their food and drink are rancid. High and low use the same implements." The travelers covered the courier route to the northeast border at a rate of 31 kilometers a day, reaching the capital of Liaodong on 2 July. They left four days later and on 12 July crossed the Yalu River into Korea.

MODES OF TRANSPORT

The Persians traveled mostly by land, the Koreans mostly by water—in vague keeping with the adage that one went by land north of the Yangzi and by water south of it. On land the horse was the fastest form of transportation for one individual traveling well-maintained roads. As the Koreans were not in a great hurry between Beijing and the border, they did not rate travel by horseback but went instead by donkey and carriage. The Persians on the other hand enjoyed the privilege of riding in sedan chairs. This device (usually carried by two, not twelve, men) was a recent invention and had been recognized for official travel only in the Yuan dynasty (see figure 9). In the early Ming, to travel by sedan was a mark of status. Thus when a censor in 1405 filed an accusation against a corrupt official, he colored the picture of the man's conduct by describing him "riding in his sedan chair into the market and buying goods at forced prices."[56] Anyone who could afford a sedan chair was free to use it, subject to color restrictions: red was forbidden, and green could not be used by officials below the fifth rank. The law also forbade coercing another into carrying a sedan chair. Such work was considered beyond the customary obligations a tenant owed his landlord, and so the landlord had to pay his tenant to carry him. The sedan chair became so much a part of elite life by the mid-Ming that its use was incorporated into residential architecture. Larger homes in Suzhou came to include a sedan hall (*jiaoting*) inside the main gate where chairs could be set down under cover. Another adaptation was the document box, a long lidded tray that rested between the shafts of an open sedan chair and enabled the passenger to read or work while traveling.[57]

Figure 9.   Because he was a filial son, the beggar Yang Yi is carried to paradise on a two-bearer sedan chair, despite his lowly status. The image appears in a popular religious text of the Qing period and can be dated to the Qing by the conical feathered hats the heralds wear.

The easiest mode of transport over long distances for people and goods alike was the boat. A wheelbarrow could handle only about 120 kilograms and "must stop when it encounters any unevenness in the terrain," nor could it "range beyond 100 *li* [58 kilometers] at the most." A four-wheeled mule cart could carry 3,000 kilograms but could not be expected to transport goods a distance greater than 300 *li* (175 kilometers). By contrast, the standard load for a grain barge on the Grand Canal was 30,000 kilograms, and a large full-sail Yellow River vessel could manage 180,000 kilograms (see figure 10). As a late-Ming observer sensibly concludes, a cart "is only a means of compensating for the want of boats in a region that lacks waterways."[58] (See figure 11.)

As Ming China was a land more of boats than carts, people made use of a bewildering range of boat types, each carefully adapted over time to its particular water environment. The standard vessel for transport on the Grand Canal was the grain barge, a single-masted freighter with a flat bottom suited to the shallow draughts of inland waterways. By government specification, grain boats were 22 meters

Figure 10.   Men hoist the mainsail on a two-masted grain tribute boat
(*Tiangong kaiwu*, 1637).

in length and 4.4 meters in the beam. The heavy sails, made of
woven rattan matting interlaced with bamboo strips, were the same
width as the boat. Dimensions increased during the course of the
dynasty in the hope of cutting costs. Whereas the standard load was
472 *shi* of grain at the start of the Ming, it was gradually increased
to 780 *shi*. Doing so reduced total transport costs, though it increased the loss when a barge sank. The quality of construction also
changed over time. Fir had been the wood used for making grain
boats at the start of the dynasty. Pine took its place. Pine was a
cheaper material, but its faster rate of decay meant that pine boats
needed to be overhauled twice as often (every three years) as fir
boats (every six years) and were worn out in five years whereas fir
boats lasted ten.[59]

The barges that transported officials up and down the canal were
of the same specifications as the grain boats, though the cabins had
larger windows and doorways and were elegantly decorated and
painted red (see figure 12). Boats that traveled open rivers like the
Yangzi were longer and slenderer, with smaller sails and more oars

Figure 11.   This pony cart is designed for elegant
but short-distance conveyance (*Nanke meng*).

to provide balance in stormy weather. "When sailing with the current, when there are no contrary winds, these boats can cover a distance of over 400 *li* [235 kilometers] in a day and a night, and even
going upstream they are capable of covering over 100 *li* [58 kilo-
meters]." These river boats were built to transport salt tax revenues,
but they were also available for private hire by "travelers who wish
to make good time."[60]

In the water country of Jiangnan, boat design was almost in-
finitely varied, with sails, oars, rudders, and draughts combined in
different measures to suit every possible boating situation. Each of

Figure 12.   Bandits attack a decorated river barge
(*Shuihu zhuan*, 1610).

the thousands of types had a distinctive regional name. According
to a sixteenth-century observer, the boats on Lake Tai (near which
Suzhou was located) illustrate this variety: there were "mountain
boats" to transport stone, "transshipment boats" to carry merchan-
dise, "embankment boats" for passengers, "patrol boats," "scout
boats" for militia, and "ferry boats." None handled in a storm as
well as the fishing boats that plied the lakes of Jiangnan day and
night in all seasons of the year. These were graded by size according
to the number of masts, from two (with a capacity of less than 6,000
kilograms) to six (able to carry 120,000 kilograms). Two- and three-
masters were more common, but four-masters combined capacity
with versatility: large enough to carry 60,000 kilograms, yet small

enough to enter most harbors and be lashed two together at night to make a sort of small floating fortress that pirates preferred not to attack. Then there were "riversiders," which had from two to five masts with capacities of up to 120,000 kilograms; "boatyard rudder-boats," which could carry up to 40,000 kilograms; "miniatures" with a capacity of less than 600 kilograms; "cut-net boats," narrow but very fast; "thread-net boats," which could hold only three people but made good speed in a wind; and rowboats, which three or four men could row faster than cut-net boats and maneuver into places other boats couldn't go.[61]

The ease of boat traffic in and around Lake Tai was not entirely due to fortunate accidents of nature. The water landscape of this region underwent considerable reconstruction in the early Ming. The most important project was the building of the East Dams south of Nanjing. The dams were built by the Ministry of Revenue to control the water level of Lake Tai, which in flood season submerged agricultural land and inundated Suzhou 350 kilometers to the east. The dams also provided Suzhou with a canal link to the Yangzi River port of Wuhu upriver from Nanjing. Even though boats taking this route had to be dragged over the lower dam and cargo had to be transshipped 6 kilometers farther west at the upper dam, this inland connection greatly improved Suzhou's water access to markets throughout Jiangnan and assured its position as the central place in the regional economy.[62] Further construction on the canal system east of Suzhou starting in 1403 would complete the task of reworking Jiangnan's rivers into an efficient transportation network.[63] The work improved state communications and control, though private commerce would reap the greatest benefits.

IDEAS INTO TEXTS

LITERACY

Like many educated men and the many more who weren't, Wang Lü found occasions to journey along the routes of the realm. Wang was born in 1332 into a physician's family in Kunshan at the mouth of the Yangzi River. What got him on the road was his search for medical knowledge. This quest took him north to apprentice with a famous doctor in Shaanxi province in the years following the founding of the Ming. Wang is better known today as a painter, and while in the north his love of landscapes took him to Shaanxi's most famous scenic mountain, Mount Hua. He made the tortuous ascent in 1381 with his personal servant. Reaching the Precipice Where [Moral Paragon] Xiyi Went to Avoid Being Summoned, he saw a narrow crevice in a corner of the cliff face and sent his servant in to find where it led. The servant reemerged to tell his master, "There are four columns of characters down there." Wang notes in his journal that "since he could not read, he could not tell what it said."

The servant was like most people of the early Ming: he knew writing when he saw it, and he realized that it was a significant cultural code, but he couldn't decipher it. He probably couldn't even read his own name. Wang identifies him only as Eldest Son Zhang. As a servant, Zhang was embedded in a social environment in which certain things, including personal names, could go without being written down, or even named. If Zhang had more than a birth-order label, his parents were probably not able to assign it a written equivalent. If Wang did not use it, it may have been because Zhang belonged to the world of servants rather than masters: to name him would have been to invite him across a strict social boundary.

Wang Lü stood toward the other end of the social scale from Eldest Son Zhang. Though not of the wealthy gentry, his was a well-established family of physicians. Wang Lü was literate in both the medical and the classical canons; he was also a producer of texts, both medical and literary. Texts posed a different sort of problem for Wang than for his servant, for after noting his servant's illiteracy he goes on to admit, "I cannot see very clearly, so I could not read it either." Wang comments elsewhere in his writings on his near-sightedness, noting that "my dizzy eyes now prevent me from painting." This is a curiously frank admission from an artist who liked to argue, rather idiosyncratically, that ideas existed only in visual form. Wang did not regard his failing vision as a handicap, and even turned it into an advantage. He claimed that if he spread his old paintings on a "clean desk by a bright window," he could see them well enough to become absorbed in them without "becoming entangled by dexterous skill, which, after all, is the same thing as clumsy slavishness."[64] Only when European trade with China in the seventeenth century brought eyeglasses—six ships arriving in 1637 included 38,421 pairs of spectacles in their cargo[65]—would such Daoist unconcern seem less compelling.

The social gap between literate and illiterate was great. The state bridged that gap by calling upon scribes and public lectors to disseminate information that it desired be known. The Hongwu emperor did not leave such communication to local initiative, but instituted a system of public pavilions where local officials or their deputies could post statements or make announcements about local matters. At the Pavilion for Declaring Goodness (*jingshan ting*) were listed and recited the names of local individuals who had displayed exemplary moral conduct. The lists were to be regularly updated at ceremonies at which those selected as model citizens were honored in person. At the Pavilion for Extending Clarity (*shenming ting*), the names and misdeeds of criminals were published as warnings to others. This pavilion was also a forum for resolving disputes having to do with marriage agreements, land contracts, and assault.[66] It was up to the local magistrate to keep the pavilions from lapsing into empty formalism or complete disuse in the face of the eternal enemy of public buildings, time. Before the first century of the Ming was over, though, most had failed. As a provincial official reported in 1432, "Today many of the pavilion buildings have fallen into disrepair, so good and evil deeds are not published, and minor matters are not handled by local elders but go directly up to the magistrate, causing a tangle of imprisonments and lawsuits."[67]

The unlettered person was not only a passive listener to state decrees. He could initiate his own communications with state representatives at the county yamen, for the Hongwu emperor provided that someone unable to write but who wished to file a complaint was permitted to recite his case to a yamen secretary, who would write it down in an "oral accusation register" for consideration by the magistrate.[68]

However numerous the illiterate undoubtedly were, there is much scattered evidence from the early Ming that indicates that this was a culture of written texts. By forbidding his subjects from using archaic salutations in their letters, for instance, Hongwu acknowledged that his subjects were writing to each other. The popularity of letter-writing guides like the early-Ming *Complete Book of Pen and Ink* (*Hanmo quanshu*) indicates that people wrote letters—but that they might need primers to help them do it.

Literacy also had its economic uses, and economic texts were part of Ming popular culture. While the government relied on registers to keep track of land ownership, the people kept their own records by writing contracts—as they had been doing for centuries—specifying the size and location of the land under transaction, its price, and the conditions, consequences, and legal responsibilities attached to the sale. The contracts bore the names of buyer and vendor as well as of witnesses, plus the scribe hired to write out the document. Each party signed under his name to verify that the document conformed to his wishes and corresponded to the transaction; the illiterate simply drew a cross. Although the state was not represented among the parties named in this document, it supported the authority of signed written documents by accepting such materials in court as the best possible evidence of ownership. The only way to trump a claim substantiated by a signed document was to produce a subsequent or more powerful document.

The land contract was not a Ming invention. Early prototypes can be found as far back as the Han dynasty, and they were in common use from the Tang dynasty forward. In her history of this document, Valerie Hansen has argued the Yuan dynasty was the age when "contractual language and ideas deeply permeated Chinese life."[69] If this is so, then the Ming was the age when this permeation gets attested in the large quantity of contracts, for only a few contracts have survived from earlier dynasties. The prefecture for which the greatest number of early-Ming land contracts survives today is Huizhou, the native place of many Ming merchants and the prefecture where our Zhang Tao served as magistrate. From this area, researchers have collected close to a thousand land contracts from the Ming. (By contrast, barely a dozen Song and Yuan contracts have survived from Huizhou.) If these instruments were sedulously preserved over so many centuries, it is because those who held them felt they were worth keeping. Without one, the right to hold a piece of land which one's family may have held for generations might be challenged, lost, or revoked. With one, a landowner could get as close as was possible to ensuring power over economic resources.

Among the the earliest Ming contracts from Huizhou that Chinese scholars have published is the following, dated 1400. It comes from Xiuning county, next door to Sheh:

> I, Hu Yin of Ward #10, Township #12, inherited from my grandfather's estate one plot of land situated in Ward #9 of the present township, [registered in Fish-Scale Map] Register Yu, #781, and measuring .848 *mu* in size. On the east side is the road; on the west, the field of Li Zigun; on the south, the field of Hu Zutao; on the north, the field of Wang Yanlun. The place is known as Tingzitou.

It happens that now I have no grain to use, and having the agreement of my aunt, Madame Zhu, I desire of my own free choice to draw up a contract to sell the aforesaid parcel of land to Wang Yougan. We have met and agreed that its current value is ten weights (*cheng*) of grain, to be handed over in full on the day this contract goes into effect.

Once this land has been sold, it will henceforth be up to the buyer to report to the officials and pay the taxes, as well as to collect the harvest and manage the property. Should the boundaries be found not to be correct, or should the land have already been sold to someone else, or should someone who is kin to, or not kin to, the vendor have taken it over, it is up to the vendor to resolve and not the affair of the buyer.

Any other documents regarding this land are no longer in effect, and should they henceforth come forward, the vendor agrees not to rely on them to challenge [this sale]. For fear that people's hearts alone are not trustworthy, this document of sale has been drawn up.

Contracted on the x day of the 9th month of the 2nd year of the Jianwen era [September–October 1400].

Vendor of the property: Hu Yin (signed)
Aunt: Madame Zhu (signed)
Witness: Wang Chougan (signed)
Uncle: Hu Longzhou (signed)
Scribe writing from oral testimony: Wu Zhigao (signed)
It is also acknowledged on that same date that today the grain specified in the contract has been received in full (signed).[70]

Consider the literate hand that wrote out this document. Wu Zhigao has left no other written records. His name does not happen to appear on the few other Xiuning contracts preserved from this time, nor is he the author of any other sort of text that anyone would have considered worth keeping. Although he was able to write, Wu was working from a formula, manipulating the set phrases of which this and all other land contracts are composed. His is not entirely a mechanical literacy, for he was capable of inserting information specific to the particular transaction and of altering the formulae to deal with such contingencies as, in this case, Hu Yin's prior discussion with his aunt. Presumably she had inherited the land from Hu Yin's grandfather and had passed it to her nephew for want of her own child to pass it to. It would seem that the buyer was keen to record the agreement of the aunt to the sale, since a claim on land by any of Hu Yin's relatives, particularly his elder relatives, was sufficient to annul the sale. This concern accounts for the signatures of both Madame Zhu and Uncle Hu, presumably her brother, on the contract: the elder generation has cleared the way. Later land contracts tend to use a simpler formula declaring that the vendor has checked with all kinsmen and that none has a claim on the land.

Wu Zhigao was not the only scribe in Xiuning county. Like every county, Xiuning had hundreds of such men, if not thousands, to meet the demand for written records. Many tens of thousands of literate professionals were distributed around the country in the early Ming to play the essential role of facilitating the textuality of economic life in the Ming. Unlike the scholars who learned to read in order to climb up through the examination system and put their literacy to more enduring uses and their names to better archived materials, these scribes have largely disappeared from our ken, breaking the surface only through the chance survival of the flimsy documents they scripted. Wu Zhigao may have started into his literacy training with the intention of serving the state but never passed the qualifying exams and for that reason ended up serving society in other ways.

One last thing: Madame Zhu's signature. If the signature was hers, this is evidence of written literacy on the part of an ordinary woman. Males did most of the writing that has survived, but some women were also literate. References to female literacy in the early Ming tend to link it to the attention of an educated father. The father of He Huilian taught her to read the texts of a basic Confucian education, such as the *Analects* of Confucius and the *Classic of Filial Piety*, and he delayed her marriage until she was twenty, marrying her finally to a poor scholar for whom she later bought books by selling her jewelry.[71] The daughter of military governor Cheng Kai, who married in 1393 at the age of seventeen, had an even more advanced education, for she was said to be "rather well versed in the *Book of History* and the *Records of the Grand Historian*," in addition to "having a virtuous face."[72]

Outside the narrow circle of the elite, it seems that few women possessed more than basic literacy. Hongwu discovered this in 1372 when he sent eunuchs to Suzhou and Hangzhou to recruit mature literate women for responsible posts in his harem, where they were to serve as educators to his concubines. Forty-four were selected for this service and brought to Nanjing. Subsequently, though, only fourteen passed the written text that was set for them; the other thirty fell short of the level of literacy being tested and were sent home. (It would appear that his son, Yongle, was less concerned about literacy in the palace. When chaste widows were conscripted in 1423 to train the concubines in his harem, the qualification for the job was childlessness, not literacy. And that restriction was reduced within a year to the stipulation that they might be married but were not to bring their children into the palace.)[73]

PRINTING

If much was written in the early Ming, so, too, much was printed, as the scattered references to buying textbooks, memorizing classics, and using published guides to write letters in the foregoing section indicate. Like contract-writing, xylography (the technology of printing from wooden blocks) was developed well before the Ming. What the Ming period marks in the history of printing is a notable expansion in the volume and variety of texts in print. Printing technology in the narrow sense of technical process did not change in the Ming except in small ways, but the technology in the larger sense—the overall social process that organized the production of printed materials—did. Paper and ink were manufactured in greater volume, woodblock carvers more widely available and working at lower wages, new fonts designed to speed up the rate of carving, new ways of compacting knowledge onto pages devised, and wider distribution systems set up. The state did its part at the very start of the dynasty by canceling the tax on books in 1368.

Even so, the expansion of printing in the early Ming was slow. Painter-physician Wang Lü is a case in point. He wrote books on medicine, astronomy, geomancy, and human affairs, and yet only his *Collection of Essays Returning to the Sources of the Medical Classics (Yijing suhui ji)* has survived, and then only in a later reprint. Much knowledge in the early Ming did not get into book form and as such remained regional, which is why Wang traveled in search of instruction. Books were not common—and accordingly they were expensive, a point made by several writers of the early Ming.[74] Those who desired books but could not afford to buy them had no choice but to copy them by hand, which they could do so long as they had connections to and the confidence of those with private libraries. Song Lian (1310–81), the eminent early advisor to Hongwu, recalled doing just this in the 1320s:

> When I was young I thirsted after study, but our family was poor. I didn't have the means to get books, so every one I borrowed from

families that collected books. I copied it out by hand and returned it within a few days,... not daring to exceed the agreed loan time by even a bit. Accordingly, many people were willing to lend their books to me, and for this reason I was able to read a great quantity of books.[75]

The art of printing was put to other uses besides book publication. One indication of the skill of printers in the early Ming is the reported success with which counterfeiters were able to reproduce items that the state had printed, notably the paper currency that the Hongwu administration experimented with briefly. Counterfeit bills were printed in large numbers, and it was said that only the most perceptive were able to distinguish true from fake. Zhu Biao, Hongwu's heir apparent who was appointed to oversee the issuance of paper currency, was said to be particularly adept at detecting counterfeit bills.[76] The same problem plagued the government tea and salt monopolies, which sold printed licenses to merchants who paid to handle these protected commodities. On each license was printed a warning of dire consequence and handsome reward: "Those who produce counterfeit tea licenses will be executed and their property confiscated, and those who report on and apprehend them will be awarded twenty silver taels."[77] Presumably the licenses were being counterfeited on a scale big enough to make the warning necessary.

Printing was a technology that the local official was also expected to use in the course of his work. He printed up annual calendars, since the designation of days was an imperial prerogative and not for private printers to undertake. He could also circulate other basic materials. A privately published handbook of 1404, the *New Mirror for Shepherding the People* (*Mumin xinjian*), advises him to draw up a pair of simple charts outlining the major rituals and laws of the dynasty and have them printed for distribution to every family, to be hung in the sitting room so as to be constantly in view.[78] More mundanely, the magistrate also had to print up multiple copies of such documents as *lijia* registration forms. Hongwu had his local officials issued with a model registration form and instructed them to "have it copied and cut onto a printing block." The magistrate was first to complete a sample form on the basis of a local household to make sure it accorded with local conditions, then have the forms printed up and distributed to all hundred captains and their subordinates. Once filled in, the forms were to be returned to the magistrate, who then bound them together into booklets known as

Yellow Registers (*huangce*). (The same procedure was followed for
land registration certificates, called "fish-scale maps" [*yulintu*] because of their appearance, which were bound into Fish-Scale Map
Registers.) Copies of these tax books were forwarded once a decade
to the administration commission in the provincial capital, and
thence to the Ministry of Revenue in Nanjing. There they were
checked and then transferred for storage to the specially constructed
storehouse by Back Lake (Hou Hu). The volume of text storage that
this system required was enormous. The ministry gazetteer of 1550
records that the ministry received 53,393 volumes "at the beginning
of the Ming," referring presumably to the 1390s.[79] Provincial administration commissions had their own Yellow Register warehouses
to handle the mountain of printed forms that accumulated at their
level.[80]

Keeping up these registers placed a considerable transcription
burden on the county. (It also involved considerable cost to the
hundred captains, enough in the opinion of one late-Ming magistrate to "enrich the country and strengthen the army" if it were put
to other uses.)[81] The original forms could be carved and printed by
nonliterates, but their completion and collation required a literate
staff. A Guangdong gazetteer indicates that, to produce a Yellow
Register for his county, a magistrate had to appoint secretaries at the
township level, plus a general secretary at the county level to tran-
scribe, collate, and summarize the data that came in. Down at the
local level, he commanded each *lijia* hundred to select one among
them who was both numerate and literate to act as scribe.[82] A
magistrate in the early Ming could expect to corvée a sufficient
number of people who had the literacy needed to produce the
registers.

The Hongwu emperor understood the ease with which ideas
could circulate in society. It would not have occurred to him to
monopolize publishing, or license publishers, or ban specific titles in
the way that states in Reformation Europe tried to do when con-
fronted with what was there a new technology.[83] Rather, the Chinese
emperor intervened by putting into print in massive numbers the
books he wanted people to read: standard editions of all school
textbooks (based on editions of the Confucian classics judged to
be "correct"), administrative handbooks (laws, rites, bureaucratic
rules, official dictionaries),[84] and moral primers. Books of his own

exhortations and reflections were made mandatory reading. Three consecutive editions of the *Grand Pronouncements (Dagao)*, in which Hongwu lashed out against what he felt was the endless evil and corruption of his regime, were issued between November 1385 and January 1387 and had to be memorized by every registered student all the way up to the National Academy. These were followed by his *Proclamation to the People (Jiaomin bangwen)*, published in the last year of his reign, in which he called on the people to join him in rooting out bad officials. These texts circulated widely, to judge from a poem written a few years after the *Grand Pronouncements* were published:

> Heaven's words are earnest, sure in guiding men's fortunes:
> Wind swirls, thunder frightens, the spirits are startled to listen.
> Hanging the text on the ox's horns, reading it at the field's edge,
> How delightful that the farmer can also read simple writing.[85]

This image of the studious farmer may be nothing more than a pleasant fiction to show that the pinnacle of state power was not entirely closed to ordinary men. Still, it was a fiction that would not have made sense had illiteracy blanketed the realm. Which it didn't. There were enough text-readers that the state could hope through publishing to bind their aspirations to its hegemony. More time would be needed before private publishing might begin to shape a world of readers larger and more diverse than the state's communicative realm. This world would take shape in the sixteenth century.

ECONOMY AND EXCHANGE

The Hongwu emperor's vision of village life, which Zhang Tao liked to replay in a romantic key toward the end of the dynasty, was of the settled and isolated village, self-sufficient in its economy and self-sustaining in its ecology. Women remained within the home to produce the cloth that their families needed, men went out to tend the crops in the fields, and those in one village had no truck with those in the next. But Chinese villages have never been hermetically closed to the outside world, contrary to modern misperceptions of preindustrial agrarian society. Nor have Chinese men and women always lived according to the ideal gender roles set for them. Gazetteer compilers liked to be able to make such declarations as, "Men devote themselves to agriculture and women to weaving," or "If one housewife does not weave, some people go cold." A compiler on the North China Plain was pleased to be able to do this for two of his more rural counties.[86]

In other local economies, however, the image of the woman indoors at the loom weaving for her family was something of a fiction. The compiler of a Hongwu-era gazetteer from Jiangxi reports that "men and women, young and old—aside from one or two who remained at home to prepare food—are all in the fields." The same writer also makes the point that these men and women inhabited a mobile world, and he was unhappy about this. "The boundaries of the county run through mountains," which should have meant that locals were insulated from corrosive influences from outside. "Because it is on a courier route, however, the people are of an inconstant nature." He notes that some locals become earnest scholars and a few achieve prominence as officials, but "there are those who pursue arguments and enjoy conflict, substituting clamor for respect."[87]

A bucolic picture of settled rural constancy reproducing itself from ancient times to the present may have comforted rulers anxious to perpetuate political stability. But even in the early Ming it was only a picture. The reality of village life was different. Not only were women in the fields, but women and men were bartering what they made for what they needed along the thoroughfares operated by the state. Once the Ming state had restored the transportation systems on which trade relied, improving the pace and ease with which goods and people could move, commerce only became more active. By the second quarter of the fifteenth century, not a few producers were sending their surplus into regional markets and some commodities were being moved long distances.

THE STATE IN THE ECONOMY

The Hongwu emperor was not ignorant of the economic functions of commerce, whatever his pronouncements in favor of an immobile self-sufficiency. He was willing to permit merchants a relatively free hand in buying, moving, and selling other than a few items controlled by state monopoly. His main concern was that merchants be registered, although he did not create a separate home-based registration category for merchants that would set them apart from the peasantry, as he did for artisans and soldiers (these statuses entailed particular fiscal duties). Rather, registration of merchants was to be done in a way that acknowledged their mobility: they were to furnish their names and descriptions of the goods they were carrying to local licensed brokers, who were to write these down in registers they submitted to the magistrate once a month for inspection. There is no evidence that this cumbersome self-reporting system was ever observed.

Local brokers were important figures in the commercial world of Ming China. A sample carriage contract from the fourteenth century indicates that a broker or "guarantor" (baoren) would act on behalf of a merchant who wanted to ship goods by engaging for him the services of a shipmaster. This agent not only served as the middleman who brought the parties together and drew up the contract, but he was responsible for guaranteeing to the merchant that the shipmaster would not defraud him while carrying his goods and would pay for any losses due to negligence. (The late-Ming almanac in which this contract is preserved advises merchants to work only with trustworthy brokers.)[88] The wholesale trade even before the Ming thus involved three distinct parties: the merchant who owned the goods but did not personally ship them, the shipper who arranged for their transportation by hiring boats and engaging boatmen on the wholesaler's behalf, and the broker who did neither but used his knowledge of local market conditions to arrange commercial agreements beneficial to both parties.

One aspect of commerce that Hongwu did desire to control was prices. Having personally experienced the inflation that raged at the end of the Yuan dynasty, the emperor regarded the stabilization of commodity prices as a major goal of his regime. He did not seek to set prices, however, but only to see that merchants bought and sold at fair market prices. The Ming Code stipulated that merchants who priced their goods unfairly would be liable for punishment under bribery laws, their penalty being based on the amount by which the selling price departed from the market price. Monopolizing goods on a local market to create artificially high prices deserved a flogging of eighty blows. To provide additional protection for the consumer, merchants were to use only the regulated weights and measures and warned to deal only in items of good quality.[89] When a price was disputed, a fair market price was to be determined by local officials, who were in any case required in the first ten days of every month to compile a list of prices on the basis of actual sales in order to govern their purchases in the local market. A handbook of 1404 reminds the magistrate to observe market prices lest the people under his jurisdiction feel he is cheating them.[90]

Hongwu's least successful intervention to manage the commercial economy was his attempt to withdraw silver from circulation. Silver was the principal medium of exchange in the Ming economy. Copper was also used, and coins were minted, but their value was small. Larger payments were made in unminted silver (measured in taels, or ounces), which silversmiths in the market cut, weighed, and melted into ingots of the required value. The emperor hoped to force silver out of circulation by lowering the limits on silver mining to restrict its flow into the market, and by replacing silver with paper money (baochao, precious scrip) as the Mongols had done. The currency never inspired confidence. The most the government could do was protect the physical bills by legally analogizing them to stamped government documents, destruction of which was illegal. When some money got torn in a fight between a husband and wife in 1384, for instance, judicial officials drew the analogy to argue they be given the full flogging of a hundred strokes by the heavy bamboo. The case came before Hongwu on 16 August. He must have been feeling indulgent that day. "This husband and wife just got into a private blow-up and did not intend to destroy the scrip," he decided after reviewing the case. "Pardon them."[91]

Despite such laws that privileged paper money, people preferred precious metals to "precious scrip." The demand for silver did not flag, nor did the attraction of smuggling it out of the ground. The revenue-hungry Yongle emperor reversed his father's policies on silver. He authorized the reopening of silver mines throughout south China and the Chinese-held portions of Vietnam and Burma, and he upped the mining quotas. Silver production boomed, reaching a rate of 10,000 kilograms a year in the second decade of the fifteenth century and continuing strong through to the fourth. (These figures reflect only the official receipts at legal mines and do not include the bits of silver that private miners were extracting from small pits throughout the hills of south China.)[92] Yongle raised the quotas because of his regime's appetite for the precious metal. A man of more expansive vision than his father, Yongle pursued grand military schemes and half a dozen large maritime expeditions into the Indian Ocean led by the eunuch commander Zheng He (1371–1433). The overseas adventures stimulated production and trade in the places they reached in Southeast Asia and the Indian Ocean, and they brought home all manner of goods both profitable and wondrous; but they were not necessarily self-financing and had to be paid for. The need for silver and the relative openness of maritime borders resulted in seepage of foreign bullion into the economy, which in turn mildly stimulated commercial activity in the fifteenth century.

Commerce expanded during and after Hongwu's reign in large part because of his own economic recovery program. Once rural stability had been restored, those producing for their own subsistence found that in good years something was left over, and they were willing to trade their surplus. If merchants simply circulated surplus where it was needed without manipulating the market to defraud producers or consumers, as the suspicious usually thought they did, then they had an economic purpose to play in the moral scheme of things. What gave merchants the power to go beyond this simple role, to identify and insert themselves into the natural gaps between abundance and shortfall and take advantage of the disparities between rich and poor, was not their cunning or greed—contrary to Confucian complaints—but alienability of property and freedom of exchange. Hongwu's schemes to reorganize the countryside as a net of closed communities may have reiterated age-old designs for ensuring egalitarian access to land and limiting the growth of a local ruling class which go back to the Han dynasty and were repeated in various ways in the Tang and Song. But as he did not prohibit buying and selling, disparities and gaps caused goods, and eventually labor, to be bought and sold. Hongwu assumed that commerce would remain within urban areas and did not consider legislating a place for it in the rural sector. This is precisely where commerce within the Chinese agrarian system found its most substantial resources.

The state did not provide institutions to service commercial exchanges, monitor commercial transactions, or guarantee financial agreements, except when called upon to adjudicate a commercial dispute. It entered the sphere of commodity circulation to ensure stability and raise money, which it did by imposing monopoly distribution and pricing on certain key commodities (salt, tea, and alum), by levying direct taxes (a commercial tax [shangshui] was levied at a modest 3.3 percent), and by imposing a transit tax at certain points in the network of state waterways (e.g., a chain of seven customs barriers on the Grand Canal between Beijing and Nanjing was established in 1429 to monitor the movement of official grain and to tax private goods). Contrary to the conventional view, Hongwu's administration was not out to suppress commerce. The emperor did hope to dampen the social power of merchants by regulating the public display of their wealth, as he did in an edict of 1381 prohibiting them from wearing silk.[93] But he otherwise showed little concern about the commercial circulation of goods.

Those living in commercialized settings shared this attitude. Despite the Confucian habit of regarding the presence of merchants in local society as a sign that something was amiss, early-Ming authors living in regions where the market economy was developed were content to note merchants' presence without expressing concern. The compiler of a late-fourteenth-century gazetteer of Yangzhou on the Grand Canal just above the Yangzi observes that "this being the major artery of communication between the Huai and Yangzi rivers, people by custom are pleased to work as merchants and do not pursue agriculture. Itinerant merchants from the four quarters live in their midst. People here are wealthier than in all other counties" in the region.[94]

FOOD SUPPLY

One item of commercial exchange in which the Ming state took keen interest was grain. The issue was not so much whether commerce was making a profit on grain as whether a shortfall might threaten the security of the regime. As the noted author Xu Wei (1521–93) would later observe, "When there are no difficulties in feeding the people, then subjects may be expected to be submissive."[95] This was the expectation that the Yongle emperor had in mind when he asked the Persian emissaries in 1420 whether the grain was dear or cheap in their country. They told him it was cheap. He replied that an abundance of food signified that the Persian ruler must be rightly disposed toward Heaven.[96] Which was just as he wished himself to be seen.

The standard method for ensuring that grain was available and affordable to the people was state-sponsored storage. By stocking grain and distributing it when needed, officials could provide direct relief in times of extreme famine. They could also let stocks onto the market to force down the price. In the first year of his reign, the

Hongwu emperor ordered that four "preparedness granaries" (*yu-beicang*) be set up in every county of the realm to prepare against famine.[97] The order was almost universally obeyed. Few of these preparedness granaries survived into the mid-Ming, however. Their decline may be a sign that local areas were achieving self-sufficiency in grain, as the Hongwu emperor hoped they might, or more likely that magistrates were too busy or too hard-pressed for funds to keep them up.

The decay of the preparedness granaries may also indicate that grain shortages, when they occurred, were being mitigated in other ways, more particularly by encouraging merchants to bring grain in from other regions where the price was lower. A vice-minister might complain that Suzhou was vulnerable to a subsistence crisis because little grain was stored there, as one did in 1432,[98] without recognizing that Suzhou usually managed fine because merchants there operated a grain market that was able to supply the city's food needs. Capital officials in the early Ming had not yet fully adjusted to the reality of the grain market, less perhaps out of a Confucian disdain for trade than because that market was smaller than it would become later in the dynasty.

MERCHANTS

The common view of merchant origins in the early Ming was that people took up trade because they couldn't survive by staying at home and tilling the fields as they were supposed to. Faced with starvation, they took to the roads as peddlers and, if they were lucky, moved up to more lucrative trade. Reports from Shanxi province, whose natives earned a strong reputation for commercial acumen in the Ming, reflect this logic: "As Zezhou is stuck in the middle of ten thousand mountains, there is not much land. Even when there is a bumper harvest, people don't have enough to eat." As a consequence, local people "without an inch of land to call their own" became merchants, ironworkers, or salt peddlers. Or again: "Shangdang is in the midst of ten thousand mountains, so merchants rarely go there, yet the land is poor and so people trade. As practically nothing is produced, one in ten takes off."[99] With levels of production too low to support the local population, areas not implicated in prominent commercial networks saw the poorest leave to survive elsewhere by engaging in small-time commerce. Taking up trade with neither example nor experience was an act of desperation. Only the exceptional ever progressed to higher levels of commercial dealing. Most remained within a permanent commercial underclass that facilitated trade but did not direct it, yet it was their itinerant retailing that lubricated the early-Ming economy.

Merchants working at the wholesale level faced the difficulties of long-distance transportation, especially in the early Ming when the infrastructure was still in the process of being rebuilt. Commercial travel took its toll. Biographies of virtuous widows in the early Ming often refer to the accidental deaths of merchant husbands. The biography of a virtuous widow in fourteenth-century Yangzhou says that she became one because "her husband went off to pursue commerce and drowned." She was not the only Yangzhou widow whose husband met this fate: the husband of another is recorded as having drowned going upriver to Nanjing.[100] Death by drowning was sufficiently common in commercial circles, or at least sufficiently feared, that it appears in the standard Ming carpentry manual as one of the outcomes of spells cast by evil house-builders. "If a boat turned upside-down is hidden in the ground to the north of the house," the manual warns, "one will perish in a river when going out to trade."[101]

The hardship of trade was made heavier by the negative attitude toward commercial gain that Confucianism voiced. To be a merchant was to be in the bottommost and least respected of the ancient "four categories of the people" (*simin*), which descended from gentry (*shi*) to peasant (*nong*) to artisan (*gong*) to merchant (*shang*). This neat and simplifying formula, which dates back at least to the Eastern Han dynasty, was disrupted when the Mongols introduced dozens of new categories for the Chinese they came to rule, but Hongwu and his advisors called it back as a template by which to fix the division of labor in society. The founder ordered his Minister of Revenue in 1385 to "inform the realm that each of the four categories of the people should keep to their proper occupations and not go wandering about to gain sustenance."[102] Hongwu was not fixated on using the fourfold classification to limit the occupations among the people or create a caste system, invoking it more as a convenient shorthand for the settled hierarchy that should prevail in local society: a moral rather than a regulatory framework. Everyone realized that lots of people didn't fit the model. The magistrate's handbook *New Mirror for Shepherding the People,* for instance, summarized "the correct occupations of the people" as "officials, soldiers, doctors, diviners, gentry, peasants, artisans, and merchants," which still managed to place the merchants in the lowest position.[103] Hongwu himself departed from the fourfold categorization when it suited him, at times specifying six categories by adding Buddhist monks and Daoist priests after the merchants.[104]

Gazetteer compilers of the early Ming tend to be much more conservative about the occupations they identify and the stigma they place on merchants. Whenever the allegation is credible, they depict local society in terms of the four categories. Best of all was to picture only gentry and peasantry on the local social landscape. Thus a compiler praised Lu'an prefecture in southeastern Shanxi by saying that "the people are hard-working and frugal and devote themselves to agriculture, and the gentry revere good breeding and apply themselves to study." Merchants and artisans simply disappear from this picture. In neighboring Qinzhou, they are mentioned but minimized: "By local custom the people are frugal and simple and devote themselves single-mindedly to plowing and reading; few engage in commerce."[105]

In any but the most backwoods counties, and sometimes even there as well, merchants were on the rise in the early Ming, even if their social prestige was limited and the gentry declined to notice them. Hongwu made mild attempts to keep the public status of merchants relative to other occupations low through sumptuary regulations. We have already noted his edict against merchants wearing silk—which wealthy merchants in any case sidestepped by wearing silk at home and either changing or putting something over it before going out. If the emperor recognized the need for disincentives, this suggests that people were more than willing to give up farming for trade if they had the opportunity. The stigma against commerce was either minor or did not exist, at least among the pragmatic poor.

MARKETS

Markets were the physical nodes in the expanding network of trade that merchants were constructing in the early Ming. They emerged wherever goods were being moved, collected, or transshipped in volume: most commonly as permanent markets open every day in county seats (only a few interior county seats lacked a permanent market at the beginning of the Ming, and all had one by the turn of the fifteenth century), but also as periodic markets (held at a rate anywhere from three to fifteen days a month) at strategic locations on rivers, along main thoroughfares, or at junctions where roads and rivers crossed. Local magistrates collected taxes at these markets, acted occasionally to oversee them, and involved themselves rarely in setting them up, but otherwise they left the existence and operation of markets to merchants.

A few larger cities like Nanjing had several full-time markets specializing in different types of trade. That city's 1395 gazetteer lists thirteen. The Great Market in the center of the city was a general market for all types of goods, while those outside the city wall specialized. For fruits in season, one went to the Sanshan Street Market; for fish and vegetables, to the New Bridge Market or the North Gate Bridge Market at Hongwu Gate; for textiles, tea, salt, and paper, to the market outside Qingliang Gate; for bamboo, to the Laibin Street Market outside Treasure Basin Gate (where Lu Li's brick was laid); for charcoal, to the Longjiang Market outside Jinchuan Gate; for grain, to the East Bank Market in the southwestern suburb; for construction timber, to the riverside market outside Yifeng Gate at the northwest corner.[106]

The power of marketing networks to concentrate resources in key regional cities like Nanjing shaped the early-Ming world in ways that the state did not anticipate. Suzhou is a prime example. That city had been the base of Hongwu's arch-rival Zhang Shicheng, as well as a major center of gentry-landlord power under the Mongols. At the start of his reign, the emperor tried to bring Suzhou to its knees by imposing crushing taxes and forced relocations, and to eclipse it by investing heavily in Nanjing and granting it extraordinary prominence as his capital. The plan did not succeed. Because of the strength of its commercialized economy, Suzhou proved able to shoulder the tax burden the emperor placed on it. Indeed, that tax burden may have helped to further stimulate commercialization by forcing people to pursue innovative strategies for making money.

The Yongle emperor abandoned his father's plan. By removing the primary capital to the north, he quickly deflated Hongwu's aspiration that Nanjing should enjoy regional preeminence. Although the Grand Canal linked both Suzhou and Nanjing to Beijing, the southern capital's connection to the canal was a side spur. The main artery flowed through Suzhou. The reopening of the Grand Canal effectively shunted Nanjing to secondary status and ensured that the Suzhou region would prosper as a nexus of interregional integration. By the middle of the fifteenth century, Suzhou had fully recovered the prosperity it had been robbed of at the beginning of the dynasty.[107] Nanjing survived comfortably as an administrative and cultural center, but it lacked the physical integration with surplus-producing regions that Suzhou enjoyed and could compete only in specialized commodities, notably luxuries as we shall soon observe. The other contender for commercial supremacy in the Jiangnan region was Hangzhou, but it lay another 200 kilometers farther down the Grand Canal and that much farther away from the center of the delta. Hangzhou appears to have served more as a feeder into the Suzhou market than as a competing market center for the region, as Ch'oe Pu sensed.

THE LUXURY TRADE

What we know of the markets in basic necessities like food and textiles in the early Ming is limited by the lack of systematic research. Easier to reconstruct, because the elite wrote about it, is the luxury trade. Early-Ming urban markets retailed expensive goods such as fine furniture, high-quality silks, women's ornaments—even sword sheaths made of yellow birch bark imported from Siberia[108]— that the wealthy wanted. These commodities were produced in few places and sold only in markets that served elite buyers in cities like Nanjing and Suzhou, and Beijing after it became the primary capital.[109] Although we have no sense of the scale of this trade, we at least know something of how the elite thought it was conducted, and through it catch a glimpse of the commercial life of the rich.

The imperial household was a major buyer of specialized manufactures, purchased or levied in great quantities. Some manufacturing was done in the imperial workshops in the capital. Cloisonné wine cups, for example, much favored by the court in the Jingtai era (1450–56), were produced by Muslim artisans from Yunnan who came to Beijing specially to make them in the palace, hence the Chinese term for cloisonné, *jingtai lan*, "indigo of the Jingtai era."[110] The imperial household also bought from workshops outside the capitals in places where artisanal specialties were well developed. Work was commissioned through eunuch agents and shipped by the transport service to the capital. From Suzhou came silks, from

Hangzhou embroideries, from Jiangxi paper (from Xishan) and porcelains (from Jingdezhen). Court demand stimulated these industries and promoted styles that nonimperial workshops quickly imitated to meet the growing demand of the status-conscious rich.

The elite were keen consumers of high-priced goods, though their dispersal makes it difficult to assess the impact of their demand on production. But the goods they coveted, and how they coveted them, are documented in *Essential Criteria of Antiquities (Gegu yaolun)*, a consumer's guide to fine cultural artifacts that reveals much about the early-Ming trade in luxuries. The author, Cao Zhao, came from a wealthy Songjiang family that actually owned many of the types of objects on which he passes judgment. His book was first published in 1388 in Nanjing, then expanded in the 1450s by Wang Zuo (js. 1427), from a wealthy family well-equipped with antiques, though from Jiangxi province. This expanded edition (bearing his 1459 preface) was published posthumously in Hangzhou three years later. *Essential Criteria* focuses on antiquities: archaic bronzes, ancient paintings and calligraphy, and old metal, porcelain, and lacquer. Ancient things bore a high cultural value, as they linked the owner to the revered past; they had a high cash value as well, a point that Cao repeats throughout the book. A devoted antiquarian, Cao Zhao rarely expresses enthusiasm for recent artifacts.[111] When he does name some recent craftsmen, such as the inkstick-maker Long Zhongdi from Taihe, Jiangxi, and the lacquer-maker Yang Hui from Jiaxing, Zhejiang, he is often critical of their work. His depreciation may be the antiquarian's prejudice against contemporary work; it may also signify that artisanal manufacture early in the Ming had not reattained the quality of the best pre-Ming work. Wang Zuo seems less troubled about referring to contemporary craftsmen.[112]

Aesthetics is the language of the book, yet Cao and Wang were not absorbed only in judgments of style, for they are keen to remind the reader that dealers were not always to be trusted to retail genuine pieces of good quality, nor to represent their wares fairly. One way of trying to increase the saleability of ordinary items was by attaching appealing but misleading names, such as calling quite ordinary Hezhou porcelains "new Ding ware" (Ding ware being highly prized, and Hezhou ware having no cachet). Cao also observes that the antique porcelain dealers of Nanjing had their own trade language: they referred to a damaged piece as *mao* ("thatch"), to a cracked piece as *mie* ("refuse"), and to a piece with insufficient glaze as *guchu* ("bones showing through"). Goods that sold well were readily imitated. The finest carved red lacquer at the beginning of the Ming came from Dali prefecture, Yunnan, but it was imitated by other producers so successfully that their wares sold well on the Nanjing market. Similarly, the solid lacquer inlaid with gold dust produced by Peng Junbao in Jiaxing in the thirteenth century was so popular that in the fifteenth century there were craftsmen producing a simpler version in both capitals.

Just as craftsmen sought to replace more expensive items with cheaper items by imitating them, so too the early-Ming market in luxuries practiced import substitution. Since many expensive objects circulating in that market were made from raw materials imported from Inner Asia, producers were encouraged to manufacture comparable objects at lower prices. In the case of objects fashioned from steel, Cao says that good steel is imported at a price higher than silver, and then notes that there is a reasonably good domestic substitute produced in Gansu called Dingxi steel from which artisans in north China make sharp knives for a fraction of the cost of real steel. Wang Zuo notes that this Dingxi steel was also being produced in his day from iron ore mined in Guangdong, Fujian, and southern Huguang, but that the Huguang steel is brittle and useless.[113]

One aspect of the luxury trade that stimulated production was the demand for luxury substitutes. Artisans wanting to sell to the rich, and the less-than-rich wanting to buy what the rich bought, conspired without meaning to in creating a brisk business in surrogate luxury goods. Canny manufacturers and dealers could push their way into this lucrative market from below by making sought-after goods cheaply using poorer materials or hurrying the production process but finishing their products in such a way that they were difficult to distinguish from the real things. At the original prices, the market encouraged both import and quality substitution, for cheaper versions could undercut the more expensive and fakes could find their way onto the market when the genuine article was unavailable or too expensive to buy. This trend alarmed wealthy collectors, of course, since buying fakes undermined the process of accumulating social capital that comes with luxury consumption. Wang offers much advice on how to avoid buying poor-quality goods. If you want to acquire lacquer furniture inlaid with mother-of-pearl, he recommends you have it made in your home under personal super-

vision to ensure you get the quality you want.[114] High culture that
ratified status through acquirable objects meant that the elite had no
choice but to interact with the market—and to figure out how to
guard against what markets do.

The knowledge that *Essential Criteria* contained thus became its
own commodity, as Craig Clunas has observed, "available in the
market-place to any player wanting to enter the search for ways of
transforming economic power into cultural power."[115] *Essential
Criteria* was particularly needed in the early Ming to educate the
new dynasty's elite, most of whom had not been born to good taste
and discrimination. They had to be told that ancient brocade curtains "are luxurious and delightful objects, but only fit for the decorating of halls or for lining walls; a scholar cannot derive pure
enjoyment from them;" or that cloisonné vases and cups "are appropriate for use only in a woman's apartment, and would be quite
out of place in a scholar's studio."[116] Inasmuch as "a wide knowledge of antiquities is the first requisite of a gentleman," the newly
ascendant had to be instructed about the right things to own and
how to own them. Cao's esoteric knowledge allows him to laugh at
the merely wealthy who pay high prices for Ding ware, the recent
manufacture and poor craftsmanship of which had reduced their
value in the eyes of the cognoscenti. Wang Zuo becomes cruelly
explicit when he names a vice-minister in Nanjing who had a screen
inlaid with stone of such low quality that it had to be touched up
with chemicals and scraped with a knife in order to make it presentable.[117] Through this rhetorical device, the text creates its
reader: someone who would not be caught dead buying a piece of
the offending porcelain or using chemicals to enhance a stone inlay
on a screen. It also coerces the reader into an identity that concedes
the authors' authority in all matters of taste. Who would not like to
think of himself as superior, in both cultural understanding and
commercial savvy, to the vice-ministerial philistine who didn't know
that he owned the wrong sort of screen?

The commodity life of expensive objects thus played a role in
shaping the hierarchies of the early Ming: in this case, bringing the
newly wealthy under the authority of the old established families,
from whom they had to learn the ropes of culture before they could
use them in turn to climb above those they regarded as falling short
of elite standards. Paradoxically, *Essential Criteria* had the effect of
redefining elite status away from those born to it, to those who had

the wealth to buy but needed to learn about what it was they were supposed to be buying. Once print put this knowledge into circulation for the price of an expensive book, any aspirant to elite status could find his way up.

THE DISTANCE BETWEEN RICH AND POOR

If the ownership and interpretation of cultural property served to enforce distinctions of status among the upper elite (and permit a measure of social mobility into that echelon), the ownership of landed property provided the foundation on which the overall hierarchy rested. Land was revered as the basis of the traditional social order. It was the source of food as well as wealth, and the primary nexus of the relationship binding rich and poor in the early Ming: those who owned or had access to it dominated over those who did not. But it was not a static foundation and accordingly was not conducive to fixed relationships. Like antiques, land was a commodity. You could buy it, sell it, mortgage it, rent it out at market rates, and make a fortune doing so, regardless of the cultural meanings ascribed to it by those who had it and those who didn't.

The Hongwu emperor appreciated that landholding was necessarily inequitable under such conditions, and he used only modest means to compensate for it. Certainly he structured the *lijia* system on the understanding that every household in the hundred should have sufficient land to maintain itself, although a supernumerary category was set aside to register the landless, and he hoped that, by placing the heavier burdens of tithing head, hundred captain, and tax captain on the wealthier households, over time the system would push households in the direction of land equality. His strongest interventions against landlordism were various relocation schemes and heavy taxation that he imposed on the large landowners of Jiangnan. When he lightened the burden of the four most heavily taxed prefectures (Suzhou, Songjiang, Jiaxing, and Huzhou) in 1380, he still warned his officials to be on guard against tax evasion scams that would mean, in a phrase that Zhang Tao would use for the dynasty's summer, that "the rich get richer and the poor, poorer."[118]

None of these maneuvers or warnings impeded the growth of a landowning elite in the early Ming. In a long memorial to the Ministry of Revenue in 1432 on the problems plaguing the fiscal administration of South Zhili, Governor Zhou Chen confirms Hongwu's fear when he observes that "big households" were sheltering people who should otherwise appear as separate taxable households.[119] Another memorial submitted to the throne four years later criticizes "the families of the rich and powerful" of Jiangnan and "tax captains in Changshu, Jiangyin, and other places"—large landowners all—for being involved in shipping large quantities of illegal salt inland to Jiangxi and Huguang.[120] This comment indicates that land was not the sole means on which the hierarchy of wealth was built in the early Ming. Smuggling is how the memorialist has chosen to represent what the rich were doing to get richer, but we could read this in a broader sense and observe that some wealthy landowners in Jiangnan were engaging in commercial speculation, albeit it in contraband, to augment land-based wealth.

The door from economic to social status was the examination system. When a man walked through that door, he converted wealth into public prestige and brought not just himself but his entire family into gentility. As the system was established and controlled by the state, the degree-holder enjoyed his elite status at the pleasure of the throne. But the bargain struck between emperor and elite was a good one. At the lowest level, the student who gained admission to the county school as a *shengyuan* benefited by gaining exemptions from corvée duties, thereby enhancing his personal status and reducing his family's tax burden. And he could look forward to the chance of an official career that could bring with it immense personal wealth and bureaucratic power, though only a select handful were able to rise to the highest degree of *jinshi*. The clearing of the slate at the new dynasty's founding meant that the elite in the early Ming rarely had generational depth going back before 1368. Some of the old notable families of the Yuan dynasty were able to perpetuate their status by relying on old established strategies such as marrying their daughters to imperial princes.[121] Otherwise, the continuity of elites over the Yuan-Ming transition appears to have been low by comparison with other dynastic transitions. It would take several generations before the gentry gained the depth and breadth needed to appear as the recognizable elite of local society.

While the gentry became established and grew, the rest of society did not stand still. In the second quarter of the fifteenth century, the Xuande emperor was aware of this movement and worried that the social world was becoming disordered. As he complained to his

Minister of Rites in 1429, "Many officials and commoners, for whom there are fixed regulations regarding dress and conduct, are transgressing ritual and offending against status."[122] However distressing this instability, most people had to deal with the more tangible devastations of drought, flood, locust infestation, and most of all famine, which overwhelmed large areas of the north, the northwest, the Yangzi Valley, and the inland southeast between 1434 and 1448.[123] The status obligations and bonds of deference that elites and subalterns had learned to take for granted as part of the Hongwu agrarian order—and which had proven durable for most of the first century of the Ming—began to appear insupportable to some.[124] The breaking point came in the hills of coastal Fujian to which many of the desperate fled. The man who led them was Deng Maoqi.

Deprivation is only part of Deng's story. The other part is silver. As commercial transacting drew more silver into circulation, officials agitated to be paid not in grain but in silver. Military officials, in particular, who frequently engaged in business on the side to ease the burden of funding their troops, were keen to have this flexibility. The government in 1436 chose to convert some of the grain tribute from the southern provinces into silver payments, an arrangement known as Gold Floral Silver (*jinhuayin*). The reform was to facilitate tax transmittance from counties where transportation was difficult, as well as provide tax relief to landowners.[125] It recognized that the economy worked more through money than barter, and that silver was available to meet the tax. The process of commuting fiscal levies from labor and kind to silver would continue subsequently through what became known as the Single Whip Reform (punning on the phrase, "reforming [tax payments] into a single item").

The government's response to the growing need for silver for paying taxes and for conducting business was to control the flow of silver onto the market: by strangling it. In 1438 the court of the child-emperor Zhengtong (r. 1436–49) ordered the closing of legal silver mines and an end to the small-scale extraction and refining of silver that went on privately in the hills of southern Zhejiang and northern Fujian.[126] Anyone found contravening the ban would be executed. But demand made illegal silver extraction a lucrative venture, and many unemployed miners and other marginal folk living in the hills carried on despite the danger (see figure 13). The decade-long series of increasingly harsh edicts against so-called miner ban-

Figure 13.   Miners scrape for small silver deposits in the mountains
(*Tiangong kaiwu*, 1637).

dits (*kuangzei*) starting in 1440 signaled that the government found
itself increasingly unable to stop the flow of silver. But unemploy-
ment, plus the desperate competition for land in the heavily populated southeastern coastal region and the corresponding vulnerability
of cultivators to high rents and other exactions from landlords,
forced many into this line of work.

The government's response to the spread of silver banditry in
rural Fujian in the mid-1440s was to militarize the *lijia* communities
by creating almost identical decimal self-defense units known as
baojia ("watches and tithings"). Liu Hua (js. 1430), the censor who
in 1446 recommended this course, suggested that small fortified
arsenals be set up in the villages so that local militia could be armed
as soon as the need arose. Local men were appointed to the post of
"small-*baojia* overseer" (*zong xiaobao*) to lead these community
battalions and organize night watches. The net of self-defense units
throughout Fujian would be so thorough that local order would be
protected.

The small-*baojia* overseers were often tough characters who used

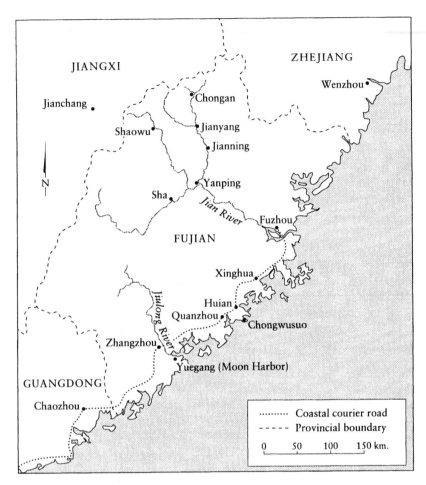

Map 4.   Fujian province.

their posts to the advantage of themselves or their local communities at the expense of the state. The Deng brothers, Maoqi (Seventh Son) and Maoba (Eighth Son), were two such appointees in Sha county in the Fujian interior (see map 4). Deng Maoqi used his position to challenge the privileges of local landlords. In particular, he pressed popular demands for the abolition of the traditional New Year's payment to landlords of grain, fowl, or fuel, known as the "winter gift" (*dongsheng*), a customary levy that landlords could impose on their tenants above the regular rent. He also insisted that absentee landlords come in person to collect rents rather than rely on agents who exacted collection fees from the tenants on top of the scheduled rents. The harassed landlords called on the county magistrate to arrest Deng in 1447, but he and his supporters resisted the attempt and killed the county magistrate and chief of police the following spring. The disturbance spilled into neighboring areas as soon as word of Deng's actions spread. The rebels organized themselves by drawing on the very community battalions the government had set up, and did so quickly enough to mobilize the forces needed to rout locally stationed troops. Many would lay the blame for Deng's brief success at the feet of Liu Hua's rural militarization scheme: if the *baojia* had not been in place, they argued, none of this would ever have happened.[127]

By the end of the summer of 1448, Deng's forces had taken over two county seats and were besieging the prefectural capital. A spokesman for the rebels declared to the prefectural officials that the rich had driven good men to desperate acts and that local officials had done nothing to alleviate their sufferings. He asked that the officials intercede on their behalf with the throne and pleaded for three years' exemption from labor service to rebuild what the petitioners called their "family wealth." The throne's response was to seek to defuse the crisis and see local conditions return to normal as quickly as possible, rather than escalate the conflict and run the danger of seeing this small shaking of the local hierarchy enlarge into a greater threat. The emperor chose to accept the appeal as an apology and not only grant the requested exemption but forgive unpaid taxes. This concession satisfied some but did not bring the rebellion to an end. Deng expanded his force to several hundred thousand and continued to enlarge his sphere of control. More county seats were captured, and when they were, the tax and household registers in magistrates' offices were destroyed.

Military households within Fujian were mobilized to fight the rebels, uprooting cultivators from the military colonies that had been set up at the beginning of the dynasty and throwing the colony system into chaos.[128] Local elites, from landlords to village elders, drummed local boys into self-defense militias using the same *baojia* organization the rebels had called upon. Neither was sufficient to put down the rebellion. Eventually, an army of over fifty thousand government troops, supported by food supplies donated by the local wealthy, was sent against them. The capture and execution of Deng Maoqi, who had declared himself the King Who Eliminates Evil, in the spring of 1449 crippled the rebellion. Resistance continued on into the autumn under his cousin until he was betrayed by a village elder. Disturbances persisted into 1450 as rebels roamed farther into the interior or out into the hills along the coast,[129] but the military occupation of the region prevented them from relinking to sustain a full-scale rebellion. The troops sent in to crush Deng's rebellion found ordinary local people easy victims. As a local author put it, "So many people died that they could not be counted."[130]

In his analysis of the uprising of 1448–49, Tanaka Masatoshi has concluded that the rebellion failed because Deng persevered in negotiating with a centralized autocracy that, by the end of the first century of Ming rule, was uninterested in protecting cultivators against the exploitation of local officials and landlords. Seeking to demonstrate his loyalty to the emperor, Deng delayed further offensive action at a time when he should have pressed his military advantage. He expected to gain imperial protection for his righteous defense of local concerns. In Tanaka's estimation, Deng should have moved rapidly to seize control of transportation arteries and secure a broader regional base for his movement, thereby preventing the incursion of troops from outside and hampering local elites from using the manpower and food supplies under their control against the rebellion. Despite its failure, Tanaka regards Deng's uprising as the first peasant rebellion that resisted the class relationship of rent rather than the depredations of officials, and therefore as the first genuinely class-based "peasant war" in Chinese history.[131]

The conflict that ignited the Fujian mountains in the late 1440s could suggest that the nature of the landlord-tenant relationship was changing as commerce and the need for silver grew. Tenants were no longer willing to think of their relationship to their landlords as a personal bond, symbolized by the obligation to give them "winter gifts." Now the relationship was simply contractual: an economic agreement that entailed no terms other than those specified in the rental contract. The rent relationship would become further depersonalized through the Ming as tenants resisted the seigneurial demands that landlords had traditionally exercised. It became more and more common for landlords to complain that it was better to have good tenants than good land. The shift from taxing labor to taxing land reinforced this trend away from personal bondage. In the future, more purely economic relationships, weighed in silver, would determine the hierarchy of power in Chinese society—just as Zhang Tao warned they would.

Spring

The Middle Century
(1450–1550)

Those who went out as merchants became numerous, and the ownership of land was no longer esteemed. As men matched wits using their assets, fortunes rose and fell unpredictably. The capable succeeded, the dull-witted were destroyed; the family to the west enriched itself while the family to the east was impoverished. The balance between the mighty and the lowly was lost as both competed for trifling amounts, each exploiting the other and everyone publicizing himself.

Zhang Tao

It was in the restless spring of the dynasty, according to Zhang Tao, that the stable repetitions of agrarian life in the early-Ming winter started to unravel as trade lured men from their fields, disrupting the foundation of wealth and disordering community life. Disorder was indeed on the minds of those alive in 1450, but disorder of a more tangible kind. The previous September the twenty-one-year-old Zhengtong emperor had been captured by the Mongol khan during an ill-considered campaign on the northern border. It is a terrible thing for an imperial system to lose its emperor: all of a sudden the center is missing. Without it the system itself threatens to fly apart. Death was manageable because rules of succession guided what should follow. But capture in battle was not something for which Chinese precedents prepared a court. There were no rules to refill the center in an emperor's absence.

An emperorless Beijing was thrown into a constitutional crisis in the winter of 1449–50 as officials jockeyed for political advantage around the question of whether to ransom the hostage emperor or remove him in favor of his younger half-brother, whom Zhengtong had appointed regent in his temporary absence. The second position won out. Zhengtong was formally deposed and the Jingtai emperor enthroned in his place. Burdened with a worthless hostage, the Mongols handed the deposed emperor over to Jingtai and six years of virtual house arrest, until Zhengtong deposed Jingtai in turn and pushed his way back onto the throne, renaming himself Emperor Tianshun ("Obeying the Will of Heaven").

THE CENTER RECEDES

The high drama of revolving emperors that ushered in the middle century of the Ming dynasty was of no interest to Zhang Tao as he penned his comments in the Sheh county gazetteer. His retrospective worries were elsewhere. Far more compelling was the disappearance of quite a different center: the self-sufficient rural community around which the Hongwu emperor had reconstructed Ming society. Land was slipping as the basis of value. A knack for commercial dealing and a keen sense of competition were proving to be more attractive than farming. As people pursued the new profitable opportunities in commerce, the mechanical solidarity that Hongwu had dreamed of reintroducing into the villages dwindled.

Even the hostage-taking of the Zhengtong emperor had commercial consequences. A junior official working in Beijing at the time noted that before he was captured, it was possible to commission a prominent writer to compose a eulogy for a deceased parent for two- or three-tenths of a tael (ounce) of silver. As of 1450, however, "the price of literary composition suddenly went up" to a half or even a full tael.[1] Officials regarded price fluctuations with almost as much horror as dethronements, as evidence that good order was seeping away. For Zhang Tao the horror was greater, for it suggested a more dangerous slippage: not from political instability to price rises (which might be only short-term), but from economic competition to the disordering of the realm. The reported rise of authors' fees in 1450 would have annoyed Zhang in another way as well. It was an unhappy reminder that, even within polite society, everything had its price.

As for decline of the old village ways in the mid-Ming, Zhang Tao was more or less correct. It was a change that the mid-Ming state accepted, and eventually promoted, through a series of reforms to the principle of corvée based on the *lijia*. Starting in the mid-1430s, the newly installed Zhengtong regime had begun looking for ways to augment revenue flows to the center. It was almost impossible to increase revenue when a good part of the levy was assessed in human labor. Only when labor had been converted into something more negotiable over distance—money—could an increase in the labor levy yield tangible returns for the central government. Collecting the land tax in grain entailed the same difficulty on a lesser scale. The grain tribute system could get more grain to the capital if more grain was demanded, but shipping bulky produce halfway across the realm was troublesome and costly. The *lijia* system may have worked to build the walls of Nanjing, but the forced contribution of labor and materials was not a reliable foundation for regime revenue in so vast a realm, especially when the capital had been moved far to the north and ordinary people were proving adept at evading *lijia* registration.

To feed its ever-growing need for revenue, the Ming state commuted some of its levies to payments in silver, of which a portion—and an ever-growing portion—got sent to Beijing. The beginning of this process can be dated to 1436 with the imposition of Gold Floral Silver, which as we noted at the end of the preceding chapter commuted a portion of the tax grain from seven southern provinces into a cash payment. Reforms in the service levy introduced during the mid-Ming installed other commutation arrangements. Local procurement (*zuoban*) came to be replaced by annual requisition (*suiban*), which required that magistrates supplying materials to the capital absorb the cost into their own budgets and forward the silver they would otherwise have paid out to the central government. Obligatory service at the local courier station was phased out in favor of a payment known as courier silver (*yiyin*), a process of commutation that began in 1490 and was made universal by 1507. These and other reforms gradually shifted the collection of state revenue onto a cash basis. By the end of the sixteenth century, practically all the services originally levied through the *lijia* system had been commuted to silver payments assessed as surtaxes on land, a process known as the Single Whip Reform (*yitiao bianfa*).[2]

The principle of corvée was thus disappearing in the eddies of the new money economy of the fifteenth century. From the point of view of revenue collection in Beijing, the center was not receding but pressing its revenue hunger more urgently onto local administrations. In another way, though, the center was pulling back from administering tax collection by leaving in the hands of local magistrates the problems of how to increase revenue. Officials in the field were obliged to come up with funding solutions on their own, which could not be formally entered into the county's books. The center did not care what went on behind the formal appearances of things so long as local magistrates met their tax quotas.[3]

How unlike the days of the Hongwu reign, when the emperor sought to arrange every detail of village life. On the surface there was little to indicate that the Hongwu order was no longer in place. His *Proclamation to the People* continued to enjoy unassailable formal authority, and subsequent emperors and central officials reminded local magistrates to make sure that everyone was still reciting their great ancestor's instructions.[4] Yet the forced arcadia the text depicted must have seemed increasingly archaic, and its recitation purely routine, to villagers and magistrates alike.

The receding center did not mean that local magistrates sat idle. Quite the opposite: activism and initiative were essential if the magistrate was to keep his county going in the growing administrative vacuum. And the activities and initiatives he took to shape his administrative world and meet his fiscal quotas had more and more to take account of the movement of commodities and the increasingly portable forms that wealth was taking. Statecraft was called for; the rigidity of Zhang Tao was not yet the style.

THE ADMINISTRATION OF WUHU

Xu Jie—not the famous and extraordinarily wealthy chief grand secretary of the same name who will appear toward the end of this chapter, but a magistrate active in the last decade of the fifteenth century—was appointed prefect of Taiping, the next prefecture up the Yangzi River from Nanjing. The seat of the prefectural government was in Dangtu, 100 kilometers from the capital, but another 35 kilometers farther upriver was the busier river port of Wuhu, which was pushing Dangtu aside as the economic center of the prefecture. Set within a rich patchwork of rice fields, Wuhu was the western terminus of the internal waterway link to Suzhou created by the East Dams project (as noted in Winter) and an important distribution point for the rice trade going in and out of Jiangnan. It was also the natural point of exit for the great Huizhou merchants coming down from Sheh county, where Zhang Tao served as magistrate. As a Sheh native described the city's relationship to his home county, "Wuhu has a stranglehold on boat and cart traffic and on tolls and trade." In the sixteenth century, the land route from Sheh to Wuhu was sufficiently well traveled that you could hire either a sedan chair or a horse to convey you whenever you wished, though you might want to time your journey in relation to the full complement of parasites that the traffic also supported. According to a Huizhou merchant who knew the route well, you could expect to be accosted by people every five kilometers. Who these people were depended on the time of day you were traveling: ruffians running protection rackets in the early dawn, transport agents during the day, and bandits at night. But these were the conditions for trade, and trade pumped the lifeblood of Wuhu. "Since the old days," as a later gazetteer compiler referred to the Ming period, "local attitudes have taken a positive view of trade and commercial travel."[5]

Prefect Xu Jie was not explicitly required to promote trade; indeed, the idea of doing so made little sense in terms of Confucian conventions of administration. But consider the four undertakings for which the prefect is praised in the prefectural gazetteer:[6]

"He built the floating bridge."

The floating bridge in question was a large wooden structure on pontoons spanning the river that flowed past the front gate of Wuhu and out into the Yangzi. Magistrates all over the country had been actively rebuilding bridges in the opening years of the dynasty in order to restore war-damaged infrastructure. The next wave of bridge building came in the latter third of the fifteenth century, especially in central and south China in the wake of the massive floods of 1465.[7] Floating bridges, being cheaper to build than permanent structures, were often favored by mid-Ming magistrates, pressed as they were to meet central demands for funds and obliged to devise their own extrabureaucratic arrangements to finance infrastructural investments, usually by soliciting funds from the local wealthy. Many a mid-Ming bridge rose or fell depending on whether the magistrate was successful in finding someone willing to pay for it.

Whereas bridge building in the early Ming seems to have been equally the work of officials and private individuals, bridges built by local people in the mid-Ming vastly outnumber those built by officials.[8] Many benefactors of bridges are identified in gazetteers as "charitable commoners" or "local residents," polite labels for wealthy merchants. To find merchants bankrolling bridge and road construction is surprising only if we cling to the notion that the Chinese state was the source of all infrastructural investment. Certainly mid-Ming contemporaries were not captive to that notion.

Consider the opinion of the noted scholar-official Zhang Yue (1492–1553), who was home on leave in the coastal county of Huian, Fujian, in 1529 and who compiled the county gazetteer, published the following year. Zhang complains in that book that local bridges and roads were in much worse repair than they had been in the Southern Song. The Southern Song had good bridges and roads, he concludes, because maritime trade had enriched the region. Looking around him at the reviving trading economy of Huian, he argues that it was time for local merchants to pay for infrastructure. "The country has been at peace for a long time now and the people have wealth abundant enough that they can put their surplus into performing their civic duties," he points out, "yet bridges and roads are not in a state of repair up to what they were in Song times."[9] As we shall see later in this chapter, trade had only just revived in the 1520s. Zhang was too impatient. Two decades later, however, a captured Portuguese sailor being escorted along the main coastal highway running from Quanzhou up to Fuzhou (Huian was just north of Quanzhou) gives a different impression: "All the roads were paved and made even: and sometimes when we went by rivers, we asked if the other roads which went on further were similar, and they told us that they were." Another member of the same party observes that "the ways eachwhere are gallantly paved with foursquare stone, except it be where for want of stone they used to lay brick." In the hilly sections of the road up the coast from Quanzhou, "wheresoever it was necessary, the road was cut

Figure 14.   An official and his retinue ride horseback
over a brick road. The axonometric rendering of the
bricks in oblique parallel lines has been a convention
of Chinese architectural drawing since the Han
dynasty (*Zixiao ji*).

with a pickaxe, and in many places no worse paved than in the plain
ground."[10] By European standards at least, these were good roads
(see figure 14).

"He reconstructed the school hall."

Prefect Xu rebuilt more than bridges. The Hongwu emperor had
ordered schools constructed or renovated at a rate of one per county
throughout the realm in the second year of his dynasty. Being the
institution at which those who reached the lowest degree of *shengyuan* had to register, if not actually attend lectures, the school

loomed large in the world of the county gentry. Many official
schools were in sorry condition by Xu Jie's time, so the mid-Ming
became a time of fixing up old buildings and as well of setting up
land endowments to cover such costs in the future.[11] Local officials
had to raise the funds for these projects from outside their annual
budgets (again, the center was not willing to fund them). Who they
turned to depended on where they could find moral and financial
support. There is no evidence of who paid for Prefect Xu's school
building, but we do know that within the decade the county magistrate of Wuhu added a library to his school, and that he solicited the
funds to build it from merchants, not the gentry.[12] Already in the
mid-Ming, local administration was becoming financially dependent
on commercial wealth. As for building a school, merchants might be
willing to come forward in the hope of seeing their own sons pass
through its gate and make the transition to gentry status.

"He sponsored the prefectural gazetteer."

Prefect Xu's gazetteer of 1497 is the sort of publication that has
made the research for this book possible. Few gazetteers survive
from the first century of the Ming because few were actually printed,
but they begin to survive in quantity from about the year 1500.[13]
Most gazetteers are redolent with an anticommercial bias, as their
compilers—for the most part disappointed moralists who did not
rise above the lower rungs of the examination system—sought to
make their subjects conform to conventional Confucian notions of
moral rectitude and good order. They underplayed and obscured
merchants' contributions to local society in the urge to make a place
seem perfectly genteel. We cannot know how the compilers recruited
by Xu Jie pictured commerce in the 1497 gazetteer of the prefecture,
as only fragments of this book survive in three Chinese libraries.[14]
Given the growing commercial sources of wealth in the prefecture, it
is tempting to think that Xu relied on merchant donations to get the
gazetteer into print.

"He equalized the burden of the courier and postal services."

"Equalization" was the standard Ming euphemism for commuting levies in labor to levies in silver, since the procedure was often
carried out in such a way that the tax burden was distributed more
equitably. In this case, the prefect was implementing the changeover
to courier silver, described above, which would enable him to pay
for the costs of running the courier service and not have to corvée
the local people. As a result of commutations like the courier silver,

magistrates throughout mid-Ming China were able to collect several hundred thousand taels annually and disburse this silver within local labor markets. This monetization increased the pressure on silver stocks, however, a development the central government was not prepared to accommodate. Official silver production between 1450 and 1490 remained modest, fluctuating between 600,000 and 800,000 taels (2,000 to 3,000 kilograms) a year. Just as the courier silver levy came into effect, however, legal silver production was cut to half that rate. The supply of silver to fund the operations of government did not meet demand. This imbalance stimulated the growing trade with Japan in the second quarter of the sixteenth century, as Chinese merchants traded Chinese products for Japanese bullion and drew silver into the Chinese domestic market.[15]

Xu Jie would not have seen any of his accomplishments as devices for promoting commerce, meeting the demands of merchants, or participating in the monetization of the economy. Neither goal lay within his responsibilities as a servant of the emperor. He was charged only with keeping the lines of communication open so that state servants, tax goods, and information flowed to the capital. Yet as a magistrate concerned with maintaining the viability of communications and finances within his jurisdiction, Prefect Xu was doing all of these things and in doing so was adding the impetus of state push to commercial pull. He did so without thinking in these terms—and without necessarily understanding the more commercial context that prefectures like Taiping and cities like Wuhu were being pulled toward.

VAGRANT AND FEMALE

To look at the official population statistics, one would never guess that Wuhu in the mid-Ming was a prosperous place. The 1391 census gave the county a population of 33,318 people. By 1522, however, Wuhu registered only 25,594, down by one-quarter. Nothing in the environment accounts for such a loss. The gazetteer indicates no disasters between 1426 and 1547 (the Yangzi flooded on both occasions) to explain this drop. Wuhu's first major calamity was not really until 1557, when the Yangzi flooded so severely that it "left no sign of the overland road from Dangtu to Wuhu, and boats passed over the tops of houses. Crops were not harvested and the people survived by eating roots and tree bark."[16] Even when disaster did strike farther up the Yangzi in the mid-Ming, it did not inflict high mortality. Flood and drought may have "succeeded one another, exhausting the people's resources,"[17] as a provincial official noted of the middle Yangzi region in 1505, yet magistrates were not reporting that people were dying of poverty.

The mid-dynasty respite from natural calamity, coupled with commercial growth, meant that population grew. Wuhu was not alone in reporting no increases in its decennial censuses. Consider the prefecture of Nanchang, 700 kilometers by water upriver from Wuhu. Nanchang filed a population report in 1412 of 1,126,119. Eighty years later it reported *exactly* the same number of residents. It did so at a time when "land scarcity and overpopulation were forcing many to live by handicraft and teaching or to wander in all directions to make a living."[18] The statecraft scholar Qiu Jun (of whom more below) believed that over half of Jiangxi males had gone west to become merchants in Huguang.[19] The Hongzhi emperor (r. 1488–1505) was aware that "the daily increase in my subjects" coincided with "the daily dwindling of registered civilians and soldiers."[20] Registered population at the end of the mid-Ming was stuck at 62,531,295.

Real population may have been double that, but people on the move were evading registration.[21] Some headed into the marginal terrain at the edges of their counties and provinces. As the 1530 gazetteer of Huian county on the Fujian coast observes, "Today the people are becoming increasingly numerous and there is not enough good land for them to cultivate, so there are many drifters and con men." Not only were Huian natives vagabonding about, but people from the prefectural capital of Quanzhou and from the next prefecture south, Zhangzhou, were drifting up the coast into Huian county to escape population pressures there. To survive, "the poor, if they live near the mountains, cut down trees to make charcoal and, if they live along the shore, burn oyster shells to make lime."[22] At the other end of the coast up in Shandong, the poor cut wood, made charcoal, fired pots, and wove mats and baskets to generate enough income to survive.[23] Inland, they moved into the hills along interprovincial borders "thickly forested and cut with circuitous valleys" where, an official reported, "there is money to be made in cutting firewood. Migrants live here without being entered on the official registers, and families occupy land without paying taxes."[24] As lowlanders pushed into the uplands, a new and more intense wave of deforestation denuded the hills, propelling China's ecology toward its current eroded state.

Those who took to the hills fed themselves by planting marginal land using hardy crop strains and agricultural techniques they brought from other areas. Early-ripening rice, which had been responsible in part for the rapid development of the lower Yangzi region in the Song dynasty, was now spreading into the uplands along the borders among the interior provinces of Henan, Huguang, Sichuan, Guangxi, and Yunnan in the mid-Ming.[25] Time layered these interprovincial spaces as early migrants took possession of what was previously waste land and later migrants worked for them as tenants or hired hands. When drought struck Huguang in the 1460s, these marginal people turned to predatory strategies to survive. The government responded with force, and the migrants fought back. In 1464, Thousand-Pound Liu and Monk Shi led hundreds of thousands eking out a life at the margins of settled society to war against the government troops. Bearded Hu led them again in 1470. All failed to hold the troops at bay. Later, in the 1530s, bands of Huguang highlanders had no strategy other than preying on each other.[26]

It was rare for a Ming monk to lead an armed band, but this needn't surprise us. Monk Shi was one of tens of thousands of itinerant clergy wandering in the mid-Ming among the people and looking for means of support. A few may have been searching for wisdom, but most were looking for a monastery that would take them in, and all begged for alms to survive. As early as 1394, the Hongwu emperor, himself a former monk, tried to restrict clerical vagrancy by ordering monks to stay in the monasteries where they were registered and not to go into towns. Only those seeking teachers or specializing in ritual services for the people were excepted. Subsequent regulations down to 1477 imposed further restrictions on itinerant monks.[27] When the vice-censor-in-chief Wang Shu (1416–1508) petitioned the throne in 1465 on security issues in Huguang, he declared that Buddhist monks and Daoist priests were among the soldiers and artisans who had moved into the uplands. "Those who have built private chapels must have them dismantled and destroyed; those who do not have ordination papers must be prosecuted and returned to lay life; those without proper documents should not be allowed to enter the mountain areas I have mentioned. As the region is scrupulously closed, the bandits will disappear."[28] The opposite process seems to have been at work, however, for settlement proceeded and, as it did, the region became more stable. After 1500, worries about wandering monks faded from central documents.

Getting monks and other vagrants back to their original places of registration was an early-Ming hope that mid-Ming emperors abandoned. The prefecture around Nanjing, from which large numbers of the people fled who had been forcibly relocated there in the early Ming, is a case in point. The Chenghua emperor (r. 1465–87) ordered his officials to draw up registers of the departed, but initiated no other procedures to bring them back. The next two emperors, Hongzhi and Zhengde, further lightened the penalties on wealthy households that had fled. When Emperor Jiajing (r. 1522–66) was apprised of the movement of unregistered migrants, his response was not to send them home but to have them be registered wherever they were now living.[29] The center thereby gave up taking the initiative on this matter and devolved the problem to local officials. Mid-Ming magistrates accepted the irreversibility of informal migration. They registered migrants alongside everyone else in their counties and adjusted the distribution of the tax burden to include them.[30]

Women should have counted as half the people registered. Rarely do they. The few local gazetteers that record population by gender report that men far outnumber women. For an example from North Zhili, the census of 1502 for Daming prefecture enumerates 378,167 males but only 226,982 females. A ratio of five men to every three women is a radical departure from the natural balance. In the most extreme county in Daming prefecture (Qingfeng), males outnumber females two to one. Even the county showing the least imbalance (Neihuang) reports seven males to every five females.[31] Additional examples from five other provinces, presented in table 1, attest to the extent of the distortion creeping into census records in the mid-Ming. Women were disappearing from view.

What does this distortion reflect? Three different explanations might apply: that the number of females reaching adulthood was decreasing, that women were evading registration on a large scale, or that household heads were refusing to register the females in their homes. The first is a factor, but hardly the entire story. Social and ritual practices did pressure families to kill infant girls. Although both male and female babies were "washed," as the euphemism went, when their families could not support them, girls were far more

TABLE I   MALE-FEMALE RATIOS FROM SELECTED CENSUS RETURNS, 1391–1614

	Date	Males	Females	Males per 100 Females
Huguang province				
Jingling county	1391	11,503	12,116	94.9
	1452	13,025	10,840	120.2
Mianyang subprefecture	1391	23,109	24,301	95.1
	1442	21,041	14,215	148.0
Hanyang prefecture	1413	15,322	17,096	89.6
	1532	19,486	12,505	155.8
Henan province				
Weishi county	1482	27,985	14,676	190.6
Xinxiang county	1502	36,760	20,511	179.2
South Zhili				
Shanghai county	1391	278,874	253,929	109.8
	1432	182,978	170,182	107.5
	1472	177,139	80,513	220.0
Huating county	1391	292,559	269,304	108.6
	1432	229,019	167,912	136.4
	1472	273,651	112,045	244.2
North Zhili				
Neihuang county	1502	22,867	16,264	140.6
Daming county	1502	13,052	7,573	172.3
Wei county	1502	24,951	13,257	188.2
Yuancheng county	1502	35,993	18,642	193.1
Qingfeng county	1502	38,070	18,749	203.1
Kaizhou subprefecture	1502	56,440	33,243	169.8
Zhejiang province				
Shangyu county	1586	23,259	12,378	187.9
Kuaiji county	1586	40,613	21,391	189.9
Xinchang county	1586	8,800	4,516	194.9
Xiaoshan county	1586	63,374	29,640	213.8
Sheng county	1586	41,203	17,514	235.3
Zhuji county	1586	112,616	45,776	246.0
Shanyin county	1586	82,399	33,110	248.9
Guangdong province				
Xuwen county	1614	9,804	4,952	198.0
Suixi county	1614	15,079	3,780	398.9
Haikang county	1614	18,620	4,553	409.0

SOURCES: *Hanyang fuzhi* (1546), 5.1a–3a; *Mianyang zhi* (1531), 9.1b, 5a; *Weishi xianzhi* (1548), 1.21b; *Xinxiang xianzhi* (1506), 22a; *Songjiang fuzhi* (1819), 28.2b–4b, *Daming fuzhi* (1506), 3.21a–27b; *Shaoxing fuzhi* (1792), 13.30a–31a; *Leizhou fuzhi* (1614), 9.6b.

likely to be killed, let die, or sold into domestic or sexual service in times of dearth. They were more expendable to their natal households than boys. Still, it is hard to imagine that female infanticide and neglect were sufficient to depress the proportion of men to women in Qingfeng county in 1502 to a two-to-one ratio or to a four-to-one ratio in Haikang county a century later.

The second possibility—that women were themselves evading registration on a large scale—seems less persuasive. Women were joining the migrations, but they were doing so in fewer numbers than men, to judge from the frequent references to single men on the move. Women also took to the roads to eke out existences as peddlers, but again not in the same numbers as men. They faced higher physical insecurity, and then there were strong cultural norms keeping them at home. One mid-Ming gazetteer from South Zhili happily reminds its readers that "women are ashamed to go out of doors."[32] So while many females died young and some took off as adults to evade registration, the main factor causing them to disappear from the census records was probably the disinclination of household heads to report their births or acknowledge their arrival at marriage. Why increase the household's vulnerability to a tax increase for the sake of girls who would eventually move away? (Getting local officials to reduce the registered number of mouths in a household when a girl left for marriage was probably a cumbersome business.) And why register a bride who might demand divorce or die in childbirth and, besides, belonged to another surname?

The decline in the number of women in census figures from 1442 onward was thus both a statistically generated illusion and at the same time a social fact: the female population was being suppressed, and so was its record. The decline may have been due more to nonregistration than to infanticide, but together they confirmed the cultural prejudice that women did not count.

Even among the women of the mid-Ming who were enumerated, there are few about whom it is possible to know anything. Historians can rescue a small number of Ming people from anonymity by reading sources other than censuses, such as the biographical sections of local gazetteers, but they rescue mostly men—which is why most of the people named in this book are men. Men simply had many more opportunities to be counted than women: for passing the exams, gaining titles, holding office, dying as martyrs, creating texts and paintings, extending philanthropy, taking the public opportunities available to them to act out Confucian virtues of righteousness and filial piety. Women, by contrast, had but one public role that would earn them a biography and through which they could be known: that of the "chaste widow" who chose not to remarry after the death of a young husband.

The following brief biography of Woman Liu in a 1540 gazetteer from central Henan province is typical of the process by which a woman was rendered into someone knowable. Born in 1477, Woman Liu (her personal name is not recorded) was married to an aspiring county school student. Her *shengyuan* husband failed to move up the degree ladder before his premature death, and left her with a young son to raise.

> She shut her doors and rarely saw her relatives. [The chaste widow was expected to close herself off from the world; male anxiety regarded the unattached female as a "gossip," someone who bypassed male-centered kinship networks in a way that could undermine male authority.] She devoted all her efforts to weaving, thereby supporting herself. [The Confucian definition of chastity ruled out financial reliance on relatives and regarded domestic textile manufacture as the only appropriate form of productive labor for the cloistered woman; refusing to remarry was noteworthy less for sexual denial than for surviving without financial reliance on men.] She used every means to raise her young son to adulthood. [Only because she had a son could Woman Liu even contemplate chastity, for as long as she kept him alive she could rely on his place within her husband's lineage and anticipate support in her old age.] Bereft of her husband at age twenty-seven, she lived thereafter as a widow for thirty-five years, surviving on gruel and an unseasoned vegetarian diet. [Woman Liu could not enjoy life as a happy widow, as that would undercut the image of suffering that gave the chaste-widow model its psychic power.] Keeping chaste from beginning to end, she won high praise in her locality. [Her reputation had to go beyond her husband's family for her to gain public merit.] In 1539, Prefect Zhang Liangzhi heard of her and praised what she had done. On New Year's Day [8 February 1540] he posted a tablet at her door which read: "The home of chaste Woman Liu, wife of *shengyuan* Yuan Xi." More than one gentry poet has celebrated her achievement.[33]

The biographer provides almost no personal details about Woman Liu, other than that she was sixty-three and still alive at the time the gazetteer went to publication. Her personality is entirely subsumed into the persona she chose to adopt, and so Woman Liu can be remembered as a type but is forgotten as a person. But no matter. In mid-Ming terms, this was a success story: a son, financial independence, and public recognition by both local gentry and officials. A woman could not ask for more, at least not at this time.

STATE AND MARKET

THE NEW PROPOSALS OF QIU JUN

The mid-Ming was an era in which people's economic calculations came to be shaped more and more by the commercial opportunities they found about them. These opportunities encouraged some to reflect on how an economy operated and to think about how the role of the state might be adjusted in relation to commercial activity. One whose thinking runs in this direction is Qiu Jun (1420–95). An independent-minded scholar from Hainan Island in the far south, Qiu rose to an influential position as policy advisor in the Hanlin Academy. Qiu was the author of *Supplement to "Expositions on the Great Learning" (Daxue yanyi bu)*, a monumental set of deliberations on state policy presented to the Hongzhi emperor when he ascended the throne in 1487. Qiu modeled his work on Zhen Dexiu's *Expositions on the Great Learning*, a Song philosophical text that had been authorized for official publication earlier in the Ming. Although Qiu questioned many Hongwu precedents, Hongzhi was sufficiently impressed with the book that he gave it his seal of approval. Published commercially, it gained recognition as having an informal place within the imperial canon and circulated widely.[34] Qiu was not personally tied to commercial circles, yet his *Supplement* voices carefully considered arguments about the balance to be struck between the functioning of the market and the responsibilites of the state.

The opening essay in the twenty-fifth chapter, on market regulations, explains that a market is a central place where people with more of one thing and less of another meet and exchange their surplus with those who, under different conditions, have different surpluses and lacks.[35] This better describes a barter market than a commercial market: Qiu purposefully leaves out both merchants and the state so that he can add them in to consider the types of action appropriate to each. Community, commerce, and state remain separate spheres for Qiu, however much each affects the others: the community is the basis of the local economy, commerce creates links among local economies, and the state intervenes to mitigate crises that threaten to overwhelm the proper operation of either. He does not believe that the state on its own can direct the economy to ensure successful guarantees for the survival of the poor. Nor, however, does he believe that an unregulated market can do this. Here he is arguing against the view popular in some official circles that exchange threatens the poor. In Qiu's view, the differentiation of rich and poor was due not to merchants, but to improperly formulated state commercial policies.[36] Forcing merchants out of the market would not eradicate the distinction of rich and poor, and might exacerbate it.

Marketing is entirely a matter for merchants. Qiu allows that merchant activity can have negative influence over popular customs, making possible the conspicuous consumption that Qiu as a good Confucian regarded as deleterious to the moral fiber of the people; but in the same breath he also points out that merchant activity determines the extent to which the state can muster the resources it needs. Without merchants, the economy that the state relies on for its fiscal viability would simply not function. For the state to take over marketing from merchants, however, would be a recipe for disaster. "When the people operate their own markets, they can readily negotiate quality and price to determine whether or not to buy something. When officials operate markets for people, quality and prices are invariably fixed, yet self-interest and hidden dealings crop up all over the place. To operate [a state market] that produces profit and avoids corruption is difficult. The better course is for state administration not to get involved."[37]

Believing that merchants did a better job of redistributing commodities and balancing supply and demand than did the state, Qiu goes on to argue against several policies that had entered Chinese state practice. First of all, the state should not run handicraft industries but should let merchants manage their production. Second, the state should not monopolize necessities like salt for the sake of raising revenue but allow salt to circulate on the open market; it should rely instead on land-based taxation for its income. (Qiu accepted the Ming monopoly on the tea trade to the Mongols because it served to procure horses for the border armies without hampering commodity circulation among the people.) If anything promotes the differentiation of rich and poor, according to Qiu, it is the tactic of squeezing revenue out of restricted commodities. Third, noting that

The Ming Code does not forbid maritime trade but only unlicensed trade, Qiu opposed bans on sea transportation and believed that the state's interests were better served by encouraging maritime trade, enunciating a view that would prevail a century later.[38]

Finally, the state should not use grain stocks to influence seasonal price variations but should leave merchants free to circulate grain at market prices in response to demand. Grain should be stored only to meet famine crises. And it should not be held in state-operated granaries, which were too vulnerable to financial mismanagement, but through noncommercial storage in locally run community granaries (*shecang*), which made grain available to the needy on condition of repayment with interest after the harvest. Qiu explains his position on grain storage policy as a response to the commoditization of grain. He notes, with rhetorical excess, that only 30 to 40 percent of the people actually grow the grain they eat, and that 70 to 80 percent rely on others for their food. They prefer to "convert grain into cash, then convert cash into clothing, food, and daily necessities." Qiu observes that "there aren't any people throughout the realm of whom this is not true, though north of the Huai River and in Shandong it is most extreme."[39] Qiu's concern is practical. He fears that reliance on the market for food will leave the people more vulnerable in times of famine, as they have no grain in hand but only money, and in amounts insufficient to buy food when dearth drives the price up.

The Hongzhi emperor was diligent in attending to the proposals of his statecraft-oriented officials, including Qiu's, but he recognized that the models of good government which Qiu and others might place before him, however laudable, ran counter to established Ming practices. His sense of the advisable was tempered by his awareness of the possible.[40] With regard to food supply, rather than overhaul Hongwu's storage system, Hongzhi required that every county have at least one operating preparedness granary in 1490 (reconfirming a decision in 1440 to reduce the number of such granaries from four to one). He also ordered magistrates to put in storage one year's worth of grain over the next three years. Success in meeting one's target was added as a criterion for evaluating performance at every magistrate's three-year review. Many officials soon came to regard this rate of storage, which might mean extracting as much as a third of a county's grain production for three years in a row, as unrealistically high. This rate of storage would have required an annual surplus of 33 percent and sucked grain out of commercial circulation; the quotas were probably never met.

In a memorial that reflected the mood among officials in the 1520s, Pan Huang (d. 1555) pointed out that the granary system was too draconian and took no account of local conditions.[41] He characterized the relationship between grain production and storage as one of root (ben) versus branch (mo). This is of course the pair of terms by which Confucian discourse prioritized the primary sector, agriculture, over the secondary or derivative sector, commerce. Pan invoked this cliché to warn against a preoccupation with storage, just as a good Confucian would warn against a preoccupation with commerce at the expense of agriculture. If the state wanted to invest in grain sufficiency, better to stimulate production by improving irrigation: in effect, expand production rather than restrict circulation. The quotas were finally reduced in 1527, to a level that was insufficient to meet a major famine.[42] By that decade, however, many counties had no preparedness granaries anyway, and many that did no longer stocked them.[43] A Shandong censor called for their revival in 1557,[44] but by this point the Ming state had abandoned its efforts to influence food supply by means of the granary system. Individual magistrates might still revive derelict granaries, particularly in counties far from commercial cores,[45] or experiment with locally operated community and charity granaries, but overall state interest had waned.

FAMINE

Neither commerce nor the dwindling capacity of the state to store grain was sufficient to meet the natural disasters that battered east-central China through the 1530s and 1540s. In Henan, a drought in 1528 deprived the people of harvests for two years running. Over half the people in some areas died of starvation (see figure 15), and many of the remainder survived by cannibalism. "In some instances," reports a county gazetteer, "fathers and sons butchered each other, as did husbands and wives." One good harvest in 1530 was followed by another drought in 1531. "The locusts that summer flew so thickly that they filled the sky and blocked out the sun.... People ate each other in large numbers and the corpses of the starved lay sprawled over each other in the streets." Drought and locusts struck again with the same intensity in 1539, paving the way for a

Figure 15.   On the left, a famine victim carries a begging bowl and a bundle of kindling for sale, as depicted in August 1516 by the Suzhou painter Zhou Chen in his *Beggars and Street Characters*. The man on the right eating a radish is another of the thousands Zhou saw living by their wits in the streets of Suzhou. Reproduced courtesy of the Honolulu Academy of Arts; gift of Mrs. Carter Galt, 1956.

large epidemic, possibly plague, that summer. The harvest again failed in the fall of 1545 because of excessive rainfall, driving up the price of wheat and forcing large numbers to flee the county ("of ten homes, nine were empty," in the conventional phrase of gazetteer compilers); those who could not leave survived on leaves, bark, and human flesh. Finally, in 1551, a severe frost in the spring destroyed the winter wheat crop in Henan province, torrential rains in mid-summer submerged the flatlands and villages under a meter of water, and a tornado in the fall demolished houses and flattened the buck-wheat standing in the fields.[46] Famine victims had no options be-sides cannibalism and flight to uncertain elsewheres.

Jiangnan was also struck by disaster. Wang Wenlu, living in Haiyan county on the coast of northern Zhejiang, reviews the pre-ceding seven years in this passage in a letter written to a friend in the spring of 1545:

> The drought in Haiyan county began in 1538 when a tidal wave crossed the sea wall in the south, inundating the fields with saltwater, and then flowed north and attacked the crops. What with the blazing autumn sun

and no sources of freshwater to irrigate, the rice put forth ears that did not turn to seed, or produced seed that then rotted. Growing plants shrank and turned to weeds, the fields yellowed: as far as you looked it was a scene of desolation. The officials did not report this to the throne. The stricken were excused from paying taxes, yet the prosperous were so pressed that they also became impoverished. Paddy rice did not come on the market and the price of rice went even higher. People fed themselves first on chaff and bean pods, then on tree bark and weeds. In 1539 and 1544 we suffered virulent epidemics. Both in the country villages and in the towns, nine out of ten houses stood empty. In any village, half the girls and boys were sold off. Now it is spring, and as we wait for the end of the summer growing season, the corpses of the starved lie everywhere—beside the monasteries, below the fords, within the suburban gates, in the middle of the roads—and everywhere the sound of wailing pierces our ears.[47]

Another Haiyan native, Xu Xian, fills in the gap in Wang Wenlu's story for 1539–40:

That autumn the plants in the fields withered and died and insects consumed most of what was left, so that the people harvested only a third of their crops. The prefectural and county officials did not report this disaster to the throne, and their collection of taxes caused an emergency. By the following spring the famine was severe and the people were eating chaff and bean fodder, foraging to the point that practically every weed was pulled up and every tree stripped of its bark. The corpses of the starved filled the roads. The children and wives sold could not be counted. It was even worse in the northern canton. The elders recalled that Haiyan had not faced a year like this since the terrible famine of 1305 over two centuries ago, when people ate each other.[48]

Severe famine struck the Jiangnan region yet again in 1543. Not a drop of rain fell between the sixth and the ninth months of 1544. The crops withered in the fields, people starved, and the weak were taken off by epidemics.[49] The price of rice skyrocketed out of the reach of most people. Whereas a *dou* (10.74 liters) of rice normally cost about 25 copper cash, in the years 1544–45 it went over a 100 cash and reached as high as 200 in some places.[50]

Commoners and officials equally were desperate for rain to fall on parched fields and implored divine assistance. The statue of the Buddhist goddess of mercy, Guanyin, in Hangzhou's Haihui Monastery was popularly regarded as the best deity to beseech. After no rain fell through the spring and summer of 1545, the prefect gave in to public pressure and set up a special altar before her statue. A day later it rained for two days running.[51] But the larger weather patterns did not change, and the region continued to suffer drought for several more years. Not until 1549 did rainfall return to normal. Then, as if nature alone had not done enough, pirates began two decades of predation along the Zhejiang coast, causing the deaths of several thousand more people in Haiyan county alone. Guanyin played a role here as well, for she appeared on the road to a gang of pirates heading up to the Tianzhu monasteries outside Hangzhou to put them to the torch. They fled and the monasteries survived.[52]

Rarely was famine a sudden disaster. It usually took months to build up, as drought or waterlogging persisted beyond what farmers could bear and private stocks of food and seed grain were gradually eaten away. By famine time most people were without the means to buy grain that merchants might bring in, particularly at the famine prices at which it was sold. Even an economically well-integrated area like Haiyan could not hope to draw in commercial grain as famine deepened. Only when the state or a wealthy benefactor subsidized its purchase and transport would commercial grain enter a famine area, though the subsidies often came too late to be effective. The only profitable trade in famine areas was in people. As Xu Xian noted, outside brokers came in to purchase large numbers of women and girls, and a smaller number of boys, for a few thousand copper cash each. These they transported north to the great commercial center of Suzhou to sell as prostitutes, concubines, and bondservants. It was a profitable trade, and some of those sold survived.

Would the famines of 1544–45 have been less devastating if the state had kept up the preparedness granaries? Probably not, when the scale of the disaster was that great. As one writer observed in 1540, people had come to expect flood every eight or nine years in a decade, drought every five or six, locust infestation every three or four, and hail every year or two, and anyway colder temperatures made it difficult to switch to other crops.[53] Under such pressures, it was difficult to believe that a few well-stocked granaries could have greatly altered the toll of suffering.

MONOPOLIES AND COMMERCIAL TAXATION

Where the mid-Ming state continued to concern itself with grain supply was on the northern border. Supplying the soldiers stationed there against the Mongols was an ongoing headache. The early Ming had sought to provide for this vast need by setting up military colonies (*tuntian*) and demobilizing seven out of ten soldiers to grow food for the army. The other method was the institution of border delivery (*kaizhong*), by which merchants shipped grain to the border in return for lucrative licenses to sell government salt. These policies were already giving way in the mid-fifteenth century as civilian transport was gradually commuted to a payment in silver that the government then used to buy grain. In coordination with this shift, a commercial market in grain emerged in the northwest.

The process of moving from levy to commerce was brought to its logical conclusion in 1492 when Minister of Revenue Ye Qi (1426–1501) proposed that the *kaizhong* trade be monetarized: henceforth, salt merchants would be allowed to purchase their salt licenses directly from the government for silver. This change was just as Qiu Jun was suggesting in his policy recommendations in favor of having the state rely on the market to meet its provisioning needs. No longer would merchants have to deliver grain to the border. Instead, the government would control the commutation rate and use the cash revenue from license sales to buy the food and other military supplies that it needed for its troops. (This reform was extended to the tea monopoly as well.)[54] Further commutation of military grain supplies from the Zhengde era (1506–21) forward increased the size of the market and intensified the level of capital that was needed to participate in the salt monopoly, and the profits that accrued from it. It also spurred the use and circulation of silver.

Outside the lucrative monopolies, the state's relationship to commodity markets in the mid-Ming was only moderately extractive. It routinely collected taxes at customs barriers along water routes and at city gates. Merchants shipping goods by water to Beijing had to pay duties (as well as increasingly extortionate bribes)[55] at the customs houses along the Grand Canal, then a further fee to bring them into the capital unless they could show that they had already paid customs fees on the Grand Canal by taking a tax receipt stamped at the customs houses in either Linqing or Hexiwu to the Ministry of Revenue.[56] Levies on commodities were set by quotas. These tended to increase in the mid-Ming, though not with the idea that commercial taxes could become a significant new tax base for the state. Quotas still served to limit state income from the burgeoning commercial trade. In this context, it is not surprising to read the praise in the official history of the dynasty for a tax collector appointed in 1521 to the mid-Yangzi port of Jingzhou, who suspended taxation after having met his annual quota in the first three months and sub-sequently allowed commercial vessels to pass untaxed. The basis for his biographer's judgment was not the extent of his contribution to state finances but rather the extent of his compassionate willingness to let the people's wealth remain in their own hands, ever a virtue in formal Chinese thinking about taxation.[57] The common assumption was that an official who went on collecting tax above quota simply pocketed the receipts and would neither reinvest what he collected in the infrastructure nor turn it over to the state.[58]

When the mid-Ming court did increase commercial taxation, it did so unsystematically—and was inevitably perceived as rapacious for having taken this step. In 1515, for example, the Zhengde em-peror ordered that new commercial tax bureaus be set up at major bridges and fords in Hanyang prefecture, Huguang, and dispatched the eunuch Zhao Tian and officers of his personal Embroidered Guard to impose levies on commercial boat traffic in the prefecture. The proceeds went directly via the eunuch to the imperial house-hold. Only after Zhengde's death did a provincial censor finally dare to memorialize his successor to ask that these bureaus be closed down "because they bring trouble to merchants." He was successful. To put an official seal of approval on their suspension, the censor erected a stone stele in 1528 with a description declaring that the bureaus were no longer in operation.[59]

Besides internal customs duties, the Ming state collected a com-mercial tax on retailers known as the "shop and stall tax" (*mentan shui*), introduced in 1425 in thirty-three larger cities to help the regime's failing paper currency to circulate. In the mid-Ming, when paper money was regarded as worthless, some officials argued that the shop and stall tax was depressing commercial activity. Censor Zhu Shichang in 1528 submitted a memorial to the emperor re-questing that in the core prefectures of Jiangnan—in Suzhou, Song-jiang, Changzhou, and Zhenjiang in South Zhili, and Hangzhou, Jiaxing, and Huzhou in Zhejiang—neither shops nor commodities be dutiable. The emperor agreed. Dropping the shop and stall tax was a generous concession for Jiangnan businessmen. Observers later in the century credited the commercial prosperity of Suzhou and Hangzhou to this decision.[60] (See figure 16.) The state thus fluctuated in its relationship to commerce, sometimes exploiting it, at other times neglecting it, without incorporating it systematically into its fiscal strategies. In this light, arguments that modern Chinese

Figure 16. Shops and stalls fill the night market at the north gate of Hangzhou (*Hainei qiguan,* 1609).

historians have made about a rapacious and anticommercial Ming state thwarting the growth of the commercial economy seem forced. The Ming state may not have promoted commerce according to a European bourgeois ideal, but at least it left it largely alone to grow as it did.

Because he had to rely on market purchasing to run his yamen, the local magistrate interacted with merchants and the market constantly. This interaction could involve large purchases. For example, after a typhoon badly damaged the Confucian school in Tongan county, Fujian, in 1459, the vice-magistrate was ordered to undertake its restoration. An appeal to the prefect for funds got him nowhere. Recognizing that "the building materials that maritime merchants sold could be readily made into beams, he approached colleagues and old friends and borrowed a hundred taels to buy [the materials], which [the merchants] shipped [to Tongan]. Then he exhorted the civic-minded among the county wealthy to make contributions to cover the labor costs." The construction work started the following year and was completed in two.[61] Similarly, when a magistrate in Huguang reconstructed the county yamen in 1499, the materials he used were "those that could be purchased on the market."[62] Purchase had superseded levy.

Local officials also found themselves intervening in commercial disputes. When Zhang Bi (js. 1466) was posted as prefect to Nan'an at the south end of Jiangxi province late in the 1460s, he discovered that through his jurisdiction passed the principal flow of traffic between Guangdong province and the Yangzi Valley. Local operators had traditionally run the porterage business down through the Nanyu mountains into Nanxiong prefecture on the Guangdong side, but rough competition from Nanxiong porters across the border was ruining their trade. Prefect Zhang called a meeting between the Nan'an and Nanxiong groups and was able to work out a compromise that split the cross-border carrying between them. While investigating the dispute, he also discovered that the thirty kilometers of narrow, steep road through the mountains to the midway station on the border made porterage difficult, so he used the commercial tax of his prefecture to pave half of this bad stretch and dig out a new road to bypass the rest.[63] Like Prefect Xu in Wuhu earlier in this chapter, Prefect Zhang found himself mobilizing the state's resources to assist a world animated and shaped by commerce.

COMMERCE

As commerce overtook mid-Ming China, the secluded community untouched by commercial influences became so rare that sighting one was something of a pastime among gentry writers unsure about the moral impact of commerce on the values of honesty and hard work that peasants were supposed to be known for. Zhang Yue in his 1530 gazetteer of Huian county was successful in finding such communities on a lonely stretch of the Fujian coast. There, villages had but a handful of families living in thatched huts and working the narrow river valleys. "They have everything they need for their livelihood without having to fish, brew salt, or engage in commerce," Zhang observes. He goes on to characterize this utopia by what it lacks when he notes that "there is little silver in these villages." When the people hold periodic religious festivals, they raise only "copper cash and rice" to pay for the costs.[64] Until a local area produced commodities for an external market, silver would not flow in. Much of rural China thus remained an economy of copper coins and rice in the mid-Ming. Even in commercially active Shanghai, rural people in the 1520s raised funds for communal rites by collecting copper cash, not silver.[65]

The incomplete circulation of silver in undercommercialized areas made silver difficult to come by—and increased its lure as formerly isolated economies began to communicate commercially with other areas. Thus the only way that locals could explain the wealth of a monk living in the hills of southeastern Henan province was by insisting he could transform base metals into silver and gold. When bandits kidnapped him and demanded his silver, the monk assured them that the rumor was false. He reminded them that backwoods areas like his saw no silver because only rice and cloth were traded, and these were bought and sold in copper and not silver. As it happens, the monk did have some silver stashed in a cave, which he earned by healing the sick.[66] The area was thus not completely starved of silver—and an adept monk could winkle it out of those who had it more easily than bandits could steal it.

Peripheral regions like southeastern Henan and the more isolated parts of Fujian could move into the commercial networks centered on prefectural capitals only if they produced something that could circulate outside the county. For example, Jianning county in western Fujian in 1543 may have produced "only fish and rice, wood-oil and varnish, and linen," yet it produced them in sufficient quantities that merchants came to deal in them.[67] Demand for something not produced locally could also pull a county into trade. In Guangshan, next to the county where the kidnapped monk lived in southeastern Henan, central policy required county residents to pay part of their taxes in linen and silk, which were fabrics Guangshan did not produce. Locals did grow cotton and beans from which they wove rough fabrics, but farmers and the local artisanate were too unskilled to produce linen and silk in sufficient quantity or quality for the tax levy. These items came into Guangshan from elsewhere, and locals had to barter with outside merchants for them using their own products. These merchants came up from southern Huguang and the Nanjing region and did well enough in that trade to buy land, marry, and live as local notables, but they were so few in the mid-Ming as to be remarkable.[68]

TEXTILES

If the acquisition of tax goods is set aside, Guangshan county is a case in which local textile production was undertaken solely to meet local needs. The number of such cases dwindled in the mid-Ming, however, as textile production and consumption were dominated more by exchange than by the clothing needs of the household. Although the classical model of men plowing and women weaving might still be discernible in less commercialized areas like southeastern Henan, elsewhere the gendered division of tasks was being adapted to commercial conditions. The compiler of the 1543 gazetteer of Shaowu prefecture in Fujian observes the old convention of dividing labor between heavy work in the fields for men and lighter work at the loom for women, saying that women "engage in weaving to clothe their husbands." Yet he then qualifies this portrait of rural simplicity when he adds that "what is left over they then trade to make a profit."[69] These women may have looked like they were cleaving to the classical ideal, whereas in fact they were producing a surplus intended for sale.

The balance between production for the household and production for the market shifted as one moved up marketing hierarchies. Closer to the Jiangnan core, for example, the women of Dehua county "only spin and do not know how to weave," according to the 1527 gazetteer of Jiujiang prefecture.[70] They were specializing in thread production and buying local "rough silk," as it was called, to meet their own needs. Further down into the humid Jiangnan core, the silk industry was booming. High-quality silk was already being widely produced in urban centers around Lake Tai, especially Suzhou, in the Southern Song. In the early Ming, silk production began moving from the city of Suzhou down to surrounding county seats. Demand skyrocketed in the 1470s and 1480s, breaking the urban monopoly and turning silk production into a predominantly rural industry.[71] A local gazetteer from the Lake Tai region records that, at that time, "in every village in reach of a town, residents were devoting their energies entirely to earning a living from silk. The poor wove, and the wealthy hired others to weave for them."[72] Not only were peasants abandoning other spheres of production to work solely at producing silk, but the wealthy were hiring labor to produce for the fast-developing textile market. (See figure 17.)

The production of cotton textiles underwent even more dramatic development. Cotton had taken root in China in the south during the Song and had spread northward through the Yuan and early Ming, first to the Yangzi Valley, and then farther north into Shandong and Shanxi. The technology to produce cotton cloth became particularly developed in Jiangnan through borrowing from silk-weaving practices of the Yuan period. During the latter half of the fifteenth century, Songjiang (of which Shanghai was the eastern part) emerged as the center of the industry, principally because cultivators had been turning their poor land over to cotton cultivation for want of anything more profitable to grow.[73] Cotton appeared as a permanent part of Songjiang's tax assessment in 1433 and thenceforth expanded as a common rural sideline. The partial conversion of taxes from kind to silver, which the prefect initiated in 1486, pushed cotton further in the direction of becoming a commodity produced for sale on the market. The same tax incentive was at work in north China as well, where raw cotton production expanded sufficiently to meet the growing demands of the commercial weavers of Songjiang.[74]

The production cycle for cotton, from cultivation to cloth, had been a unified process for most Chinese weavers in the early Ming. The cotton had been grown, ginned (the process of removing seeds), spun, and woven all within a single household, principally by women. Itinerant merchants bought the cloth, and sold raw cotton only when the producer's own household could not grow enough,

Figure 17. Cocoons soften in a tub of water in front of a laborer, who detaches the ends of the threads from the cocoons and winds them through a silk-reeling machine. Note that the reeler is male (*Tiangong kaiwu;* 1637).

but the division of labor was minimal. By the mid-Ming, however, the production of cotton cloth was becoming more specialized. The 1512 Songjiang gazetteer provides a description: "The textile industry is not limited to the rural villages, but is also seen in the city. Old rural women enter the market at dawn carrying yarn and, after trading it for raw cotton, return home. The next morning they again leave home carrying yarn. They don't have a moment's rest. The weavers finish a short bolt a day; some stay awake all night [to finish]."[75] Although the women who spun and wove continued to live in farming households, they specialized in parts of the production process by relying on urban markets. They were not simply producing household surplus but were working now on a cottage-based piece rate.

Similarly in Fujian, women in the hinterland wove at home and sold to merchants working out of the prefectural cities along the coast, who traded the cloth to Zhejiang merchants who in turn distributed it outside the province. In Xinghua prefecture, it was said that a skilled weaver could weave a bolt of cotton cloth in four or five days and sell it for a *shi* of unhusked rice at the market in Xianyou county. Evelyn Rawski, who has researched this market, says that "this represented one sixth the annual harvest from a *mu* of excellent land." Although this rate of return provides a rather too optimistic scenario for women's work, at a much lower rate of return it can still be argued that "the incentives for keeping women at the loom in this area were high, and the profits from intensive cultivation had to be considerable before it was profitable to put these women to work in the fields." The presence of a merchant-serviced market for textiles meant that "peasants in the coastal area found it more profitable to grow alternative cash crops, ship them to other markets, and import rice. The coast enjoyed the advantages of cheap water transport, which made it possible to export lichees, oranges, plums, and timber as well as textiles, iron and wine."[76]

The growth of the cotton and silk trades induced Jiangnan people to plant cotton and tend mulberry trees on a scale beyond personal consumption. The northern Zhejiang silk market, for instance, was sufficiently developed that people could sell not only silk thread, which they produced by feeding silkworms on mulberry leaves they grew themselves, but the leaves as well. In Chongde county, for example, by the sixteenth century some peasants did not plant just a few mulberry trees in order to raise silkworms to "survive through lean harvests" but were growing fields of them so as to be able to sell the leaves commercially to mulberry leaf traders who in turn sold to other silk-producers. Merchants and producers both calculated to take advantage of fluctuations in the price of mulberry leaves as supply and demand shifted. The Chongde gazetteer records a case in 1522 of two brothers who each raised fifteen baskets of silkworms. They did not grow enough mulberry leaves to feed this number, but estimated that they would be able to buy the leaves they needed. Although they did not anticipate a price rise, they knew how to respond to it when it came: "When mulberry leaves became extremely expensive and the two brothers were running out of leaves, they said to each other, 'The leaves are expensive and hard to buy. Buying leaves to get silk is certainly not as good as selling leaves to get money.' So they dumped their silkworms in the sewage tank."[77]

As cultivators of the mid-Ming came to produce for the market, so also they relied on it to buy what they didn't make. In less commercialized areas in south China, for instance, they bought such "sundry items" as betel nuts, sugar, oil, wax, shell jewelry, wood, incense, rain cloaks fashioned from bamboo leaves, and even grain. "None of these items is produced in the local area, yet not one commands a very high price,"[78] reports a Guangdong gazetteer. Thus local markets in less commercial areas managed to supply at low cost items produced elsewhere. In more highly commercialized areas such as Jiangnan, textile producers went to market for more basic items, most importantly the rice that they no longer grew. Their demand was strong enough to pull rice down the Yangzi River in a long-distance trade that became a permanent link between rice farmers in the central interior and Jiangnan consumers.

MERCHANTS

As exchange networks gained in scale, merchants became more visible. A typical description of their activities is given in the 1540 gazetteer of Hejian, North Zhili:

> The merchants who transport commodities within Hejian prefecture deal in silk fabrics, grain, salt, iron, and wood. Silk merchants come from Nanjing, Suzhou, and Linqing. Grain merchants travel the imperial thoroughfare from Weihui and Cizhou and go as far as the region along the river at Tianjin, buying up grain when the harvest is good and selling it when the harvest is poor. Iron mongers deal mostly in agricultural

implements, coming here in small carts from Linqing and Botou. The salt merchants come from Cangzhou and Tianjin, the wood merchants from Zhending. Those who sell porcelain and lacquerware come from Raozhou and Huizhou. As for local merchants, most come from the prefectures and counties north of the Yellow River: they are known as "shop households."[79]

The author goes on to explain which counties in Hejian prefecture are on the Grand Canal and can ship grain to Beijing by water, and which must transport their grain overland. The commercial traffic along the Grand Canal was so heavy in the mid-Ming that officials became concerned about obstructions to state traffic. In new guidelines on the maintenance of state waterways drafted by a senior bureau director in the Ministry of Works in 1530, it was alleged that merchants were not only choking the Grand Canal with their barges but making illegal use of courier and postal facilities by bribing the staff. (People working at courier stations and post houses would have found servicing the private traffic far more lucrative than handling the unpaid state traffic.) This bureau director singled out bamboo and wood dealers for obstructing the Grand Canal with their cargoes and for hiring thugs to intimidate local officers along the route into letting them pass.[80]

The foregoing sketch from the Hejian gazetteer focuses on the activities of regional dealers but notes as well the presence of wholesale and retail merchants from outside the prefecture. Identified by their home prefecture or county, outsiders from certain places had by the mid-Ming gained reputations for specializing in certain types of commodity or exchange. The compiler mentions Raozhou merchants, who distributed the porcelains produced in the kilns of Jingdezhen in Jiangxi. He mentions Huizhou merchants, who became the most prominent and prosperous commercial dealers in the dynasty (and whom we shall consider in some detail further on in this chapter). He also mentions that Nanjing, Suzhou, and Linqing merchants dominated the silk trade, as also did Hangzhou merchants. The one prominent group he neglects to name are the merchants of Shanxi province (notably from Fenzhou and Zezhou prefectures) who were widely engaged in dealing in salt, grain, and other commodities, including silk. Even up in the border town of Xuanfu, two hundred kilometers northwest of Beijing, the silk shops that ran along most of the main market street for over two kilometers were run by merchants from not only Nanjing, Suzhou, and Linqing, but also Hangzhou, Fenzhou, and Zezhou.[81]

Although some succeeded spectacularly in trade, commercial dealing was speculative. Agents and business associates stole capital, looters emptied shops, bandits and bad weather closed routes, and porters helped themselves to the goods they transported. Stories of boatmen in league with robbers abounded.[82] In the less commercially developed regions, people stayed away from commerce, not out of moral reproof but because they saw business as an uncertain, high-risk pursuit. A gazetteer compiler in eastern Huguang expresses this attitude in 1531 by saying that the local people "resist the lure of commerce and fear to travel afar as merchants and would rather die in a ditch of starvation than become bandits,"[83] as though banditry were the next option after commerce. Even in Suzhou's Wujiang county, through which the Grand Canal passed, the compiler of the 1488 gazetteer declares that local people "do not travel great distances. Merchants grimace when they have to go more than a hundred *li* from home, leaving their families to stick to their home villages and carry on the farming. Those who go off as merchants to other places, leaving their homes in search of profit and letting the years pass without ever returning, are looked on as faithless men." Sixty years later, the editor of the next edition removed this passage from the gazetteer. The mid-Ming gazetteers of nearby Shanghai reveal the same adjustment on either side of the Zhengde era. In 1504, Shanghai men regarded commercial travel as shameful; twenty years later, Shanghai merchants were traveling as far as Beijing, Shandong, and Huguang.[84] By the 1520s commerce had become more attractive to the people of the lower Yangzi region, and home truths in Shanghai and Wujiang changed accordingly.

MARITIME TRADE

Ming ideology did not celebrate China as a commercial seafaring realm. Ming law nonetheless permitted maritime trade so long as it was licensed. Other than what were considered strategic items, such as horses, weapons, ironware, copper coins, or silk, Chinese goods could go abroad. (Judges were able to ban other goods by analogizing them to items listed in *The Ming Code*; for example, in 1524 an official memorialized against allowing Chinese boatbuilders to build trading ships for foreigners "according to the law that deals with people who are discovered taking forbidden weapons out of the country."[85] Naval use meant that boats could be deemed weapons.) Foreign goods could be imported, but only so long as they came through designated ports and were assessed for import duty. *The Ming Code* did lay down certain restrictions on two-masted boats that did not apply to smaller boats, the intention being to limit the wealth that big maritime merchants could accumulate. The penalties for infringing on these restrictions were greater than they were for contravening the regulations governing domestic trade. Anyone who bought or warehoused uncertified foreign goods, for instance, faced heavier fines than if he had just been evading domestic commercial taxes. According to a commentary in the *Code,* this difference in penalties was intended originally only so that the state could collect its share of the high profits of the trade, but the intention later shifted to one of actively discouraging trade with foreign countries.[86]

The commentary reflects a larger ideological shift that gained ground about the turn of the sixteenth century. Qiu Jun in 1487 had argued in favor of removing the ban on maritime trading and offering a three-year moratorium on the levy of customs duties precisely to stimulate that trade. Such opinions soon lost their champions. Foreign trade came to be viewed with suspicion, the grand maritime expeditions of Zheng He and his eunuch commanders regarded with distaste, and Chinese merchants abroad suspected (justifiably) of impersonating imperial envoys to gain audiences with Southeast Asian rulers.[87] Typical of this disdain for foreign trade was that of an official who, on a visit home to Zhangzhou in 1506, learned that his kinsmen had built a large boat which they intended to use to carry on unlicensed trade with foreigners. Zhangzhou's port of Yuegang (Moon Harbor) was the center of the licensed (and unlicensed) maritime trade on the southern coast of Fujian. "I should report you to the authorities," the official stormed. He never made his report. The threat was sufficient to put an end to the venture, the kinsmen implicitly acknowledging the right of the state to legislate foreign trade. Indeed, this antimaritime attitude became so firmly entrenched, at least in court circles, by the turn of the sixteenth century that the copies of Zheng He's expeditionary charts preserved in the Ministry of War were burned by ministerial order.[88]

Knowledge of maritime routes—and the desire to use it—was not, however, lost within mid-Ming society. Route maps and rutters (charts of maritime compass bearings) dating from the fifteenth century continued to circulate among navigators in handmade copies in the sixteenth, as Portuguese discovered when they came into contact with Chinese mariners.[89] Regardless of the state's withdrawal from maritime commerce subsequent to Zheng He's voyages and its increasingly antitrade posture, merchants along the harbor-studded coast of Fujian engaged actively in trade with Southeast Asia during the fifteenth century, and were still doing so after Zheng's charts were reduced to ashes in Beijing and the outraged Zhangzhou official ordered his kinsmen to give up their dreams of maritime shipping.

In 1617, a customs official stationed in Zhangzhou commissioned and published a survey of the countries and trade of Southeast Asia. Reflecting the revenue-collection concerns of his patron, local author Zhang Xie observes in his survey:

> In the Chenghua and Hongzhi eras [1465–1505], members of powerful families and wealthy households boarded huge ships to engage in trade across the seas. Immoral people secretly got up to corrupt practices. Officials were unable openly to share in their profits, though as the former came in time to enjoy extraordinary gains, they enticed the latter and thus threw [customs collection] into chaos. By the Jiajing era [1522–66] corruption reached the extreme.[90]

Reports such as this indicate that overseas trade between coastal Fujian and Southeast Asia grew in scale and profitability through the mid-Ming. This impression is confirmed from the other end of the trading relationship. The regional economy of Southeast Asia into which Chinese merchants traded experienced a boom through the latter part of the fifteenth century, when Chinese demand for cloves, pepper, and sappanwood stimulated production and trade in Southeast Asia. Chinese trading communities sprang up in entrepôts throughout the region to handle the business.[91]

The trade to and from the Zhangzhou area became so profitable, according to the county gazetteer, that merchants would rather put to sea in a typhoon and run the risk of capsizing and losing their ships and cargo than delay sailing and lose business.[92] This observation suggests an ever-intensifying competition to get into the trade with Southeast Asian buyers and suppliers. This competition helps to explain the rise of smuggling and piracy starting in the 1520s. When merchants bribed officials of the closing decades of the fifteenth century, it was in order to evade paying customs duties, though the more important concession they were buying was covert agreement to allow the volume and range of goods they were bringing into the country to expand beyond the regulatory limits. Anecdotal evidence from Zhangzhou suggests that by the turn of the sixteenth century, the number of merchants in the import-export trade was growing faster than the volume of trade. As competition intensified, so did rivalries and turf wars; by the 1520s this had become an armed trade.

The rise of commercial conflict along the Chinese coast may also be linked to the disastrous arrival of the Portuguese on the Indian Ocean. Seeking to take over the extensive maritime trading networks that Muslims and Chinese operated before they arrived, the Portuguese plundered or sank almost every trading vessel they encountered between 1500 and 1520 in order to force their competitors out of the market. When the Portuguese captured the major regional trading center of Malacca in 1511, they butchered the large community of Chinese merchants living there. The Chinese memory of this massacre was long. Zhang Xie recalled it a century later in his survey of Southeast Asia with this understated but vivid comment:

> Of old it was said that people along the coast fear the tortoise dragon [crocodile]. It stands four hands high, has four feet, with a scaly body and long protruding teeth. It bites people whenever it encounters them, and no one can escape death. In the mountains they fear the black tiger [leopard]. It is slightly smaller than a tiger, rather like human form. It slinks into marketplaces in broad daylight and if discovered is caught and killed. Today these could, along with the Portuguese, be called "the three terrors of Malacca."[93]

Portuguese piracy temporarily paralyzed the existing trade in Southeast Asia and drove the regional spice economy into a slump, from which it would recover only after the 1520s.[94] The timing of the recovery of the Southeast Asia trading economy with the rise of piracy along the Chinese coast is probably more than coincidence, though we still know too little to reconstruct the connections with confidence. In part it may have been the simple response to opportunity, as Fujian merchants rushed to grab a piece of the renewed trade. But possibly as well the disruptions and losses that the Portuguese caused may have had a temporary deflationary impact on the coastal economy during the early decades of the sixteenth century, to which Chinese officials responded by closing the border more tightly than they would otherwise have done. It may also be that the

Portuguese presence forced merchants to arm themselves, and that this arming of the trade increased the violence among participants.

Whatever the explanation, Chinese officials from the 1520s called for tougher restrictions on foreign trading. The Ministry of Justice published a new set of restrictions in 1524 imposing punishments on those found trading with, borrowing money from, and provoking disturbances with foreign merchants. This was followed the next summer by an order from the Ministry of War that every two-masted ship along the Zhejiang coast be seized, inspected, and destroyed. "Even if they do not carry any barbarian goods," declared the order, "the people aboard ship shall be banished to the frontier as guards for [defying the restriction against] carrying barbarian goods."[95] Only fishing boats would be exempt from the destruction (and even they were banned in 1551).[96] The intention of the ban was to suspend foreign trade, not shut down trade among Chinese up and down the coast, which went on in full view of Chinese officials along the coast. In the early summer of 1548, for example, one official tracked the movement of boats along the Zhejiang-Fujian coast over a period of thirty-nine days. He enumerated 1,172 boats and noted that 30 of these boats were at sea at any one time, most of them engaging in legal coastal shipping.[97]

The bans against foreign commerce were counterproductive and further intensified the violence associated with the trade. Chinese and foreign merchants continued to gather in considerable numbers in the lees of offshore islands to trade out of sight of piracy-suppression officials. As trade increased, so did suppression, culminating in the so-called *wokou*, or "Japanese pirate," raids of the famine-troubled decades of the 1540s and 1550s, when bands of Chinese sailors working with Japanese and other foreigners raided where they could not trade. The tension between trade and closure would not be resolved until the reopening of trade in the 1560s.[98] The Jiajing-era closure is usually attributed to a Chinese continentalist orientation based on a deep-seated aversion to foreign contact and a failure to appreciate the benefits of maritime contact in the southeast. Chinese, so the explanation goes, have always been culturally oriented to the continent. The sea was a foreign element, a barrier beyond which the world made little sense and had no claim on Chinese attention. I suspect that this rationalization will eventually cede place to a fuller understanding that we do not yet have of conditions of trade and fluctuations in the local and regional economies affected by the trade. Chinese officials and high Confucians may have believed profoundly in the inferiority of the non-Chinese world and feared whatever corrupting influences they thought came from abroad. But culture is what people do, not what they think they should do. The people of Zhangzhou did not subscribe to this alleged cultural aversion to foreign contact.

As for the Portuguese, they first reached south China in 1513 in a ship from Malacca commanded by Rafael Perestrello, none other than a cousin of Christopher Columbus. A larger second expedition was undertaken in 1517 to trade at Guangzhou. While there the expedition dispatched a delegation to the Chinese emperor from the king of Portugal seeking trade relations. The diplomatic initiative failed and the Portuguese assigned to it languished and eventually died in prison, but clandestine trade proved profitable to both sides, and European ships came more frequently into China's coastal waters. Seasonal trading between Chinese and Portuguese had become a regular occurrence by 1549, when traders met to trade on Shangchuan Island (which the Portuguese called Sao João), southwest of the Macao peninsula. From there they stepped to Macao and established a legal treaty port in 1557, a first small but long-term European toehold in the China trade.

COMMERCE AND CULTURE

THE SIMPLE AND THE OBSTINATE

The proliferation of both domestic and maritime trade was troubling to the scholastic Confucian commitment to social hierarchy resting on settled village life. Commentators of the mid-Ming remark on the decreasing distance between the urban world of markets and traders and the rural world of agricultural production, worrying about the invasive expansion of the former and the corruption of the latter. A gazetteer compiler for a county in Shanxi province describes a separation of town and country that was still much alive as an ideal at the middle of the sixteenth century, and does so to complain about the destabilizing mobility of townsfolk:

> Most rural residents are simple, upright folk, whereas in the city soldiers and civilians mingle, and some are fond of cheating others, dressing in

fancy clothes and taking pleasure in making luxury articles. By nature they are obstinate and bad-tempered and prone to throw themselves suddenly from cliffs or into rivers. When they meet catastrophe, they toss their satchels over their shoulders and cross the boundaries, calling it "going to harvest."[99]

Hysterical suicide was hardly as rampant as the compiler implies. Yet elsewhere as well it was becoming harder and harder to find "simple, upright folk" in the countryside where the urban elite believed they might still exist. Rural habits were not acting, as they should, to brake the erosion of customs in urban areas. In the mid-Ming, rural styles followed urban. The compiler of a Henan gazetteer from the same decade observes that the people of the markets and villages alike are "boastful and extravagant"; only those living up in the hills were still "rough and parsimonious."[100] The author of a Guangdong gazetteer published the next decade catches the same urbanization of rural styles, noting that urban and rural women differed only in the material from which they wove their hats. Otherwise, he regrets to report, women from even the most distant corners of the countryside "in their personal adornment are almost indistinguishable from those in town." Another Guangdong gazetteer published slightly earlier reports that dress in the prefectural towns was in turn aping the fashion in the provincial capital.[101] The dissemination of urban-based styles and customs was eroding the conventional separation of town and country and structuring a hierarchy in which the town enjoyed the edge.

These and other observations about the breakdown of rural styles were not simply the work of an overactive Confucian imagination. Life in mid-Ming cities was departing from rural norms in more than style. One sign of the difference was the attitude toward security of property, as towns became places where people had to guard against theft to a degree that was not known in the countryside. One mid-Ming tale tells of a Buddhist monk living alone in a small temple in Hangzhou. We know he kept the temple locked, for when he went out to recite sutras in private homes he gave his key to his cat. The cat hid it in a hole and retrieved it only when his master returned. By contrast, a Buddhist retreat in rural Yangzhou in the latter half of the fifteenth century was "without latch or lock."[102] Such trusting habits had become unimaginable for urban residents.

THE MERCHANTS OF HUIZHOU

Those made to bear the moral disapprobation that accompanied these changes were merchants, eminently urban-based and perceived as unattached to rural life. To survey what was happening among merchants, we shall consider the group that rose to national prominence and notoriety in this period, the merchants of Huizhou. Huizhou was the prefecture to which Zhang Tao was appointed when he became magistrate of Sheh county. This prefecture gained a unique reputation in the mid-Ming as the native place of some of the greatest merchants in the land. The prefecture was in the anomalous position of being adjacent to major regions of population and consumption like Jiangnan, yet separated from these regions by mountainous topography. Huizhou was not completely isolated, however, for it was fortunate in having two rivers that could serve as transportation arteries for moving its bulky local produce (tea, timber, and wood products) into two of those provinces. The Dagong River flowed westward to Jiangxi province and down through the porcelain center at Jingdezhen, and the Xin'an River, which formed where several smaller streams converged at the tea-trade market of Tunxi, flowed in a southeasterly direction across the Zhejiang border, feeding eventually into Hangzhou Bay. Though both these rivers were Huizhou's lifelines, the main route for export traffic went out to Hangzhou. Transport boats taking the Xin'an route could be down to Hangzhou in a week, though shoals, sandbars, summer flooding, and uncertain weather conspired to make the journey arduous. Because of this pattern of single avenues between production areas and distribution points, trade in Ming Huizhou remained export-oriented and did not proliferate into a hierarchy of intermediate marketing centers as would be expected in a highly commercialized region.[103] Internal dialect barriers attest to this orientation, for as late as the seventeenth century a native of one Huizhou county could not make himself understood in the next.[104] Huizhou people flowed out, not across.

The early commercialization of Huizhou agriculture, which was prompted by the rapidly increasing pressure on land in the twelfth century, had facilitated the shift to producing local export commodities. Tea was one of these. Huizhou tea production was aided by the shift in taste from powdered to leaf tea at the beginning of the Ming. Powdered tea was processed by milling tea leaves into powder which was then compacted into transportable cakes that didn't grow stale or spoil and were easier to ship than leaf tea. The Jiangnan elite in the early Ming preferred powdered tea, but popular taste favored leaf tea. The Hongwu emperor personally preferred leaf tea and declared that it alone would suffice as tribute from those areas where tea was furnished to the court, though his decision was motivated in part by his desire to disturb the patterns of corruption surrounding the levy of powdered tea.[105] Huizhou benefited from this shift, as its leaf tea could be shipped to the nearby centers of tea marketing and consumption in Nanjing, Hangzhou, and Suzhou more quickly than tea from other regions up the Yangzi or farther down the coast.

What catapulted Huizhou merchants into the highest echelon of merchant wealth in the Ming was not the tea trade, but the border delivery (*kaizhong*) trade supplying grain to the border in exchange for salt licenses. With the conversion of grain deliveries to payments in silver starting in 1492, Huizhou merchants were increasingly able to dominate the lucrative salt monopoly (based in the city of Yangzhou, near the coastal salt yards) and be counted among the wealthiest merchants of the age.

Coinciding with the restructuring of the border delivery system, as Harriet Zurndorfer has discovered in her studies of the region, was a change in the tax policies of the Ming government. Huizhou came under intense fiscal pressure in 1494 when the requisitions of varnish and tung oil required by the Ministry of Works were no longer levied as deductions from land tax proceeds but were set apart as separate, annual levies in addition to the land tax. This change effectively increased local taxes by 3,777 taels. In 1515 the Ministry of Works imposed a further levy on Huizhou of 20,000 pine trees, followed in 1523 by an increase in the tax on trees cut. When the formerly insignificant miscellaneous tax surcharges were sharply increased in the Jiajing era (1522–66), the cost of securing income from agricultural land became so heavy that many preferred to get out of landowning altogether in preference for trade.[106]

The wealth that Huizhou merchants amassed and the reach of their commercial dealings brought them much attention, not all of it admiring. The image that ordinary people developed of the Huizhou merchant was that of the grasping pawnbroker who sued anyone he disagreed with and spent vast amounts of money on commercial sex. However distorted the image, Huizhou merchants did dominate pawnbroking, which is a business that requires the capital and the careful accounting procedures that Huizhou merchants commanded; as sojourners, they did buy sexual services more than other people and had the cash to do so; and as people accustomed to frequent lawsuits over property rights in land-scarce Huizhou, they did incorporate litigation into their business strategies.[107] Their greatest vulnerability was not poor public regard, however, but the image that officials had of them. Those involved in the monopolies in particular worked hard to develop cordial ties with officials so as to limit the danger of bureaucratic predation and to have officials' support should conflicts with other merchants arise. To do so, they made great efforts to find points of entry into the cultural world that officials occupied. Often they succeeded. Thus, when the Huizhou salt merchant Fan Yanfu (1448–1517) chose in the mid-1490s to retire from Yangzhou, where he had conducted his business, he was presented with a collection of writings by several prominent regional officials and scholars.[108] Fan had learned that he had to have such contacts in order to pursue his business successfully.

Accordingly, Huizhou merchants proved adept at participating in high-cultural circles, particularly in Yangzhou. That city gained a reputation in the mid-Ming as a place where "the people by local custom value scholarship and refinement, and the gentry promote literary production. In the sounds of their [zither] strings and their chants, and in the style in their clothing and hats, they quite surpass people of other prefectures."[109] The description is of the quintessential gentry cultural life, but it is difficult to imagine how Yangzhou could have afforded such elegance had Huizhou merchants remained outside this social world. And indeed they did not. The tea-trader Fan Jizong (1412–61) played the zither. His cousin, the big grain merchant Fan Yuqing (1402–1464), composed poetry in his later years. Bao Song (1467–1517) built up a collection of rare books numbering over ten thousand *juan*, some of which he had printed with his commentaries.[110] These undertakings did not just signal personal interests but demonstrated a long-term commitment to participating in the cultural and educational practices of the gentry elite. Only partly was this course linked to a strategy of nurturing candidates for bureaucratic office. A degree within the family was an asset, but degree-getting was less important than ensuring that the family continued to prosper in its dealings with officials.

Mid-Ming culture was aware of the fragility of preserving commercial wealth over successive generations. The children of merchants "who are content with their station," notes the Guang-dong provincial gazetteer at midcentury, "just consume their wealth and pay no further attention to the cost of living, while the ex-travagant and wasteful ones get up to all manner of licentious and drunken behavior, gathering together and throwing dice. Accord-ingly, few are able to pass on [the family fortune] to the next gen-eration."[111] As it happens, the Huizhou Fans just mentioned were able to maintain the family's fortune but were notably unsuccessful in fielding examination candidates, though not for want of trying. For the Ming merchant, there could be no advantage to culturally isolating one's family from the world of the gentry and much to gain by crossing the status barrier between commerce and gentility.

COMMERCE AND KNOWLEDGE

Commerce spilled into the world of gentry cultural practices in ways more concrete than many gentry may have realized: books, for in-stance. It was still common in the mid-Ming for books to be pub-lished on a sponsored, noncommercial basis. A magistrate might pay for the printing of a book by an eminent local son, the publication of which brought credit to the county.[112] Increasingly, though, it was commerce that produced the texts that circulated among those who read for exams as well as those who read for pleasure. As one scholar living in the second half of the fifteenth century noted, "In the Xuande and Zhengtong eras [1426–49], printed books were still not widely available, whereas the printed editions we have today increase by the day and the month."[113] Many commercial pub-lishers who emerged into prominence at this time to supply this market did so by reprinting textbooks and the many editions of the classics and other reference works that the palace had published in the early Ming. Shendu Studio, for example, in 1505 brought out the first commercial edition of the voluminous *Comprehensive Gazetteer of the Ming Dynasty* (*Da Ming yitong zhi*), which the Classics Workshop in the Forbidden City had issued in 1461. It must have been a financial success, since within three years a Beijing publisher produced a second edition.

Shendu Studio was one of the largest publishing houses of the mid-Ming and specialized in historical works. It was located neither in Beijing nor in one of the great commercial centers of Jiangnan where the bulk of its educated readership lay, but in the specialized

Figure 18. Papermaking. Bamboo is trimmed and steeped in water to produce a mash, which is then spread on racks and dried into sheets (*Tiangong kaiwu*, 1637).

printing district of Jianyang county, Fujian.[114] Situated deep in the hills of the southeast interior near the border with Jiangxi province, Jianyang enjoyed proximity not to markets but to sources of abundant raw material. Inexpensive paper was made from the fibers of bamboo, and bamboo forests were abundant in the hills along the Fujian-Jiangxi border.[115] (The process of papermaking is illustrated in figure 18.) Jianyang paper was shipped all over the province, but it was also retained within the region to produce books, notably in the Jianyang towns of Masha and Chonghua. The area was known for its paper and printing in the Song, and by the Ming Jianyang publishers were turning out books in great volume and retailing them all over China. According to the county's gazetteer of 1553, "every house" in the town of Chonghua "sold books, and merchants from all over the realm traded in books as though they were handling textiles, gathering for market on the first and sixth of every ten-day cycle."[116] Even though the shipping distance from Jianyang north to the book-buying public in Nanjing was 1,050 kilometers, the low cost of raw material offset the cost of transport. The route from Jianyang to Nanjing, although broken with portages, was reasonably good. Known as the Chongan route (because it ran through the county of that name directly to the north of Jianyang), it had been developed in the Southern Song to handle the cargo coming down from northeastern Jiangxi to Quanzhou, when that city was China's major port in the southeast for international maritime trade.[117]

The commercial reprinting of classics and palace editions by publishers like Shendu Studio inadvertently helped the state to establish a core set of books that "most scholars" could be expected to own, according to Zhang Yue, whom we have encountered above as the author of the 1530 Huian gazetteer who complained about the lack of private investment in bridges and roads. This basic set included the Hongwu recensions of the Confucian canon and the standard histories as well as *The Ming Code* and *Ming Regulations*.[118] Commercial publishers went well beyond the curriculum, however, producing all manner of popular texts cheaply and in large volume to sell to a broader reading public than aspiring officials. How broad it was is difficult to say, though there are indications that literacy was widespread. Ch'oe Pu insisted that "even village children, ferrymen, and sailors" could read.[119]

The expansion of printing in the mid-Ming did not have the effect that it would soon have in Europe: what Italian historian Carlo Ginzburg has called "the historic leap of incalculable significance that separates the gesticulated, mumbled, shouted speech of oral culture from that of written culture, toneless and crystallized on the page."[120] In China, by contrast, oral and print cultures had coexisted for centuries and become partly fused. This is not to deny that many rural Chinese of the mid-Ming still had no contact with the world of print. But the culture of print was not a world apart from the oral context of everyday life, and character primers, almanacs, and etiquette guides could circulate and be partly understood. The ease with which printed knowledge traveled among the people did not please everyone. A mid-sixteenth-century gentry author was scandalized, for instance, to find that popular law books were widely available and thus likely to be used by those who would manipulate the law to their own advantage.[121]

A sure sign that books were increasingly available in the mid-Ming was the growing presence of book collections in the lives of mid-Ming intellectuals. Qiu Jun, the policy advisor to the Hongzhi emperor who advocated the freer operation of markets, recalls that in his early childhood on Hainan Island, his family owned several hundred *juan* (fascicles, or chapters) of books, which would have amounted to several dozen titles, not an insignificant private library. His father died when he was six, and friends helped themselves to the collection. Qiu was able to recover only a portion of it when he grew older. He borrowed books from booksellers to pursue his education, though he complained that "the books on the market were mostly low-brow, miscellaneous works, so those [of any academic merit] that I was able to acquire amounted to only a handful." Later, when he was on leave from his research post in Beijing in 1472, he built a library for the use of students at the prefectural school. Built of stone to withstand moisture, Qiu called it Stone Chamber. It was "a narrow place from which one can grasp the breadth of all within the four seas," and the books he placed there were the means "to grasp the world for ten thousand *li* from within the space of one room." His choice of distance metaphors shows his awareness of the problems that distance imposed on the communication of knowledge, particularly for those far from the centers of academic knowledge production. Stone Chamber housed the collection of books that Qiu deposited there, including all his own works, for over a century until another library was built for the county school in 1614 and the books were moved to the new location.[122]

Among the wealthy of Jiangnan, the expansion of printing was making it possible to assemble large private collections. The prestigious goal was to own ten thousand *juan* and house them in a library.[123] Two families that amassed impressive mid-Ming collections, the Feng family of Ningbo (whose collection was later bought by the Fan family and became the core of their justly famous Tianyi Ge library) and the Yu family of Shanghai, each named the buildings in which they housed their collections Wanjuan Lou, or Library of Ten Thousand *Juan*.[124] This number would be regularly exceeded only in the late Ming, as we shall see in Summer.

Books became more numerous in the mid-Ming, yet knowledge still did not circulate without restriction. Craft knowledge tended to be protected as the preserve of specialists or known only locally. For instance, the compiler of a North Zhili gazetteer reminisces at the end of the section on local products that in his younger days he walked with a local doctor into the hills north of the prefectural capital and had pointed out to him a wild herb called "road shoulder indigo" which relieved consumption. He says that the efficacy of this herb is not generally known. He also mentions learning from a friend he stayed with in Beijing that there was a kind of plant growing in the region known as "green rush grass" that could be used to make inexpensive writing brushes. He experimented with both claims and found them to be true, and included them in his gazetteer because he thought that knowledge of them would benefit others. He conceded, though, that there was always the gap between local knowledge and general use, and that knowledge had to overcome people's natural resistance to new information before it could yield benefits.[125]

Mid-Ming writers often portray the uneven distribution of knowledge in moral terms, setting their own informed attitudes and practices in contrast to the backward ignorance of rural folk. Medical knowledge was a common matter of complaint in this regard. Many a gazetteer compiler of the mid-Ming observes disparagingly that rural people consult shamans and witch doctors for medical assistance and not those who have a good knowledge of medicine. "Nowhere in the countryside are there either doctors or medicine," Zhang Yue notes of his native Huian county, Fujian, in 1530. "When someone is sick, people butcher a goat or pig and pray to the spirits."[126] At least in this case he credits their reliance on spiritual healing to lack of access to other knowledge rather than obstinace, as many writers of the time chose to do.

Zhang Yue was aware that knowledge of other technologies was not universally available. In his gazetteer of Huian, he notes that the cultivators made twenty-four-hour use of both well-sweeps (see figure 19) and water wheels to irrigate their fields during drought. Later in his career he took that knowledge with him to a post in southwestern Guangdong, where well-sweep technology was not practiced. By introducing the well-sweeps from his own county, Zhang Yue benefited the local people.[127] Even minor adjustments in how things were done between one region and another could make a difference. The compiler of another Fujian gazetteer observes of his county that "the plows and hoes used locally are not all that unlike those in South Zhili and Huguang," the two great agricultural provinces in the Yangzi Valley. He goes on to point out, however, that cultivators lack weeding hoes and are obliged to weed the fields on their hands and knees, and regrets that this back-breaking work

Figure 19.   This well-sweep is of the sort that Zhang
Yue sought to introduce into southwestern Guangdong (*Tiangong kaiwu,* 1637).

consumes so much labor.[128] Coupling this observation with his
comment on plow design, he indicates an awareness of the effect of
distance on knowledge, and of the continuing pressure to improve
conditions for its transfer.

COMMERCE AND CONNOISSEURSHIP

The strictest Confucian model of Chinese society placed the gentry
on the top rung and merchants at the bottom, but the distance

between the rungs lessened in the mid-Ming as some merchants gained entry into gentry circles and some gentry accepted them and searched the scholarly tradition for precedents to justify commerce. A county magistrate in Henan in the early 1540s, for instance, invokes a well-known passage in "The Great Treatise" of *The Book of Changes,* in which markets are regarded as part of the good order of society, to declare that "the people gain advantage from the circulation of commodities." He goes on to argue, in classical fashion, that merchants should be taxed lightly. To do otherwise sets the state in competition with the people for the advantages they may gain from commerce. This magistrate does accept the corollary to the Confucian view, which is that the state's interest in regulating markets is to prevent bad people from driving out good. But he does not assume, as earlier Ming commentators might, that merchants are among the bad. Failure to regulate markets as places of honest trade will not only drive merchants away from local markets but will drive them into smuggling to carry on their trade. He concludes with the strong judgment that "forcing peasants to become merchants is within the acceptable; forcing merchants to become bandits is not."[129] He does not privilege agriculture as absolutely superior to commerce, and he accepts that his role as magistrate includes ensuring the good operation of markets.

The experience of living within the commercial environment of the mid-Ming may not have induced most gentry intellectuals to espouse procommercial attitudes. Yet it was broadening the range of items that commerce brought into the gentry's reach. This the gentry did not resist. They happily absorbed these items into their cultural pastime of discriminating and appreciating fine things, at the same time stimulating their production. These things were not only antiques of the sort we saw listed in *Essential Criteria of Antiquities* in Winter. The list of collectibles branched out to include rare plants and exotic foods as these items entered commercial networks. Consider, for example, the unusually long list of local products in Zhang Yue's 1530 gazetteer of Huian. He discusses each with loving attention. In the opening entry in the section on fruit trees, Zhang tells us that the best lichees are produced just up the coast in Fengting and just down the coast in southern Quanzhou. Huian produces none of the exotic kinds, only two varieties whose main virtue is resistance to wind and cold, ordinary lichees that fruit growers can depend on to ripen even when the weather turns bad rather than the more finicky luxury varieties. Longans, he tells us, must be distinguished according to three sizes: "dragon eyes" (*longyan*), "human eyes" (*renyan*), and "ghost eyes" (*guiyan*—Chinese ghosts have small eyes). He complains that the local people fail to make these distinctions and simply call them all "dragon eyes." Under citrus fruits, Zhang enters the pomelo but notes that it is not mentioned in the geographical classic, *The Tributes of Emperor Yu* (*Yu gong*). Lacking a textual basis in the classics, the pomelo is excluded from the category of ancient things and unable to bear an investment of high-cultural meaning. Zhang tells the reader that the best citrus fruits in any case are produced in Zhangzhou to the south, and that the local fruit, which is grown only in limited quantities, is inferior.

Moving from citrus to flowering trees, Zhang reports that Huian has four varieties of cherry trees, each of which blossoms in a different month between June and September. He does not mention the importance of month-by-month flowering, but that would be obvious to his gentry reader: for the laying out of gardens. Cherry blossoms have a better color than plum, he says, whereas plum blossoms are more fragrant than cherry. He suggests that the age-old battle over which is the more beautiful may be resolved by taking the view "that one has no choice but to consider both to be the most beautiful." He notes that several varieties of Yangzhou plum grow in Huian, and that these are better than the plums grown elsewhere in Jiangnan.[130] Zhang goes on to evaluate other fruit trees, along with every other local product. (In the section on fish, he takes a tangent to tell the reader how a certain kind is cooked in Nanjing.)

Zhang Yue goes well beyond the standard lists of plant names that one usually finds in the "local products" section of a mid-Ming gazetteer. Why this intense interest in the flora of Huian county and how should it be properly appreciated? A plausible answer emerges if we think of him as concerned with something more than just botanical identification. Zhang was identifying plants in the county ecology, but he was also signifying them to his readers as elements in the cultural production of the county gentry. To know which plants to appreciate was not neutral knowledge but part of what someone needed to command in order to share in the cultural world of elite life, where such things mattered. To discriminate between plums as better or worse was also a way of discriminating between social betters and everyone else.

The irony here is that this sort of discrimination became possible in the mid-Ming because commercial networks were moving plants and fruits just as they were moving commodities. For a plant to be rare in a county meant that it had at least been made available. Availability was a function of mobility: the plant had to get to the county, and when one did it was often as a residue of commercial travel. It was also a function of the plant's viability as a commodity in the new environment; that is, someone had to take the trouble to produce it for purchase within the county. But availability had to have its limit: the rare plant had to be produced in small quantities so as not to devalue its cultural—and economic—value. The type of lichee that was ubiquitous in Huian county, for example, might generate a profit for those who grew it in bulk, but being both common and cheap it had no cultural cachet. This aesthetic exercise put Huian at a disadvantage, for the best was mostly absent, and much of what was good originally came from elsewhere. A gentleman in Huian accordingly would not want to be seen eating ordinary lichees like any commoner. For this reason, Zhang tells his educated readers which six varieties of lichee a gentleman would prefer to consume. He notes that only a few of these varieties are grown in Huian. The rest had to be brought in from elsewhere—through networks of commercial transaction, of course. The rarity of these lichees combined with elite demand in a way that compounded their cultural with their economic value.

This sort of discrimination of taste is still unusual in mid-Ming gazetteers, but it becomes all the rage in the late Ming, as we shall see in Summer. We can see it in fact in the 1609 Sheh county gazetteer that Magistrate Zhang Tao edited. This Zhang was a practical sort and not inclined to pose as a gentleman of taste. Still, even he would have enjoyed Zhang Yue's discussion of fruit trees had he been able to read it eighty years later. (Zhang Tao knew of Zhang Yue—he mentions him at one point in the Sheh gazetteer—but perhaps not his gazetteer. Huian was down on the Fujian coast, far to the south of inland Sheh, and Sheh was as southward as Zhang ever got in his career. Still, a water and land route did link Sheh to Jianyang,[131] the center of the Fujian publishing industry, so who knows what Fujian books got carried north?) In his own gazetteer Zhang Tao too indulges in discussions of local plants. His eye was caught by, among others, thickly flowering citrus trees, fragrant teabushes that produced more flowers than leaves, green pome-granates, white hibiscus, and a local plum blossom that had recently been crossbred to darken its color and make its fragrance more intense. He too neglects the local botany. Such flowers as magnolia that can be found in any of the surrounding counties are not worth mentioning, are they? Every plant that is worth mentioning came originally from outside the region: the hibiscus from Kaifeng, the pomegranate from Beijing, the teabush from Sichuan, and the citrus tree from Fujian. Sheh being a county of merchants, it would appear that all these plants were residues of Huizhou commercial travel that found niches in the local ecology, though Zhang Tao reverses the process by saying that the local soil had adapted to the plants rather than the other way round.[132] Zhang Tao shies away from talking about the economic value of the plants he records, though he does say that the fruit of a certain citrus tree he liked could be candied and that it was used to produce medicine.

Eighty years earlier down in Huian county, Zhang Yue is a somewhat cannier observer of the conditions of daily life. Perhaps it was living at an earlier phase in the growth of Ming garden culture, before the commodity value of picturesque trees was suppressed in gentry writings,[133] that kept Zhang Yue from succumbing to the connoisseur's static view of the world. For he was aware that the lack of fine fruit trees in Huian county was not a cultural or moral failure on the part of stupid peasants, even if it did serve to keep them beyond the pale of refined society. Concluding the section on fruit trees, he observes these trees required considerable care: fertilizing and watering had to be done at the right times, and rot and parasites had to be treated. But the critical complicating factor was the recurrent threat of drought. Exhausted from tending their modest plots, the peasants of Huian could not protect themselves against that. "So who has the extra labor for growing fruit?" he asks. Zhang Yue thus acknowledges that investing in fruit trees would be an expensive gamble against which local conditions stacked the odds. Without large local demand, these odds were not worth trying to beat. Fruit gardening in Huian was an indulgence only the rich could afford—and the rich mostly preferred to keep it that way anyway. To discriminate nicely among things was at the same time to discriminate sharply among people. Of what use were Yangzhou plums if everyone could afford them?

THE ZHENGDE DECAY

Zhang Yue spoke with the voice of unwavering authority on fruit trees as on many other matters. He was able to do so on the strength of his exalted position as the leading member of the Huian county gentry. Being a sociocultural rather than economic category, the gentry defies precise definition. At its core were those who held titles granted by the state principally through the examination system. But the status that degree-holders enjoyed extended to various educated relatives and to those whose cultural attainments and social networks gave them entrée into the world of scholarship and connoisseurship that marked off the elite.

The local gentry of Huian, as in many places in the mid-Ming, was a small privileged group just taking form. In the fifteenth century, Huian natives captured a *jinshi* degree at the triennial national examination in Beijing only once every quarter-century, and rarely did they pick up more than one or two provincial *juren* degrees a decade. This pattern began to change into the 1500s. The numbers of *juren* rose sharply: a spectacular six Huian *juren* in the three exams between 1501 and 1507, three in the second decade of the sixteenth century, four in the 1520s, and eight in the 1530s, rising to a noteworthy eleven in the 1540s. Getting to the *jinshi* was naturally a harder and slower process. When Zhang Yue won his *jinshi* in 1517, he was the first Huian native to have done so in over forty years. He was eventually followed by three more *jinshi* in the 1530s and another four in 1547. Of the five families that stand out in the mid-Ming degree lists, the Fragrant Hills Zhangs (as Zhang Yue's lineage was known) won more titles than any other, beginning with his great-grandfather's *gongsheng* degree in the 1460s.[134]

Such dazzling success was never a straightforward accomplishment, given the lottery-like character of the exams. In 1530, when half of those degrees had still to be earned, Zhang Yue wondered aloud whether it wouldn't be a good idea to bring back recommendation as a supplement to the exam system[135]—just to ensure that the exams didn't randomly knock families like the Fragrant Hills Zhangs out of elite echelons too quickly.

The first half of the sixteenth century is thus the period when a degree-based gentry peopled by men like Zhang Yue emerged to form an elevated elite in Huian county. A local gentry had been in formation in prefectural core counties in the fifteenth century, but only in the mid-Ming did such a group accumulate size and presence in semiperipheral counties like Huian (the process would proliferate in peripheral counties in the late Ming). The Huian gentry were not alone, therefore, for gentry elites were in formation for the first time in similarly located counties throughout central and southeast China in just these decades.[136] Their emergence was not an easy matter, however. As they emerged, many in this new elite agonized over their identity. Gazetteers and essay collections of the mid-Ming, particularly its latter half, reveal them writing on topics and in self-conscious ways that their early-Ming counterparts didn't. They struggled to come to terms with what they conceived to be their responsibilities for Confucianizing local society, but without the political means to meet them. To put their predicament simply, the mid-Ming gentry had to make sense of who they were in local society in the absence of formal opportunities to undertake public action. In relation to the emperor, they were his obedient servants whose conduct conformed to Confucian principles. But with reference to the local context, they held no formal franchise. Their social mobility gave them an informal power, but that was hard to justify in terms of Confucian ideals of deference and obligation to the imperial order that the magistrate represented. At the same time, the social forces that had propelled them into prominence were throwing up more competitors from below. The rhetorical strategy they used to escape from this predicament was to bewail the decay of the age and portray themselves as civilization's last great hope.

If we go back to the beginning of the mid-Ming, elite authors—mostly officials, for that matter—wrote of decay as a future possibility to be averted rather than as a present reality to be corrected or shunned. At that time the spokesman for Confucian morality was usually the county magistrate. Consider, for example, the following "Song to Promote Agriculture," which a county magistrate in Henan composed in the 1460s. He wrote it for the rural illiterate to hear, memorize, and hopefully heed:

> I urge you to revere filial piety,
> I urge you to be in harmony in your villages,
> I urge you to be diligent in agriculture and sericulture,
> I urge you to be at peace,
>   Whether you go or whether you stay.

Let the poor scholar have his books,
Let the peasant have his land,
Let the artisan and merchant follow their separate callings.

Then when I see you in no matter what place,
Each will be devoted to his own calling,
Without animosity or envy,
   Whether you go or whether you stay.

This text went into local lore, for two centuries later a local scholar was able to report that "the common people sing it even today."[137]

The picture of settled rural order in this song would have warmed the Hongwu emperor's heart. By its very existence, however, the song doubts the presence of Confucian social harmony. If the magistrate wants to get the local people to chant it while they work, it can only be because they were living in ways that didn't conform to what the song describes. A magistrate in the 1460s could still blame the lower orders for nonconformity. Half a century later, the picture was not so simple, as the harvest scene in the 1537 manual, *Annotated Illustrations for the Convenience of the People*, suggests (see figure 20). Many a peasant no longer "had his land" but had to stock the granaries of gentry landlords, who sold their tenants' crops into the commercial grain trade.

Even so, the magistrate's hopeful vision of a constant fourfold social order is often repeated by local gentry in the gazetteers they compiled in the mid-Ming. The editor of the 1506 gazetteer of Daming prefecture (from which some of the skewed male-female statistics earlier in this chapter were taken) reports of one county that "the gentry know to orient themselves to study, the peasantry know to devote themselves to agriculture, and the merchants, while adept at trading, do not go beyond their station." Of another county he happily declares that the people "are content to remain in their fields and villages and do not undertake travel to distant places."[138] In the same spirit, a writer in rural Jiangxi within the same decade could declare: "The gentry devote themselves to nothing as thoroughly as the Confucian undertaking," while "among peasants and merchants, artisans and traders, each undertakes his proper undertaking." As a result, he insists, "there are no mines, and no vagrants." (The one was thought to attract the other in the tradition of Deng Maoqi.) "This is nature at its most natural," he concludes.[139]

Figure 20.   Tenants deliver harvested grain to the landlord's granary.
Baskets of grain are carried in on poles to be measured using the three
containers on the granary porch. The largest on the left is a *dou* (10.7 liters,
one-tenth of a *shi*), the next a *sheng* (one-tenth of a *dou*), and the smallest
a *he* (one tenth of a *sheng*) (*Bianmin tuzuan*, 1592).

Naturalizing the social order hints at a slight sense of anxiety that
things might be other than as depicted. In the last two decades of the
mid-Ming, approaching the middle of the sixteenth century, that
sense has grown into an unhappy certainty that exceptions are disrupting the picture. For instance, after duly describing the devotion
of scholars to study, the hard work of the peasants, and the solid
morality of everyone else, another county gazetteer compiler at
midcentury is moved gently to note that "nowadays some of these

characteristics are gradually changing."[140] Of particular concern
was the wide cordon between the gentry at the top and merchants at
the bottom. The eminent and unconventional Gui Youguang (1507–
71) would go further to state: "In ancient times the four orders of
commoners had their distinct functions, but in later times the status
distinctions among scholars, peasants, and merchants have become
blurred." This change appears not to have worried Gui. When he
praises a Huizhou merchant family for being "gentry yet merchants,"[141] he indicates that he is willing to accommodate the
blurring. For their part, Huizhou merchants were keen to see the
boundary between them and the gentry dissolve. Merchant Wang
Hong (1491–1545), for example, instructed his son that "gentry and
merchants pursue different methods but share the same commitment." The biography of a kinsman goes further. "The ancients did
not differentiate four categories of the people," the author insists
against the grain, "so why should merchants be regarded as inferior
to gentry?" Indeed, he presses on to ask: "How do we know that
merchants can't be gentry?" This author feels that they can be, for
he declares the subject of his biography to have been "a merchant
who acted like a Confucian."[142]

Gui Youguang's notion of gentry-yet-merchant marks an extreme
position in the gentry discourse of social order at this point in the
Ming, though the notion would gain ground in the late Ming. For
more conventional writers concerned to assert their Confucian identity in what struck them as increasingly un-Confucian times, the
attempt to claim ancient authority for the nondiscrimination of
merchants had no appeal. The model of strictly divided occupational
categories was still regarded as the true and ancient way, and any
deviation could only be construed as a regrettable modern departure and proof that "the present is not equal to the past,"[143] as
the compiler of the 1543 gazetteer of Fujian's Shaowu prefecture
phrased it. The best was in the past.

Antiquity was not the only patina one could give to prescriptions
for social order. Rural life was also susceptible to being held up for
idealization, for some gentry took the lower degree of commercialization in the countryside as evidence that rural people, unlike
urbanites, were "close to ancient," as a gazetteer compiler said of
his quiet backwater in eastern Huguang.[144] The Shaowu gazetteer
compiler could likewise speak well of three of the prefecture's four
counties, where "the people work hard at planting their fields and

rarely become merchants," by saying, "They do not let extravagance
enlarge their desires or corrupt their minds." The reason they remained uncorrupted was that the rural economy in these counties
had not been extensively linked through commercial networks to the
outside world; or in his own words, "Resources here are meager and
so the people are content with eating rice and plain vegetables....
Few gentry or commoners ride horses, and when the rain soaks their
clothes they all hold their own umbrellas and take off their own
shoes" rather than have servants do these tasks for them.

But the Shaowu writer found himself obliged to observe that a
change was under way. "I have heard that ten years ago goose was
never served to a guest, but these days it sometimes happens, and as
many as several tens of dishes may accompany the rice. Rare styles
of clothing and hats are gradually being worn. And there are even
those who become merchants!" Sumptuary customs were in disarray, and this advertised a more profound moral disarray. Still, the
chaos was under control in those three Shaowu counties where "the
people work hard at planting their fields and rarely become merchants." In Jianning, Shaowu's capital county, however, local customs were altogether different. In Jianning "men parade themselves
in concave hats and silken garments with wide sleeves that hang to
the waist, and regularly change their styles." Consumption was so
competitive that public display got prohibitively expensive. As a local
saying put it, "A family with a thousand ounces of silver that holds
three weddings is wiped out, a family with a hundred ounces of
silver that hosts ten dinner parties is destroyed."[145] As the compiler
of the prefectural gazetteer saw it, wealth alone determined status in
Jianning, with little prospect of the classical model interfering with
this determination.

Those who agreed that society was in decline in the mid-Ming
tended also to agree when the turning point had happened. Almost
invariably writers in Jiangnan and the southeast pinpointed the
Zhengde era (1506–21).[146] Blaming the Zhengde reign became
fashionable almost as soon as the alcoholic emperor was dead at the
age of twenty-nine. Officials serving in the first years of the following
Jiajing court looked back on the previous reign as a period when
moral conventions governing social life began to erode.[147] The
Zhengde decay was quickly conceived as universal, and the world
before Zhengde mobilized for all sorts of nostalgia, much of it

misplaced but all of it powerful in shaping how people felt about the age in which they lived.

The first and most consistent nostalgia was for a world in which the ancient four orders of the people still applied. He Liangjun (1506–73), the great cultural arbiter of Songjiang in the 1560s, saw the Zhengde era as the time when conflict and status-seeking finally destroyed the fourfold model. He blames the poor for causing the collapse. "Up until the Zhengde era, ten percent of the population worked in government offices and ninety percent worked in the fields. The four classes of people each had their own fixed occupations, and the commoners were contented with farming and did not have any other ambitions." Since Zhengde, however, those once bound to the land were fleeing agriculture, some serving the wealthy families, others going into commerce and handicrafts, yet others becoming drifters. He declares, with a touch of exaggeration, that 60 to 70 percent of Songjiang peasants have left farming, the foundation on which he believed China's socioeconomic order rested.[148] He neglects to note that in Songjiang the land from which they fled was under the control of his fellow gentry landlords, who might regret the decay of the old order but profited by it.

The common people were not the only culprits, however. A member of the greater gentry just across the border in the northen Zhejiang prefecture of Huzhou charged the gentry with leading this process of decline. There was a time, he dreamed, when members of even the great rural gentry families would walk into the city, but once the Zhengde era was over, they never went anywhere except by sedan chair.[149] In fact, most had given up traveling between their rural estates and the cities, since they had left the countryside for good and moved into lavish residences in fashionable urban neighborhoods.

These judgments together projected another nostalgia back before Zhengde, and that was the harmony of class relations in the countryside. Returning again to Songjiang, we find its most prosperous native son, Chief Grand Secretary Xu Jie (not the earlier Xu Jie featured at the start of this chapter), declaring that one had only to go back to the late-fifteenth century to find ideal relations between landlords and tenants: "The large households had land they could not cultivate themselves, so they entrusted it to the tenants. The tenants wanted to farm but had not enough land to support themselves, so they relied on the large households." From the landlord's point of view, which idealized the relationship of landlord to tenant as being like "the mutual sustenance between father and son," it was a perfect and rational match. This was certainly the view of Xu Jie, Songjiang's largest landlord. But that paternalism faded in the Zhengde era, when "the mutual support and mutual sustenance of former times began to turn into mutual suspicion and mutual enmity."[150] Never mind that landlordism was something the Hongwu emperor disliked and would have banished from his ideal arcadia. From Hongwu's point of view, the chief grand secretary was embracing the wrong nostaliga, but then he lived in an age when only the most zealous rural Confucian fantasized the return of universal owner-cultivators.

The sense of growing disorder in rural relations inspired a further nostalgia, which was that people submitted to state control more obediently before the Zhengde era. To quote again from the 1543 gazetteer of Shaowu prefecture in interior Fujian:

> Up until the Zhengde era, the people were all fearful of officialdom. They met their tax payments on schedule, and the idle were whipped. Some urban dwellers did not know the yamen gates, and some villagers died without ever going to the market in town. There were absolutely no lawsuits, so that all [an official] could report is that the people were honest and affairs simple. Today debts and lawsuits have led to perverse habits and officialdom is not feared. Pacifying [such people] is not the Way. Does this not show the speed at which the world is changing?[151]

On the coast of Fujian, Zhang Yue saw the same process of decay in Huian county from the other side and wanted to blame the officials. He waxes so nostalgic that even the weather seemed better in the Hongzhi (1488–1505) era that preceded Zhengde:

> Up until the Hongzhi era, the weather varied according to the progress of the seasons through the year. At that time officials and petty officers also obeyed the laws and respected the responsibilities of their offices. They were at peace with the people and did not create incidents. For this reason the period is popularly called "neoclassical" (*jingu*). Starting at the beginning of the Zhengde era, however, harsh exaction was taken for administration, and then after six years of ruthless exploitation came several disastrous droughts. With the people impoverished, deception gradually took root. Local customs have undergone a sea change.

In the case of Huian county, Zhang Yue had some reason to blame the weather for the growth of mismanagement, for a flood and famine in the sixth year of Zhengde (1511) did start a cycle of decline.[152] Of course, Zhang Yue was not a fan of the Zhengde era anyway, for that was when he was demoted to a teaching post for refusing to bend to the emperor's whims. As he penned his comments into the gazetteer, he could comfort himself with the observation that there were still people in Huian who had not lost the timidity and frugality that the romantic vision of the countryside liked to ascribe to a hard-working and settled peasantry. He also sensibly warned his readers that in this age of decay (*moshi*) the poor could not be counted on to tolerate their poverty forever.

One other nostalgia popular among gentry on the Fujian coast was that foreign trade was better managed and more peaceable than it had subsequently become. The prominent coastal official Zheng Xiao (1499–1566), for one, complained that in the Zhengde era Chinese merchants (and gentry too) along the southeast coast expanded their illegal trade with the Japanese. As already noted, foregn trade along the southeast coast appears to have suffered a recession in the first two decades of the sixteenth century, coinciding exactly with the Zhengde era. The response of the new Jiajing regime was to close the coast, which only further intensified competition and militarized seaborne trade. The result was a long bout of piracy that lasted through midcentury.[153] Some liked to blame the Japanese for the unrest, though coastal officials came to recognize that most pirates were Chinese seeking to expand trade opportunities in the face of antitrade prejudices at court. In other words, the problem that blew up in the Zhengde era was rooted in China, specifically in the contradiction between the rapid expansion of commercial production in the early decades of the sixteenth century and the state's desire to stem the unfettered accumulation of wealth that foreign trade made possible.

If, as many gentry of the sixteenth century worried, China rounded a downhill corner in the Zhengde era, none offered a more comprehensive or stern summary of this rounding than Zhu Yong. Zhu Yong was a native of Huian, Zhang Yue's home county. Zhu was not part of the greater gentry residing around Zhang in the county seat, however, but lived down on the coast in the military town of Chongwusuo, the Fort Where Martial Skill Is Revered (see figure 21). Chongwusuo had become a town in its own right in the mid-Ming, and Zhu honored it with a gazetteer in 1541. Under "Customs and Fads," Zhu lays out a moral history of Ming society

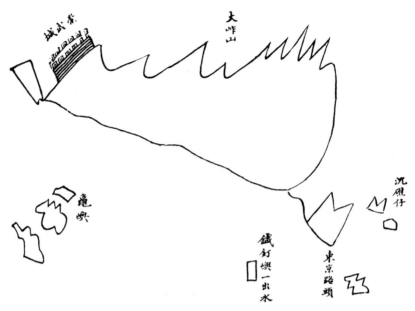

Figure 21. Zhu Yong's walled hometown of Chongwusuo is depicted
on a hand-drawn coastal navigator's map derived from a Ming original.
The note at the upper right identifies this as "the region of Quanzhou,"
the major city just down the coast. The large jagged mass is Dazuo
Mountain; the smaller shapes mark islands that the navigator should
avoid (*Gu hanghai tu*).

in terms and tone that all the preceding authors would have understood and approved—with the possible exception of the cultivated
Huizhou merchants.[154]

Zhu Yong begins his declamation by offering his vision of society
in the early Ming:

> At the beginning of the Ming dynasty, when people had just emerged
> from the disaster of the military overthrow, the lean and the wounded
> were just getting on their feet again and prosperity had not yet returned.
> Those who could devote themselves to studying for the examinations
> were few in the extreme. Once peaceful days lengthened, literary teach-
> ings gradually spread. It was at this point that people began to take
> up study. This was an age when teachers were valued, a time when
> gamblers and wanderers were not tolerated. Between elder and younger,
> respected and mean, there was gradation; between close and distant,
> honored and base, there was moral distinction. Some who were careful
> of their resources gained great wealth through commerce; some who
> were hard-pressed to find food earned bumper harvests through agri-

culture. Everyone cultivated or worked according to his proper occupation, and so there were no bandits in the hills.

Families were self-sufficient, so few people filed complaints. They valued benevolence and deference and did away with rancorous conflict; they strove for simplicity and happiness rather than style or decorativeness. Silks were rarely worn in the homes of officials, and meat was prepared only for entertaining guests. Marriages were arranged to achieve accord and avoid unsuitable mates. When the bride was sent off, her family did not dare to despatch her with such pomp as to compete with the groom's family and were embarrassed only lest it be done without sincerity. In the affairs of the living and the dead, everything was undertaken according to the methods of ritual. This was the lingering style of the ancient past, and the fine intention of our glorious dynasty.

The reader at this point will have sensed that Zhu Yong's picture of the early Ming is halfway to total nonsense. Like Zhang Tao half a century later, he compounds the Hongwu emperor's nostalgia with his own. Thus the early-Ming world that Zhu thought he had lost has become an "ancient" time free of conflict and observant of the natural hierarchies of age, kinship, and status. The public realm was not an arena for competition but a community where wealth and social prestige blended seamlessly. Even the merchant had his place and could earn rewards appropriate to his efforts.

Since the Zhengde era, however, the moral register of status had been replaced by an economic register as conspicuous consumption removed the patina of polite elegance from wealth:

> In the past few decades, local practices and people's hearts have gradually lost this. Even families where the *Book of Poetry* and *Book of History* are read and households where [ancient] rites and music are performed are mad for wealth and eminence and loathe poverty and meanness. Taking delight in filing accusations, they use their power to press their cases so hard that you can't distinguish between the crooked and the straight. Favoring lavishness and fine style, they drag their white silken garments as they roam about such that you can't tell who is honored and who base. Rites are excessive and indiscriminate, costumes and texts insincere.

Differentiation through clothing, ornament, and text now prevailed over the reabsorption of differences into a solidary social unity that had still perhaps been possible in the early Ming. Private persuasion had given way to public lawsuit; the distinctions of rich and poor, once subtle because clear and well understood by all, or so Zhu

Yong believed, had become exposed and raw. Moral order had departed from public culture.

Family life witnessed the same erosion. The naturalized hierarchy of elder and male over younger and female no longer held:

> Husbands and wives look on each other with contempt, forgetting the bond between them. Those who come from the same womb and were suckled at the same breast dare sunder the amity between brothers. The childless wealthy raise other people's children, and the lineage says nothing about the matter. Those who have many daughters drown the very girl babies they gave life to, and the mother shows no emotion.[154]

The lineage—the collectivity of families acknowledging group cohesion through their male members—was the kinship unit above the family with which most people identified, and to which they became increasingly bound by ties of moral and financial obligation in the mid-Ming as the lineage acquired shared assets and a corporate identity.[155] Zhu Yong saw the breakdown of kinship order occurring at the three points of greatest structural weakness in the lineage system: the link between husbands and their wives who came from a family outside the agnatic network of male kinsmen, the lateral link between brothers in the same generation, and the link between generations when adoption from outside the lineage was preferred over naming an heir within.[156] All were sensitive points of emotional connection. So too, and more to the point, all had property implications, each one threatening to undermine the concentration of lineage resources. Wives might bring dowries that their husbands' families aspired to divvy up after the man's death; brothers might split up family resources and weaken the lineage; and sons adopted from outside could threaten to remove their adopted father's property from the control of his agnates, which was often the reason outsiders were adopted in the first place. And at the heart of the entire system of association through males, and the desperate desire to prevent property from escaping through female ties, lay the practice of female infanticide.

The interface between family and public culture was marked by ritual, and there the disruptions among relatives and neighbors were exhibited together as failures to observe ritual:

> When wealthy householders hold a funeral, they invite guests and attend only to pleasing the living with liquor and food. The poor take loans and follow their example, preferring to skimp on the coffin and burial clothes. When someone is sick, he does not take medicine but does as

the spirits direct: this is called "the way of the spirits." When someone dies, [his descendants] do not bury the body by the prescribed time but store the coffin until an auspicious site has been divined: this is called "Heaven's truth is not equal to earth's." Some are so mad and reckless that they profane their forebears and openly declare: "The rites were not established for our generation."[157]

The funeral, the key moment for recertifying relations among the still living, was no longer reinforcing kinship solidarity but providing instead an opportunity to buy status and set the wealthy apart from their poor kin. The culture of such occasions only victimized the poor,[158] while the rich could declare that their generation had achieved independence from the old conventions. The moderns were at war with the ancients. An elder Confucian like Zhu Yong could read these changes only as signs of moral collapse. His sole remedy was to drill the people with counterideals from a more settled past in the hope of reabsorbing the conflict breaking out on all sides. Moral rearmament had little chance, however, against the main source of this conflict, which was money. By the Zhengde era, elites and commoners both could afford to buy their way out of simplicity and obscurity and into pleasure and notoriety.

Gentry complaints about decline are fraught with irony, for the main beneficiaries of the new prosperity were the gentry themselves. Prosperity may not have felt like a good thing, and yet it was making possible the conditions under which certain families could afford the education and cultural training needed to move into the world of the gentry elite. The gentry were taking it upon themselves to worry about the decay of the age at the very moment when they themselves were emerging to restructure and redefine elite life. One senses behind their protests a desire to identify and control anxieties arising from a social nexus in which they have the most to gain, if perhaps also potentially the most to lose. Certainly the old elite stratum and the established great families who inhabited it were under threat in the gradually commercializing whirl of the mid-Ming, and yet without that threat men like Zhu Yong and Zhang Yue might never have been able to break into the ranks of the gentry. Once there, they had then to be concerned about justifying their position and preserving their status in the rough-and-tumble world since Zhengde, and so they appealed to Confucian education (Zhu) and even to restrictions on the exam system (Zhang) as gatekeepers against the growing tide of upwardly mobile commoners pressing for entry.

It was a rare mid-Ming writer who could take a benign view of the changes going on about him—but a few did. One who stands out in this regard is the Shanghai literatus Lu Ji (1515–52), who spoke *in favor of* extravagance rather than against it. Unable to justify lavish spending with a moral argument (that terrain was already well occupied by the opposing viewpoint), Lu opted for an economic argument to support his opinion that spending was a good thing. He argued that when great merchants and wealthy families (like his own) "are extravagant in their food, then cultivators and cooks will share the profit; when they are extravagant in their silk clothing, then cloth dealers and weavers will share the profit."[159] Lu is sufficiently confident of his view to round off his argument with a quote from Mencius about the value of balancing surplus and need. If Lu was blithe about the moral dimension of consumption, it was perhaps because he was the heir of the leading landlord-gentry family in sixteenth-century Shanghai and felt secure in his position and secure in the conviction that his wealth need not be a moral burden.

The extraordinary declarations of Lu Ji as much as the more ordinary complaints of Zhu Yong testify to the power of the changes sweeping China in the mid-Ming, changes that the Confucian order could suppress only through rhetoric by calling up contrived memories of the world before Zhengde. But the moral center had long ago receded. It had no power to reestablish the old ways or initialize the new, as it might have done under Hongwu. That power had passed to the local gentry. Even if the old rules were caving in as commerce grew, the gentry better than anyone stood to gain from the new sum of wealth that commerce was generating and the new channels of status and power that the accumulation of wealth was digging across the landscape of Chinese society. Few gentry were willing to celebrate what was overtaking them as the right patterns of public demeanor disappeared from view, and most were appalled. Confucianism did not provide them with any ready rules to transform what was taking place into something that made sense. The challenge for those who found themselves living in the late Ming, among them Zhang Tao, would be to figure out what the new rules might be.

Summer

The Last Century
(1550–1644)

Those who enriched themselves through trade became
the majority, and those who enriched themselves through
agriculture were few. The rich became richer and the poor,
poorer. Those who rose took over, and those who fell were
forced to flee. It was capital that brought power.... Trade
proliferated and the tiniest scrap of profit was counted up.
Corrupt magnates sowed disorder and wealthy shysters
preyed.... Purity was completely swept away.

Zhang Tao

As they crossed into the latter half of the sixteenth century, many felt
they were entering a new world, Zhang Tao among them. They saw
the old models coming apart in the flux of change that more people,
more money, and more competition were bringing about. They
found the experience of being Chinese less predictable and less uni-
form. For upper gentry, large landowners, and rich merchants, the

late Ming was a time of cultural brilliance, innovative ideas, and endless pleasure—also a time of confusion and anxiety. At the other end of the social scale, the anxious poor survived at the edges of this prosperity as short-term tenants, wage laborers, domestic servants, woodcutters, and seasonal migrants. Hongwu's orderly image of owner-cultivators living in self-contained villages had strained credulity even as he strove to put it in place. By the late Ming, when many cultivators plowed the fields of others and some found they could not even claim a place in the village economy, it was little more than a nostalgic and impossible ideal.[1]

THE GOD OF COPPER CASH

COINS AND BUDDHAS

Zhang Tao attributes to this hot summer of the dynasty a passion for counting up the tiniest scrap of profit. For all but silversmiths and accountants, that scrap usually took the form of a cash (wen), the thin copper coin with a hole in the middle that served as the lowest denomination of money. Silver was fine for the wealthy, but a laborer earned too little to be paid in anything but copper coins. The Catholic Grand Secretary Xu Guangqi noted in 1619 that the going rate in Beijing was 24 or 25 cash for a day's work, and that this was barely enough to keep a man alive.[2] For someone selling a day of his labor for two dozen coppers, the god of copper cash against whom Zhang Tao is about to warn us was a thin and miserable deity.

At the other end of the spectrum, the god was growing fat. One of his avatars looms that way today in the main hall of the Royal Ontario Museum in the guise of a bare-chested Vairocana (see figure 23).[3] This Buddha was probably cast in bronze around the turn of the seventeenth century. His flat face is peaceful, benign, almost abstract in its concentration on what lies within. It feels as though the artist had no particular face before him as he sculpted the sharply delineated mouth and eyes. For the elite patrons of the monastery in north China where he once sat, this Vairocana gave expression to the serenity they sought to find in the Buddhist realm and usually didn't find out in the streets of real life. To those who stood outside this pleasant construct of withdrawal, a statue of this size was literally a mountain of cash, a Buddha only temporarily,

Figure 22.   Copper coins are made by pouring
molten copper into molds (*Tiangong kaiwu,* 1637).

always ready to be made to yield up roughly six-sevenths of its
weight in pure copper.

For this statue to have survived the four centuries from the late
Ming to the present goes against the odds. All too often objects
made of so much metal were melted down. The list of lost metal
Buddhas is long. The famous iron Buddha in Iron Buddha Monastery of Universal Illumination in Hangzhou, for instance, was
melted down at the end of the Yuan dynasty by Zhang Shicheng,
Zhu Yuanzhang's main rival before he became the Hongwu emperor.[4] Zhang had wanted the iron for arms. Bronze statues, on the

Figure 23.   This late-Ming bronze statue of Vairocana Buddha was
acquired in the years just before 1920 from a temple in north China by
George Crofts, a British fur dealer based in Tianjin. It was one of about
thirty objects that Crofts sold to the Royal Ontario Museum, Toronto,
for $15,000. The photograph was probably taken in Tianjin in 1920 just
prior to shipping, reproduced courtesy of the Royal Ontario Museum
(921.31.30), Toronto.

other hand, were good for making both weapons and coinage. For
that matter, coins and weapons were good for making each other.
Lu Rong (1436–94) recalled seeing copper coins of the Hongwu era
circulating when he was a boy, but observed that by the time he had
grown up these had entirely disappeared for arms manufacture.[5]

A tradition of confiscating and melting down bronze Buddhas
goes back at least to 955,[6] and the Ming continued on this course.
The first large confiscations occurred in the Zhengtong era (1436–
49), when the government targeted bronze figures and other objects
in Buddhist and Daoist monasteries to make the weapons needed for
the massive campaigns on the northern border in which the Zhengtong emperor himself was finally captured. Confiscatory moves were
not always successful, as the gazetteer of Shengshui Monastery in

Hangzhou records. A large bell hanging in the main hall of Sheng-shui was one of those earmarked for melting. While laborers were removing the bell in the main hall, the assembled monks prayed for divine intervention. Suddenly the great bell slipped from the laborers' grasp and fell to the ground. It was found to be unharmed, a sign from heaven that Shengshui should keep its bell.[7]

Further attempts to confiscate religious objects were made in the Jiajing era. In 1528, Minister of Rites Huo Tao (1487–1540) advocated the closing of convents, which he regarded as covens of illicit sex, and recommended as part of the moral cleansing that the bronze statues in these convents be melted down for state use.[8] This moral emergency gained little support and left most statues intact. Far more destructive was the military emergency in the 1550s, when coastal officials were struggling with pirate attacks. In 1554, the provincial governor of Zhejiang ordered the bronze bells in all Buddhist monasteries in the region confiscated to be melted down for firearms, literally "Frankish machines" (*folangji*).[9] The gazetteer of the Tianzhu Monasteries in Hangzhou says the order was supposed to apply to the bells only of abandoned monasteries, but that overly zealous junior officers got carried away and took down the bells of functioning monasteries as well. Only the abbot of a place as important as Tianzhu could appeal over their heads to stop the requisitioning. Guanyin was able to stop a band of pirates from burning down this monastery, as we noted in Spring, but the abbot couldn't match her in trying to protect the bell in the main monastery. It too was melted down.[10]

The Ming state was not the only entity to have an eye for idle metal. Private interests saw the copper in bronze Buddhas just as clearly. Three men carried off a bronze statue of the Daoist deity Zhenwu from a newly built temple in Shanghai in 1607 with the explicit notion of selling it for the metal. At 600 catties (approximately 360 kilograms), this was a small statue by Buddhist standards, which required three to four times that much metal for a really imposing Buddha, but it was certainly enough to fetch a good price from a metal dealer. The thieves managed to get the statue onto a waiting boat and set off, but were later discovered and foiled in their plan.[11]

The mutability of metal Buddhas did not discourage pious Buddhists of the late Ming from having them cast. One merchant who came down from Sheh county to the commercial port of Wuhu, which was discussed at the beginning of Spring, gave two Buddhas to Yuanzhao Monastery which lay just northwest of the city, one of iron and the other of bronze.[12] As Yuanzhao came to be known as Iron Buddha Monastery, at least the iron Buddha survived. The bronze Buddha on the other hand seems not to have withstood the hunger for copper.

All this thieving and confiscation suggests a copper shortage in the late Ming, or at least an increase in its value as compared to silver at a time when the importing of Spanish and Japanese bullion was expanding silver stocks.[13] As silver came in, copper (actually bronze) coins went out to Japan, Southeast Asia, and the Indian Ocean despite the legal prohibition against their export.[14] The value of copper in bronze coins became so much greater than their face value that counterfeiters found it profitable to melt down good coins and recast them in debased form. It appears that practically all coins circulating in the Wanli era were cheapened counterfeits. The economy was too active to leave precious metals idle.

And yet this is exactly what patrons of Buddhist monasteries did in the late Ming every time they wanted a fat Buddha or a giant bell cast in bronze. These could be enormous objects. A single bell made for a Zhejiang monastery in 1602, for example, consumed over 2,300 catties of the finest copper plus over 400 catties of tin, a prodigious amount of metal weighing over 1,600 kilograms.[15] The patrons who paid for this bell—just like the putative patrons who paid for the Vairocana Buddha in the Royal Ontario Museum— were sufficiently powerful to keep these religious objects from slipping away into coins or cannons. A different type of acquisitiveness dislodged the Vairocana from his monastic setting in the second decade of the twentieth century, but perhaps it rescued him from a more severe fate later in the war-torn decades that followed. At any rate, this god of copper cash has survived to gaze dispassionately through his lidded eyes—then upon the wealthy men who poured their money into him, now upon the patrons of the museum.

PATRIARCH MIAO

Casting one's resources into the religious body of Buddhism was one way of stopping the restless movement of money, commodities, and statuses in the late Ming. It also had the added advantage of rendering the authority of a higher power visible to the common people over whom it held sway. But there were other ways to stem the tide of change, or better still, get it to flow in beneficial directions. One of the most popular in the late Ming was to gather together the resources of one's own family with those of one's agnatic (male) kin into the communal body of the lineage. The lineage bound people and their land together into a unity that commercial opportunity could not so easily undo; not only that, it gave them the means in common to participate with greater advantage in the networks through which goods were traded and money changed hands. The lineage also served as the site within which the hierarchies of deference and obligation that one feared were being lost could be reinstated and the status of the senior members enhanced.

The "Family Instructions" of a Miao lineage of Guangdong province, preserved in the late-Ming edition of that lineage's genealogy, show how one rural elder conceived of what he was up against in this money economy, and how he thought his relatives should respond to the changes going on around them in society.[16] The rules set down by the unnamed head of this branch of the Miao lineage—we shall call him Patriarch Miao—promote the usual values of diligence and obedience and are imbued with the nostalgia for order that one might expect of a family elder. But Patriarch Miao was also sharp enough to understand that his advice had to bear some relationship to the real world. In his instructions we can detect his quiet adjustments to the changed circumstances of the late Ming.

Patriarch Miao's argument for the role of the lineage is an argument against urban living. "For generations, this family has dwelt in the countryside, and everyone has had his set profession; therefore our descendants should not be allowed to change their place of residence." He warns that "after living in the city for three years, a person forgets everything about farming; after ten years, he does not even know his lineage." Cities induce an "extravagance and leisure" that few can resist. He declares that "the only legitimate excuse to live in a city temporarily is to flee bandits."

Just as he distrusts cities, Patriarch Miao dislikes consumption for pleasure. "All our young people" are not content to "wear cotton clothes and eat vegetables," whereas in fact "a diet of vegetables and soups provides a lifetime of joy." So too, when a guest is entertained, "we should not have many dishes and should not force the guest to drink too much." Keep the menu to "not more than five dishes or more than two soups. Wine and rice should also be served in the right proportion." Raise your own fish and harvest your own vegetables and fruits, he advises, for "to purchase everything needed for the morning and evening meals means the members of the family will merely sit and eat" rather than labor for what they eat. "Is this the way things should be?" Perhaps not, but only in an economy in which production and consumption had not yet been separated. If the younger generation felt "ashamed of their coarse clothing and coarse food," it was because the economy had freed them from the necessity to dress or eat coarsely.

In the background behind these comments lurks money, and contrary to his pose of the simple rural man, Patriarch Miao is always ready to talk prices. Gifts among relatives, which should be exchanged no more than twice a year, should not cost more than a tenth of a silver tael. In return for gifts presented to the family on ritual occasions, he is quite specific about the amounts that should be given: a tenth of a tael if the gift is a pig's head; three-tenths for two geese and wine; half for a lamb and wine; a full tael for a pig and wine. "In addition, one-fiftieth of a teal should be placed in an envelope and presented [to each guest] as a token compensation for fruit and wine." These costs were recouped by a silver levy on those who attended at the same rate, one-fiftieth of a tael per person. Clearly the Miao lineage was wealthy enough not to be a copper community. Silver may have been only the unit of record, with actual payments tendered in copper cash equivalents, but it is likelier that silver was the actual medium through which ritual responsibilities were assessed and social obligations paid out.

The insinuation of money and commodities into family life was altering the terms of daily life for women, whom the patriarch pictures participating in the money economy just as much as the men. He instructs them to execute the tasks of the housewife with the same attention to detail expected of men in the fields. For instance, they should make sure that the store of firewood is sufficient, so that "even if it rains several days in succession, they will not be forced to use silver or rice to pay for firewood, thereby impoverishing the family." Even though the housewife is advised to avoid relying on the market, she must conduct the domestic economy according to a careful economic rationality: to "closely calculate the daily grocery expenses and make sure that there is no undue extravagance." His advice against wasting resources made sense only in a commercial economic environment that permitted what he would regard as overconsumption. Finally, Patriarch Miao warns that "women from lower-class families who stop at our houses tend to gossip, create conflicts, peek into the kitchens, or induce our women to believe in prayer and fortune-telling, thereby cheating them out of their money and possessions." If Miao women could be cheated out of money, they had to have had some on hand.

Finally, Patriarch Miao is sensitive to the changing structure of society. He invokes the standard fourfold model to organize his opening advice for each of the "respectable occupations" that a lineage son might take up, as well as to summarize his advice at the end of the document. All seems conventional: "Scholarship ranks the highest; farming is next; and then craft and business." And yet something about the mold has radically changed. He declares that Confucian scholarship, for example, is a "hereditary occupation," yet he says that "it should be up to the individual to measure his ability against his aspirations as well as to find the most suitable occupation for himself." In other words, choice of occupation, and the social mobility implied in this choice, has been thrown wide open. An occupation turned out to be hereditary only if a son happened to follow his father's line of work.

However suitably old-fashioned Patriarch Miao's advice was meant to look, and must have looked to all the subsequent generations of Miaos through the Qing dynasty, it took full account of the ways in which the world had changed since the mid-Ming. Silver had its place. Only when the tail wagged the dog by tempting lineage members into selling family property does the patriarch fulminate against it. He concludes by stating that "these family instructions attempt to show the correct procedures to be followed in everyday life." Such procedures would have been inconceivable, and most certainly judged morally incorrect, in any time before the late Ming.

SUBSISTENCE IN AN AGE OF PLENTY

Patriarch Miao was careful to see the resources of his lineage husbanded properly. The family was reasonably prosperous, though whether that had anything to do with his instructions is a matter of pure speculation—perhaps the lineage simply held good investments. So too the laity who contributed several hundred taels of silver to have the Vairocana Buddha cast in bronze must have been prosperous men and women. But the wealth of the late-Ming economy was not evenly distributed. The pressure of population during the final century of the dynasty made wealth for all impossible.

Determining how many people were actually alive in the late Ming involves calculations with absurd margins of error. The official census records were hopelessly out of touch with demographic reality. The compiler of a Zhejiang gazetteer of 1575 insisted that the number of people off the official census registers in his county was three times the number on.[17] A Fujian gazetteer of 1613 similarly dismissed the impression of demographic stagnation conveyed by the official statistics: "The realm has enjoyed, for some two hundred years, an unbroken peace which is unparalleled in history," the editor pointed out. "During this period of recuperation and economic development the population should have multiplied several times since the beginning of the dynasty. It is impossible that the population should have remained stationary." A Fujian contemporary agreed: "During a period of 240 years when peace and plenty in general have reigned [and] people no longer know what war is like, population has grown so much that it is entirely without parallel in history." Another official in 1614 guessed that the increase since 1368 had been fivefold.[18]

China's population did not grow between 1368 and 1614 by a factor of five, but it certainly more than doubled. The standard estimate suggests that China was approaching 150 million by 1600, though working from a modestly higher base figure suggests that it may have approached 175 million.[19] It is possible that rising mortality may have slowed this rate of growth in some areas. So too did human choice, for it seems that some attempt was made to space pregnancies. A possible example from the 1590s is the wetnurse Yao of Tongxiang, Zhejiang, distressed to find herself pregnant by her husband before the proper "interval between the union between husband and wife" had expired, which was three years. Despite the assurances of the family where she worked that shortening the interval was not a shameful matter, Yao committed suicide by drinking mercury ("liquid silver"). This is the only reference to spaced pregnancies I have found in Ming sources, and it may apply only to wetnurses who had to coordinate their pregnancies with the production of milk for their employers, for which the standard contract appears to have been three years. Yet the stress of shame suggests that she had internalized birth spacing as a moral norm that was more powerful to her than her contractual responsibility to her employer.[20] The more consistent method of discouraging population growth, however, was infanticide. Infants of both sexes were "submerged" to limit family size, despite the efforts of magistrates to curb the killing of children, and girls of course were overwhelmingly vulnerable.[21] Some families were known to practice female infanticide repeatedly over successive generations in order to restrict births entirely to boys.[22] Female infanticide was illegal, of course, and the Chongzhen emperor reiterated the prohibition in 1629, but without any visible consequence.[23]

However Chinese sought to limit births, this did not stabilize China's population, which in the late Ming far exceeded any it had previously had. This growth was testimony to the growing capacity of the Ming economy, but it entailed as well a mounting pressure on resources. Recurring cycles of flood, drought, and cold from the 1580s forward had devastating effects. During a famine in Jiangxi province in 1637, for example, people stripped the landscape of everything that even approached edibility, and then when that was gone they filled their stomachs with fine soil dug deep from the ground. They called it Guanyin's flour, in the hope that the Buddhist goddess of mercy would save them in their extremity.[24] The consequences of particular famines remained relatively short term until the great epidemic of 1641. Entering into China from the northwest, it raced down the Grand Canal to infect most of densely populated Jiangnan, then made a second pass through many of the same areas the following year. A gazetteer in northern Zhejiang records that over half the population fell ill that year, and that in 1642 90 percent of the local people died. Another gazetteer across the border in South Zhili records that in 1642 the corpses of epidemic victims were scattered everywhere. The devastation was shocking, and when crops could be neither grown nor harvested, the pressure on food supply and tax revenues became unbearable.[25] Two years later the dynasty fell.

DISASTER IN AN AGE OF UNCERTAINTY

The threat of devastation found its way into a popular almanac of 1599, The Correct Source for a Myriad Practical Uses (Wanyong zhengzong). (See figure 24.) This almanac was compiled and printed by the successful Jianyang publisher, Yu Xiangdou, whom we shall

Figure 24. Selected omens from the section entitled "Heavenly Perturbations" in the first chapter of *The Correct Source for a Myriad Practical Uses*, published in 1599.

Wind on Qingming portends that the price of paper will rise; a wind on Guyu portends that the wheat harvest will fail; a wind on Chongyang portends that the price of grain will rise.

Thunder in the absence of clouds: The *Commentary on the Five Elements* says that thunder is the beating of heaven's drums. Thunder in the absence of clouds means that violent soldiers will come.

Rain in the absence of clouds portends frequent drought for a generation.

A wisp of cloud across the sun in the shape of a snake if green portends epidemic; if white, military uprising; if red, treason; if yellow, battle; if black, flooding rains.

If the sun shoots forth flames, it portends a great drought lasting three years.

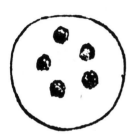

If one sunspot appears, it portends a storm; two sunspots, no wind; three sunspots, no rain; four sunspots, drought; five sunspots, famine.

If a bird flies out from the sun, it portends drought.

Should a yellow toad appear at the bottom of a full moon and move upward, it portends cannibalism.

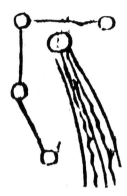

If a comet enters the Sieve constellation, the people of the realm will suffer hunger and disease and the price of rice will rise.

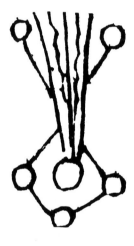

If a comet enters the Ox constellation, a woman will cause the government of China to change.

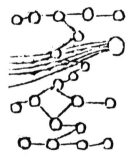

A comet in the Dawn constellation portends an epidemic among the people that will strike one in ten.

meet again in this chapter. The first chapter of *The Correct Source* includes a section entitled "Heavenly Perturbations." Yu says nothing about where he got these omens, but presumably they circulated as secret lore among the people. Here we can discern what disasters late-Ming Chinese most feared.[26] The two most frequently named are warfare and starvation. After these comes epidemic: a comet in the Dawn constellation, for instance, portends an epidemic that will strike one person in ten. Other disasters include treason, banditry, murder, foreign invasion, frost, snow, tornado, and something called "a chaos of women." Yu does not explain what this final disaster entailed: Imperial concubines misleading emperors? Women overturning gender norms? We can only guess.

The mutation of portents by month suggests that disasters were thought of as coming not singly but in sequential combination. This after all was often what happened in real life. For example, a comet during a lunar eclipse in the first or sixth month portends drought; in the third month, a rise in grain prices, and in the tenth, a rise in all prices; in the fourth month, starvation, and in the eighth, famine; in the fifth, fire; in the seventh, the death of livestock. As this example indicates, one of the anxieties was vulnerability to price fluctuations. Wind on the midspring festival of Qingming heralds a rise in the price of paper, a disaster for publishers like Yu Xiangdou; wind on the midautumn festival means that the price of grain will go up, a disaster for everyone else. A lunar eclipse on the fifth day of the twelfth month portends that grain will become dear, though in the tenth month it means business will prosper.

PRINTING IN AN AGE OF INFORMATION

Foretellings of the future were restricted knowledge, for only the emperor was permitted to divine heaven's will. Yu Xiangdou may have been courting treason to include "Heavenly Perturbations" in *The Correct Source,* but he did nothing to hide what is the best illustrated section of the almanac. Its inclusion underscores the commercial nature of the publication. Yu was an entrepreneur willing to make information of any provenance available for a price without concern for legal consequences. A large popular audience wanted to know how to read the future, and his almanac aimed to supply that demand. In this regard, the book is typical of what the mass-market industry in the Fujian interior produced: primers, moral tracts, law texts, novels, plays, erotica, joke books, route guides, accounts of foreign customs: compendia of any sort of knowledge that might interest a buyer and cheap abridged editions of any sort of book that sold well.

Even gentry were lured into this market. Thus it was said of a Jiaxing *jinshi* of 1559 who was a passionate bibliophile, "Not even books on medicine, pharmacology, divination, and shamanism would he fail to inquire after."[27] These were the bodies of knowledge outside the "correct" or canonical (*zheng*) literatures that a Confucian was expected to read and master. But people read them as well as the books they were supposed to read; in fact, volumes on medicine and divination were even being included in the libraries attached to prefectural and county libraries. A 1607 gazetteer compiler in north China allows their inclusion by resorting to the notion of taste: "The world could not do without them—they're just as important to scholars as are literary and historical books. It is just that people have different tastes. We may not want to have them in the collection, but that does not mean that we should destroy them."[28] Confucian teachers were right to fear that noncanonical reading would bring students under the wrong influences, for popular literature did corrode the edges of the canon. Editors appointed to vet the imperial library in the eighteenth century looked over the texts that came to them from the Ming and complained that the taste for sensational reading in the late Ming had encouraged all sorts of erroneous interpolations into serious literature.[29]

The new types of information getting into print were not only of a sensational variety. In his preface to *The Exploitation of the Works of Nature* (*Tiangong kaiwu*), from which many of the illustrations in this book have been taken, Song Yingxing (1587–1666?) worries about the charge of defying the canon and modestly declares the knowledge of technological processes his book contains to be of no significance. It was only because his friend Tu Shaokui (1582?–1645) prevailed upon him to publish it, he insists, that he allowed the book to see the light of day. Song notes that Tu "believes that in any piece of writing, whether by a contemporary or a past author, if there be one worthy sentence, or one iota of merit, then this work deserves to be completed and made known." Song is defending himself against having written about matters that are "in no way concerned with the art of advancement in officialdom," but he is also voicing the new attitude of the age: that there need be no barrier between what can be rendered into text and what should be put into print. Song adds that books are important for people like himself who don't have wealth enough to collect rare objects or access to scholarly circles where knowledge of such objects is shared.[30] (Song was right to doubt the appeal of his material, for the book went out of print and almost out of existence, preserved only in Japan.)

Whether technological, divinatory, or canonical, books of all sorts were being printed, and in numbers and variety beyond what had been produced at any previous time. The Italian Jesuit missionary Matteo Ricci (1552–1610) marveled at the world of books he discovered in late-Ming China. Coming from a culture to which printing had just been introduced, he was amazed by "the exceedingly large numbers of books in circulation here and the ridiculously low prices at which they are sold."[31]

The commercial publishing industry developed regional specializations, which a late-Ming bibliophile sketches:

> There are three places for publishing: the Suzhou region, Zhejiang, and Fujian. Sichuan editions were most prized in the Song but in recent times have become very rare. Beijing, Guangdong, Shaanxi, and Huguang all now have publishing ... but are not as productive as the three places I have mentioned. In quality, books from the Suzhou region come first; in quantity, Fujian books are tops. Zhejiang comes second on both counts. In terms of cost, books from the Suzhou region are most expensive, from Fujian cheapest, and from Zhejiang at neither extreme.[32]

The high-end publishers in the Suzhou region were scattered among Nanjing, Wuxing, and Sheh county (though there were complaints that the keen commercial publishers of Sheh did not maintain editorial standards equal to their technical skills).[33] The low-end publishers in Fujian, such as Yu Xiangdou, clustered in Jianyang county, where we met them in Spring.

Given the greater volume of books in print, serious scholars and bibliophiles no longer dreamed of stopping the desire to possess books at ten thousand *juan* (chapters). Private libraries in late-Ming Jiangnan now ran to thirty, forty, even fifty thousand *juan*. The largest may have been that of Yangzhou scholar Ge Jian, who owned ten thousand *titles*, not *juan*.[34] As the books mounted up, they had to be stored. The collection of Yao Han was said to fill forty large bookcases; Shanghai scholar Shi Dajing (jr. 1585) had so many books that the catalog ran to four volumes and was over five inches thick. Huzhou scholar Shen Weijing needed a building more than ten beam-spans in size to accommodate his collection. And for his tens of thousands of books, Mao Kun (1512–1601) built a library that had dozens of rooms.³⁵ The Jesuits who saw these collections and thought of the miserable private libraries back in Europe were duly impressed with "the great number of Libraries in *China* magnificently built, finely adorn'd, and enrich'd with a prodigious Collection of Books."³⁶

Late-Ming collectors were keen to publish rare works in their collections, often doing so as a series of matching editions known as a collectanea (*congshu*). The Nanjing scholar Sima Tai (js. 1523) is credited with having compiled five separate *congshu* of between thirty and a hundred *juan* each.³⁷ None was printed, however, until commercial publishers decided that there was a strong enough market among the well educated to justify the expense of printing these multivolume editions. The best-known commercial collectaneae, the *Shuo fu* (*The Domain of Texts*) and its continuation, *Shuo fu xu*, were put into print for the first time by a Hangzhou bookdealer sometime between 1607 and 1620. When the publisher tried to recoup his losses in the great Hangzhou fire of 1621, he sold off those woodblocks that survived to other publishers who then incorporated them into yet other collectaneae of their own devising.³⁸ The shift from scholarly to commercial publishing among scholars encouraged many to publish more of their own work serially while they were still alive, rather than wait for disciples or descendants to do a posthumous collected works.³⁹ As the grandson of Ai Nanying (1583–1646) said of his prolific grandfather, he "published as he wrote."⁴⁰ It made good business sense in this environment, for the writings of an author like Ai Nanying were so much in demand that Suzhou and Hangzhou booksellers paid him to come and write something—anything—they could publish.⁴¹

Both the court and local officials banned books, but only occasionally and unsystematically. The best known case is the banning of the works of Li Zhi (1527–1602), a strong critic of Confucianism whose notoriety derived in part from his skill in getting his books into circulation and read. Even his letters with prominent debating partners he got into print as soon as he was able to collect enough for publication. Zhang Wenda, the censor who lodged the impeachment memorial against Li that led to his suicide in a Beijing prison, expressed concern as much over the ease with which Li's ideas were circulating among the younger generation of provincial elites as over the ideas themselves. He took the position that a man's ideas were, within reason, his own business, but that it was when they were communicated to others that they assumed a political character that demanded state intervention. Li Zhi's coy titles, like *A Book to Be Burned* (*Fen shu*) and *A Book to Be Hidden Away* (*Cang shu*), anticipated what in fact would happen to his books. The Ming state found bans difficult to enforce, however. As a Sichuan provincial censor reported to the throne in 1625, officials many years previously had received the imperial proscription declaring Li Zhi's writings uncanonical, had burned all copies in their possession, and had forbade bookstores from selling them; "and yet, even though their circulation is prohibited, many gentry enjoy his books and have hidden them away, so that even today they have not been exterminated."[42] Commercial publishing made prohibition almost impossible. Readers were not persuaded not to read.

NEWS

Not only the volume of information carried in books but the amount of data processed by the bureaucracy grew vastly. Late-Ming officials felt themselves inundated under an ever-widening flood of paperwork. About 1640 a secretary in the Ministry of Revenue estimated that the volume of memoranda submitted by his section was 50 percent greater than it had been in 1628, and 70 percent greater than it had been a decade before that. He interpreted this increase in state communications as a sign of moral failure, an overabundance of paper suggestions sapping what energy officials had for actually getting things done.[43] The hunger for information in the capital also affected the Beijing Gazette. Handwriting had been the copying technology through the first two centuries of the Ming, but it was failing to produce enough copies to meet demand. Intermittent attempts were made in the Wanli era to bring out a printed edition using woodblocks, but the cost of cutting blocks on a regular basis was judged to be more expensive than hand-copying. People who wanted the news could do it themselves. But popular demand won out, and in 1638 the gazette began to be published in movable type.[44]

The gazette could satisfy the demand only for certain types of news. The body of literate people in the late Ming grew larger (seventeenth-century sources report that, even in backwoods counties, "many read books, and few even of the common people in the poorest villages are illiterate"),[45] and this growing body came to demand current information that went beyond carefully worded government documents. That demand gave rise in the late Ming to commercial news production. Information about China's first "newspapers" is scattered. A reference in a short essay on border policy by Grand Secretary Yu Shenxing (1545–1608) is both explicit and negative. Probably writing during his retirement from public life after 1591, Yu expresses concern about panic caused by false information about the military situation on the northern border. He complains of "news bureau entrepreneurs (*baofang guer*) who are out for the most miniscule profits and give no consideration to matters of [national] emergency." In the spirit that has come to dominate the relationship of politicians to journalists, he asks, "Why aren't they strenuously prohibited?"[46]

The first Ming newspaper publishers were not printers at all, but small-time entrepreneurs who made up sheets of news stories copied out by hand and sold to whoever would pay a few cash. They began working in Beijing probably no earlier than the Wanli era. The first dated record of their existence is on a list of thirty-two trades nominated for tax concessions by the minister of revenue in 1582. Newspaper publishers appear alongside booksellers, stationers, and tofu-makers as running businesses insufficiently profitable to pay the shop tax. The terms that came into use for private news merchants were borrowed from the gazette system: *baofang* ("news bureau") had been the term used for the offices that provincial administrations set up in Beijing to make copies of the Beijing Gazette; *chaobao* ("newscopying") literally meant "copying the gazette." Most of the material in the early newspapers was taken directly from the gazette. The newspapers provided summaries of official news for those who were not in the upper echelons where copies of the gazette circulated. Private newspapers appear to have carried their own news as well, sometimes augmenting official stories, sometimes contradicting them. Producing news remained a hand-to-mouth business at this time, though, an opportunity for small operators rather than big merchants, a quintessentially urban-based service enterprise.

TRAVELS AND LETTERS

Is it a paradox to find more people traveling and more commercial agents servicing that travel at the very time when local officials are successfully petitioning to reduce the courier service and shut down transport offices they could no longer afford to keep open?[47] Probably not, since the resources that one tapped were not available to the other. Magistrates tended to keep the post houses in good order, otherwise they could not communicate with the official world beyond their counties' borders.[48] But they did let courier stations in their jurisdictions decay, having little incentive to expend precious local resources to keep a national service in good running order. The result was that wealthy officials on assignment might choose to stay in private inns rather than official hostels. As Gu Yanwu grumbled in the early Qing, courier stations in the late Ming ended up being "really no better than holding pens for criminals."[49] All the court could do to encourage the proper maintenance of the system was to ask its officials on assignment not to make the burden on local administrations heavier by exceeding their travel entitlements. The Chongzhen emperor in 1632 and again in 1633 tightened the rules governing the use of the courier system and ordered his officials to show consideration for the local people who had to serve in the vain hope of keeping the service running—but he had no way to see this enforced.[50] The appeal had no appreciable effect. Starting in 1629, Chongzhen approved the closing of as many as a third of all courier stations, with the goal of saving the central treasury 100,000 taels and relieving the local people pressed into service.[51]

The desperate need to funnel all available financial resources into military funding plunged the Ming government into a vicious cycle. As communications became impossibly understaffed, the discharged courier soldiers—like the future rebel leader Li Zicheng—preyed on those who traveled the official roads that they themselves had once serviced. Roads linking county seats were particularly vulnerable to predation, breaking the state's communications network at its most basic level. The late-Ming magistrate had to rely on his own ingenuity to raise local funds to lubricate state communications; so too he had to look to local militias to control the roads, thereby fueling the militarization that swept China in the final years of the dynasty.[52] Gu Yanwu read back from this grim denouement to the decline of official travel services and declared the closing of courier stations to be the reason the Ming fell.[53] This is too simple an explanation on its own, though the failure to maintain communicative means adequate to rule an extensive realm was certainly part of what slid in the larger collapse.

PRIVATE TRAVEL

If anything compensated for the erosion of state travel services, it was the corresponding growth of commercial services, which accommodated private travel in the late Ming, and at costs lower than those needed to maintain the official systems. According to *The Comprehensive Illustrated Route Book* (*Yitong lucheng tuji*), a route book published by Huizhou merchant Huang Bian in 1570, you could "hop a boat" outside the city of Yangzhou and sail down the Grand Canal to the north gate of Guazhou, the canal's port on the Yangzi River, for 3 copper cash. You walked through Guazhou to the south gate to catch another boat that for 2 cash would ferry you across the Yangzi and past Jin Mountain monastery to the wharf at Zhenjiang on the other side. From the wharf you entered the west gate of Zhenjiang, walked 1.5 kilometers down to the south gate and caught another boat heading down the Jiangnan portion of the Grand Canal. If you were traveling with baggage, a porter could be hired at the wharf for about 15 cash per carry. South from Zhenjiang, the rate for boat passage was only 2 copper cash for every 20 *li* (11.7 kilometers). The day's journey from Zhenjiang down to Wujiang, one of Suzhou's counties on Lake Tai, involved a relay of six boats. From Wujiang you could take either a day or night boat to Jiaxing, and from there a day boat up to Songjiang or a day or night boat down to Hangzhou. From Hangzhou east to Ningbo the route was well serviced to handle the pilgrims going out to the Buddhist island of Putuo, and commercial boats plied the route day and night. However, if your destination from Suzhou was westward into Huizhou prefecture, you could get a night ferry to Huzhou, and then another night ferry from Huzhou to Sian on the Zhejiang–South Zhili border. There you had to switch to land travel; commercial carriers in Sian offered a choice of sedan chairs, carts, and horses for those going to Sheh county (see map 3).[54]

Along routes that bore heavy commercial traffic, commercial travel services were available and cheap. Every port had a fleet of

Figure 25.   Officials are ferried across a river
(*Shuihu zhuan*, 1610).

boats available for hire, as well as an army of travel and warehousing agents and organized transport workers. Jianyue Duti
(1602–79) was one of many Yunnanese monks who came east in the
late Ming to seek instruction—and in turn contribute to the revital-
ization of Buddhism in that era. He discovered the fever of competition among these agents in 1637 when he arrived at Danyang
midway along the Zhenjiang-Suzhou stretch of the Grand Canal and
found himself besieged by passenger agents trying to entice him onto
their barges. Distracted by the hubbub of the fare hustlers, Duti
discovered that someone had stolen his satchel. He reported the theft
to the wharf manager, but it was not returned.[55]

Although transport labor was not as well organized off the heavily traveled routes, services were usually not difficult to arrange. In his now famous travel diaries, Xu Hongzu (1586–1641) provides a close record of his journey from his home in Jiangyin near the mouth of the Yangzi to the great Buddhist complex on Jizu Mountain in Yunnan between 1636 and 1640. Xu makes frequent reference to the business of hiring boatmen, carters, and porters along the way. On the morning of 3 December 1636, barely 30 kilometers out of Hangzhou, Xu discovered that his longtime bondservant Second Son Wang had deserted him. After breakfast, he asked around for someone to replace him. He complains that this took some time, though a man was found and the party able to set out before noon.[56]

In less traveled areas of China, securing porters proved more difficult. On 14 June 1638, Xu was about to cross into Yunnan from Pu'an, Guizhou's westernmost subprefecture, but found he couldn't secure a porter. After four days' delay, a merchant from Huguang tried to recruit one on Xu's behalf, without success. In the end, Xu was obliged to go through a local labor boss, who charged what Xu called "an extortionate price." (In his diary entry for 19 June, the day the deal was concluded, Xu declared this labor boss to be one of the three most evil people he had ever met.) Once he had his porter, Xu was also able to secure a horse the same afternoon, though again at a heavy price. His exasperated diary comment: "There wasn't anything to be done!" The next morning he bade farewell to the merchant who had tried to help him (he gave the merchant a letter to his uncle to take back with him to Huguang and send on down the Yangzi through his own contacts) and set off with his hard-earned porter and horse into Yunnan. While in Yunnan Xu was able to make use of his gentry status to get a military mount permit, which allowed him to use the horses stabled at military courier stations at no cost. This was an extraordinary privilege normally restricted to officials on imperial commission. Xu seems to have been able to arrange it because he impressed local officials in out-of-the-way places with his personal status as a gentleman from Jiangnan. Xu was fortunate in being in a position to call on their support, for he fell ill while in central Yunnan and was able to return home reasonably quickly in the summer of 1640, thanks to the courier service. He traveled 150 days by sedan chair as far as Wuchang, which for a distance of roughly 4,500 *li* (2,600 kilometers) meant a daily progress of 17 kilometers. Once he reached Wuchang, a magistrate there provided him with an official boat down the Yangzi. He covered the distance to Jiangyin, just short of 3,000 *li* (1,700 kilometers), in a mere 6 days, traveling at a rate of close to 280 kilometers a day.[57]

Not everyone in out-of-the-way places was keen to accommodate the growing numbers of travelers. A merchant author notes that in Huguang, villagers who did not want to put up travelers hung a sign with the single character *qu*, meaning "Go!" As he explains to the uninitiated, "In places where there are 'Go!' signs you cannot stay the night."[58] While commercialization improved travel services in places where traffic was heavy, it also accentuated the social gap that already existed between these areas and others—as between the travelers in their ever greater numbers and the local people. Their resistance to what sedentary villagers regarded as the unfair power of transient outsiders could take other forms. In the hillier parts of coastal Fujian, it was expected that travelers riding on animals or in sedan chairs should dismount when they reached a village, walk through, and only then remount. Those who declined to follow this custom might get off lightly by being ridiculed or laughed at, or they might be pelted with stones.[59] The custom appears to have started in the late Ming, when more and more people were on the move. If not a gesture of resistance, then it was at least a comment on the indifference and disrespect that travelers might feel for the places they passed by. Those who could move thus had their wings clipped ever so slightly by those who could not. At least in peripheries, the local refused to be submerged into the supralocal, and commoners refused to toady to those with the wealth to travel.

The greater disincentive to overland travel was banditry, a worry often repeated in late-Ming writings. It was sufficiently well fixed in people's minds that in many places they did not dare to travel by night, even in parts of the well-traveled Jiangnan core. According to route-book author Huang Bian writing in 1570, the area south of Lake Tai was so secure that most of the boats out of Huzhou left at night, permitting commercial passengers to get to their destinations without losing a day's worth of business; but no night boats went north from Suzhou, nor did any service the eastern prefecture of Songjiang.[60] The author of another route book of 1626 was less confident of the region half a century later, when conditions seem to have been less settled. He agreed that the densely settled area close to Hangzhou, which lay directly south of Huzhou, was safe for

Figure 26.   This small river ferry carries a mat shed
mounted on the back. The picture illustrates the re-
venge of Zhang Shun, one of the rebel leaders in the
novel *Water Margins*, against ferryman Zhang Wang
for having robbed him during an earlier crossing
(*Shuihu zhuan*, 1610).

travel, but advised against traveling at dawn or dusk and warned his
readers not to go into the area at all in times of dearth. As for the
area around Suzhou, he noted that banditry was rife in years of poor
harvests and that one could travel in rural Suzhou only with an
armed guard.[61]
    Travel was even less safe north of the Yangzi. Huang Bian de-
clared that where the Grand Canal met the Yangzi River south of
Yangzhou, which was a favorite congregation point for both salt

and cotton merchants, there were no bandits day or night; but he warned that salt smuggling in the region north of Yangzhou made night travel on the Grand Canal impossible. He advised merchants to be cautious when hiring the local boatmen, of whose honesty he had a low opinion (see figure 26). North of the Yellow River, the problem was not that the men you hired would steal your goods, but that they would sign on for a lump sum fee in order to pay off their debts and then disappear halfway to the capital. In the final stretch between Tianjin and the capital, security again became an issue. You could travel by night along this route, though Huang advised caution. Going by the Grand Canal was far safer than taking the overland route. For the northern segment of that route, Huang advises more than caution. He recommends recruiting an armed guard for protection against the mounted bandits who roamed the North China Plain, and in some places (he mentions the stretch from Yingzhou to Daming) even an armed guard might be insufficient. By contrast, merchants who went west from the Grand Canal via Kaifeng to southern Shanxi faced no such problems. The area west of the town of Qinghua, the major transport nexus in northern Henan for Shanxi merchants trading southward, was so secure that you could not only travel at night but do so, Huang asserted, even under the light of a full moon. The constant flow of commercial traffic made predation there too risky.

ROUTE BOOKS AND PROSPECTS

Security of travel was enhanced by knowing how to get where you were going and what facilities were available along the way. When Xu Hongzu set out from Jiangning county in South Zhili on 17 October 1636 to travel to Yunnan with the monk Jingwen, the only text he took to guide them into the uncharted southwest was the bulky *Comprehensive Gazetteer of the Ming Dynasty*, ninety *juan* of official geographical knowledge first produced in a palace edition in 1461.[62] Xu almost lost it late in the evening of 7 March 1637. He was sitting quietly on the deck of his boat on the Xiang River in Huguang, gazing at the moon on the first clear night in well over a month. As he was about to go to sleep, he heard a mournful wail from the shore, piercing as the cry of a child. He lay down and began composing couplets on the sadness of life when bandits struck. They boarded the boat waving torches and swords, hoping to frighten Xu and Jingwen into fleeing and giving up the boat and their possessions. Xu managed to thwart their plan by throwing the sail overboard, but his foot got caught in the towrope and he went overboard with it. Jingwen stayed onboard and beat the bandits back. Xu notes in his diary that Jingwen's bravery saved three texts: a copy of the Lotus Sutra that Jingwen had copied out in his own blood, Xu's now-famous diaries, and his copy of the *Comprehensive Gazetteer*.[63]

In the late Ming, the increasing number of travelers needed better route information than what was in the *Comprehensive Gazetteer*, and arranged in a more portable format. Simple lists of courier route stations available to official travelers circulated beyond those entitled to courier service, though people taking other routes to other places needed a more comprehensive guide. This need was met by a new genre, the route book. The first extant route book, Huang Bian's *Comprehensive Route Book,* was published in Suzhou in 1570.[64] Huang relied on the routes in courier handbooks, imitating their placename/distance format, but added many others that didn't conform to the network of administrative routes radiating out of Beijing or Nanjing. Most were within the Yangzi Valley or in and out of his home prefecture of Huizhou. Huang Bian also added advice to clarify difficult turnings and explain the advantages of alternate routes, and he inserted information regarding famous sites, inns, ferries, and the daily or seasonal security of routes. As a Huizhou merchant working in Suzhou for his family's business, Huang had personal experience of commercial travel. He says he was moved to compile the book because he once found himself "in a great hurry to get home, but the road in front seemed endless and we had difficulties asking the way. It pained me to think of all the people throughout the realm who like me get lost on byways."[65] Another Huizhou merchant (working out of Hangzhou rather than Suzhou) compiled a second route book; Cheng Chunyu, possibly its author, has included it as the first half of his 1626 merchant manual, *Essentials for Gentry and Merchants at a Glance (Shishang yaolan)*.[66]

These route books were produced by and for merchants. Cheng Chunyu was still justified in naming the gentry among his potential readership, for the late Ming was a time of widespread enthusiasm among gentry for travel—not on official assignment but for their own pleasure. (See figure 27.) Previously the gentry had not widely embraced travel as a form of recreation. By 1547, however, it was

Figure 27. An official says farewell to his wife as he sets out on a journey. A porter transports his cases on a carrying pole (*Zixiao ji*).

possible for an unsuccessful examination candidate to entertain "the idea of leaving all the mundane involvements and indulging in distant travels," even if his sober friend told him, "To travel to distant places is not as good as to strive in learning."[67] Such denunciations of touring as a morally dubious pleasure quickly faded thereafter. By 1596 the poet Yuan Hongdao could happily declare that travel was the gentry's "one great weakness."[68] Travel had been absorbed into the gentry project of cultural refinement.

Since officials were obliged to travel extensively, it was easy for late-Ming gentry to use travel-on-assignment as the base from which to justify the new delight in travel-for-pleasure. "From youth to old age, I have gone back and forth in the dust and noisy tumult of cart traffic and horses' hooves," a man observed in 1614 after a long career as a provincial official. "Yet even when traveling in my official capacity, I indulged rather often my craving for misty mountain scenery."[69] He associates his private touring with his public travel, yet he invokes two devices to invest it with a different, and purely gentry, meaning. The first is to speak of the scenery one sees on tour in painterly terms ("misty mountain"). The second is to label the pleasure of travel as a "craving" or "obsession" (*pi*). This term had a precise meaning in elite circles where it communicated an obsessive enthusiasm for a culturally approved activity. One could crave books and collect them beyond reason or the capacity to read them. One could crave strangely formed rocks and spend a fortune buying them and putting them all in a garden.[70] So too one could crave to gaze at perfect landscapes (which were often preformed in sets of eight, ten, or more "prospects" (*jing*) from which they were considered best viewed). Not only were these cravings acceptable, but they set apart the truly inspired (and truly wealthy) gentleman from ordinary gentry. Craving for travel set the gentry traveler apart from the laboring merchant and the common sightseer.

TRAVELING WOMEN

Like so much else in Ming China, traveling was a gendered undertaking. Xu Hongzu had a burning passion to travel and explore sights enshrined in ancient texts that would take him as far as Yunnan. He quietly chafed at home to care for his aging parents, then to observe mourning for his father. Once that duty was completed, his mother released him to travel. She put her permission—and justified his desire—in gendered terms by telling him, "Setting your sights on the four quarters is a man's business."[71]

Women were not free to roam, with the notable exception of pilgrimage. Men too went on pilgrimage, but women were particularly drawn to it as an extension of their devotional role in Ming society. They, far more than men, prayed, tended local shrines, and called in shamans. In doing so they forged communicative affiliations among themselves in a realm partially apart from the male realm (see figure 28). This apartness disturbed some men, who criticized women who

Figure 28. An elder woman oversees two younger women lighting incense before Buddhist statues (*Zixiao ji*).

visited temples or joined banned religious sects. Such activities were barely excusable only when "crones and that sort of person"— women old enough not to matter in male eyes—were involved.[72] A late-Ming novel depicts such a pilgrimage to the sacred Mount Tai in Shandong organized by two "crones" and exploits male distress to comic effect. The excitable Xue Sujie, married to a student in the Imperial Academy, has bought a place on the pilgrimage for ten taels of silver. She discovers that her co-pilgrims are tenants' wives and servants but decides to go anyway. The day before her departure, her brother tells her that gallivanting about the countryside in public view will reflect badly on her husband. He decides that her husband, Di Xichen, must go with her.

> Sujie rose and completed her toilet. She put on a short over-jacket in white silk, a lined jacket in pale pink damask, a silk blouse worked with sky-blue damask, a pale shirt of thin twill silk in white, leggings in the same material with white embroidery, cotton-lined shoes in satin with scarlet uppers. On her back she carried incense wrapped in a blue silk handkerchief, and on her head she wore Buddha images printed on paper. She insisted on riding a large donkey hired by the society. When the farmhand detailed by Di Xichen came up and attempted to lead it along she drove him off some distance away with a lash of her whip round his neck and made Di Xichen walk along leading the beast for her. This brought men and womenfolk down both sides of the street straining for a glimpse.

The author makes his women travelers a ridiculous sight:

> Like a pack of wolves and dogs, the whole herd of women stampeded their donkeys, overtaking one another turn by turn. As they rode on donkey-back, some of them had babies in their arms, some had their hairnets jolted off; some fell off when their saddle slipped sideways, some squealed and shrieked when the animal ran off; some, before they had gone more than a mile or two, said their bowels were unsettled and wanted to get down and find a lonely spot to relieve themselves; some said they had their period and wanted to pull cloths out of their bed sack to go between their legs; some wanted to suckle their children and asked the man with the whip to lead them along by the reins; some said their leg-bones were getting numb and asked people to pull their feet out of their stirrups; some dropped their perfume sachet and asked people to look for it on the ground; some had forgotten their toilet box and told people to go home and fetch it for them. All this stampeding about sent the dust rising up to heaven and the rank smell of bodies spreading far and wide.[73]

The chapter ends with what looks like a satire against women, yet the satire is really ridiculing male anxiety about women's public conduct. It is not the indiscreet female but the fretting male the author targets, for he assures the reader that Xue Sujie had a wonderful time on her journey and once home felt a new freedom to break whatever male barriers stood in her way.

Pilgrims, tourists, and itinerant merchants—"coming and going like shooting stars," as a stele at a ford in Shaanxi expresses it, "arriving and then setting off again without taking a day's rest"[74]— were remaking not just China's map, but its society. By the 1630s, Song Yingxing in the preface to *The Exploitation of the Works of*

Nature (*Tiangong kaiwu*) could turn his back on Zhang Tao's anxieties about restless mobility and regard himself as living in a fortunate age "when carriages from Yunnan are freely traversing the northeast, and officials and merchants from Guangdong and Guangxi are traveling at will north beyond the capital." All this movement was cause for celebration: "People group by status and goods differ by place of origin, but by trading and moving back and forth they compose the world. If everything remained permanently where it was, how would each find its proper place? Even those of high rank must set out, and so they travel despite their concern that the journey will be long. Even cheap goods are needed, and so they are retailed to the places where they are in short supply."[75]

When Europeans visited two centuries later, they found China such a mobile and commercial place that they assumed it had ever been so:

> As regards to traveling, nowhere can there exist greater freedom and in-dependence of motion; each citizen may wander about among the eigh-teen provinces and settle where he pleases, undisturbed by any public functionary. No one interferes with the traveler, who is sure never to encounter a gendarme demanding his passport. The liberty to traverse the various parts of the country unobstructed is almost indispensible to these people, continually as they are engaged in commercial operations. Of course the least impediment to free motion would check the great system of commerce which is the life and soul of this vast empire.[76]

MAIL

As people moved, so they needed to keep in contact with each other. China had been a world of letter writing long before the Ming. People wrote letters to convey greetings to one another, to conduct business, and to communicate fresh ideas and evolving beliefs in a function like that served by literary and scholarly journals today. And they wrote them in great volume. The scholar and cartographer Luo Hongxian (1504–64) described his long correspondence with the philosopher Wang Ji (1498–1583) as "nine years through which our letters went back and forth in a great flood."[77] Two things happened to alter the practice of letter writing in the late Ming. One was the publication of letters by eminent people as a way of com-municating new thoughts and arguments. The other was the provi-sion of commercial mail service.

Figure 29.   A prefectural courier carries away a letter. The courier's satchel reads Jiangzhou prefecture,
the name of Jiujiang prefecture in Jiangxi during the
Song dynasty, which is when the novel *Water Mar-*
gins is set (*Shuihu zhuan*, 1610).

We know little about how letters circulated. Sometimes they were
sent with servants, though hand-delivering over a great distance was
not practical. Letters traveling over long distances would more likely
be entrusted to a traveler, preferably a relative or friend, going in
that direction rather than specially dispatched with a messenger.
They might also be given to an itinerant merchant, a yamen runner,
a post soldier, or a state courier for a fee (see figure 29). Couriers and
post soldiers were legally forbidden from carrying private correspondence, but just as private carriage by the tribute boatmen on the

Grand Canal was essential to small-scale shipment of goods, so too the delivery services they provided facilitated the circulation of private letters. A sense of the strategies used to get letters to their destination is suggested by the following two examples, which are drawn from letters preserved in manuscript by their authors' families.

Zhuang Yuanchen was a member of a Jiangnan gentry family living in the commercial town of Nanxun in northern Zhejiang. He traveled to Beijing in 1603 (it took him forty days) to sit successfully for his *jinshi* degree the following year and pursued a brief career until called home to observe mourning for his mother. His "miscellaneous writings," which are preserved in manuscript, include letters he wrote to his son while he was in Beijing between the summer of 1603 and the summer of 1605.[78] These letters reveal that correspondence was not as regular as he might have liked. Zhuang's first letter from Beijing, written on 15 June 1603, reports that he is living in Amitabha Monastery outside Chongwen Gate and that letters can be sent to him care of the manager Zhang at Wu Zhonggeng's residence. In his letter of 14 September, he writes that he received his son's letter dated 22 July on 26 August (it took thirty-six days). In his next letter, written on 14 October, he tells his son that he entrusted his 14 September letter to the manager Zhang and asks whether it ever reached him. The flow of letters slowed that winter, for Zhuang received none until three, dated 19 September, 10 November, and 27 December, reached him at the same time. It slowed again, for a letter dated 2 June 1604 asks in distress why he has received nothing since the 27 December letter; eleven days later he wrote again to say that his four compatriots had all received letters from home but he hadn't. Finally on 27 June, a friend arrived bringing a letter from his son dated 29 May (that one took twenty-nine days).

Zhang appears to have been Wu Zhonggeng's business manager, whose duties included sending out and receiving his master's (and his master's fellow-countrymen's) letters. Presumably Zhang sent them with commercial travelers, although this is not revealed. Zhuang indicated that he relied on other channels besides Zhang, for he was able to send at least one letter with the servant of a fellow student in Beijing who was being sent home. This sort of personal connection with the bearer was the only assurance that permitted Zhuang to trust that a letter would arrive as directed. In another letter, Zhuang advises his son that three- to five-tenths of a tael was an appropriate amount to pay someone carrying a letter to the capital—not an insignificant fee. He also stresses that on no account should his son send letters with someone he doesn't know. Sadly for us, Zhuang is silent about who such a person might be: a chance acquaintance? a traveling merchant? a government courier? a commercial letter carrier?

The more eminent Xu Guangqi (1562–1633) was in Beijing just after Zhuang Yuanchen, and his letters back to his son in Shanghai reveal further details surrounding the business of correspondence. Unlike Zhuang, who kept track of his letters by the dates on which they were written, Xu and his son numbered their letters by year in order to keep a running tally of which had been received and which hadn't. He notes in a letter written in the spring of 1607, "Letter number 23 also arrived; of last year's, only number 27 hasn't arrived"; and again in the summer of 1615 (or possibly 1616), "Last year's letters and this year's letters before number 4 have all arrived at the capital, but none has reached me after the third month"; and again on 20 November 1616, "A servant of Mr. Fu's went back, and letter number 19 that I sent with him certainly must have arrived." Of carriers he mentions only friends' servants. Xu's correspondence appears to have moved more erratically than Zhuang's, depending not on the good offices of someone's manager but on the chance of whoever was going south. As Xu advises his son in his letter of 27 June 1616, "Watch for anytime to find a convenient messenger to send a letter to us."

Xu's letters also make frequent reference to the sending of items other than letters. He relied on his son to send up food and other items for personal consumption from their farm in Shanghai, for he tells him in the fall of 1606 to "still send rice and other assorted articles up on the cloth boat," then asks in the spring of 1607, "What things did you send up by the Canal from the family? With whom did you send them?" The security of shipped goods was ever in doubt, for he goes on to write: "Why didn't you write all the details to me? It is indeed regrettable." Still, provisioning a household in the capital by shipping food up from Shanghai must have been sufficiently reliable to meet daily needs, and sufficiently inexpensive to be more economical than purchasing it in the Beijing markets, even with a tip of several taels thrown in.[79]

Xu also refers several times to the sending of money by commercial means—and reveals his sensitivity to the fluctuating value of silver. In 1611 he reports to his son that "the money order also came, but since I was afraid that the Imperial silver would be sure to be capital issue, for the time being I didn't get it." by 1616 money was going in the other direction, for he writes, "I'm sending you a money order today. When you get it, give it to Uncle Jiao for family expenses." The earliest recorded instance of transmitting money over distance in the Ming dates to the Yongle era, when an agency in the commercial city of Ningbo handled money orders or "flying money"—as well as letters, it seems. The cost varied, depending on the distance covered, from several tenths of a tael to several taels.[80] By the late Ming, money order service was available at least between Beijing and county capitals in Jiangnan, and probably elsewhere as well.

Not until the 1660s is a commercial agency dispatching private mail from Beijing specifically named in a source, and it is none other than a *baofang,* a news bureau. The commercial production of news and the commercial circulation of letters could occur together because this news bureau was involved not just in compiling news broadsheets but in sending copies out to provincial capitals to sell. It was a simple matter to attach the couriering of letters to the regular distribution of news. Soon thereafter in the seventeenth century, "ticket [stamp] agencies" (*piaohao*) specialized in handling mail become visible in the sources.[81] Commercial mail services may well have existed before this time, but only as adjuncts to other services.

Of commercial mail service in busy Jiangnan, the earliest evidence is again from the 1660s. A collection of model letters published in Hangzhou in 1663 carries a notice from the publisher asking readers to mail in interesting letters to the bookstore that sponsored the publication for consideration in subsequent collections. Sequels duly appeared in 1667 and 1668. The 1668 sequel includes a letter from a woman painter written to a woman poetry editor suggesting that a poets' circle of like-minded women could be formed without actually meeting by asking the women to mail poems to each other on spring and fall holidays; she also wonders whether their poems might be mailed to the editor to produce an anthology of their poetry.[82] A similar call for submissions by mail can be found in the prefatory material to a poetry anthology published in 1672. The editor announces that a second volume is planned and asks readers to mail their poems to his home in Taizhou or to one of four addresses he gives in Yangzhou, Beijing, and Nanjing. A second anthology appeared six years later. In yet another commercial anthology of women's poetry published in 1689, the editors thank contributors from six widely separated provinces who "relied on mail [you] to send manuscripts from distant places."[83]

Jiangnan commercial networks carried parcels as well as letters. The biography of a *jinshi* of 1588 living in the city of Yangzhou records that a friend in Zhejiang, probably Hangzhou, sent him "an old book box" full of books for safekeeping. The man stored it away without closely examining its contents. When the friend in Zhejiang died ten years later, the man in Yangzhou shipped the box of books back to the deceased's son. The son emptied the box to discover over 500 taels of silver hidden in the bottom.[84] The biographer does not disclose the arrangements either man made to send the box. These facts would have been of no interest to him or his readers, who would have known how to ship a box of books from Yangzhou to Hangzhou. It is only we today who have forgotten how it was done.

CONSUMPTION AND PRODUCTION

GRAIN

The most traded consumption item in the late-Ming economy was grain. As consumption and production increasingly occurred in different places, more and more people needed the food (and clothes) that in earlier times they might have produced themselves but now didn't. Regions such as Jiangnan and the southeast coast produced the fabrics that "clothed the realm," as the saying went, regions such as Shandong and Henan produced the raw materials for the weavers, while yet other regions such as Huguang and Guangxi grew the grain the weavers ate. An interregional economy—and maybe even a "national" economy—was emerging.

Among officials in service, grain storage was of little real interest, and most of the old preparedness granaries were defunct. Abandoning this part of Hougwu's plan for the realm disturbed some commentators. Li Le (1532–1618) was a long-serving scholar-official from Tongxiang county in northeastern Zhejiang. In a collection of candid observations of life in and out of office he compiled just before turning seventy, Li complains about incompetent magistrates doing nothing but calling on the local wealthy to provide relief in time of famine. When the great famine of 1588 struck the neighboring prefectural city of Huzhou, he observes, the prefect did nothing but tell the poor to get rice from the wealthy. Mobs quickly gathered outside the gates of the rich and were ready to riot when the rich did not make rice available at a reasonable price. The prefect's next move was to order the rich not to take advantage of the situation but to sell rice for one tael per *shi*, already well over twice the price of what it would normally sell for. This order only caused the price of rice to rise to 1.6 taels. Li declares that setting minimum prices is no way to deal with famine. The only reliable method is to go back to the early-Ming model and set up granaries. When "the sole contemporary method for dealing with famine is to exhort people to lend grain," only small numbers of people can be fed.[85]

What Li neglects to acknowledge is that the practice of exhorting the wealthy to feed the starving had in fact become standard procedure in the Wanli era.[86] This was the simplest and least expensive course. It also accepted that the market could make grain available in the quantities and at the speed needed. When Zhang Tao had to deal with a famine in Sheh county in 1608, he did not simply tell the wealthy that they had to feed the poor. He told them to *buy* the grain to do so—that is, to acquire grain from elsewhere through commercial mechanisms and then sell it well below famine prices. The state did not need to stockpile grain when grain could move in response to demand.

Individuals who sought to alleviate famine followed the same course of using the market. Buddhist master Hanshan Deqing (1546–1623) recounts his experience during the massive famine in Shandong province in 1593: "The corpses of the starving covered the roads. We had already distributed all the food that had been donated to the monastery as relief to those living in the vicinity, so I took a boat that was going to Liaodong and bought several hundred *shi* of beans to save them. Because of this action, not one person in the four wards around the monastery died of hunger."[87] Although this famine was relieved with commercially available food supplies, relief in this case relied on a noncommercial subsidy. Merchants were not shipping beans to Shandong on their own initiative for there was nothing to be made in the foodstuffs market when famine had reduced the ability of the starving to pay. The philanthropist had to intervene from outside the market to take a loss, not the merchant. In the late Ming, magistrates counted on finding enough county residents willing to subsidize the import of commercial grain to fend off angry mobs and keep the local economy from collapsing, though as the Huzhou prefect discovered it required more than an abrupt order to achieve results.

The negative side of this arrangement is that sometimes relief arranged in this fashion was simply not enough, even in commercial Jiangnan. Or should we say, especially in commercial Jiangnan? When famine struck there in 1587–88, and floods inundated the region two decades later, many of the destitute starved to death. Neither solidary *lijia* communities nor state granaries were there to ensure they would be fed. As these institutions disappeared from village life and commerce saw to it that fields once planted in rice were now yielding inedible cotton, the irrigation infrastructure that had supported paddy agriculture fell into decline.[88] Distressed gentry and officials of the late Ming, like Li Le, hankered for Hongwu-style self-sufficiency, or if that was inconceivable, even mid-Ming-style landlord paternalism. They feared that these failures signaled not simply a breakdown of institutions but a structural crisis, and they searched about for solutions that made sense.

The regions producing commercial grain in the late Ming were in the interior, away from the coast. Jiangnan received its grain from the two interior provinces up the Yangzi River, Jiangxi and Huguang, as well as from the western part of South Zhili. In his economic geography of China written in the 1580s, the Hangzhou scholar-official Zhang Han (1511–93) pictures boatmen coming down the Yangzi from Huguang to Nanjing who "transport grain, singing as they scull, heading for the capital."[89] Rice also came up through Zhejiang, as Xu Hongzu discovered in 1636 when he was 160 kilometers upriver from Hangzhou and encountered a convoy of a hundred grain barges moored at the side of the river waiting to get the rice milled before proceeding to Hangzhou.[90]

The pattern was different in the north, as there was no grain surplus in the west to feed the consuming coast. North Zhili (outside Beijing, which was supplied by the grain tribute system) imported much of its rice from Shandong (called "eastern rice"). Some commercial rice also came up the Grand Canal from Jiangnan (called "southern rice"), though the cost of transportation limited quantities and favored the import of higher-priced glutinous rice (called "Yangzi rice") used for gifts rather than daily consumption.[91] In more general terms, grain production in parts of late-Ming China was being carried out on the basis of knowledge of demand in other parts, and merchants were taking regular advantage of consistent gaps between supply and demand.

Supply and demand were not always so neatly coordinated. Officials were aware that excessive demand in one place could provoke a crisis of supply elsewhere. When a county in Yangzhou was besieged by bandits during a two-month emergency in the winter of 1636–37, the magistrate forbade merchants from buying up local grain and shipping it out of the county, and he posted an official schedule of grain prices.[92] That same winter a magistrate in rural Jiangxi tried to keep rice in his county by closing the floating bridge that linked the county seat with the outside world. Xu Hongzu, who reports the closure in his diary, observes that brandishing an official document was sufficient to intimidate the bridge keeper into opening the bridge.[93] Despite such efforts, neither the magistrate nor the state sought to organize or direct the grain market. That was left to commerce. Consumers themselves sometimes acted on their own initiative, however, blocking grain and boycotting merchants who were driving up local prices. A story from 1589 displaces the role of popular justice to a deity. The drought in Jiangnan drove up the price of rice that year. A Huizhou merchant handling the shipping of grain from Huguang was able to realize a fourfold profit at this time, but decided to hold the grain off the market to see whether the price would go up any farther. He even consulted a Daoist priest who asked the Great Lord of the Southern Ultimate. In good populist fashion, the god was so annoyed with the merchant's greed that he caused the man's entire stock to burn but left every other granary in Suzhou untouched.[94]

The economic historian Wu Chengming has argued that most of the grain on the market in the late Ming and early Qing was not produced as a commodity but came onto the market as surplus. Merchants were handling rent paid to landlords, not a commodity, and this, Wu claims, limited the potential of the grain market to transform the Chinese economy.[95] While managerial landlords who were growing for the market can be found in the late Ming,[96] Wu is largely correct in seeing the commercial movement of grain as a process of collecting and redistributing surplus. Still, the logic of his argument is more formal than descriptive. Much of the grain that was marketed may not, strictly speaking, have been produced as a commodity, but it was collected by landlords with the expectation that it could be sold, and more significantly its consistent availability for sale in rice-deficit areas meant that people could rely on the market for food. The grain market thus enabled the emergence of commodity production of other goods, particularly textiles.

Jiading, the county immediately to the northwest of Shanghai, illustrates the relationship between commercial consumption and commodity production. Many grain growers had converted their land to cotton-growing by the end of the sixteenth century, cotton fetching a much better price than rice. Since what they ate had to come from elsewhere, "when the summer wheat has ripened and the autumn rice been gathered in," says the 1605 county gazetteer, "merchants' boats sail in, one following the next,"[97] taking out cotton and bringing in rice. Although the cotton could not have been grown were rice unavailable, Wu Chengming makes the economic argument that it was cotton rather than rice that led the development of the late-Ming market.

TEXTILES

The production of cotton was indeed changing the nature of the Chinese economy. For the trade between rice and cotton was not a matter of simple barter. Merchants who handled it were not just creating links between areas of surplus and areas of deficit, as we have already noted in Spring. For some products and in some regions, they were inducing people to produce commodities, not just sell their surplus when it became available. In late-Ming Jiangnan, however, they were further organizing the various stages of the production process. Few Jiangnan weavers were going from raw material to finished product, except when producing rough homespun. Each stage of production—from the growing of industrial crops (cotton, mulberry) to the production of raw materials (thread) to weaving and finishing—was becoming an independent activity. Moving up through these stages usually implied moving from countryside to market town to city, and merchants moved up and down regional marketing hierarchies to link these stages into a consecutive production process.

The first stage of textile production was visible in the fields. The silk industry's demand for mulberry leaves was so strong that many cultivators throughout Jiangnan turned their entire fields over to mulberry bushes. Mulberry production became a specialty of northern Zhejiang. In the diary of a trip he took that way in June

1567, Wang Zhideng (1535–1612) observes that south of Jiaxing "the area is rich with mulberry fields. The threads of the silkworms create a market, and great merchants from the four quarters come in the fifth month every year to buy up the thread, piling up hills of silver in the process."[98] Further southwest toward Hangzhou, a resident of Haining county writing in about 1610 recalled that in his youth in the 1550s little mulberry was grown in his home village of Yuanhua. "Where the present excels over the past is the astonishing production of raw silk. Originally Yuanhua had little mulberry. It occupied only a small percentage of land, never more than one or two *mu*. Now there is mulberry everywhere. The tenants even plant several dozen cotton plants on the hillsides to make two or three taels in the spring to cover some of their farming expenses."[99] Farther east in Haiyan, according to the county gazetteer published fourteen years later, "mulberry stalks cover the fields, and there isn't anyone who doesn't raise silkworms."[100] And when Xu Hongzu was traveling on the far side of Hangzhou in 1636, he passed Inner Mulberry Village, then Outer Mulberry Village, and then noted, "From here on south, every family specialized in mulberry."[101]

Silk was produced in agricultural households throughout these areas of northern Zhejiang. The center of commercial production was Huzhou, and the natives of that prefecture made a career of their craft knowledge. When Xu Guangqi was advising his son in letters about the family's domestic production in 1611, he suggested that his son "should probably have someone from Huzhou to take care of the non-select silkworm eggs." He repeats this advice twice, then tells his son that if he can't find a reliable Huzhou native silktender in Shanghai, he should go all the way to Huzhou (a journey of 451 *li* or 262 kilometers) to recruit someone. Xu's purpose was to ensure that the family's silkworms were properly tended. Productivity depended on maintaining the right temperature "at the time they ascend the cocoon holders and begin to spin" (see figure 30). He also was hopeful that the women in his family would learn the best techniques from their employee.[102]

As impressive, and possibly more extensive, was the cotton-growing that took over the region just to the north of Jiaxing. Half of Songjiang prefecture was said to be devoted to growing cotton, and the rate went even higher in its county of Shanghai. In parts of Jiaxing itself, the claim was made, with some exaggeration, that cotton was grown on close to 90 percent of the land. Equally sig-

Figure 30.   A woman tends silkworms as they spin
their cocoons on racks warmed by charcoal braziers
below (*Tiangong kaiwu*, 1637).

nificant for the region's economic development was the amount of
cotton cloth that Jiangnan weavers were weaving from this cotton.
In fact, as labor moved from growing cotton to the more profitable
venture of weaving it in the late Ming, Jiangnan quickly fell behind
in raw cotton production and had to import raw materials from
outside the region. By the Wanli era, merchants were shipping
additional supplies of ginned cotton. Some of it was brought down
the Grand Canal from Shandong and Henan provinces, the rest came
up the coast from Fujian and Guangdong. The two regions fed the

Jiangnan textile industry in different ways. The raw cotton grown in south China was produced by small landholders and tenants working on small plots, whereas much of the cotton grown in north China came from larger plantations using hired labor to plant and process the cotton. The rapid commercialization of the Shandong and Henan economies in the late Ming, which the increase in rural markets there reflected, was stimulated in part by the levying of taxes in silver by the state, but this was secondary to the demand of the Jiangnan market and the inexpensive link the Grand Canal afforded.[103]

Merchants who brought processed cotton to Jiangnan to sell to weavers carried Jiangnan textiles back with them to other provinces. The stimulus to textile production in Jiangnan was tremendous. The Songjiang prefectural gazetteer of 1630 notes that the weaving of fabrics for everyday use was so well-established and so specialized that "every village and market town has its own varieties and names" for the types of cloth it produced: "the list is inexhaustible."[104] Suzhou and Hangzhou, by contrast, were the centers of the luxury textile trade. The Hangzhou scholar Zhang Han, whose family wealth derived from a successful weaving enterprise started four generations earlier, noted in the 1580s that textiles were the product drawing most merchants to that city. "'Even the big merchants from Shaanxi, Shanxi, Shandong, and Henan don't consider several thousand *li* too long a journey" to buy in Hangzhou.[105] The compiler of the 1579 prefectural gazetteer, published while Zhang Han was home in retirement, dramatized the unprecedented scale of urban growth by recalling Hangzhou back in the 1520s as a place of deserted lanes where "grass grew over a foot tall" and "rabbits and foxes thronged." As of 1579, however, houses were jammed together along these same lanes "and the city has become very populous and prosperous."[106]

The same could be said, and more, of Suzhou, which continued to outclass Hangzhou in the late Ming as a production and consumption center. The city was filled with the exquisite garden residences of the wealthy, the luxury-trade workshops of skilled craftsmen, the warehouses of great merchants who moved goods in and out of Suzhou in vast quantity, and the canal bridges that not only knit the city together but doubled as specialized pickup spots for day laborers. The bridge by Guanghua Monastery, for example, was where spinners gathered before dawn in the hope of being hired for a day's work.[107] The concentration of hired labor served Suzhou's needs as the center of national trading networks.

COMMERCE IN THE PRODUCTION PROCESS

As the foregoing examples have already suggested, textile production was organized as a sequence of activities. Rarely were the two main stages of production after the raw cotton had been ginned—making thread and weaving cloth—unified into a single process. More commonly, especially among rural spinners and weavers who supplied the majority of textile labor, activities were organized consecutively, each linked to the next by an act of exchange conducted (and largely controlled) by merchants. Merchants bought the ginned cotton to sell to spinners, bought the yarn to sell to weavers, and bought the weavers' output to wholesale to cloth retailers. Zhu Guozhen (1557–1632) describes this sort of arrangement in his native Huzhou, where cloth merchants from neighboring prefectures sold ginned cotton to people who "spin it into yarn or weave it into cloth. They go to the market early in the morning, exchange it for raw cotton, and then return home where they again spin or weave it, taking it back the following morning to exchange."[108] The Jiangnan market was so dependable that households could rely entirely on weaving to survive. The weaver "weaves cotton into cloth, exchanges cloth for silver, uses silver to buy rice, and tenders rice to the soldiers to transport" as grain tribute to the capital. "A family's rent, food, clothing, utensils, and what it spends for social occasions, for raising children, or for burying the dead," notes the memorialist, "all come from cotton."[109] To increase daily output, some households wove at night by lamplight.[110]

Historians of the Ming are aware of the importance in Europe's transition to industrial capitalism of the putting-out system, by which merchants advanced capital to rural workers in the form of raw materials and controlled their product. Some have suggested that Chinese textile workers were likewise being absorbed into a putting-out system and likewise entering capitalist relations.[111] In the passage from Zhu Guozhen, the use of the term "exchange" (*yi*) rather than "sell" might suggest that producers were not negotiating the sale of their products daily but working for a single agent who handled all stages of the process from the buying of ginned cotton to the distribution of finished cloth. Similar hints can be found in other reports of the Jiangnan cotton industry.[112] Capitalist logic stresses that merchants control the production process on the strength of their capital, not their manipulation or monopoly of the local market. The putting-out merchant wasn't simply taking advantage of the division of labor by selling to weavers one morning and buying their product the next. He was purchasing their labor power by providing raw materials and setting the pace of production, controlling the production process from *within*. In the late Ming, however, merchants who exercised control over household textile production did so by extracting their profits from *outside* the production process: that is, by buying cheap and selling dear, by monopolizing the local markets in which spinners and weavers could exchange their products,[113] and by binding producers to them through usury.

Tanaka Masatoshi, who has argued this view most cogently, insists on the distinction between the European putting-out system and the Chinese system of exchanging product for raw material. The latter "cannot be regarded as a stimulus to development" (meaning here, development toward capitalism) since it was not altering the relations of production.[114] This point of view doubts that the textile industry was propelling China in the direction of capitalism, as many Chinese historians have liked to think by speaking of "sprouts of capitalism" in the late Ming. What was taking form within the commercial economy of the late Ming was unlike the subsistence economy of the early Ming, to be sure, and different from the large-scale redistribution of surplus going on in the mid-Ming; but it was even more unlike what was emerging at this time in Europe.

Moving out of Jiangnan, the picture of the late-Ming economy becomes simpler, for most local economies were only weakly linked into national markets. Ye Chunji, magistrate of Huian county, Fujian, in the early 1570s ranked his county's products in terms of importance within the local consumption economy: "greatest" (*zui*), "great" (*zhong*), and "lesser" (*ci*). Of "greatest" importance was grain—a rating that applies to almost every county in late-Ming China—which was not traded out of the county. Of "great" importance were mulberry, cotton, hemp, and ramie—the raw materials for local textile production. "Less important" were salt, cloth, vegetable oil, lumber, sugar, fruit, vegetables, fish, and livestock—the only products traded out of the county (mostly to the prefectural capital of Quanzhou nearby). Ye observes that outsiders handled the trade, as they did in many Fujian counties,[115] and concludes that commercial profits tended to be repatriated out of the local economy. He does note that linen was produced from hemp fiber brought into the county and "brings money in from outside." Otherwise, trade in Huian was in "the profits of hill and ocean," primary resources rather than manufactured goods.[116] The impression Ye gives is of a largely self-sufficient agrarian economy consuming most of what it produced but little engaged in regional commodity networks.

In his account of the growth of commerce in early-modern Europe, Fernand Braudel has argued that two distinct types of economy existed side by side. The market economy drew rural surplus into regular patterns of exchange, while the "infra-economy, the informal other half of economic activity," was "a world of self-sufficiency and barter of goods and services within a very small radius."[117] The two economies coexisted in an integrated fashion, the market economy relying on the prior operation of the infra-economy to extract surpluses and redistribute them. Adjusted for scale, the model fits late-Ming China rather well. Most villagers produced and consumed within infra-economies. Some of their product and some of what they consumed left and came in via the market economy, as seems to have been the case in Huian county, but not to an extent that could enable the market economy to take over and eventually dissolve the infra-economy. The situation was different to some extent in Jiangnan, where the separation between production and consumption in weaving households pulled them away from their infra-economies. A writer in Huzhou exposes this separation when he puzzles over the popular late-Ming paradox that "Huzhou silk is all over the realm, yet there are people in Huzhou who live out their lives without ever wearing a single thread of silk."[118]

Braudel formulated his model of the growth of commerce in early-modern Europe within the larger intellectual problematic of understanding the development of European capitalism. He has argued, sensibly, that capitalism does not appear automatically as the market economy expands. Rather, it forms within the social hierarchies constructed on top of the market economy. From this point of view, capitalism is the outcome of the interaction between a particular social structure and the market economy. Its evolution in Europe is thus unique to European history. Another social structure would not necessarily lead to the same outcome. This is where our interpretations of the histories of early-modern Europe and Ming

China, with their different contexts of elite composition and state power, must diverge. China was not generating capitalism in the late Ming. This is not to say that China "failed" to generate capitalism. Rather, it created something else: an extensive market economy that used state communication networks to open links to local economies, organized rural and urban labor into consecutive production processes in certain regions without disrupting the rural household as the basic unit of production, reorganized patterns of consumption without entirely severing consumption from production, and knit itself slowly but surely to gentry society in ways that would erode the Confucian disdain for commerce and result in a powerful condominium of elite interests in the Qing. But this was not capitalism in the European sense.

WOMEN IN THE COMMERCIAL ECONOMY

The family regulations of the Miao lineage at the head of this chapter show women as consumers buying goods and services on the local market. One way to assess the scale of their market involvement would be to know how much silver they used within the domestic economy. We don't. We do know that when the Jesuit house in Nanjing was shut down in 1616, it was found to have 17.6 taels of silver on hand, presumably to cover day-to-day domestic expenses. This seems a rather large amount, but it may have been the sort of sum that a reasonably well-off housekeeper kept to meet the expenses of running a household. Women were not only consumers, of course, but figured in the market as producers of goods and services, most conspicuously as textile workers, peddlers, and prostitutes.

Zhang Tao idealized the early Ming as a time when "women spun and wove, and men tended the crops." As we noted in Spring, this classical trope was beginning to wear thin in the mid-Ming, or at least to misconstrue what women weavers were up to. Women were producing textiles not just for domestic consumption but to sell on the market. These textiles could be sold as surplus, but they could also be produced as commodities. Engagement with the market deepened in the late Ming as the weight of domestic production shifted from surplus to commodity and as more women participated. This trend was vivid in the cotton industry of Jiangnan, but it was true as well of the periphery. The 1619 gazetteer of Hainan Island, for instance, reports that women there wove cowrie shells into cloth, which they sold to merchants who marketed it elsewhere. The commercial character of their production is suggested by the compiler's remark that women did this work because of a lack of hired labor.[119] They were engaging in work analogous to wage labor in the sense that they were producing commodities the sale of which contributed to household income. Their cowrie cloth was not surplus being sold for pocket money.

The position of women within the domestic economy of textile production was far from stable, however. Francesca Bray has argued that a long-term process of shunting women to secondary positions in textile production began in the late Ming so that men could take their place. In silk, men took over the work of weaving and left the more poorly paid steps (such as silk reeling) to women. Song Yingxing mirrors this trend by having the illustrator for *The Exploitation of the Works of Nature* picture women tending the silkworms and working the spinning wheel (see figure 31) but put men behind all the looms.[120] Rural women were still weaving cotton, but larger value was being added in the cities by calenderers and dyers, all men. By the end of the Qing dynasty, Bray argues, the only aspect of cotton production that women controlled was the production of homespun for household use—which meant that they were not earning cash income as they had been in the late Ming. The development of a money economy, which initially drew women into the cottage-based textile industry, in the longer term promoted the marginalization of their labor and reduced their place in production.[121] Despite this marginalization, women's labor was essential to the process of commodity production in the late Ming and some may have benefited from their craft skills in ways that were closed to women in the early Ming.

Turning from production to commerce, women became more visible as petty merchants in the late Ming. Working at the low end of the market, they rarely figure in contemporary accounts. A Songjiang writer does include a brief notice on "tradeswomen" in his turn-of-the-century essays about his native prefecture:

> Of those who came from other prefectures, there were only a few in any one year. In recent years, women of poor families who have a bit of enterprise and go outside have suddenly been dubbed tradeswomen. Some barter gold and pearl head ornaments, some deal in kerchiefs and thread, some specialize in making up the face and combing the hair, and

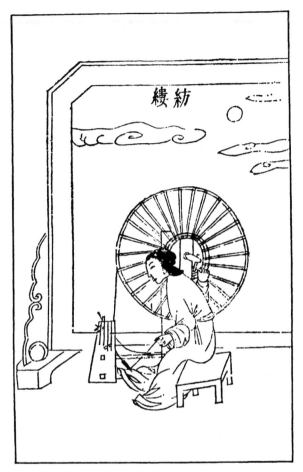

Figure 31. In cotton production, spinning cotton
thread was sometimes all that remained to women
(*Tiangong kaiwu*, 1637).

some pretend to be go-betweens discussing matches. If it promises profit
there is nothing that they will not do.[122]

The author goes on to insinuate that the step from trade to prostitution is a short one. Other gentry linked women in trade to moral
debasement in other ways. In nearby Jiaxing prefecture, Li Le
praised his prefect for "forbidding local people from gambling and
women from selling in the market," as though the people in these
two categories were equally depraved.[123]

The other commercial livelihood open to poor women was to sell sexual services in "willow markets and flower streets," Chinese terms for our equally euphemistic "pleasure quarters."[124] Prostitution had flourished earlier in the dynasty and did not need to wait for the full development of the commercial economy. Already in the mid-Ming it was asserted that the larger provincial capitals had several thousand brothels, while even small cities had them in the hundreds.[125] These estimates seem exaggerated, yet brothels may have grown to this scale with the growth of cities, whose male residents habitually outnumbered female and were too poor to marry. Although concentrated in urban areas, prostitution was practiced anywhere migrant males passed. Herders on the winter sheep drive from Shanxi down into Huguang, for example, were followed by "prostitutes and porters bearing wine and food." We learn that "the shepherds pay them by shearing off some wool."[126] Seasonal temple fairs were also occasions for mobile brothels to set up shop.[127] Women who worked as prostitutes were usually bound to service through their sale by fathers or husbands (unless they were acquired as famine orphans) and could only gain their personal freedom by working off the bond. Almost invariably it was men who held the bonds and owned the brothels. Prostitution may have been a way for women to earn a livelihood, but as an economic opportunity it was principally for men. Engaging female labor at close to subsistence cost was a way for entrepreneurial males to enter the commercial economy.

TRADE

FOREIGN TRADE

A lubricant of all this consumption and production in the late Ming was silver. Weavers used it to pay taxes. Jesuits in Nanjing and housewives in Guangdong kept some on hand for domestic purchases. Large merchants handled it in sums in the hundreds and thousands of taels. Everyone saw it and almost everyone used it. Silver had been flowing into the Chinese economy from Japan during the middle decades of the sixteenth century, when it was augmented by bullion from South America. The lifting of the ban on maritime trade in 1567 to all but Japan (in response to the petition of Fujian governor Tu Zemin to legalize the large foreign trade coming in and out of Moon Harbor on the south Fujian coast)[128] coincided with the Spanish conquest of the Philippines in the late 1560s and the opening of the huge silver mines in Potosí (in present-day Bolivia) in the 1570s. Through Acapulco, the Spanish organized the shipment of much of their South American silver to their base in Manila to pay for Chinese exports. How much silver flowed through Manila late in the sixteenth century is impossible to determine, though reports from Mexico in 1597 and 1602 indicate that between 150,000 and 345,000 kilograms (between 4 and 9 million taels) was shipped from Acapulco annually. Most of this silver was destined for China, where the Spanish bought goods that Chinese merchants brought out to Manila to trade. The Portuguese also brought silver to China through Macao, at a rate in the thousands rather than the millions of taels, but still not insignificant.[129]

The first Spanish galleons laden with silver arrived in Manila to trade for Chinese silks and porcelains in 1573. These luxury goods, which fetched high prices in Europe and made their carriage there profitable, especially as silver became cheap, were what drew this silver into the Chinese market where it could buy so much. Antonio de Morga, president of the *audiencia* at Manila, describes the full range of goods that the Spanish were buying:

> raw silk in bundles, of the fineness of two strands, and other silk of coarser quality; fine untwisted silk, white and of all colors, wound in small skeins; quantities of velvets, some plain and some embroidered in all sorts of figures, colors and fashions, others with body of gold and embroidered with gold; woven stuffs and brocades, of gold and silver upon silk of various colors and patterns; quantities of gold and silver thread in skeins; damasks, satins, taffetas, and other cloths of all colors; linen made from grass, called *lençesuelo*; and white cotton cloth of different kinds and quantities.

Besides these textiles, Chinese merchants brought a wide range of goods from the Chinese domestic market to sell to the Spanish:

> musk, benzoin and ivory; many bed ornaments, hangings, coverlets and tapestries of embroidered velvet; damask and gorvaran tapestries of different shades; tablecloths, cushions and carpets; horse-trappings of the same stuffs, and embroidered with glass beads and seed-pearls; also pearls and rubies, sapphires and crystal; metal basins, copper kettles and

other copper and cast-iron pots; quantities of all sorts of nails, sheet-iron, tin and lead; and saltpetre and gunpowder.

De Morga continues his inventory of Chinese trade goods at Manila with an even longer list of processed foods and other supplies that Chinese merchants sold for the daily use of the Spanish residents:

> wheat flour; preserves made of orange, peach, pear, nutmeg and ginger, and other fruits of China; salt pork and other salt meats; live fowl of good breed and many fine capons; quantities of fresh fruits and oranges of all kinds; excellent chestnuts, walnuts, and *chicueyes* (both green and dried, a delicious fruit); quantities of fine thread of all kinds, needles and knick-knacks; little boxes and writing cases; beds, tables, chairs, and gilded benches, painted in many figures and patterns. They bring domestic buffaloes; geese that resemble swans; horses, some mules and asses; even caged birds, some of which talk, while others sing, and they make them play innumerable tricks. The Chinese furnish numberless other gewgaws and ornaments of little value and worth, which are esteemed among the Spaniards; fine crockery of all kinds; *canganes,* or cloth of Kaga, and black and blue robes; *tacley,* which are beads of all kinds; strings of cornelians and other beads, and precious stones of all colors; pepper and other spices.

De Morga closes his list with the generic category of "rarities which, did I refer to them all, I would never finish, nor have sufficient paper for it"[130]—surely the wrong rhetorical flourish, since his paper came from China as well.

Undernoticed in De Morga's list is porcelain, which is curious because it was in such great demand back in Europe. It surfaces only among the goods that Chinese merchants supplied to the Spanish for their personal use in Manila. Other Manila sources, however, itemize porcelain as an export item.[131] As well they should, for the underglaze blue ware that the kilns of Jingdezhen were producing in the late Ming was so desired in Europe that fine porcelain came to be known as china. Much was shipped to Europe: between 1602 and 1682, for example, the Dutch East India Company alone handled over 6 million pieces.[132] Yet we should not overestimate the effect of European demand. By one estimate only 16 percent of late-Ming ceramic exports went to Europe; the rest went to Japan and Southeast Asia.[133]

Like the exporting weavers, potters adapted to the demands of foreign markets, decorating the surfaces of their wares with foreign motifs and fashioning their shapes in imitation of Japanese and

European objects. For Jingdezhen, once the flourishing supplier of endless orders of porcelain to the palace, the growth of the export market was well-timed. A reorganization of the levy of kiln labor in the 1560s in favor of private kilns enabled Jingdezhen to increase production. The kilns were kept busy through the Longqing and Wanli eras (1567–1620) supplying the high-spending court. But when imperial orders fell off after 1620, Jingdezhen kiln masters had to look elsewhere for markets. Declining court demand plus a limited domestic market [134] encouraged them to adapt their designs to foreign tastes.

Exporting high-priced porcelains and silks in large volume required much capital but yielded enormous profits. It was said of those involved in the export trade to Japan that they made a tenfold profit on their business.[135] The insistent repetition of "tenfold" in late-Ming writings suggests this estimate has more of cliché than of cost accounting to it. Actual returns were not that high. Raw Chinese silk could be sold in Japan for about double its Chinese price; cotton thread and ceramics fetched between two and three times their price; high-quality silk fabrics sold for almost three times; licorice more than tripled its price. Other evidence indicates that profits realized through the trade with Japan rose to the range of 100–200 percent.[136] Given that the rate of profit on domestic wholesale trade was usually under 100 percent,[137] the proceeds to be garnered from international trade were satisfying—if less impressive than the tenfold level they reached in the overheated imaginations of poor scholars.

SILVER

All these profits were reckoned in silver—and made possible by it. Without silver, the global export of Chinese goods in the late-sixteenth and early-seventeenth century would not have happened. Japanese and Europeans were unable to produce goods more cheaply at the same level of quality to sell into the Chinese market, but they did gain access to vast supplies of silver. Fortunately for the foreign merchants, silver traded at a much higher value in China than it did in either Europe or Japan. Its value was so strong that Chinese merchants in Zhangzhou in the 1620s or 1630s imported from Japan the copper dregs left over when silver ore was refined, which contained trace amounts of silver that Chinese refiners found profitable to extract.[138] The higher value of silver in the Chinese market served to enhance the great profits that foreign traders earned in turn by selling Chinese goods in their home markets.

Silver entered the late-Ming economy at an annual rate in the millions of taels. The inflow of this amount of silver must have boosted the economy, and its disruption could induce at least short-term crises. Chinese merchants in Zhangzhou certainly got a taste of the latter in 1623 when Dutch traders turned to violence and blockaded Moon Harbor to force the Chinese government into opening trade. Three hundred Zhangzhou merchants petitioned the provincial governor that they "be allowed to traffic with us," as one of the Dutch captains who took part in the blockade reports. "By reason of the war they had lost their goods, and should the war continue they were in fear of being brought to poverty altogether; therefore they resolved urgently to beg of the before-mentioned Combon [governor] to consent to peace and traffic with us."[139] Whether the influx of silver was responsible for price rises along the coast; whether the volume of silver entering China declined late in the 1630s (South American silver dwindled, but Japanese silver continued to flow); and whether that decline precipitated the collapse of the dynasty in 1644: these are questions currently under debate.[140]

Whatever its economic or even political effects, the enlarged flow of silver through the late-Ming economy induced changes in social behavior that disturbed the moral constitution of Zhang Tao and others like him. Ye Chunji, magistrate of Huian county on the Fujian coast in the 1570s, worried about silver disrupting norms. He decided to impose a voluntary restraint program on the county and set what he thought were reasonable limits on what people should spend on weddings and other ceremonies. "The frugal man with only one tael of silver can have something left over," he reminded them, "whereas the extravagant man with a thousand can still not have enough."[141] This sort of restraint had no appeal to the silver-laden elite of Huian and all the other counties along the Fujian coast, who were content to accumulate silver and untroubled about spending it.

As the Wanli era unfolded, committed Confucians could not rest content with trying to tilt the balance of value against cash through such moral reminders, but were driven to seek more active ways of leveling money and morality. Yuan Huang (1533–1606), a native of coastal Jiashan county up the Zhejiang coast, stands as an example. Yuan developed and popularized the use of ledgers of merit and demerit as a Confucian form of moral self-cultivation. The earnest Confucian who used this system wrote down all his good and bad deeds, attached numerical values to them, and thus could sum up the quality of his moral life—in what looks suspiciously like a commercial ledger. Yuan was not simply aping the accounting procedures of the commercial world but, following a long Buddhist tradition designed to encourage financial patronage, searching for a system to strike parity between wealth used for charitable purposes and moral worth. His exchange rate was one merit point for every thousand copper cash spent in charity. Although Yuan insists that money was not necessary for accumulating merit, his system puts the man of wealth in a stronger position to gain merit. He does not extend this logic to the point of celebrating wealth, observing (through the voice of a Daoist priest in an incident he recounts from 1594) that even if a man "distributes 200,000 taels of pure silver, his good fortune will not be complete."[142] The important thing for Yuan is the purity of his mind, not the purity of his silver. Nonetheless, the possibility of calibrating goodness in terms of the expenditure of precious metals opened the way for finding a legitimate place for silver in the Confucian moral economy.

Many late-Ming gentry were already acting out this possibility in their home localities by donating large sums, sometimes in the hundreds of taels, for the building and restoring of Buddhist monasteries (including bronze bells and statues) and other public institutions,[143] as well as for other charitable projects. At the hands of a Confucian activist like Yuan's fellow Jiashan native Chen Longzheng (1585–1656), public philanthropy was undergirded by a morality of social recompense that went both ways. Aiding their communities demonstrated that the wealthy deserved their natural-born right to elite status. At the same time it reminded the destitute of their duty to accept the paternal relationship to which the surplus of wealth in elite hands obliged them. Social recompense did not deprive the elite of the right to spend for their own pleasure, however. It may in fact have redeemed it.[144]

Yet other intellectuals in the late decades of the Ming took a different approach, not investing moral value in silver but arguing that moral and monetary values are separate and not to be confused with each other. Across the border from Jiashan, in Shanghai, Xu

Guangqi seems to do this when he observes in the 1620s that silver was not wealth but a means for assessing wealth. His purpose is to point out the standard Confucian notion that silver has no intrinsic value but depends for value on the agricultural economy within which it circulates, yet by stressing its role as a medium of exchange rather than as something of intrinsic worth, Xu wants to demystify silver. His fellow-prefectural, friend, and editor Chen Zilong (1608–47) amplified the point in 1639 by agreeing that silver did not create wealth (again, from a Confucian viewpoint, only land can do that). The role of silver was to concentrate and direct resources.[145] By arguing against confusing monetary and moral values, which Confucians a century earlier would have rushed to do, Chen and Xu were acknowledging that silver was a fact of late-Ming life and indicating that they were comfortable with that fact.

MERCHANTS

The role of merchants in the Chinese economy and their visible presence in society only increased in the late Ming. They furnished the human links in the production processes of particular commodities, in the interregional networks through which commodities circulated, and in local retail distribution. Wholesalers, brokers, middlemen, retailers, commercial agents, small shopkeepers, and peddlers worked the commercial landscape to an extent and in such numbers as never before.

Most merchants, even those in retail businesses, were sojourners, and sojourners from certain prefectures or provinces gained reputations in particular trades. Northerners from Shanxi and Shaanxi, enriched through the border trade, dominated salt and other commodities in the interior. In Sichuan, for instance, the local people "are poor and their capital resources thin, so most of the salt merchants here are natives of Shanxi and Shaanxi."[146] The merchants of Huizhou, who also grew rich on government monopolies, dominated interregional trade along the Grand Canal as well as wholesale and retail distribution in most Jiangnan cities. They shared this region with merchants from Suzhou, Fujian, and Guangdong, in roughly descending order.[147] Jiangxi natives tended to work at lower levels of capitalization and were conspicuous in the central interior provinces of Henan, Huguang, and Sichuan.[148] In few places, however, did any one provincial or prefectural group monopolize all trade. Merchants in the city of Jiading, near Shanghai, hailed from Hangzhou and Huizhou, from Shandong and Beijing, from the provinces of Shanxi and Shaanxi, and even from the Liaodong frontier in southern Manchuria. The Huizhou merchants were powerful in the key sectors of salt, cotton, and pawnbroking and located themselves not just in the Jiading county seat but in all the market towns as store managers and itinerant commercial agents. Their presence was so strong that when the Huizhou merchants vacated Jiading's largest town, Nanxiang, to get away from a protection racket run by local predators, the economy of the town collapsed.[149]

Gentry did not like to appear entirely easy in the presence of merchants and preferred to draw a disdainful line between the market and the study. In keeping with this style, a scholar-official from Huizhou draws this line in a poem commemorating his visit to the market at the City God Temple in Beijing:

> The galleries around the hall fill with people, and you crave a little space,
> Craftsmen and merchants try to make a sale, and you tire of their patter;
> Seeing so many strange and ingenious objects, your vision becomes a
>   blur,
> Hearing so many different dialects, your ear ends up recognizing
>   none.[150]

The pose of the gentleman whose sensitivities are overwhelmed by the hubbub of the market is slightly forced, for as a native of Huizhou he should have been used to barter. For that matter he should have been able to pick out his native Huizhou dialect from among the hawking voices. His real problem with the marketplace is that it was thronged with the lower classes.

Gentry accommodation to trade is evidenced directly in the writings of many gentry who hailed from commercial families. Zhang Han, a scholar from a Hangzhou textile family, was willing to argue that commerce performed a necessary function for society and that the state should facilitate trade. This he does in his essay "On Merchants," penned probably during his retirement in the 1580s. His portrait of merchant activity is incomplete, but it does convey a sense of China's unity as a realm of commodity circulation. Zhang uses the essay to advocate lightening internal transit duties, not just to reduce the tax burdens of merchants but to speed up the rate at which goods circulated. While he was a bureau secretary in the Nanjing Ministry of Works in the late 1530s, his first posting,

Zhang says he took the initiative to reduce commercial taxes at the Longjiang customs house by 20 percent. The effect was positive on all sides: commercial traffic into Nanjing increased, and the overall customs receipts went up 50 percent.[151]

Other officials can be found making similar changes, notably in the south. In Fujian, a local official in 1603 responded to local complaints about the 3 percent commercial tax, which were coming to him *from the gentry,* by getting rid of it.[152] In Leizhou, Guangdong, a vice-prefect imposed a temporary ox tax in 1600 to pay for regional military campaigns against the Li people, which was levied on each ox brought to a market, or on grain, pigs, or chickens in markets where no cattle were traded. It came into general use, exciting widespread opposition, and not just among merchants. "Markets were originally for facilitating trade, not for levying an ox tax," complained a writer in the neighboring prefecture. "Where merchants gather is never constant, and tax quotas are hard to control." In other words, commercial taxes drive business elsewhere and are a dangerous temptation for a state wanting to feed a constant tax hunger. Its effect, he concludes, was to harm the economic life of the people. To prove his point, he distinguishes between twenty-one markets in a local county where "recently the market tax was imposed by quota" and nine that "now are all closed."[153] By implication, the latter nine markets closed because the tax ruined business.

With success and wealth expanding to levels their mid-Ming forebears could only have dreamed of, merchants of the late Ming sought entry into higher social echelons. They were proud of the success that their hard work and ingenuity in the marketplace had brought them, and they were more willing than earlier generations to acknowledge in public the commercial origins of their wealth. One did not have to be, nor even pretend to be, from the old, somewhat idealized rural gentry to feel able to enter polite society— though the acquisition of a landed estate was always an attractive asset for staking a claim to social status. One can understand why old rural gentry resented merchants, since landless merchants were able to evade the service levy that the gentry as landowners had had to bear;[154] their exclusive attitude had a fiscal as well as ideological basis, but that was changing as big merchants moved into landowning. In any case, the old gentry were fast disappearing as such, as the wealthier abandoned their rural manors and used the profits of commercial landowning to acquire urban residences, usually in the county or prefectural seat but if possible at the provincial capital.[155]

In this atmosphere of shifting identities, merchants desired gentry status and happily expended resources to make the transition from commerce to gentility. One strategy was to act like gentry. This we can see Jianyang publisher Yu Xiangdou, who included the heavenly portents in his 1599 almanac *The Correct Source for a Myriad Practical Uses,* doing before our eyes in figure 32. Yu was not content to affect a scholar's style by putting his literary epithet Santai on the title page and the first page of each chapter, nor by gracing the preface and the colophon on the last page with his personal name. He went further and inserted an idealized portrait of himself at the end of the table of contents. This portrait presents him seated at his desk in a garden. The pose is of scholarly endeavor, with several volumes stacked at his left hand, a book open in front of him, and an inkstone and two brushes ready at his right hand: posed, but not engrossed, for he is gesturing to one of the three serving women standing nearby, while a maid sweeps the garden and a boy fans the brazier on which tea water is heating. We are not looking merely at vanity, but at the social aspiration to look like gentry, and as well the commercial motive to present the almanac as the reading matter of a man of culture. The books, the elegant garden, the fine furniture, and the tea being served in a dainty porcelain teacup communicate a refinement to assure the purchaser that when he buys a book published by the Santai publishing house, he is getting an emanation from the world of the gentry. The plaque over the pavilion, "Santai's Office," slightly mars the image of gentility. However, it subtly reminds the viewer that Yu was running a flourishing business.

Wealth was the precondition for rising to genuine gentry status. How a merchant family became wealthy was potentially problematic in Confucian moral terms, and is often told in merchant family histories by a plot device that might be called the initiating moment. This moment arises in a context of hardship, often unexpectedly or mysteriously. It signals the turning point in the family history, invariably from peasant or artisanal poverty to commercial success. Because the initiating moment marks the point of transition to a commercial life, it is a troubling link in a narrative of success that the narrator strives to bring into conformity with Confucian expectations for moral action. The Hangzhou scholar Zhang Han locates the initiat-

Figure 32.   Yu Xiangdou's self-portrait depicts the businessman as scholar (*Wanyong zhengzong*, 1599).

ing moment in the time of his great-grandfather, a liquor-maker.
During a flood, the man's stock was destroyed. "One evening as he
was returning home, someone suddenly called him from behind. My
great-grandfather turned to greet the man, and was handed something warm. Suddenly the person was not to be seen. When he got

home, he lit the lamp and shone it on what turned out to be a small ingot of silver."[156] This inexplicable piece of silver became his ancestor's capital for entering the weaving business. How the original seed money was acquired is left untold, a past perhaps to leave discreetly buried.

The prominent Huizhou scholar Wang Daokun (1525–93), whose grandfather entered business using his wife's dowry as start-up capital, liked to explain that commerce was not in contradiction with scholarship and often funded it. He notes that many Huizhou families alternated between the two vocations: "It is not until a man is repeatedly frustrated that he gives up his studies and takes up trade. After he has accumulated substantial savings he encourages his descendants, in planning for their future, to give up trade and take up studies. Trade and studies thus alternate with each other."[157] Wang concludes this passage by likening the alternation of careers within a family to "the revolution of a wheel, with all its spokes touching the ground in turn. How can there be a preference for any one profession?" Wang's argument for a convergence of gentry and merchant would not have impressed every gentry reader of his collected works, Zhang Tao among them.

MERCHANT VALUES

Most merchants lived farther down the social ladder than these wealthy men from Huizhou. There, working with limited means and within more restricted social networks, middle merchants looked up at gentry status as something almost impossibly remote. What dominated their thinking was how to succeed in business, not how to get out of it. We can trace the formulation of such thinking in texts that merchants began to produce for their own readership. Moral guides for merchants appearing in print early in the seventeenth century furnish sober statements that illustrate the conservative tendency of thought among this middle group. One of these texts, *Bringing Merchants to Their Senses* (*Shanggu xingmi*), is a series of short maxims with longer commentaries. The maxims sound like old merchant lore, while the commentaries have the feel of being more contemporary statements on the sensible conduct of commercial life. *Bringing Merchants to Their Senses* appears to have been first published as an appendix to the 1635 edition of Huang Bian's famous route book. The book's editor, an otherwise unknown Fujian merchat named Li Jinde, is likely the author of the commentaries.

The main theme drumming through *Bringing Merchants to Their Senses* is that morality is more important than the single-minded pursuit of profit. This Confucian theme is turned to commercial purpose by the equally strong message in the commentaries that stable, long-term profit requires honesty, not deceit. The immoral businessman who sinks to corrupt schemes will ultimately fail in his enterprise, however successful he may be in defrauding those around him. Profit, in this commercial adaptation of Confucian morality, is morally neutral so long as it is garnered through honest means and remains within community standards. For instance, commercial and personal loans should be offered at an interest rate of 20 to 30 percent, which was considered normal. Under certain circumstances, interest might run to 70 or 80 percent, but never on a long-term basis, otherwise the financier will be condemned in public opinion as a usurer, his borrowers will feel justified to default, and his capital will disappear.[158] Better to turn down the possibility of high profit in the short term in favor of moderate profit in the long term. On this point, Li Jinde concurs with the standard gentry critique that the ruthless pursuit of profit is evil. But the issue is not the maintenance of Confucian morality. It is the sustainability of a business venture.

Li Jinde also offers the simple wisdom of ensuring that expenses not exceed income. This necessary task, he says, may be accomplished in three ways. First of all, be diligent: attend to the smallest details, exercise caution in all business dealings, and be early to bed and early to rise.[159] Second, conserve the wealth you have: watch against waste, avoid ostentation, and don't associate with people who waste their money on sex and gambling. If you are careful in these ways, then wealth will do what it is naturally supposed to do: beget more wealth. The third thing to do is to keep careful accounts. "Measure income in order to keep control over expenses, and to the end of your life you will never lose your wealth. If you fail to budget, you will certainly have a shortfall."[160] This advice tallies nicely with Confucian concerns about diligence and modesty translated to the commercial sphere. Like Confucianism's promise that dedicated study will be rewarded, Li's homily was backed with the assertion that the merchant who conducts his life in these ways will be rewarded with success.

The late-Ming world was often otherwise, of course. Even the sympathetic Zhang Han was ready to take both merchants and consumers to task for not conforming to this sort of commercial Confucian morality. Zhang was proud of the commercial vitality of his native Zhejiang but nonetheless worried that "the people are clever and their customs extravagant," and he decries the culture as "lavish." The merchants from Jiangxi over the border "are inwardly stingy but outwardly lavish." And the many who "live by speculative trade" in Li Jinde's province of Fujian are trapped in a competitive consumption so severe that "were someone to find his food, drink, bedding, or clothing insufficient to meet his own needs at a time of poor harvest, his neighbors would despise him, even though he might be a high official or a person of importance. Hence, these people treat miserliness with contempt and value lavishness. In Tingzhou and Zhangzhou the people are ruthless coveting profit."[161]

Li Jinde, small-time Fujian merchant, and Zhang Han, big-time Hangzhou official, saw eye to eye on these matters of limiting lavishness and condemning ruthless practices in profit-taking, though they did so from different positions. Zhang wanted merchants to conduct themselves according to gentry norms (as he must have felt his own family had done) so that the sociopolitical order he served would not be disrupted by the disharmony that aggressive self-promotion stimulated. He was also moved by Confucian standards of probity and deference that fierce competition could threaten. Li Jinde hoped that merchants as much as gentry would internalize Confucian standards, but his moral concern was the more immediately practical one of promoting a business code of self-regulation. Li understood that a healthy commercial economy could operate only in a climate of trust and recognized that commercial fraud not only undermined trust but raised transaction costs. He knew also that Ming law lacked workable mechanisms to deal with commercial fraud (in any case, merchants would have hesitated before taking their complaints before a magistrate and being bled by the cost of pursuing litigation). In the absence of effective and available state protection of property rights, the only way to reduce transaction costs was through internally imposed standards. It was in everyone's interest to meet public expectations regarding good business practices. Yet this wisdom was hard to ensure when itinerant trade brought complete strangers together for commercial dealings. Accordingly, much of Li's advice is about handling commercial agents, who were expected to work diligently and honestly for their employers while out of their reach but who also had to avoid being duped by the brokers who provided the links they needed to the local economies in which they bought and sold.[162]

FASHION

Against the sensible and conservative advice of Li Jinde was the contrary urge among merchants and gentry alike to pit themselves in an endless struggle of status competition, and there is no site in which to watch this struggle played out in the late Ming that is more colorful than the volatile arena of fashion. The readiness of late-Ming people to follow fashion was not a complex matter of moral lapse, as the author of *Bringing Merchants to Their Senses* might like to think. It was the simpler effect of commercialization at a time when the numerous and newly wealthy sought status: there were more expensive things for sale, more people who could afford to buy them, and more anxiety about the reliability of established status markers. This is the perfect combination for fashion. To resolve these anxieties, people buy things.

If the impulse for fashion in a commercial economy is simple, it gets played out in complex ways. To begin with, fashion operates on the principle of constant disappointment and failure. For fashion to discriminate between the elite and the mediocre, most people must fail to make the grade; otherwise, everyone becomes fashionable and discrimination does not occur. Fashion is never static. Its boundary constantly moves as new standards are set to frustrate those who are moving within reach of the current standards. The connoisseur must remain one step ahead of the mere collector, the truly elegant one level above the merely presentable.

Fashion-setting is not an open process, however. It is arbitrated by established elites. Its standards are set not by the aspirants coming up from below but by those who have already arrived and need to protect their status as the established elite. They draw the lines, and do so in ways that exclude most of those who seek entry into elite status; otherwise, their status becomes diluted and their symbolic capital devalued. This exclusion does not occur without resistance from below. Commercial elites will seek to impose their own fashions on society, to undo the standards set elsewhere and beyond their reach. Accordingly, those above who set fashions and those below who follow them are engaged in a constant skirmish, as those below seek to expand the realm of the fashionable in ways that will include them and those above seek to place new barriers to entry. The stylist must therefore from time to time make it clear to the crass consumer that he is wearing or collecting the wrong thing, or wearing or collecting it in the wrong way, or otherwise falling short of elegant living; and he must refuse attempts to formulate new styles from below, except to incorporate them in ways that put them out of the common reach.

Not surprisingly, given the control that they have over fashion, the elite profit. Fashion facilitates a redistribution of wealth away from the merely wealthy, who must spend their cash in ever-growing amounts to capture the expensive tokens of high status. Some of this wealth flows, in ever-increasing amounts, into the hands of artisans who produce luxuries and merchants who distribute them. Some drains back into the hands of the established elite who identify symbolically valuable items to resell in the fashion market and who even produce the items themselves, as many late-Ming literati did by penning funerary inscriptions or reproducing the paintings of famous masters. The connoisseur may disparage what the mere collector collects while occasionally selling him things from his own stock.

THE FASHIONABLE BUSINESS OF CLOTHES

Late-Ming people felt the sartorial restrictions and simple tastes of an earlier era slip from their grasp as commoners dressed above their station and used clothing to renounce the anonymity of membership in a class community. In the early Ming, state regulation forbade certain styles of clothing and restricted permissible styles to certain ranks of people. Even as late as 1541, the government was still banning particular styles. The minister of rites that year denounced the "cloud" style of headgear and shoes and was successful in getting local officials to see that people didn't wear it. By the 1560s, though, such bans had become untenable as gentry and commoner alike wore whatever extravagant garments they chose.[163] This was especially true in urban Jiangnan, where fashion display became an important element in the discourse of social interaction in public and private settings, and the restless changing of fashion the ground upon which status was constantly challenged and rescheduled.

Anxious gentry were quick to connect fashion in dress with the commercial environment in which clothing was worn and produced. Writing in the 1570s, the scholar Chen Yao (js. 1535) notes with dismay how fashion in clothing emerged over the course of his own lifetime in his native region of Yangzhou. He invokes the Zhengde reign (no surprise!) as the turning point:

> In the Hongzhi and Zhengde eras, it was still the style to esteem agriculture and devote oneself to practical matters. Most gentry living at home wore clothes of simple weave and hats of plain black fabric. Students prided themselves in the study of texts; they also wore plain robes and unadorned footwear. Commoners wore hemp in summer and cotton in winter, clothes inexpensive in price and unadorned in character. The customs of frugality and simplicity were like this.

But no longer: "Now the young dandies in the villages say that even silk gauze isn't good enough and lust for Suzhou embroideries, Song-style brocades, cloudlike gauzes, and camel serge, clothes high in price and quite beautiful." The issue for Chen is only partly the regrettable replacement of modesty by ostentation. It is also the instability of consumption patterns. "Long skirts and wide collars, broad belts and narrow pleats—they change without warning. It's what they call fashion," to translate *shiyang*, literally "the look of the moment."

Chen's despair is at its most complete when he goes on to observe that the escalating fashion in luxurious clothes has canceled the earlier clear distinctions between rich and poor, town and country, gentry and commoner, elite and base. Social status was no longer readily clear in the street. Chen reads the evidence of clothes to express his anxiety that these distinctions in the 1570s are fast fading: "Take simple clothes to a country fair, and not even country people will buy them—they'll just laugh. Brokers and the common run of insignificant and base people wear gentry hats, while actors, lictors, bankrupts, and peddlers wear courtiers' shoes. They traipse right down the road like that, one after the other, and no one thinks it strange."[164] This parade of inappropriately dressed commoners is proof to Chen that social norms have been overturned. The momentum of consumption has overwhelmed the normal standards of status. Lurking beneath this rupture of his imagined tradition of a sober, plainly dressed gentry and a diligent peasantry clad in homespun is the working of commerce. Expensive embroideries from Suzhou are now sold on rural markets, and brokers and peddlers can dress themselves up to appear as the gentry's social equals. The market for simple peasant dress has disappeared.

Zhang Han notes the same process of fashion diffusion outward from the luxury production center of Suzhou two decades later: "Popular customs are in general more extravagant south of the Yangzi than north, and south of the river [Jiangnan] none are more extravagant than Suzhou. From early times the people of Suzhou have been habituated to rich adornment and have favored the unusual, so everyone is moved to follow fashion. If it isn't splendid Suzhou-made clothing, it isn't refined; if it isn't a beautiful Suzhou-made artifact, it isn't valuable." Zhang goes farther than simply noting the cachet of Suzhou style. He suggests that the escalation of fashion Chen Yao deplored was not just a sign of collapsing sumptuary limits but a feature lodged in the working of the market, again to Suzhou's benefit:

> People from all over favor Suzhou clothing, and so Suzhou artisans work even harder at making it. People from all over value Suzhou artifacts, and so Suzhou artisans work even harder at making them. This drives the extravagance of Suzhou style to even great extravagance, so how is it possible to lead those who follow the Suzhou fashion back to sensible economy? By inclination people can go from parsimony to extravagance easily, but to go from extravagance back to economy is difficult. The present having become so decadent, how could we now return to a simpler beginning even if we wanted to?[165]

Zhang Han invokes human nature to emphasize what he is up against, but he recognizes that the fashion process had become installed as a component of commercial production. Once the Suzhou textile industry had become dominant, demand generated not simply supply, but supply of ever-escalating style. This escalation in turn pushed demand up a notch, creating a cycle of product sophistication and supersession that no one who wished to rank in this social environment could break.

Fashion traveled through the social structure just as it did through the marketing structure. As style in Shanghai had to follow style in Suzhou, yet always fall short of it, so style among the common people aped the style of the gentry, and usually did so incompletely. The early-Qing essayist Ye Mengzhu, thinking back to his native Shanghai under the late Ming, puzzles over the movement of fashion. "If we go back to the beginning," he speculates, "it probably started with the gentry families. Their maidservants and concubines copied their style, then it spread to their relatives, and then it got to the neighbors." From there it was out of gentry hands and into the world of the common people. Once a style had been diffused, the process had to be set going again to render the formerly fashionable unfashionable, as Ye recognized: "At first the rich admired the novelty of it, then they had to go beyond it to achieve a look that was considered beautiful."[166]

In Chen Yao's time at the "start" of the late Ming, it was still possible to imagine gentry out of the fashion circuit. Their dress could be imagined as a timeless style, which their social inferiors since the Zhengde era had begun to plagiarize. By the time of Ye Mengzhu, born more than a century after Chen, this posture was no longer feasible. Ye saw the gentry as quite as vulnerable to the lure of fashion as everyone else and contributing to the craze by spreading new and extravagant styles to the rest of society. By the end of the Ming, the gentry were simultaneously agents of change as well as bulwarks against it, asserting their privileged position against newcomers by constantly rewriting the rules of taste as soon as everyone was starting to learn what they were supposed to pursue. This perpetual retreat to higher fashionable ground had the numbing effect of denying enduring value in established styles to anything: clothes or shoes, hats or ornaments, furniture or food, values or beliefs. The constantly destratifying terrain of fashion in the late Ming was thus as constantly being restratified as clothing went in and out of fashion, entering the ken of commoners as it left high society.

For a capital censor in 1628, the distress of observing "uneducated women and the wives of low-class characters dressed up in long gowns and draped in gold and silver" was a matter not of deplorable style but of deplorable transgression of status boundaries. The Chongzhen emperor in the closing reign of the dynasty was willing to respond by ordering the police in Beijing to arrest commoners who were outlandishly dressed.[167] But this was hardly a process that a few policemen could reverse.

THE FASHIONABLE BUSINESS OF THINGS

Moving into the realm of expensive things, the circle of fashion participants narrows. The untiring shuffling for status here involves only those who could afford to convert large amounts of cash into esteemed objects. Culturally meaningful objects such as antiques and paintings, which circulated among only the tiniest number of elite in the early Ming, were brought in greater numbers into the morally vacant world of money. To those invited to view or use them they displayed their owners' discernment and good taste.

The wealthy of the late Ming were under almost constant commercial pressure to take part in the fashionable business of things. In his diary, the artist and official Li Rihua (1565–1635) happened to jot down for the year 1603 thirteen visits by antique and art dealers trying to sell him something (how many did he neglect to record?).[168] Li lived in Jiaxing, which was on the water and land routes connecting Hangzhou and Shanghai, and so not surprisingly the dealers that visited him came from those two cities, as well as one from Jinhua prefecture southwest of Hangzhou. One Shanghai art and calligraphy dealer brought such a large stock of scrolls that Li was able to view forty or fifty. He also mentions a book dealer selling newly engraved editions.

For Li Rihua, the decision not to buy what these dealers offered him was easy. (Traveling salesmen are suspect in most cultures.) He had other and better sources for reliable things. Wealthy individuals outside Li's circle did not have his control of the standards of acquisition, however, and would have been readier to put down money for things that looked expensive and high-class. In the world of decorative objects, the simplest way to know what value was built into an object was to acquire things that were literally made of money, that is, of silver or gold—such things as gold tableware, silver incense-burners, and brocade worked with gold thread. These objects certainly set their owners apart, for only the fabulously wealthy could afford to own them. Gentry arbiters of taste in the late Ming responded defensively by denying them symbolic value and declaring their possession a sign of hopeless vulgarity. The elegant Songjiang bibliophile He Liangjun (1506–73) makes this point when he reports on visiting a wealthy gentleman in Jiaxing:

> The household used silver braziers and golden spittoons. Every guest had a set of golden dish and dish-stand, and a great golden cup with a pair of dragons. Each set contained about fifteen or sixteen ounces. I passed the night there, and the next morning washed my face in a silver basin chased with plum blossom. The hangings, curtains and bed clothes were

224   Summer

all of brocaded gauze, and my sight was assaulted to the point where I could not close my eyes at night.

He came away from this visit concluding that "the richest family in Jiangnan" was "the acme of commonly vulgarity incapable of being outdone."[169] All that physical wealth certainly dazzled ordinary folk, but in the eyes of those who represented high-cultural taste, it was simply a waste of money: the bid for status had failed.

The second impulse of the wealthy was to ask cultivated gentry for direction. They got it, in a guarded sort of way, from books. As Craig Clunas has noted in his study of these texts, authors of taste manuals exploited "an explosion of publishing interest in the fields of what might loosely be called luxury consumption, encompassing not just high-status and high-value works like painting, calligraphy and early bronzes, but also a whole range of contemporary products necessary to the presentation of self in elite life."[170] The authors all moved in the cultivated environment of urban Jiangnan, most as literati, some as merchants, and they clearly enjoyed displaying their discretion as they tutored their readers in what was elegant and what wasn't. The merely wealthy could now go to these texts to learn about the fashionable business of things: what things to collect, how and when to display them, what to appreciate in them, how to grade their quality—in other words, how to act so as to appear elegant (see figure 33).

The learning process could not have been easy. These texts were written for readers who were already inside the elite social networks where the "superfluous things" of the gentlemen were valued on cultural rather economic terms (although their economic value always lurked just beneath the elegant surface). They reconfirmed the cognoscenti in their knowledge and reaffirmed the importance of that knowledge in their interactions with a world of things that commerce, by increasing the sheer volume of things that could be bought, had made more unstable and confusing. This literature of taste also quietly suggested that ownership (and therefore the ability to purchase a valued item) was not the most important aspect of connoisseurship. The elegant always knew better than the rich.

Under the pressure of competition for status, fakes flooded the luxury market and buyers had to beware. This aspect of late-Ming life caught the attention of Matteo Ricci, who noted while in Nanjing, a city with a large art market, that the Chinese "are greatly given

開塲敦衍家門

Figure 33.   The delicate rosewood folding chair
signals this gentleman's wealth and status to readers
of this libretto (*Zixiao ji*).

to forging antique things, with great artifice and ingenuity, so that
those who do not know enough can spend great sums of money on
things which then are worth nothing."[171] Liu Tong (d. 1637) in his
detailed guidebook to Beijing published in 1635 goes to great lengths
to explain to those interested in connoisseurship (he uses the precise
term *shangjian* to indicate more than amateur collecting) the standards by which to judge the authenticity of objects sold in the city's
markets. He assures the reader that the sheen on a Xuande (1426–
35) bronze can't be faked as long as you know how to recognize it.
And recent imitations of fiercely expensive porcelain cups of the
Yongle era (1403–24) he says give themselves away by their thick-

ness.[172] The apparent ease with which faked objects circulated in the
late Ming was a response to the large number of mostly indiscrim-
inate buyers. Some literati were not disinclined to take advantage
of the situation. Trained to paint and write in perfect imitation of
the ancient masters, they had the skills needed to forge in these media.
Many Suzhou literati in the Wanli era were involved in turning out
famous paintings and calligraphy for a price, sometimes acknowledging that they were copies, other times not. A few prominent
scholars relied on this sort of work for regular income.

In a market in which things were not always what they seemed,
the less well schooled had to rely on simpler criteria of judgment.
Liu Tong advised porcelain buyers in Beijing to judge by the reign
date stamped on the bottom of pieces fired at imperial kilns (a
practice that achieved some regularity in the Yongle era). Liu tells
his readers how to rank: Chenghua first, then Xuande, Yongle, Jiajing, Zhengde, and Hongzhi, and finally the more recent reigns of
Longqing and Wanli.[173] This method of choosing the right porcelain
was not foolproof since, as he reminds the reader, high-quality
pieces can be found in all reigns and, more pertinently, reign dates
can be faked. Faking the reign date became so conventional that
late-Ming potters blithely penned anything on the bottom that might
seem reasonable for the type of piece they were dating. Xuande was
a particularly popular reign mark (Yongle pieces were too rare by
the late Ming for the Yongle mark to fool most buyers).

Another way in which objects were given identifications to compete on the market was to mark them with the name of the master
craftsman or workshop that made them. The quality associated with
a craftsman's name became more important to the purchaser who
lacked the discrimination to tell good from bad than the quality of
the object. A maker's mark served as a brand name: an easily
learned shortcut for purchasing quality items without having to
master a thorough knowledge of how to discriminate one object
from the next. The wealthy Shaoxing scholar and cultural arbiter
Zhang Dai (1597–1689) provides a list of many artisans whose
names one would want to look for, craftsmen whose work made
them "the social equals of gentlemen of the gentry": for pewter pots,
Huang (or, sometimes, Wang) Yuanji of Jiaxing; for lacquerware,
Zhou Zhu and the Hong family of Jiaxing; for bronzes, the Zhang
family of Jiaxing; for bamboo ware, Pu Zhongqian of Nanjing and
the La family of Jiaxing; for lacquered bamboo ware, Wang Er;

for speckled bamboo furniture, Jiang Huayu of Suzhou; for fans, Ma Xun and the Lotus-Leaf Li family; for ceramics, Wu Mingguan of Huizhou; for lined silk garments and curtains, Zhao Shiyuan; for gold- and silversmithing, Zhu Bishan; for zithers, Zhang Jixiu; for three-string lutes, Fan Kunbai; for jade carvings, Lu Zigang; for vessels carved from rhinoceros horn, Bao Tiancheng; for combs, Zhao Liangbi.[174] Zhang's list is limited to Jiangnan craftsmen. Writing a little earlier, in the north, Liu Tong presents a completely different set of names that one would look for on quality goods sold in the markets of Beijing.[175]

Clunas observes rightly that the names Zhang Dai lists are formulaic and can be found in other Jiangnan sources of the late Ming and early Qing. In fact, they had become so standardized that people muddled them: a century earlier, Wang Shizhen (1526–90) thought the comb-maker Zhao Liangbi to be the finest maker of pewter, and Gu Yanwu a decade or two later praised him for producing the finest knife blades![176] Inasmuch as no surviving artifact of any sort can be credited to Zhao Liangbi, we are left with no greater evidence of his skill in making combs/pewter/blades than the intensity with which connoisseurs insisted that owning a comb/pewter/blade by Zhao Liangbi placed the owner safely above the great vulgar mass of rich and poor beneath. It seems it didn't matter what Zhao Liangbi actually made, only that one knew the name. Clunas perceptively sees this naming exercise as an indicator of "the increased need of the elite to fix bench-marks of discrimination between different types of goods" at a time when the boundaries of elite status were in flux and the elite's traditional ability to discriminate was under siege. For such reasons, Zhang felt compelled to refix boundaries of quality as a way of allaying his "fascination and unease about the fluidity of social boundaries," as Clunas has put it.[177] Of course, the mere act of recording brand names diluted their exclusivity, since those trying to cross social boundaries had only to memorize brand names to be confident of having purchased the right objects. A comb maker just had to assure his customer that this was a Zhao Liangbi comb to make a sale, and the pewter maker down the street had only to make the same claim to achieve equal success.

The right things alone were not enough to effect social discrimination. They had to be possessed and displayed in the right ways. To the burden of things was thus added the burden of connoisseurship. This sort of knowledge too was available in books. The following example of advice on the care and display of things is taken from a posthumously published manual on art and object appreciation by the great painter Dong Qichang (1555–1636):

> Calligraphy, famous paintings, old rubbings, and ancient zithers should be locked and sealed in a small casket before the onset of the rainy month [June] and again of the eighth month [September]. The casket should be made of pine boards, but do not lacquer the inside—glued paper will prevent dampness. Seal up the lid four times around with paper in such a way that no air can get in so things don't get moldy. Once past these two periods, it is acceptable to set the things out in a bedroom and allow them to be in the presence of people. If you set them out in an open hall, keep them well away from the ground.
>
> Another matter: at normal times calligraphy, paintings, and rubbings should be displayed every ten days or so and mildly exposed to breeze and sun; keeping them rolled up for a long time encourages mold. A zither is best hung in a brocade sack on a wooden wall in a place where the air circulates, but not near a plaster wall exposed to humidity or sunlight. Preserved in this way, it will long outlive its owner.
>
> In displaying calligraphy or painting, there are five don'ts: don't show it under a light, on a rainy day, after drinking, in the presence of a vulgar person, or in the presence of a woman.[178]

Dong's advice goes beyond the simple problems of storage, of course, to imply standards governing the social interactions of gentlemanly life—a life from which women were clearly excluded.

Just as the right use of a thing communicated status, the wrong use canceled it. Zhang Dai tells the story of an antique bronze goblet that was in his family's possession until a persuasive antique dealer induced them to sell it for a hundred taels of silver. (So the story goes; more likely, a smart Zhang smelled a fine price and was not averse to letting the market convert symbolic capital into real when the price was right.) Zhang learned later that a merchant from Sheh county had bought it and placed it on the altar in his family shrine.[179] Zhang tells the story to laugh at the faux pas. The merchant should have known, and didn't, that an altar was not an appropriate setting for an antique bronze. He was too far outside the ranks of the elite to know what to do with the thing, exposing his social climbing to ridicule. Yet beneath Zhang's humor lies his anxiety that someone like a boorish Huizhou merchant could acquire objects that only connoisseurs should own, and that only the mistake of wrong use separated them.

Figure 34.   An illustrator in Fujian depicts the pursuits of a gentleman for readers who had little access to the world of the gentry: collecting books in the upper left, playing the stringed *zither* in the upper right, appreciating fine paintings in the lower left, and playing chess in the lower right (*Wanyong zhengzong*, 1599).

THE FASHIONABLE BUSINESS OF SEX

Passion too had its fashions. Lavishing money on commercial sex was one way to show the world that such expense meant nothing, and the Huizhou merchants gained something of a reputation as big spenders in this regard. But commercial sex could be constructed to display not just wealth but, again, a sense of discrimination by pushing the margins of moral notoriety. No symbolic capital was garnered from patronizing prostitutes, since any male with a little cash could buy female sexual services in any Ming town. Desire needed other guises to participate in the fashion struggle.

One of these guises was courtesanship. Briefly in the closing decades of the dynasty, some late-Ming gentry acquired educated women as courtesans outside the institutions of both marriage and concubinage. Courtesanship was made to bear a cultural significa- tion specific to the age. It rewrote the purely sexual relationship of prostitution as a literary, even companionate relationship. This re- writing happened from the male perspective—although women might well aspire to courtesanal status—as men sought soulmates with whom they could enact the notion of heroic love popular in the romantic fiction then on the market and not accommodated in the realm of arranged marriages and dowry transfers.[180] At another level, it was an opportunity for some men to remove women from certain cultural constraints—to gentrify them, even masculinize them—by requiring that courtesans have male-level literacy and be trained in the predominantly male-gentry arts of calligraphy, painting, and poetry. Men did not do this alone, for the courtesan fashion formed at a time when the gender limits on literacy and the arts were being removed by gentry women themselves. Courtesanship also formed at a time when the luxury trades could supply the fashionable costumes and ornaments through which gentry could crossdress their courtesans as members of the elite.

Most famous of late-Ming courtesans is Liu Shi (1618–64), lover of Chen Zilong, whose comments on silver we have noted. Liu began her career as maidservant Yang Ai working in a brothel in the town of Shengze. A retired chief grand secretary acquired her as a concubine and trained her in poetics and painting. A sex scandal obliged the old man to release her in 1632 at the age of fourteen. She moved to Songjiang, where her refined manner and skills in poetry and painting brought her into the circles of the Songjiang elite. Liu Shi and Chen Zilong became lovers in 1633. During their cohabitation in the spring and summer of 1635, both wrote their finest poetry. Chen's wife forced him to give her up, but Liu went on to become the concubine and soulmate of the eminent Qian Qianyi (1582–1664), with whom she remained and continued to write until his death, shortly before her own.[181] Of other well-known gentleman-courtesan couples,[182] all the men were of high social status and, with the exception of Qian Qianyi, were born in the opening decades of the seventeenth century and came of age in the last decades of the Ming.

The acting out of the cult of romantic love did not survive much beyond the first decade of Qing rule, except as a nostalgia. The literature on late-Ming courtesans, both then and now, has tended to romanticize this small group of fortunate women—then for their talent, now for what they did that appeared to challenge traditional conventions of subordination. From another perspective, though, the men who treasured romantic love glorified what these women did in an attempt to rescue themselves from the loss of official recognition and sense of powerlessness to which the factionalism at court had consigned them toward the end of the Ming. The ideal of romantic love invested their withdrawal into relationships with courtesans with the sense of moral greatness that was missing from their failed careers and political insignificance. Taking a courtesan became an act of allegory. Highly cultured males could fictionalize their dilemma as tragic men by buying women trained in certain culturally admired ways and taking on the courtesan's persona of the suffering female to express their sense of victimization.[183] The close association after the fall of the Ming between the romance of loyalty to a lover and the romance of loyalty to the fallen dynasty[184] confirms this allegorization and underscores the extent to which the cult of romantic love was a male narrative that set the thinnest upper stratum of the gentry apart to personify the nation (as opposed to the state). Companionate relationships between gentleman and courtesan may have echoed change in the lives of gentry women in the direction of greater education and freedom of movement,[185] but the brief flare of romantic love at the end of the late Ming neither led nor redirected changes in women's lives. Girls trained as courtesans gained individual access to literacy, mobility, sexuality, and intellectual life, but among women they remained marginal. No amount of romanticizing of suffering made these realms accessible to most women, nor was it intended that it should.

Another, rarer gesture in the fashionable business of sex in the late Ming was the buying of sexual services of boys. The practice of hiring "singing boys" to entertain at banquets and then letting the guests fondle them after their performance was already known in the most exclusive circles in the capital in the mid-Ming,[186] but few subscribed to this confusing pleasure. Coupling with a catamite *as a fashion* rather than as a matter of private desire seems to have fully entered the repertoire of status competition only in the late Ming. Ming customary law frowned on "taking the male member and sticking it in another person's anus in licentious play," male or female, yet sex between men was not expressly forbidden in written law, as Matteo Ricci was dismayed to discover when he learned that gentlemen in Beijing were engaging in "unnatural perversions." Pederasty was openly talked about, and Ricci seems to have been as distressed by the public nature of elite homoeroticism as by the practice itself. But then he had his own concern on this point, for the celibate Jesuits were rich food for sexual speculation among the Chinese.[187]

Although pederasty caught Ricci's attention in Beijing, it had greater play in the social world of the Jiangnan elite. Many within that milieu viewed pederasty as corrosive to the moral values of Confucianism. They saw it as substituting for the teacherly relationship of elder male (protective, paternal) to younger (deferential, filial) a dominance that was openly sexual. Some late-Ming writers sought to diminish the power of pederasty to parody Confucian principles of hierarchy by insisting that it happened to other people or in other places (the usual gambit was to externalize it as a Fujian practice). Fujian writer Xie Zhaozhe (1567–1624) parried the allegation by insisting that "nowadays," regardless of where the practice may have started, "from Jiangnan and Zhejiang to Beijing and Shanxi, there is none that does not know of this fondness."[188] Like Ricci, Xie acknowledged that sexual fondness for boys was a matter of public knowledge, not something kept hidden as a secret act. This public exposure was essential to the social purpose of homoeroticism in the late Ming. Like the buying of rare displayable artifacts, it marked off the truly rarefied at the pinnacle of elite status.

The power attached to that marking derived substantially from its commercial character. Whatever other pressures directed male desire toward boys, and however men construed that desire to themselves, homoeroticism was a commercial as much as personal relationship. Sodomy in this context was not a private act between consenting adults but a contractually documented act performed in the public setting of the purchase or rental market. Entrepreneurs acquired boys, usually as orphans or famine victims, trained them in entertainment skills, then hired them out as prostitutes or sold them to patrons. The arrangement was basically no different than it was for girls, whom entrepreneurs could hire out as prostitutes or sell as concubines, though the purchase price for boys was higher. Li Le mentions, for example, that a county magistrate in Fujian—Li repeats the Fujian stereotype—paid fifty taels of silver for "a beautiful boy" in the 1580s, for which his upright provincial governor had him fired.[189]

What lent pederasty social power, and set the catamite apart from the concubine, was not strictly money. Fifty taels was not a sum out of the reach of most gentry. It was wealth entwined around the social and psychological pressures in Chinese culture against *nanse*, "male colors," or less literally, "erotic attraction to the male body." These pressures distinguished homoerotic love as an exclusive gesture within reach of only a tiny minority of those able to afford a catamite or a courtesan. This fashion was accordingly differently constructed than courtesanship: more daring, repugnant to sexual norms, indifferent to ideologies of self-cultivation and loyalism.[190] While it may be that the expression of natural homoerotic desire could only burst forth with the peculiar erosion of Confucian norms in the sixteenth century, those norms paradoxically ensured that pederasty was a sexual fashion beyond the emotional reach of most people, and for that reason rich in social credit.

Zhang Dai wrote obliquely of his own affairs with boys serving in his household, which he names among the many passions he pursued as a young man.[191] He does so not to explain his individuality (he went after the maids as enthusiastically as he went after the serving boys) but to illustrate to a later, more sober age the decadence of that time. Yet the moral of this revelation (as for much of what Zhang chose to write about his late-Ming youth) is more complex than that. Even as he condemns late-Ming decadence and seeks to expiate the sin of witnessing and therefore allowing the collapse of the dynasty, he writes with deep nostalgia for a lost age when he moved effortlessly in the highest social circles in which making love to a boy distinguished those at the very top of the social heap.

A FLOATING WORLD

Zhang Dai divided his late-Ming youth between his native Shaoxing and its provincial capital and marketing center, Hangzhou. Hangzhou was many things. To merchants it was the main southern port on the Grand Canal, the collection point for commodities coming up the coast and east from the Huizhou hinterland, a major producer of textiles and books, and home for a large community of sojourning Huizhou merchants. To the gentry it was an ancient capital filled with grand monasteries, a lakeside resort to stroll through, a place to buy luxuries, and the site of elegant private gardens. The gentry's Hangzhou and the merchants' Hangzhou were not separate, of course. Their worlds overlapped every time a gentleman bought a merchant's wares or a merchant bought a gentleman's calligraphy; their paths intersected on the grounds of monasteries and in the houses of the pleasure quarters.

Zhang Dai is one of the best guides to the floating world of Hangzhou in the closing decades of the Ming. His "dream essays" as he called them, written after the fall of the Ming, are filled with recollections sharpened, perhaps distorted, by a painful sense of loss and the knowledge that the late-Ming world in which he had lived, moving through the fashionable monde of "aristocrats and consort families, senior statesmen, colleagues, Buddhist monks, great litterateurs, and famous concubines,"[192] existed nowhere but in his memory. Under the glare of dynastic collapse, even the memory of relatively uncomplicated pleasures such as eating fruit troubled him.

Take oranges. Back in Spring we read Zhang Yue, in the 1530 gazetteer of Huian county on the Fujian coast, discriminating between the fruit that a gentleman would eat and the fruit he would not dare to be seen eating. He declared the citrus in Huian to be undistinguished and advised getting oranges from Zhangzhou further down the coast. Zhang Dai too ate Fujian oranges, as well as a delicious pastry made from them, a century later in Hangzhou. Hangzhou was perhaps too far from the Fujian coast for its residents to worry about which county their oranges came from, but it was close enough that commercial suppliers could deliver Fujian citrus on a regular basis. "Distant [foods] arrived [in Hangzhou] annually, nearby [foods] arrived monthly or even daily. Every day I anxiously and eagerly planned what would please my mouth and my stomach." Zhang Dai looked back on such commercially sustained pleasures with intense guilt, as though his indulgences had brought the dynasty down: "My sins are indeed heavy." But he is not entirely disabled by the memory. At the end of this little essay on late-Ming delicacies, he cheers up enough to observe that being able to eat "the foods of the four quarters" had been a nice bit of luck.

Zhang Dai's favorite season for enjoying Hangzhou was spring, when the Buddhist monasteries on the shores of West Lake held a pilgrims' fair that lasted from the middle of the second month to the beginning of the fifth. The women of Hangzhou went out to the monasteries at this time to burn incense, tour, and sleep over in the residents' quarters—despite the special prohibition against "licentiousness" that the provincial surveillance commissioner, unable to imagine women sleeping in a monastery except to have intercourse with monks, promulgated in 1603.[193] It was also the season when northerners trekked their way south through Hangzhou to reach the pilgrimage mecca on Putuo Island off the Zhejiang coast. During these months, the monasteries of West Lake were thronged with visitors. The pilgrims came from as close as neighboring prefectures

Figure 35. In a stylized depiction of the great temple fair at Zhaoqing Monastery in Hangzhou, the man at the first table is selling fans (*Hainei qiguan,* 1609).

and from as far away as Shandong province. Zhaoqing Monastery, the great Vinaya center of Jiangnan, was turned into a vast market of curios and souvenirs (see figure 35):

> Every inch of space was used inside and outside the halls, above and below the raised paths, to the left and right of the pond, and within and beyond the front gate. Where there were rooms, [dealers] set up stalls; where there weren't, they put up sheds; in front of the sheds were booths with awnings and behind them were yet more stalls. Here everything was

available, from cosmetics, hair ornaments and earrings, ivory, and scissors to scriptures, wooden gongs, and children's toys.

Zhang enjoyed rubbing shoulders with the hoi polloi at times like this, with "country women in their village dress" and townspeople who came out in the hundreds of thousands to poke about for treasures and bask in the warm weather. At other times he preferred the elegant gatherings in the gardens of gentry residents. The wealthy families of Zhejiang all kept residences in Hangzhou, as did the Zhangs, and spent as much of the year there as they could. This was a world of "famous courtesans and idle monks," as Zhang tells it. When the gentry were not at home, they went on outings to spots around West Lake, most famously Dragon Hill just south of the city wall. It is here that many of Zhang's stories of the 1620s are set. In one of them, Zhang tells that he and his younger uncle in 1622 joined a cock-fighting club that met on Dragon Hill. He was so good at betting on the winning bird, and his uncle so bad, that he ended up winning all manner of things from his uncle—antiques, paintings, brocades, fans—before deciding that he had better give it up lest he become addicted to gambling. In the winter of 1626, three feet of snow fell on Hangzhou. Zhang walked up Dragon Hill one moonlit night and settled himself in the entrance hall of the City God Temple to gaze out over the snowy scene while female attendants served him wine and played music.

Zhang Dai's longest description of Dragon Hill is of the Lantern Festival, an annual four-day celebration held there in the middle of the first month. On that day, people had lanterns made and displayed them along the path between the City God Temple and Penglai Ridge. Each lantern owner sat out on mats spread beneath his lantern with kinsmen and friends, singing and drinking wine they could buy from the wine sellers plying the festival. The high point of the evening was to go up to the small temple on the peak of Dragon Hill. Patrons might order their servants to clear a path for them through the throngs of people heading up, but in the crush of merrymakers it was impossible to do anything but let oneself be borne along with the crowd. After the festival was over, Zhang recalls, the litter was swept into great mounds. The only refuse that didn't go into the piles were ladies' slippers, which were hung up in the trees to titillate all with the thought that sexual encounters had taken place on the hill under cover of night.

In his memoir of the Lantern Festival, Zhang retells a story he heard about a "vagabond" who took over an empty building on the east side of the City God Temple and installed boys he had bought in a "screened alley"—a male brothel. Male prostitution did a good business for the vagabond and his brothel prospered. On the night of a Lantern Festival when the world was too busy to notice, a young man showed up at the entrance to the screened alley and put down money for the services of one of the boys. As soon as the client was ushered with the boy into a room, he snuffed out the candle, drank some wine, and tore the boy's clothes off. But when he undressed himself, he turned out to be not a he at all, but a cross-dressed woman. Here was the true inversion of the sexual order, with the woman putting herself in the position of the buyer of commercial sex. Yet here also was its restoration as she conferred on the boy the power of genital sex that the commercial exploitation of his physical beauty had denied him. She made love to him until just before dawn, then slipped away undetected.

The moneyed pleasures of Hangzhou were soon gone as well. In the spring of 1640, Zhaoqing Monastery, site of the great pilgrims' fair, burned to the ground. That same year Hangzhou was struck by famine. Even the wealthy were reduced to eating rice gruel, and the rural poor cooked and ate their silkworm cocoons to stave off starvation.[194] The disaster dragged on for two years, by Zhang's report leaving half the people of the region dead. Emaciated corpses lay where they fell in the city streets. The flow of northern pilgrims dwindled, and when the Manchus attacked Shandong on an early raid in 1642 it dried up completely. The fair disappeared. Three years later, the military forces of the new Qing dynasty reached Hangzhou. Zhang fled with a few boxes of books into the hills of his native Shaoxing, leaving behind the rest of the 30,000 volumes in his library. The occupying troops used them as fuel to keep themselves warm in the winter of the new dynasty. The culture of the late Ming was over. Or was it?

Fall

The Lord of Silver
(1642–1644)

One man in a hundred is rich, while nine out of ten are
impoverished. The poor cannot stand up to the rich who,
though few in number, are able to control the majority.
The lord of silver rules heaven and the god of copper cash
reigns over the earth. Avarice is without limit, flesh injures
bone, everything is for personal pleasure, and nothing
can be let slip. In dealings with others, everything is
recompensed down to the last hair. The demons of
treachery stalk.

Zhang Tao

Or so it seemed to one earnest Confucian scholar who came out of
political oblivion in the late Ming with an appointment as magistrate to the county of Sheh. Sheh was the wrong point of reentry for
a moralist like Zhang Tao. How could he greet the commercial
world into which he had been released from his forced retirement
with anything but disapproval? Sheh was at such distance from

238

Confucian ideals. It was the home of the great trading empires of the late Ming, the inner sanctum of the successful Huizhou merchants, where money was the prime standard of value and where learning and virtue were practiced under its shadow. For Zhang Tao, the moral year of his dynasty had turned so far from the quiet winter of 1368 that the wheel of order was wobbling off its axle. It was the end of the world as he had known it.

So much for metaphors. After 1609, when the Sheh county gazetteer was published, things got worse in the real world as well. Zhang Tao never got to see the end of it all. He retired back to his home county of Huangpi roughly a decade later and lived out a quiet retirement. He probably missed the decade of bloody factional struggles at court between eunuchs and literati in the 1620s, and he was safely dead when the disasters of the 1630s struck. But his heirs weren't. Huangpi county in 1636 suffered its worst drought in decades. Six years later, the fields dried out again and clouds of locusts descended to strip them bare. The great epidemic that burst into north China in 1641 arrived in Huangpi the following year. There were no crops to harvest, nothing to eat but the bodies of plague victims. Did the people of Huangpi observe the festival of the City God, which fell that year on 10 August? Did they parade his statue through the streets to ensure his blessings, or did they whip his wooden corpse for failing to protect them from the lord of famine, the god of locusts, and the demons of plague?[1]

Of course Zhang Tao had something quite different in mind when he called up his metaphorical demons. The demons stalking through China in 1642 were anything but metaphors. They were real people: unpaid soldiers, discharged couriers-turned-bandits, men without land to till, boys orphaned by the epidemics, refugees without food, marauders hiding in the hills and preying on the valleys below. Some moved in small gangs, others in large armies. They bore down on defenseless villages and swarmed across the plains, plundering wherever state security evaporated and elites failed to muster their tenants into makeshift militias. Then came the Manchus, disciplined and deadly horsemen who had moved down from Manchuria toward the Chinese territory of Liaodong, where Zhang Tao had held his last post, and raided across the Great Wall almost with impunity.

In this chaotic time, the roving army of another rebel leader, Li Zicheng, made a long-shot bid in the spring of 1644 to grab Beijing. They were successful. The Chongzhen emperor slew his daughter so that she would not die a more miserable death and then hanged himself in the pleasure park behind his palace. The rebels took what they could not keep. In less than six weeks they had to give up their prize when the Ming army charged with defending the northeast border against the Manchus struck a deal with the enemy and led them through the Great Wall and down to Beijing. The rebels fled south. The Manchus marched into the capital, enthroned their child khan as the Son of Heaven, and declared the Ming dynasty over.

Which demons ended the Ming dynasty? Were they the lord of silver and the god of copper cash? Zhang Tao might have liked to think so, but he was dead when the end finally came. What did the living think? Ding Yaokang and Li Tingsheng were among the millions that made it through: we shall ask them.

THE FALL OF THE MING

ON THE COAST

Late in the fall of 1642, the Manchus launched a short but devastating raid by boat across the Gulf of Bohai into Shandong. Ding Yaokang was in Beijing at the time and raced home as soon as he heard the news to save his family in Zhucheng, a backwater county in the impoverished southeastern corner of the province.[2] Ding had a *gongsheng* degree, a respectable certification that opened some doors but was not grand enough to guarantee an official post. He had been hanging around the capital on the off chance of picking up an appointment, but that fall it seemed hopeless. The epidemic the year before had weakened the regime's finances and the constant rebel alarms were bleeding the treasury dry. In any case, Ding was from an obscure and insignificant county that gave him no faction to call upon and no patron to open a back door into the capital bureaucracy. The raid convinced him that it was time to go home.

Manchu horsemen had raided Shandong three years earlier. Although they had gotten no farther than the western prefectures, they had inflicted much damage and more terror. Ding had been home in 1639 and had wanted to evacuate his family southward down to the walled safety of Nanjing, the city to which gentry throughout eastern China were fleeing.[3] But the raid had thrown the province into such turmoil that it was impossible to make the arrangements to transport them southward out of harm's way. That time, fortunately, the horsemen had not pushed as far southeast as Zhucheng county. This time it would be different.

When Ding Yaokang arrived home, he found the region in some disarray and the county administrators nervous. It looked as though the magistrate did not have the resolve to withstand a siege by Manchu horsemen. Ding urged his kinsmen to leave the county seat and take refuge somewhere else. The lineage, known as the Cangma Dings, was large and locally prominent. A military ancestor had served the Hongwu emperor and been modestly rewarded with a hereditary posting to this miserable stretch of coast. The Dings had moved into gentry status in the mid-sixteenth century (their first *jinshi* was 1565). Ding Yaokang himself never got that far, but he did enjoy a reputation in local society for his calligraphy, poetry, and fiction (his oeuvre includes a well-known sequel to the late-Ming erotic novel *Golden Lotus*). The Cangma Dings were not outstandingly wealthy, but Ding Yaokang and his brothers had been able to expand the family's landholdings in the 1620s and 1630s.

Ding's kinsmen were not convinced of the need to flee. They were more fearful of losing their property to rapacious neighbors than losing their lives to the Manchus. So he decided to take his own counsel and move his part of the family out of the county seat to the family's rural estate in the hills down toward the coast. He mustered four hundred able-bodied tenants to make up a family militia and got together fifty draft horses and donkeys with carts and enough weapons and firearms to arm everyone (see figure 36). Many other powerful families were also moving south. Watching "strings of carts and horses going on without a break," he decided that his family was not safe even in the countryside. In January he went down to the coastal port of Andong, situated just above Shandong's border with South Zhili, to arrange for a ship to carry a store of provisions out onto an island in the ocean. Then he returned to organize his family's departure.

In the predawn of a snowy February morning, one of the tenants spotted three Manchu scouts. The militia wanted to fight, but Ding sensed that such action was hopeless and immediately took off with the two dozen family members who would go with him down to the coast. The ship he had chartered had not yet returned to pick them up and he became frantic to arrange passage. As he was being jostled among the waterside crowds, he ran into a friend who had engaged a place on another ship. The friend introduced him to the

Figure 36.   These fowling pieces (*niaochong*) are of
the sort that Ding Yaokang probably had among his
store of firearms (*Tiangong kaiwu,* 1637).

captain, who for the extortionate price of fifty silver taels was willing
to take his family aboard. That night (6 February) Ding looked out
from his ship through the rain and sleet and saw fires on shore
spreading in all directions as the Manchus pillaged and torched every
village. Next day they learned that the county seat had fallen. They
set sail.

   Ding had lost track of the supplies he had sent ahead and had
only a small stash of silver with which to keep his family alive. But
they reached an island where a scholar befriended them and took

them in. The Manchus remained in Shandong for three months, during which time the Dings survived on this islander's kindness and starvation rations. Once the Manchus had withdrawn in the spring, the Dings returned to the mainland. Ding Yaokang left his family on the coast and went on alone to inspect the family estate and see whether the winter wheat crop could be harvested. He discovered that half his land had been taken over by neighboring lineages. Losing the land was only half the problem, for he notes in his diary that "the markets were empty of people." With no labor there was no one to harvest the wheat. He could do nothing but leave it to rot in the fields.

Ding later reestablished his family on the half of their property that remained, but the banditry of these difficult times forced them into the county seat. In the spring of 1644 their fortunes turned again. With the Manchu invasion, the rebel troops of Li Zicheng retreated from the capital southward into Shandong. Ding resolved to escape to sea a second time. On 22 April he took his family and a supply of grain to another coastal island where friends of the scholar who had befriended him the previous winter provided them with a refuge. He was not alone, for he discovered that over a hundred eminent families from southeastern Shandong had moved out onto the islands along the coast and bought up land in anticipation of a long stay. One retired official had acquired over 400 *mu* of land and was living quite comfortably on an annual rent in excess of 100 *shi* of grain.

News soon arrived that the Manchus had founded a new dynasty. Ding slipped back home to see how matters stood. The rebel forces of Li Zicheng were still roaming Shandong, and besides that the neighbors had swallowed up the other half of his estate. He decided to head back to sea, but on his way ran into an old scholar friend who had raised a small cavalry force. Ding helped him recruit another four thousand men from the private militias of the great families of the region to drive back the rebels, but he saw no future in staying with the resistance movement and returned to his family.

Conditions were harsh in Shandong that next winter. The land went uncultivated and merchants abandoned the province.[4] By the following summer, however, it seemed that the new Manchu order was there to stay. Ding felt he had no choice but to return to Zhucheng and make peace with the Qing dynasty. The following October he went a step further and traveled to Beijing to reconfirm his status as a *gongsheng* under the new regime. He then returned to Zhucheng to spend several years trying to secure his future, even contemplating a move to South Zhili, but with little success. Finally he made the momentous decision to take service under the Manchus. At the end of August 1648, he went by ship to Tianjin and overland to Beijing (covering almost 500 kilometers in only three days) to seek a post. There he met up with old friends who were already in Manchu employ and found a comfortable niche in the new order.

After a few years in educational posts, Ding earned a strong promotion to serve as magistrate of none other than Huian county in Fujian, where Zhang Yue in Spring learned the value of well sweeps and pontificated on fruit, and Ye Chunji in Summer tried to get the people to cut down on wedding expenses. The prospect of traveling so far south may have daunted him, or perhaps he had tired of government service. Whatever the reason, Ding never went to Huian. He gave up his promotion and chose instead to retire. He went back to Zhucheng's small gentry society, edited the Ding genealogy, and in 1656 wrote *A Brief Account of My Escape from Disaster (Chujie jilüe)*, from which we know his story.

Writing a decade and a half later, Ding regarded his instinct to flee in 1642 and 1644 as having been the smart thing to do. It had meant going against the authority of his kinsmen and losing control of the family estate, but there had been benefits. It had ensured the survival of part of his lineage. It had gained him an entrée into official service, something he'd never been able to manage under the Ming. And it had enabled him to retain his status among the Zhucheng gentry. He had survived the transition and gone on to mild prosperity within a gentry world that had quickly resurrected itself after the troubles were over.

INLAND

To Henan province, 1642 brought not Manchus but the rebel forces of Li Zicheng. While Ding Yaokang lived through the dynastic transition at sea, a student named Li Tingsheng spent these years on the south end of the North China Plain, that millennial mainstage of military conquest and dynastic war, skipping back and forth across the Yellow River to escape contenders for the Chinese throne.[5] Li Zicheng's army had moved into western Henan the year before along the transportation routes cutting across the province. Their arrival coincided disastrously with the great epidemic of 1641 that ravished Henan and, it was claimed, left only three people in ten alive in some counties.[6] In the spring of 1642, the rebels threatened the northeastern corner of Henan province, which included Qi county where Li Tingsheng was enrolled as a *shengyuan*. When the magistrate of Qi abandoned his post, the gentry chose discretion over valor. Li joined the exodus. He spent most of the next twenty-two months moving about with friends and family, mostly north of the Yellow River, evading rebel forces at one turn and government armies at the next. (See figure 37 for what he might have looked like.)

Li lived the life of a refugee, but a gentry refugee. The descriptions of that life in his diary convey the sense that hardships were more psychological than physical, and that the world of gentry inter-action—and gentry money—remained intact. He communicates this in a simple way by his frequent references to the circulation of silver among the gentry. In the summer of 1643, two education officials in Jun county just over the border in the south end of North Zhili "bestowed gifts of silver and words" on Li. Later that fall, the magistrate of Hua, the next county to the south of Jun, gave Li and two fellow students five taels of silver when they met—though Li is sufficiently candid, and ashamed, to admit in his diary that they had gone looking for the magistrate to connive for a gift because they had run out of money for wine. When Li returned to Jun in January 1644, a patron presented him with a travel gift of silver. At least as many times as he received cash gifts, he gave them: to teachers and patrons, often to the very people who would later give him travel money. These gifts were conventional gentry gestures in the late Ming. If the late-Ming gentry were able to survive the interdynastic war, it was not only because they looked out for each other, but also because in extremity they kept up the appearances of their status. The disruptions of the 1640s did not eliminate either the niceties of gentry intercourse or the silver to see that they were carried out.

Li Tingsheng proved adept at adjusting to life on the road, surviving from day to day but also taking the odd day off to visit scenic places along the way. He writes that on 18 May 1642 he and seven family members found a former neighbor living in a village on the Henan-Shandong-North Zhili border and decided to stop there. They had nothing to support them but two oxen, but the border

明邑庠生楊公茂林神儀

Figure 37. This early-Qing ancestor portrait of a *shengyuan* identifies the young man as "Yang Maolin of the Ming dynasty." Dressed in the regalia of a student at a Confucian county school, Yang was of the same status as Li Tingsheng in the Ming-Qing transition. An ancestor portrait of so young a subject with his dynasty indicated in the inscription may signify that Yang was killed in the Ming-Qing transition. Reproduced courtesy of the Royal Ontario Museum, Toronto.

location provided Li with an inspiration about how to support his family:

> When taking advantage of the cool shade under the four willows behind the village, I saw the comings and goings on the highway. The tracks of carts on the road were numerous and dense. I conceived the idea of turning this into a road to life. Finally, I inquired and found out that the markets in the two towns [joined by the road] met on different days, so that trading occurred on alternate days and traffic through here was constant. Thereupon I sold one ox to get capital to start a business. I instructed my family to prepare some rustic food and other items so that we could "fish for profit" under the trees. With disheveled hair, bare feet, and [when not going to market] no shirt, I sat or lay there all day with father while my younger brothers and children led the servants in gathering fuel and carrying water to assist with the business. Every day we heard only woodsmen's chants and whistles and saw only herdsmen driving their calves. Our daily contacts were with peddlers plying their wares and itinerant merchants passing through.

Disguised as a roadside food vendor, Li Tingsheng thus spent the summer of 1642 working the flow of herdsmen and the merchants who moved constantly between two alternating periodic markets. The threat of rebel overthrow did not interrupt this sort of petty commerce, which provided opportunities for destitute gentry willing to cross-dress as rustics to make a temporary living.[7]

In August, Li and two cousins returned briefly to the family's estate in Qi county to collect what harvest they could. They impersonated carters and mixed in with a group pushing carts south to avoid notice (see figure 38), hence the diary heading, "Inspecting Agriculture Dressed in Disguise." As Roger Des Forges points out in his commentary on the diary, once Li arrived back home, he had to use extra effort and money to coerce the locals to do what otherwise he would have expected them to do for little or nothing: "We used warm words to charge the house servants," Li says, "and gave heavy rewards to the porters."

Back with his family, Li Tingsheng hears of a good melon crop twenty kilometers to the north. He and a gentry friend decide to go into melons. Once again, clothes remake the men. "We changed into the garments of carters. Taking turns pushing the cart, we left." Halfway there, dusk came on and they found shelter with the family of a *shengyuan* of Li's acquaintance. The man's uncle owned a peach orchard there, the proceeds from which he divided with a neighbor who jointly operated the irrigation system that watered the

Figure 38.   Carters push two-wheeled barrows of
the sort Li Tingsheng probably used in the summer of
1642 (*Shuihu zhuan*, 1610).

trees. Li and his friend decided to switch from melons to peaches
and asked the uncle if he would be willing to sell some of his share.
The uncle was pleased to unload the peaches rather than market
them himself (which he had been away doing when they first
arrived) and gave them a good discount, declaring, "How can we
engage in trade with people of our class?" He may simply have been
giving them the usual wholesale discount, but it was pleasant to
construct the discount as a sign of class solidarity. Li and his friend
filled their cart with peaches and marketed the fruit at a good profit.

Li went back to the roadside food stall until the middle of the fall,
when the area was again threatened. Searching for a safer environ-

ment, he and his friend "took on the appearance of merchants"—presumably people would harass gentry but not merchants?—and headed north for Jun county. There, Li was invited to tutor the children of a local landlord and failed scholar and give up his commercial dealing. He experienced the invitation as a moment of crisis, expressed again as a dilemma of how to dress: "I thought: having suffered from being crowded together with woodsellers on the road, I had already come to regard brushes and ink slabs, garments and other [scholarly] possessions as another world. How could I now change my clothes, set up a study, and discourse on the arcane forms of classical literature?" He does because he sees this tutoring post as providing him with a more stable income for supporting his family. He was also under pressure from his father "not to squander my proper profession ... and not get mired in trivial [commercial] pursuits." The choice achieves what his father had hoped. "This," Li says, "was the first time I had been recognized in this time of difficulties." Gradually he returned to his suspended studies and resumed the life of the examination candidate, relieved not to have to play the merchant again. As he put it squarely: "I was back among people like myself."

Li represents commerce over and over again as an act of impersonation. The impersonation was temporary and opportunistic, especially when it became evident that the roving military bands on the North China Plain were targeting gentry families for attack.[8] But impersonation was also pleasurable until the opportunity to dress again as a scholar arose. The diary account is thus structured around not only the adventure of escape from calamity and return home but also the adventure of commerce. Just as the tension of Li's experience of hardship is resolved by returning home and affirming the common cause of the gentry (his last sentence says that he and the man who had employed him as tutor "swore that we were together in the same boat"), so too the tensions excited by having dipped into commerce are resolved by reaffirming the value of landlordism and gentry status.

Li's experiences suggest that gentry society survived the potentially fatal transition because individuals developed skills, attitudes, and a relationship to the economy that enabled them to find food and income. He and his peers knew how to search out commercial opportunities to survive. At the same time, they did what they needed to do to see that gentry culture was kept alive: living as gentry but cross-dressing as merchants. It was partly a matter of generation. Li was born just about the time the Wanli era finished in 1620. From birth these boys lived their lives under the shadow of the lord of silver and were easy in his presence. Unlike Zhang Tao's generation, born before the Wanli emperor was enthroned in 1573, Li's generation was not fazed by the competition for resources that Zhang decried as "avarice without limit." Nor did they find the calculating attitude that Zhang called "recompensing down to the last hair" philosophically troubling or morally reprehensible. It was just sensible dealing. Li Tingsheng did note some of the ways in which commercial dealing could demean the dignity of individuals, but he would never have worked himself up into the high rage about demons of treachery as he and his father set up their lunch counter to "fish for profit," the stock Confucian phrase Li uses to lend an apologetic touch to the whole business. If Li wanted demons of treachery, he had only to look at the marauding soldiers from collapsing Ming armies and the thugs who attached themselves to local warlords. But not commerce. Commerce was simply his way of making money, and anybody could do it.

LIVING THROUGH THE FALL

Zhang Tao's remark about demons of treachery was not a literal prediction that his dynasty would fall. Had he lived until 1644, he might have been tempted to see the collapse of the Ming as evidence of the decadence of the age. Would he have been right to do so? Was the unbridled pursuit of profit and pleasure the motive force behind the dynasty's destruction? Zhang argued that commerce had undermined the founding emperor's vision of an autocratic Daoist arcadia by reducing all social relationships to their financial cores and stripping the Ming personality of the Confucian urge for reciprocity. He judged its social effects—class polarization, exploitation, impoverishment—as corrosive of the moderate Confucian vision of class hierarchy, paternalism, and subsistence. And he predicted that that vision was threatened with complete annihilation. Yet the demons he had in mind were not people at all, neither the rebels stalking Li Tingsheng nor the Manchus putting Ding Yaokang's county to the torch. They were the uncontrolled lust for gain. Was that enough to destroy the Ming dynasty?

Some analysts after the fall were ready to cast it in moral terms.

The great seventeenth-century scholar Gu Yanwu, for instance, compiled *The Strengths and Weaknesses of the Various Regions of the Realm* (*Tianxia junguo libing shu*) to document the geostrategic reasons for the fall of the Ming, yet he too was bound up with the disasters he lived through and was quite willing to include Zhang Tao's diatribe among his texts. He knew nothing about Zhang, but he must have liked the uncompromising tone and brooding anxiety that precociously foreshadowed decay at a time when the realm was still reasonably well governed. The passage certainly appealed to Gu's own instinct for nostalgia, for both Gu and Zhang position the present in relation to better pasts. Gu was thirty years old when the Ming fell. Later in life he would look back across that divide with a rosy gaze, not unlike Zhang Tao's idealizing of the early Ming. For Gu, though, the ideal age was the late Ming:

> When I was a boy [in the 1620s] I saw old people in the rural areas who had never seen an official, were content to remain in the fields, and had never gone into the city; whereas now, with commerce in full flood, corvée burdensome, and lawsuits numerous, half the year has to be spent in the offices of officials. The common people have a saying, "When a family has 200 *mu* of land, you sleep in the yamen."[9]

Should we take Gu at face value? As we noted in Spring, the image of the contented old peasant never straying from his home village and passing his entire life without once going to the county seat was already a tired convention in the mid-Ming.[10] Gu Yanwu went to yet other lengths to romanticize the Wanli era: he describes it as a time when

> the autocrat did not intervene [*wu wei*] and disturbances within the four seas were few. Those who went to the capital from the counties were largely enrolled officials, and the servants who accompanied them numbered no more than three or four. Other than them there were a few *juren* and *gongsheng* and tax-forwarding households charged with bringing tribute rice [to the capital]. It was close to the description of ancient times in the *Talks on Salt and Iron* in which it was said, "Few traveled the roads and weeds sprouted in the marketplaces."[11]

Given all that we learned in Summer, Gu's image seems a little off the mark. Weeds were trampled as soon as they put up their shoots in the markets, the roads were crowded, almost everyone went to the cities, and an official who traveled with a retinue of only three or four was a laughingstock.[12]

The two authors picture the late Ming differently, but do so by using the same chronology of moral time, regretting the present and wishing for the past. Zhang Tao's adulthood had brought him into a world of treachery, avarice, and pleasure from which the solid virtues of an earlier time had been lost. So too, Gu's adulthood was a time of commerce, burdens, and litigation when few were content to live the simple life he thought he remembered from his childhood. It didn't matter that the effect of the same moral chronology was to induce them to write about the Wanli era in completely opposite ways. Both were striving to resist the influence of commercial ways of thinking over the habits of consumption and social deference once taken as essential elements of right living.

Was Gu Yanwu right to accept Zhang Tao's judgment on the effect of commerce on Chinese life? He complained about the commercialism of his own day, but had commerce altered the conduct of public and private life in fundamental ways? Had such alteration provoked the apparent crisis that China faced in the late Ming? Or had mobility and commerce, by broadening the realm of the social without fundamentally transforming its structure, guaranteed that the world the gentry commanded would hold together even as the dynasty fell apart?

The experiences that Ding Yaokang and Li Tingsheng record in their diaries suggest that China had indeed changed by 1642, but not to the final detriment of the gentry.[13] In fact, it was the very changes in mobility, money, and status in the late Ming that enabled them to make their way across the dynastic transition intact. Both took advantage of communication networks of the late Ming to evade danger and seek out opportunities. Rebels and Manchus traveled the same routes, so Li and Ding had to take care to use them when they could and get off them when danger approached. But they could cover protective distance when they had to.[14] Both men were able to take advantage of the money economy, which continued to function. Li in fact did quite well in both retail and wholesale trade. Ding stuck with the elite's traditional income source of landlordism, yet his cash wealth in silver enabled him at key moments to pay for food and transportation.

More important than either of these factors is the continuing status that the gentry could trade on to weather the storm. Both Ding and Li connected at several important moments with other gentry, both fellow refugees and those who were able to maintain a more stable existence through the transition years. Without that solidarity, either man and his family could have come to harm. Gentry status earned them respect in the eyes of others, though Li was quick to disguise his status when status anonymity seemed wiser. It may also have given each man confidence in navigating around immediate obstacles and making choices for the long term.

The social personality they assumed as gentry of the 1640s was not the same as what Zhang Tao might have looked for in a gentleman forty years earlier. Times had changed and the gentry had learned to change with them. Li and Ding understood how to look for financial opportunities without feeling demeaned. They knew how to calculate advantage without feeling petty. They had an adaptability to circumstances that Zhang Tao would not have wished to muster. They were confident in the knowledge that they were the masters of the social order and would triumph as a social class, even against the new lords from Manchuria.

The deepening evolution of gentry identity from the sixteenth through the seventeenth century argues against assigning too much significance to 1644. In this sense, the history of China during the Ming dynasty was about more than the fortunes of one emperor's family. Its rise and fall had something—but not everything—to do with the evolving interaction between a market economy and a social structure dominated by the gentry. What was decisive about the late Ming was not the eruption of some irresolvable contradiction between gentry and merchants, even if this was how Zhang Tao responded to the confusions of pleasure that commerce brought to the gentry. Rather, it was the subtle knitting together of their two societies. If anything, 1644 wound the strands of the educated and moneyed elites more tightly together. Despite Zhang's worst warnings about the lord of silver and the demons of treachery, the social distance between gentry and merchant was being resolved in a way that strengthened rather than diminished gentry society.

LAST GLIMPSES

This evolution was well advanced even while Zhang Tao was alive. It can be teased out of the mountain of reminiscences that the late-Ming gentry wrote for themselves and their friends. Before leaving the Ming to its defeat, I would like to go back to one voice in particular, a voice we heard in Summer (worrying over the conundrum of Huzhou silk weavers never wearing silk). It is a voice of candid opinion, though not otherwise notably distinct from the other voices of the Wanli generation. For our purposes, though, Li Le will finish this book nicely.

Li Le was born a decade or two earlier than Zhang Tao, and he came from a wealthier Jiangnan family. His home was Tongxiang county, part of the great silk-producing prefecture of Jiaxing in northeastern Zhejiang. More exactly, he lived in Qingzhen, which was Tongxiang's main commercial town on the border with Hu-zhou, the wealthy silk-marketing prefecture to the west. (Qingzhen was twinned with the equally vibrant market town of Wuzhen just across the river in Huzhou, and together they became known in the late Ming as Wuqingzhen.) Li Le "crossed the pond" in front of the county school, as the saying went for gaining *shengyuan* status, in 1550. Eighteen years later he gained his *jinshi* degree, and with the patronage of Chief Grand Secretary Xu Jie went on to a successful career as a local and capital official. Once back in Qingzhen to enjoy a long retirement three decades later, he compiled a gazetteer of the twin towns, published in 1601, and in the same year assembled the first edition of his commonplace book, *Miscellaneous Notes on Things Seen and Heard (Jianwen zaji)*. The moralistic tales and wry stories in this book include many anxious portrayals of crumbling gentry status. The Wanli era was a time when, in his opinion, the three most terrible things in the world (next to the disregard of Confucian ethics) were blocked transport routes, natural calamities, and foreigners.[15] Four of Li's stories will provide us with some last reflections on the state of the late-Ming world. Each has to do with a different class of person, each allows Li to agonize over a boundary-crossing that would not have occurred earlier in the Ming, and each leads him to a "wrong" analysis of what was going on and where the world was headed.

THE BONDSERVANT

Li Le recounts the story of a gentleman whom two officials visited one hot summer's day. The gentleman called in an old bondservant from his fields to wave a fan and cool the threesome. Turning to his guests, he didn't immediately notice that the bondservant had casually pulled up a stool behind him, which placed the servant in a

position above, and therefore superior to, his master. When Li at
last noticed, he chided the old man for failure to keep his place.

"You're getting all the breeze you want," the bondservant shot
back. "Why fuss if I happen to be sitting in the master's place and
you in the servant's?"

The tension dissolved when the master laughed at his own petty
insistence on proper places: dissolved, but not resolved, for Li Le
agrees that the bondservant was not acting according to etiquette.
Like the master in the story, Li excuses the bondservant's conduct by
allowing that outspokenness was a sign of the healthy simplicity and
frankness of "hillfolk,"[16] who in that status could be expected not
to pose any real challenge to the lords of the lowlands. Being a hill-
billy, the bondservant was deemed not to have resisted his master's
authority. This excuse was a fanciful one for the late Ming, for hillfolk could no longer be idealized as naturally virtuous residents of
an unspoiled upland arcadia. Most were marginal people who had
recently been pushed there by commercial agriculture and rising
land prices, and there they survived by engaging in such commercial
practices as planting tea, harvesting medicinal plants, gathering fuel,
and cutting timber.

Li Le's more significant "error" has to do with bondservice, not
hillfolk. Indentured service was becoming an anomaly in the commercialized environment of the late Ming, a holdover from earlier
times when relations between rural capital and labor were less contractually defined. As commerce undid the culture of rural relations
dependent on "Confucian values such as propriety, benevolence,
and loyalty,"[17] servitude was not only unprofitable to the bond-
master but a source of much trouble. It is not surprising to hear a
bondservant dressing his master down at a time when the structures
of deference that supported such labor bonds were disappearing.
Bondservice would die out in most parts of China in the early
Qing, though its disappearance inspired an anachronistic romance
of bondservant loyalty as a popular theme in gentry texts. A nice
example is the biography of a bondservant named Shining (his surname is not recorded) preserved in a Huguang gazetteer. During the
dynastic transition, Shining preserved his master's land contracts,
got him and his family to safety, found wage work to support them,
returned after the fighting to reclaim the family's property, managed
his lands, and found teachers for his son who attained *shengyuan*

status and went on to have children and grandchildren of his own.[18] No gentry master could have hoped for more, and indeed few did. (Local gazetteers also record tales of bondservants murdering their masters.)[19]

THE HIRED HAND

A fellow member of the Tongxiang gentry was traveling by boat, and one day his quilt was not put away. When one of his hired servants (not someone bound to hereditary service) took a nap, he used it by mistake. When this use was discovered, the gentleman was so distressed that he had the quilt burned.[20] Li recognizes that burning the quilt was an excessive response, given that the servant had not consciously intended to cross the boundary that such things marked between himself and his master. However, the story seems to stick in Li's mind as testimony to the ease with which important distinctions could be eradicated when vigilance was relaxed.

Li's "mistake" is once again to have made an outmoded assumption about the contemporary condition of social relations. The master-servant relationship had been altered by commercialization. Some servants were still lifelong attendants (changsui fu)[21] and therefore treated if not cordially then at least consistently by the men they worked for. By the late Ming, however, many more servants were simply wage-workers, engaged and dismissed as needed, particularly when attending a traveler. Living on short-term hire, they were not bound by the same investments of obligation, nor did they hold their employer in any deference greater than was necessary to fulfill their functions well enough to earn their wages. It was hardly surprising that the servant in the boat did not recognize the master's quilt, nor take the trouble to figure out whose it was before he pulled it over himself. If Li Le and the man's employer were "right," and from their class perspective they couldn't be anything but right, it was in believing that their place as elite required the constant patrolling of status boundaries.

STUDENTS

The third story taken from Li Le's commonplace book tells of students who went to the capital of Fujian province to the juren examination of 1579. Li was in Fuzhou at the time in his capacity as a county magistrate. He discovered to his great dismay that, when these students were not studying or writing exams, they went out into the marketplace without their hats or gowns, thereby failing to mark themselves as distinct from ordinary folk. Li expressed his dismay to the young men of his household. They assured him that there was nothing strange about such conduct. Students attending the provincial exam in Hangzhou had been acting that way—cross-dressing as commoners (or was it not cross-dressing as gentry?)—for the past twenty years, they told him.[22] Li was hardly comforted to learn that the essential distinction between lower gentry and commoner was being maintained less and less, that those who aspired to gentry status did not think it necessary to prepare their conduct to assume elite status, or that the epicenter of this erosion was up in Hangzhou. He thought back to his own youth when he sat in the county school and dared do nothing but what his teacher told him to do. That style had long ago given way—he dated the change to the early 1550s—and the junior gentry had now sunk to indiscipline.[23]

What Li Le neglects to consider in this reminiscence is the growing competition for gentry status in the late Ming. The spread of literacy was partly responsible, as more found access to the primary skill needed to aspire to gentry status. More to the point was the increasing wealth circulating in the late-Ming economy, which in turn increased the number of families that could afford to educate sons and field them as candidates in the examination system. Much of this wealth derived from landlordism, but this landlordism was profitable because it operated within a commercial economy that converted agricultural surplus into silver and guaranteed markets for those who moved into the production of industrial crops. But even merchants were training their intellectually gifted sons for the exams as an investment in their families' long-term futures. Li Le has no notion of whose sons these students were. He expects them to act like gentry, yet many were not from families in which one would have been fully trained in the gestures and public conduct that the gentry adopted to set themselves apart from those of lesser status. All that would have to be learned. After all, the self-professed point of recruiting through exams was to bring new blood into the dynasty's service, even if that rarely happened.

Li Le was not alone in judging the students of the 1570s harshly. Zhang Tao himself says as much in his essay on education in the

Sheh county gazetteer. He declares that, as of the 1570s, "most students who went into county seats to register at the county school were the children of wealthy families, and poor scholars who hoped to get a place were dismissed by the officials as though they were famine refugees." Money mattered more than it should, at least as far as Zhang was concerned. This meant that merchants' sons could infiltrate the gentry, beating their sons at their own game. Zhang concludes that, as a result, "the organic body of superior and inferior has completely disintegrated."[24] He might have concluded differently, recognizing that status will always attract wealth. But to do that would have been to deny his own vision of the way the world should be.

THE GENTRY

Our final story from Li Le's commonplace book is set among the upper gentry. When the much admired Suzhou gentleman Zhou Yong died about 1580, his relatives approached Li's patron, retired Chief Grand Secretary Xu Jie, whom we encountered at the end of Spring running a vast landlord operation in neighboring Songjiang, to script an epitaph in his own hand. There may have been professional and personal ties between the Xus and Zhous, though Xu Jie was of higher rank than Zhou Yong. The request more likely involved a financial transaction.

The epitaph declares that Zhou Yong had died in Beijing in such poverty that he didn't have enough money to cover the costs of his funeral. This trope was an old one, a standard device for declaring someone to have been so extraordinarily honest that he did not enrich himself while in office, as most other men would (and Xu Jie did himself). Li Le lived less than forty kilometers from the deceased's family and was familiar with their circumstances. He was entirely skeptical of this claim. The family was too well off (hadn't they been able to afford an epitaph by Xu Jie?) to have left its most eminent member in poverty. "The epitaph is not to be believed," Li concludes with disgust. "Filial children and grandchildren should most certainly not have to concoct this sort of story for their fathers and grandfathers."[25]

But they did, not to alter the truth (although truth may have found itself altered) but to enhance the status the Zhou family was acquiring for itself by buying an epitaph from Xu Jie. Li Le's complaint that the claim was unbelievable was to him an entirely reasonable judgment, but it was a bit beside the point. The point is that the Zhous were inescapably involved in unrelieved competition with the other gentry families of Suzhou (and even beyond, since the story reached Li Le in neighboring Zhejiang). The death of a family member was an opportunity to publicize the family's position, wealth, and uprightness, and also its connections. Such publicity had to be carried out when elite society was constituted not of fixed statuses and permanent identities, as Li Le alleged was true in the past and should still be in the present, but of ever-changing membership and shifting terms of entry. Commercial wealth had removed the fixity Li ascribed to gentry status. This is not to say that wealth and gentry status were at odds. Xu Jie not only was Suzhou's most eminent retired official but had possibly the largest investment in land in all of Jiangnan, for which he was held in awe by his peers and in contempt by the common people. He was not a merchant, but his income relied on the smooth functioning of the foodstuffs market in Suzhou to convert his tenants' produce into cash. His case would seem to suggest that the liquidity of wealth only further strengthened the social hierarchy, thus obliging individuals and families to fight that much harder to move into and hold on to positions within it. In a commercial economy, the reality of elite status is that rungs on the social ladder break easily. The Zhous could not rest content remembering their virtuous elder: they had to buy him an epitaph that went over the top.

Li Le's bed-tempered conclusion at the end of a late-Ming gentry lifetime of watching boundaries being crossed at every level of the social structure was that you can tell people to "rest content with your status and you will suffer no shame" but that doesn't mean they will act accordingly.[26] But we can read Li Le's observations in a contrary way: as evidence not of distinctions collapsing, but of distinctions being reinforced, even widening. If the bondservant usurped the master's position and felt free to speak out against him, it was a temporary moment that highlighted and reconfirmed his inferiority. If the gentleman burned the quilt his hired man had napped under, his extreme response underscored the castelike social exclusion between wage-giver and wage-earner. If students taking the provincial exams didn't bother to impersonate gentry, it was because they knew that only a few from outside the established families ever gained access to that status. And if there was an inflation in epitaphs, it only reminded the purchaser that the seller set the terms and the rules of the game.

What I wish to suggest here at the end of this account of Ming life is that, however thoroughly commerce had replaced paternalism and deference with a wage relationship, or however well some individuals managed to step over social barriers and move up the social ladder, or however deeply the successful were troubled as standards and distinctions seemed to dissolve beneath them, the class system of overlordship and deference that held the Chinese world together at the beginning of the Ming was still there at the end. It had been much transformed by commerce, as merchants found their way into the elite and gentry turned to business to augment their income. But it had not been dismantled. For all the busy mobility that communication and commerce induced within Ming society, the structural distinction between those who ruled and those who were ruled was not weakened. Individuals suffered through the crisis of 1644, but the system survived. In fact, it may have grown stronger. The patriarchs of fall held sway over the people under conditions vastly different from the circumstances that had shaped the patriarchs of winter, but still they held sway and would continue to do so into the next dynasty.

THE AUTUMN OF THE MAGISTRATE

It was ironic that Zhang Tao should have been released from political disgrace to be made magistrate of Sheh county. Suddenly the Confucian moralist was in the heart of the Huizhou beast after having spent fifteen years in forced retirement in Huangpi county. Huangpi suited his disposition, being a minor center of reformist statecraft thinking,[27] and Zhang must have imbibed some of that activist spirit in his youth and again during his exile from politics. He could not have resisted rising to the challenge he found in money-minded Sheh and building from his reaction an indictment of the failings of his age. His stridency was out of step with the attitudes that prevailed in Sheh county, but his bureaucratic superiors liked his style and promoted him quickly up to Beijing.

Zhang Tao came into his own at the end of his career when he was made governor of Liaodong. He took a righteous stand on the need to intensify border defense and refused to make concessions to buy breathing space from the Manchus. At the same time he did everything in his power to alleviate the enormous financial burdens that ordinary people had to bear to maintain a forward defense policy.[28] Once up there on the border, did Zhang ever give the Huizhou merchants and their commerce a thought? Or did he look back and think that his worries as magistrate of Sheh paled in comparison with his troubles as a governor? Did the gathering Manchu forces across the border confirm him in his old desire to recapture the lost order of Hongwu? Or did that vision of rural innocence become less persuasive under the demands of holding the border against invasion? Was the rise of the Manchus to be blamed on China having lapsed into commercial ways? Or did silver lose its power in his imagination against the looming presence of more palpable demons of treachery?

We have no answers to these questions. He edited no gazetteers in Liaodong. He did publish his memorials on border defense and military supply after he retired, and that book may have contained some hints of what he thought about commerce in his later years, but *Memorials While Governing Liaodong* (*Fu Liao zoushu*) seems not to have survived. It is not surprising that we do not have his book. Huangpi was laid waste in the interdynastic fighting and almost all texts and records in private hands were destroyed.[29] Zhang's writings disappeared with them. The Manchus would in any case have banned this book had it survived, as it must have included remarks that they would have judged disrespectful to them.

So we shall never know whether Zhang Tao changed his mind about the commercial erosion of the age in his last years as he sat at his desk putting his papers in order to the whine of summer cicadas, or as he lay on a lattice cot waiting for death. Perhaps he had not yet finished speaking to us in 1609 and in those papers was moderating his judgment on the dynasty's autumn in favor of an assessment of dangers lurking elsewhere. More likely not. He probably had nothing to say that he hadn't already voiced back when he was magistrate of Sheh, and nothing he would have wanted to change. Had he lived to see the coming of the Manchus, likely he would have said that the barbarians from the northeast were simply completing the process of China's decay that silver had started.

Other eyes saw it differently, as we have discovered. From the perspective of Ding Yaokang and Li Tingsheng, Zhang Tao was wrong to fear the lord of silver. They learned to absorb commerce into their lives without coming apart in a decadent blaze of autumnal glory, and they made good use of it to ensure that they didn't go out in that style. The Qing gentry whose ranks they joined would go on in time to worry about moral decline—elites usually do—but they would not frame that worry so explicitly as an anxiety about the moral degeneracy of trade. The crisis of 1644 was not therefore a judgment on commerce. Without commercial networks, many gentry would not have survived the dynastic transition and the gentry-merchant fusion of the Qing might never have taken place. In another way, though, perhaps Zhang was right: not to argue that commerce was evil and that China should revert to the wintry order of Emperor Hongwu, but to hope that the seasons would turn again and, in turning, reinstate the conservative values of patriarchy, hierarchy, and ruling-class justice that have sustained China's social structure well beyond the Ming.

Notes

ABBREVIATIONS

DMB   L. Carrington Goodrich and Chaoying Fang, ed., *Dictionary of Ming Biography* (New York: Columbia University Press, 1976)

TJL   Gu Yanwu, *Tianxia junguo libing shu* (Strengths and weaknesses of the various regions of the realm; 1662)

TLT   Danyizi, *Tianxia lucheng tuyin* (Illustrated guide to routes of the realm; 1626)

TSL   Huang Bian, *Tianxia shuilu lucheng* (Water and land routes of the realm; 1570)

PREFACE

Regarding Jean Nicolet, see the *Dictionary of Canadian Biography*, vol. 1 (Toronto: University of Toronto Press, 1966), p. 517.

INTRODUCTION: SEASONS OF THE MING (1609)

1. Other scholars have cited this text from Gu Yanwu (*TJL*, 9.76a–b) without tracing it to the original source, e.g., Willard Peterson, *Bitter Gourd*, p. 70; Frederic Wakeman, *The Great Enterprise*, p. 9; Harriet Zurndorfer, *Change and Continuity*, pp. 52–53.

2. The county name is normally romanized as She. I use Sheh to avoid confusion with the English feminine pronoun.

3. *Shexian zhi* (1609), 6.10b–12a.

4. Ye Chunji, *Huian zhengshu* (1672), Ye's preface, 4b.

5. *Ming shi*, vol. 19, p. 5,776.

6. Biographies of Zhang Tao appear in *Huangpi xianzhi* (1871), 8.7b–8b, and *Shexian zhi* (1771), 4.16b–17a. The mid-Ming quote is taken from the Huangzhou prefectural gazetteer of 1500; it and the two quotes from the 1591 county gazetteer and the reference to women staying indoors (also from the 1591 county gazetteer) are reprinted in *Huangpi xianzhi* (1871), 1.25b–26a.

7. *Zhongguo jin wubai nian hanlao fenbu tuji*, p. 75.

8. *Shexian zhi* (1771), 4.17a.

9. A different Zhang Tao of the same name, a Christian convert, was active in defending eastern Shandong against the Manchus in the 1620s but was executed in 1633 for failing to suppress a rebellion.

10. Wakeman, *The Great Enterprise*, pp. 59–66.

11. *Shexian zhi* (1609), "Zhaogao chenghuang biao," 1a, 1b.

12. *Shexian zhi* (1771), *shou* 1a, 1.22b.

13. Communication is the processes by which ideas are disseminated, knowledge processed, and goods and people transported. In a realm as extensive as China, the state had a strong interest in seeing that its communicative means were equal to the task of administering such a far-flung realm. Commerce refers to the trading, selling, or buying of goods. Commercialization is the transformation of trade from the collection of surplus to the circulation of commodities produced for commercial sale; it alters the distribution not just of economic resources but of social power as well, and this alteration is manifested in culture, among other spheres. Culture signifies the practices, attitudes, and discursive constructions by which action and thought are invested with meaning: it is how people do things in common with others and how they make sense of what they do. Culture is neither constant nor unitary but under constant revision as practices diversify and conflict arises.

The study of Ming commerce and its social effects was initiated in the 1950s by the Japanese historian Nishijima Sadao (his first essay on the cotton industry appears in translation in Linda Grove and Christian Daniels, *State and Society in China*) and the Chinese historian Fu Yiling. Fu was part of a school of research on Ming socioeconomy that concerned itself with detecting signs of an emerging capitalism. Only in the 1970s did Western scholarship on the Ming dynasty begin to move away from its dominant interests in institutional and intellectual history to consider socioeconomic questions. Early examples of such scholarship are Evelyn Rawski's *Agricultural Change and the Peasant Economy of South China*, published in 1972, and Michel Cartier's *Une réforme locale en Chine*, in 1973. Only in the 1980s did problems of culture begin to be addressed, though almost invariably without sustained reference to the economy. Thus far the sole attempt by a cultural historian to address cultural issues in relation to the economy is Craig Clunas's *Superfluous Things*.

14. S.A.M. Adshead, *China in World History*, p. 174.

15. Chinese Marxist scholarship on the Ming places the dynasty in the "feudal" period, which started in the fourth century B.C.E. and was suspended with the Opium War in 1840. The language of feudalism continues to be popular even after the influence of Marxism recedes from Chinese

historical analysis. The Western convention is to locate the Ming within the "late-imperial" period, beginning variously in the Song, Yuan, or Ming dynasty and ending with the fall of the Qing in 1911. In this book I avoid this designation as undertheorized and potentially of only random significance, despite my own extensive use of the term in all my previous work. "Late-imperial" is problematic in ascribing lateness to the Ming. There is also the additional difficulty of associating the Chinese realm with the European notion of "empire." The association began by analogy with the Roman empire, the only historical unit that struck Europeans as spatially equivalent. "Emperor" came into use for *huangdi* early on, but "empire" (for *tianxia*, "all under heaven") appears not to have been fixed until the mid-seventeenth century. The Italian Jesuit Matteo Ricci (1552–1610) used the term "imperatore" to designate the ruler of China but declined to speak of China as an empire, using instead "regno," a reign or realm; thus he translated *Zhongguo* as "Regno nel Mezzo," the Middle Realm (see Pasquale d'Elia, *Fonti Ricciane*, vol.1, pp. 12, 51–54). The first striking use of "imperio" appears to have been in the title of *Imperio de la China*, Faria i Sousa's 1642 Spanish translation of a book on China that Álvaro Semedo (1585–1658) wrote in Castillan in 1638. Semedo's own title speaks more modestly of the "reyno da China" (*DMB*, p. 1,158).

To write history in terms of a dynasty rather than a period defined in relation to more fundamental forces may strike some readers as hopelessly retrograde. I do not advocate the dynasty as the sole meaningful unit of analysis, but wish only to suggest that the dynasty conforms to the Chinese experience of historical time and thus seems apposite for writing cultural history, in particular the history of Chinese constructions of their cultural identity.

16. There is no convention among Ming historians as to how to periodize the dynasty. Most accept the notion of an early-Ming period shaped by the interventions of the Hongwu and Yongle emperors, and all recognize a late-Ming period that includes the Wanli era, when everything seemed to come apart. There is no agreement on a mid-Ming period, though a recent Chinese study roughly distinguishes such a period from the 1460s to the 1560s (Zheng Lihua, *Mingdai zhongqi wenxue*). After completing this book, I found that Richard Britnell in *The Commercialisation of English Society 1000–1500* also divided his period of study "into three approximately equal parts." These, he writes in the introduction, are "employed for ease of exposition, and do not represent clearly defined historical stages of development. It is tempting, when working with a structure of this kind, to shape the evidence so that each period looks different from the previous one. I have tried to counter this, where necessary, by stressing continuities between one period and the next." His comments could have been my own.

WINTER: THE FIRST CENTURY (1368–1450)

1. *Huangpi xianzhi* (1871), 1.26a; the description of the Spring Festival is not precisely dated.

2. Frederick Mote, "Chinese Society under Mongol Rule," pp. 585–86. The circumstances of the fourteenth-century plague are summarized in Adshead, *China in World History*, pp. 148–52.

3. *Chaozhou fuzhi* (1547), 5.7a, referring to a prefect appointed in 1375; *Yangzhou fuzhi* (1733), 27.2b. A magistrate on Hainan Island was praised for attracting back no less than thirteen thousand refugees on the strength of his reconstruction; *Qiongzhou fuzhi* (1619), 9b.77a.

4. The outer limit of 20 *li* for a day's travel is implied in an edict of 1394 releasing monasteries from size restrictions if they were at least 20 *li* from a settlement; *Jinling fancha zhi* (1607), 2.24a–27b. Regarding the English limit, see Britnell, *The Commercialisation of English Society*, p. 83.

5. *Ming lü jijie fuli*, 4.5b, 15.5a. A soldier exceeding the 100-*li* limit was punished for absence without leave. The fullest study of the social order Hongwu sought to legislate is Edward Farmer, *Zhu Yuanzhang and Early Ming Legislation*.

6. Brick making is described in Song Yingxing, *Tiangong kaiwu*, pp. 184–87; Sun and Sun, *T'ien-kung K'ai-wu*, pp. 137–38.

7. Xie Zhaozhe, *Wu zazu*, 3.20a–b; Jiang Zanchu, *Nanjing shihua*, pp. 105–106; regarding Hongwu's confiscation of furniture, see Zhu Yun-ming, *Ye ji*, 18b.   •

8. On the *lijia* system, see Tsurumi Naohiro, "Rural Control in the Ming Dynasty." Its integration with other spatial units is discussed in Timothy Brook, "The Spatial Structure of Ming Local Administration," pp. 29–35.

9. Near Lu Li's brick is another bearing the name of Wang Ruolin, the assistant magistrate of Fengxin county, Nanchang. As Wang (coincidentally a native of Sheh county) served in this position between 1372 and 1374, we can date that brick to those years (*Nanchang fuzhi* [1588], 14.9a). Wang's brick can't be used reliably to date Lu's, however, since many bricks in the Nanjing city wall have been moved around and recemented, possibly several times.

10. Forty per barge was the loading rate for bricks shipped to Beijing later in the dynasty, given in Song Yingxing, *Tiangong kaiwu*, p. 188; Sun and Sun, *T'ien-kung K'ai-wu*, p. 144. Song notes that the rate for private boats was half the public rate.

11. Anren county (*Raozhou fuzhi* [1873], 4.55b); Dangtu county (*Taiping fuzhi* [1903], 25.13b); Linchuan county (*Fuzhou fuzhi* [1876], 20.27b); Gan county (*Ganzhou fuzhi* [1536], 12.1b); Huangmei county (*Huangzhou fuzhi* [1500], 4.46a); Taiping county (*Ningguo fuzhi* [1919], 14.35a); Yongfeng county (*Guangxin fuzhi* [1873], 2:2.18a; *Yongfeng xianzhi* [1544], 4.19a). The Guangfu monasteries in Gan and Dangtu counties are noted in Xiancheng Ruhai, *Canxue zhijin*, 1.57b, 2.15a. The monastery in Dangtu closed down in the Yuan dynasty but was rebuilt early in the Ming. The rebuilding is dated 1380, which may mean that the monastery was still defunct when Lu Li was firing his bricks; however, 1380 is likely to have been the date the reconstruction was officially completed, suggesting that the work was going on through the 1370s.

12. *Yongfeng xianzhi* (1544), 2.1b, 3.4b, 3.8b. Yongfeng in the mid-fifteenth century had 69 *li* (Li Xian, *Da Ming yitong zhi*, 51.2a), and that was further reduced by the mid-sixteenth to 67 (*Yongfeng xianzhi*, 3.1a). Given that Yongfeng had a household population in 1391 of 16,229, the number of hundreds in the Hongwu era should have been double. It was common to reduce the number of *lijia* hundreds in the fifteenth century to lighten the county tax quota.

13. *Ming shilu*, Hongwu, 236.8a.

14. The 1381 and 1391 totals appear in Liang Fangzhong, ed., *Zhongguo lidai hukou*, p. 185, citing *Ming shilu*, Hongwu, *juan* 140 and 214. Figures from the 1393 adjusted census are given in *Ming huiyao*, pp. 937–41, reprinted in Ping-ti Ho, *Studies on the Population of China*, p. 10; also Liang Fangzhong, *Zhongguo lidai hukou*, pp. 203–204.

15. In the standard study of population in Ming-Qing China, historian Ping-ti Ho has suggested revising the 1393 figure up to 65 million, noting that some areas (in North China) and some communities (notably frontier peoples) were left out of the census; Ho, *Studies on the Population of China*, pp. 8–9, 22, 259.

16. Qiu Shusen and Wang Ting ("Yuandai hukou wenti chuyi," p. 120) derive a population in the early 1340s of 90 million by multiplying the official household total of 19.8 million by a factor of 4.5 (average mouths per household). This reconstruction has been criticized by Mote, "Chinese Society under Mongol Rule," p. 622, n. 8.

The official figures for 1381 and 1393 imply an average size of household that suggests consistent nonregistration of family members. According to the 1393 data, the average household had 5.68 members, yet early- to mid-Ming local gazetteers consistently reveal larger households. Changyuan county, North Zhili, reported just over 6 mouths per household in 1442, rising to just under 9 in 1492, with another slight increase over the following decade (*Changyuan xianzhi* [1541], 1.17a). In Henan province, Lanyang county registered 7 mouths per household in 1412, rising to 9 by 1482 (*Lanyang xianzhi* [1545], 2.8b). Southwest of Lanyang, Lushan county had a household average of 10 members in 1412, rising to 11 in 1502 (*Lushan xianzhi* [1552], 2.13b–15a). For similar ratios in central Henan in 1492, see *Xuzhou zhi* (1540), 3.7b–8a. To modestly correct for the underreporting of household members, I have taken the average household size from the censuses in the Chenghua era (covering enumerations for 1464 to 1486) of 6.82, and use that, rather than 5.68, as the factor to estimate a total population of 75 million. Censuses underreported children, especially female children. In a rare case of breakdown by age, *Funing zhouzhi* (1593), 7.1b, reports that of the 11,245 males registered in 1391, 1,321 were "not adults" (*bu cheng ding*), a ratio of 1 boy to 7.5 adults. The ratio for females is even more skewed: only 50 of the 7,120 females registered were "small" (*xiao*), one girl for every 141 women.

17. *Ming shi*, p. 1,881. A longer extract from Xuande's lecture appears in *Ming huiyao*, p. 942. Xuande was referring obliquely to his grandfather, the Yongle emperor, whose glorious excesses (such as sending imperial

armadas into the Indian Ocean) he desired to bring under control for fiscal reasons.

18. Zhou Chen, "Yu xingzai hubu zhugong shu," 2.11a.

19. Official census statistics register this shift. Provincial returns for 1393 indicate that 35 percent of all Chinese lived in the eastern provinces of South Zhili and Zhejiang, whereas a century later these two provinces accounted for only 25 percent of the population. Over the same period, the five north-central provinces (North Zhili, Shandong, Shanxi, Henan, and Shaanxi) increased their share from 26 percent to 39 percent. In other words, people were moving out of more heavily populated regions into the north and northwest.

20. Liang Fangzhong, *Zhongguo lidai hukou,* p. 185; also Mote, "Chinese Society under Mongol Rule," pp. 618–19. Mark Elvin has argued from the 1290 data that south China had filled to demographic capacity by this time, forcing a subsequent rebound to dry-land farming in the north. He suggests that this rebound signaled a demographic limit on China's economic development and induced "an alteration in the causal patterns at work over the long run" (*The Pattern of the Chinese Past,* p. 203). Elvin's argument requires three assumptions: that the demographic decline in the Yuan was real, that it was an outcome of pre-Yuan trends, and that the subsequent expansion of population into the northern and western frontiers in the Ming and Qing signifies what he calls "relative stagnation." All three assumptions are problematic. The 1290 census exaggerates demographic decline in north China inasmuch as soldiers and those attached in bondage to Mongol appanages were not enumerated. Further, what decline there was may be better attributed to the particular conditions of Mongol occupation than taken as evidence of long-term secular change. Finally, one could interpret the post-Yuan peopling of the frontiers as an indication that growth was continuing. Admittedly, the dwindling of free space meant that this growth was at a slower rate than in the Song, but Elvin's implied involutionary argument may obscure the extent of creative adaptation of labor to resources that enabled the Ming and Qing dynasties to sustain productive economies.

21. Some of the forced relocations are listed in *Ming huiyao,* pp. 944–46. The 1364 order was imposed on wealthy households of Suzhou prefecture to weaken the base of Zhu Yuanzhang's rival, Zhang Shicheng. The 1389 relocation to Fengyang, fourteen years after Zhu had given up his dream of making it his capital, was purely punitive, directed against families the emperor felt were resisting his rule. In 1391 an estimated 45,000 wealthy households were moved from northern Zhejiang to Nanjing as wealthy hostages; Ping-ti Ho, *Studies on the Population of China,* p. 137.

22. Xu Shiduan, *Ming shilu leizuan: funü shiliao juan,* pp. 6, 9. Difficulties associated with military widowhood, such as fear of being without financial support, led some to commit suicide; see ibid., p. 14.

23. The first two forced relocations to Beijing in 1370–71 moved 70,000 households in from north of the Great Wall to weaken the Mongols' economic base. In 1403–1405, over 50,000 households were moved from

Jiangnan. Through the next decade, close to a quarter of a million soldiers and their families were moved as well (Edward Dreyer, *Early Ming China*, pp. 190–91). Conscripted laborers were also sent to build the new capital. Some remained to settle there as peasants (*Hengyue zhi* [1612], 2.1b); others disappeared (*Ming shi*, p. 4,436).

To coastal North Zhili, people were moved voluntarily from neighboring Shandong province, the Suzhou region, Fujian and Guangdong in the south, and southern Huguang; *Tianjin fuzhi* (1899), 26.1a. To southwestern North Zhili and northern Henan, most migrants came from Shanxi, which had escaped the dynastic war. The first relocations, conducted by the Ministry of Revenue in 1369 and 1370, moved residents a short distance from Hongdong and Zezhou in southern Shanxi to Mengxian and Jixian in northern Henan. The flow out of Hongdong county was so sustained that a special relocation office was set up adjacent to a prominent Buddhist monastery to process those who wished to leave. Migrants were issued with ministry passes permitting them to move to specific locations, designated "civilian colonies," in Henan, North Zhili, and Shandong, and could relocate only between the ninth and eleventh months; Wang Xingya, "Mingchu qian Shanxi min dao Henan kaoshu." For the last relocation of southern Shanxi peasants in the early Yongle era, see Peter Seybolt, *Throwing the Emperor from His Horse*, pp. 1–2.

The relocations were not always successful. The colonists often found themselves given poor land and could not make a go of it. One northern gazetteer admits that "all colony land is bare and thin"; *Hejian fuzhi* (1540), 8.21a. Two centuries later, an elderly resident of Wei county at the south end of North Zhili told Gu Yanwu that in most counties in the region, about 30 percent of the people were migrants' descendants; Yin Junke, "Mingdai Beijing jiaoqu cunluo de fazhan." *Baoding fuzhi* (1607), 16, 6b, reports a similar percentage for the second decade of the fifteenth century.

24. *Da Ming huidian*, 104.5a, citing an edict of 1433.

25. On the continuing illegal movement of people, see *Ming huiyao*, pp. 946–47; Huang Miantang, *Mingshi guanjian*, pp. 376–77.

26. *Ming shi*, p. 4,436.

27. "In recent years," declared the Zhengtong emperor, "officials have been unsuccessful in encouraging agriculture, so cultivators have decreased and vagrants increased"; quoted in Chen Baoliang, *Zhongguo liumang shi*, p. 156.

28. *Da Ming huidian*, 149.8a.

29. Zhu Yunming, *Ye ji*, 10a.

30. Xu Shiduan, *Ming shilu leizuan: funü shiliao juan*, p. 15. Between 1368 and 1372, Hongwu imposed a series of sartorial regulations for women of the imperial family, based on what were loosely described as "Tang and Song styles"; ibid., p. 826. See also *Ming shi*, pp. 1,641–46.

31. Zhu Yunming, *Ye ji*, 11a.

32. Zhu Yuanzhang, *Ming taizu ji*, p. 305; *Ming shi*, p. 3,987.

33. *Hejian fuzhi* (1540), 7.7a.

34. E.g., *Ming shi,* pp. 7,189, 7,191, 7,193, 7,215. Impeachment was a difficult business. When commoners in Xiuning county criticized magistrate Zhou Decheng (1339–91), thirty members of the county elite traveled to Nanjing to intercede successfully at court on his behalf; Zurndorfer, *Change and Continuity,* pp. 89–90.

35. For examples of memorials submitted by the director, see Xu Shiduan, *Ming shilu leizuan: funü shiliao juan,* pp. 684–87.

36. Quoted in Yin Yungong, *Zhongguo Mingdai xinwen chuanbo shi,* p. 28.

37. For example, when the great painter Dong Qichang was appointed to edit the Veritable Records of the Taichang reign, he went to Nanjing in 1622 to consult the gazette, copies of which he found preserved in the Office of the Henan Circuit; *Rongtai ji,* 5.50a. The compiling of the Veritable Records has been a two-edged legacy for historians, for although the process produced carefully checked records of court activities, each editing ended with the burning of all the notes and court records that had been consulted. For a Ming scholar's distressed reaction to this destruction of original documents, see Zheng Xiao, *Jin yan,* p. 56.

38. Didier Gazagnadou, *La poste à relais,* provides a detailed study of the Yuan courier service and its influence on Europe.

39. These figures are given in Shen Dingping, "Mingdai yidi de shezhi," p. 78; see also Su Tongbing, *Mingdai yidi zhidu,* p. 15. As of 1587, when the *Da Ming huidian* was published, the number of stations had been reduced to 1,036.

40. The passages cited come from Hafiz Abru, *A Persian Embassy to China,* pp. 27–28, 33–36, 43–44, 49. Distances have been taken from *TSL,* pp. 23, 82–83, 127–32.

41. *Da Ming huidian,* 149. 11b.

42. On the last morning the party covered "four to five farsangs." The Persian diarist estimated that one side of the Beijing city wall measured one "farsang." Assuming he was referring to the north or south wall, each of which was roughly 7 kilometers in length, four to five farsangs indicates a distance of about 30 kilometers.

43. Abru, *A Persian Embassy to China,* pp. 118–19. The diary says the envoys' bags were searched at Ping'an, a place I cannot positively identify. There was a Song fort of that name on the road between Ganzhou and Xiaozhou, but that location does not fit well into the diary's chronology. The diarist records only that the embassy arrived at Ping'an a month and a half after leaving Beijing, and that "all the officials and grandees of the town did honour to the envoys and came out to receive them. It was a very fine and orderly town." Possibly Xi'an, or its county name of Changan, has been mistranscribed.

44. The passages quoted may be found in John Meskill, *Ch'oe Pu's Diary,* pp. 58, 66–69, 88, 111, 113, 135, 153–57. Distances have been calculated from *TSL,* pp. 1–2, 100–101; and *TLT,* pp. 395–97, 484–85.

45. *Ming lü jijie fuli,* 17.8b–10a.

46. This chart is reproduced in Huang, *A Complete Book,* p. 86.

47. Quoted from *The Historie of the great and mightie kingdome of China*, the 1588 translation of Gonzáles de Mendoza's *Historia de las cosas más notables, ritos y costumbres del gran Reyno de la China*, in C.R. Boxer, *South China in the Sixteenth Century*, p.lxxxvi.

48. *Wujiang xianzhi* (1561), 1.10b.

49. Fu Yiling, *Mingdai Jiangnan shimin jingji shitan*, p. 42, citing a text from the Zhengde era.

50. Ray Huang, *Taxation and Governmental Finance*, p. 50; *Nanjing hubu zhi* (1550), 10.1a–1b. The system is thoroughly examined in Hoshi, *The Ming Grain Tribute System*.

51. Chen Jian, *Huang Ming congxin lu* (1620), 18.18b.

52. Ray Huang, *Taxation and Governmental Finance*, pp. 53–56. For the reference to Gu Yanwu (*TJL* 15.9a), see p. 336, n. 48.

53. Yu Xiangdou, *Wanyong zhengzong*, 2.40a–b. For another song of the same route, see *TLT*, pp. 397–98.

54. This dangerous passage was corrected when a lock was built there at the end of the fifteenth century; see Yang Zhengtai, "Ming-Qing Linqing de shengshuai," p. 17.

55. André and Baslez, *Voyager dans l'antiquité*, p. 400. The distance of a Roman relay was 9 to 10 kilometers, slightly longer than the standard Chinese distance between post houses (6 kilometers).

56. Xu Shiduan, *Ming shilu leizuan: funü shiliao juan*, p. 685.

57. E.g., Royal Ontario Museum 909.11.1.

58. Song Yingxing, *Tiangong kaiwu*, p. 253, 259–60; Sun and Sun, *T'ien-kung K'ai-wu*, pp. 173, 180, 182–84; Ray Huang, *Taxation and Governmental Finance*, p. 57.

59. *Ming shi*, p. 1922.

60. Song Yingxing, *Tiangong kaiwu*, pp. 234–50; Sun and Sun, *T'ien-kung K'ai-wu*, pp. 172–78; Joseph Needham, *Science and Civilisation in China* 4:3, pp. 411–12. For comparison's sake, a Yuan handbook on the Yellow River gives rates of canal travel as 35 to 50 *li* per day (depending on their burden) upstream, and 100 to 200 *li* downstream; Shiba Yoshinobu, *Commerce and Society in Sung China*, p. 35.

61. Zheng Ruozeng, "Taihu tu," quoted in *TJL*, 4.3a–b.

62. *TLT*, p. 385.

63. Michael Marmé, "Heaven on Earth," p. 31.

64. Kathryn Liscomb, *Learning from Mount Hua*, pp. 37, 71; regarding writing ahead, see p. 12.

65. C.R. Boxer, *The Great Ship from Amacon*, p. 195.

66. The resolution of marriage disputes at a *shenming ting* is mentioned in *Hejian fuzhi* (1540), 4.5b.

67. Gu Yanwu, *Rizhi lu jishi*, 8.11a.

68. *Da Ming huidian*, 177.1.

69. Valerie Hansen, *Negotiating Daily Life*, p. 146. For a study of land contracts from the mid-Ming forward, see Yang Guozhen, *Ming-Qing tudi qiyue wenshu yanjiu*.

70. *Ming-Qing Huizhou shehui jingji ziliao congbian*, vol. 2, p. 19. This

is the main collection of published land contracts from Huizhou, of which 685 date from the Ming. Another 11 contracts are published in Fu Yiling, *Ming-Qing shehui jingji shi lunwen ji,* pp. 243–48. See also Valerie Hansen, *Negotiating Daily Life,* pp. 109–11, regarding contracts from Huizhou prefecture.

71. *Huizhou fuzhi* (1542), 11.28b.

72. *Qiongzhou fuzhi* (1619), 10b.93b.

73. Zhu Yunming, *Ye ji,* 12a.

74. The Yongle emperor posited a connection between wealth and books when he observed in 1406 that "few gentry or commoner families have the extra resources" to collect books (*Ming shi,* p. 2,343). The biographer of a 1391 *jinshi* from Hangzhou makes the same connection when he notes that "the man's family was rich and he collected books"; so too does the biographer of another Hangzhou bibliophile who, "when he died, had no wealth set aside, but the books he had collected amounted to several thousand *juan,*" (Wu Han, *Jiang Zhe cangshujia shilüe,* pp. 9, 50).

75. Song Lian, "Song Dongyang Ma sheng xu," *Song xueshi wenji, juan* 73, quoted in Ōki Yasashi, "Minmatsu Kōnan ni okeru shuppan," p. 13.

76. Zhu Yunming, *Ye ji,* 10a.

77. *Nanjing hubu zhi* (1550), 12.39a.

78. Zhu Fengji, *Mumin xinjian,* 1.15a; I am grateful to Thomas Nimick for sharing this text with me.

79. *Nanjing hubu zhi* (1550), 5.15b.

80. *Nanchang fuzhi* (1588), 4.21b.

81. Li Yue, *Jianwen zaji,* 5.63b.

82. *Qiongzhou fuzhi* (1619), 5.66a.

83. Brook, "Censorship in Eighteenth-Century China," pp. 179–80.

84. E.g., in order of their production, *Da Ming ling* [The Ming statutes] (1368), *Da Ming jili* [Collected rites of the Ming dynasty], *Xiangang shilei* [Regulations for the censorial system] (1371), *Da Ming Lü* [The Ming code] (published 1373–74 and reissued in a revised standard edition in 1397), *Hongwu zhengyun* [Correct rhymes of the Hongwu era], *Zhusi zhizhang* [Handbook of government posts] (1393).

85. Xie Yingfang, *Guichao gao,* 8.13a, as translated (with one minor emendation) in John Langlois, "The Hung-wu Reign," p. 156. On early-Ming imperial publishing, see Brook, "Edifying Knowledge," pp. 103–7.

86. *Baoding fuzhi* (1607), 16.8a, 9a.

87. Quoted in *Nanchang fuzhi* (1588), 3.28b, 29b.

88. Shiba, *Commerce and Society in Sung China,* p. 37.

89. *Ming lü jijie fuli,* 10.1a–10b; *Da Ming huidian,* 37.28b ff; see also Su Gengsheng, "Mingchu de shangzheng yu shangshui," p. 436.

90. Zhu Fengji, *Mumin xinjian,* 1.6a.

91. Xu Shiduan, *Ming shilu leizuan: funü shiliao juan,* p. 680. Regarding the destruction of documents, see *Ming lü jijie fuli,* 3.4b.

92. William Atwell, "International Bullion Flows," pp. 76–77.

93. *Ming shi,* p. 1,649.

94. Quoted in *Yangzhou fuzhi* (1733), 10.10a.

95. *Kuaiji xianzhi* (1575), quoted in So, *Japanese Piracy in Ming China*, p. 123.

96. Abru, *A Persian Embassy to China*, p. 62.

97. The preparedness granary system is outlined in Gu Ying, "Mingdai yubeicang jiliang wenti chutan."

98. *Ming shilu*, Xuanzong, *juan* 69, quoted in Zheng Hesheng and Zheng Yijun, *Zheng He xia xiyang ziliao huibian*, vol. 1, p. 221.

99. Li Weizhen, *Dabi shanfang ji*, juan 15; *Lu'an fuzhi* (1659), juan 1; both quoted in Zhang Zhengming and Xue Huilin, *Ming-Qing Jinshang ziliao xuanbian*, pp. 2, 10.

100. *Yangzhou fuzhi* (1733), 34.7b, 8a.

101. Translated in Klaas Ruitenbeek, *Carpentry and Building*, p. 301.

102. *Ming huiyao*, p. 340. The comment appears in the context of reminding the people not to dress above their station.

103. Zhu Fengji, *Mumin xinjian* (1404; 1852), 1.18a.

104. In his *Proclamation to the People*, Zhu Yuanzhang observed that the four categories belong to the time of the sage-rulers Yao and Shun, and that two categories of Buddhist monks and Daoist priests can now be added. Collected in Zhang Lu, ed., *Huang Ming zhishu*, 10.12b–13a.

105. Both passages are reprinted in *Shanxi tongzhi* (1682), 26.4a, 5b.

106. *Hongwu jingcheng tuzhi* (1395), 49b–51a.

107. Zheng Lihua, *Mingdai zhongqi wenxue*, p. 190; Marmé, "Heaven on Earth," p. 30.

108. Re birch sheaths, see Percival David, *Chinese Connoisseurship*, p. 153.

109. In the 1450s one could get painting-quality silk in both Beijing and Nanjing; Wang Zuo's commentary translated in ibid., p. 18.

110. Wang Zuo's commentary translated in ibid., p. 144.

111. E.g., David, *Chinese Connoisseurship*, p. 142, where Cao disparages new Cizhou porcelains.

112. E.g., Wang names three contemporary brush-makers in ibid., pp. 145, 203, 209.

113. Ibid., p. 137.

114. Ibid., p. 148.

115. Clunas, *Superfluous Things*, pp. 12–13.

116. David, *Chinese Connoisseurship*, pp. 143, 150.

117. Ibid., pp. 5, 143, 161–62.

118. *Ming shi*, p. 1,880.

119. Quoted in Wei Qingyuan, *Mingdai huangce zhidu*, p. 202.

120. Zhu Tingli, *Yanzheng zhi*, 7.1b.

121. Xu Shiduan, *Ming shilu leizuan: funü shiliao juan*, p. 8, from an entry dated 15 October 1371.

122. *Ming huiyao*, p. 340.

123. Denis Twitchett and Tilemann Grimm, "The Cheng-t'ung, Ching-t'ai, and T'ien-shun Reigns," pp. 309–12. This source leaves out a large famine in Fujian in the 1440s; see *Anxi xianzhi* (1552), 3.15a.

124. James Tong, *Disorder under Heaven*, pp. 45–49.

125. Ray Huang, *Taxation and Governmental Finance*, p. 52.
126. *Da Ming huidian*, 37.20b.
127. This argument, broached by censors shortly after Liu's death, is repeated in *Yanping fuzhi* (1526), 23.16a. Liu's descendants were duly punished.
128. *Huian xianzhi* (1530), 6.12a, where Deng's rebels are referred to as "Sha county bandits."
129. *Huian xianzhi* (1530), 4.9a, reports that extra defenses were mounted in the hilly areas of the county against roving remnants of bands from Sha county.
130. *Gutian xianzhi* (1606), 14.19a.
131. Tanaka, "Popular Uprisings," pp. 201–204.

SPRING: THE MIDDLE CENTURY (1450–1550)

1. Ye Sheng, *Shuidong riji*, 1.3b.
2. Ray Huang, *Taxation and Governmental Finance*, pp. 112–18. On courier silver, see also Hoshi Ayao, *Min Shin jidai kōtsū shi kenkyū*, ch. 4. Courier silver proved vulnerable to appropriation for other purposes. The beginning of its erosion may be dated to 1558, when the emperor approved a memorial requesting a portion of local funds set aside for maintaining the courier service be forwarded to the Ministry of Revenue to pay for military supplies. This expedient was canceled five years later, yet the damage had already been done; see Su Tongbing, *Mingdai yidi zhidu*, pp. 426–29. See also pp. 429–34 regarding further reductions in the funds available for the courier service in the Wanli era.
3. The transition from government by intervention and decree to administration by routine and formalism in the mid-fifteenth century is noted in Nimick, "The County, the Magistrate, and the Yamen," p. 5.
4. Gu Yanwu, *Rizhi lu jishi*, 8.11a, regarding an edict of 1453; Yu Ruwei, *Huangzheng yaolan* (1589), 4.66b, regarding a memorial of 1529.
5. *TSL*, p. 255; *Wuhu xianzhi* (1919), 10.2b, 8.1a.
6. *Taiping fuzhi* (1903), 26.18b.
7. E.g., in Qiongzhou, Guangdong, bridge building (which often amounted to the replacement of wooden bridges with stone) was strong between 1466 and 1475: *Qiongzhou fuzhi* (1619), 4.83b ff; regarding the flooding in 1465, see 12.3b. Elsewhere in south China, bridge building flourished slightly later. To cite some prefectural examples at random: in Shaowu, Fujian, from 1481 to 1505 (*Shaowu fuzhi* [1543], 6.19b–45b); in neighboring Yanping, from 1489 to 1499 (*Yanping fuzhi* [1526], 3.17b–25a); in Jiujiang, Jiangxi, between 1487 and 1504 (*Jiujiang fuzhi* [1527], 2.27b–34a). On bridge building in southern Fujian in the mid-Ming, see Lin Renchuan, *Mingmo Qingchu siren haishang maoyi*, pp. 143–44; Susan Canfield, "Bridge Construction and Repair," pp. 34–35. By contrast, bridge building and repair in north China seems to have occurred later and become widespread only after the turn of the sixteenth century. The provincial gazetteer for Shanxi records much bridge building at the turn of the

sixteenth century, and even more in the second quarter of the sixteenth century; *Shanxi tongzhi* (1682), *juan* 5a–5b. In North Zhili, however, the pattern of bridge building corresponds more to trends in south China, perhaps because of its links to the Grand Canal system; e.g., *Daming fuzhi* (1506), 2.21a–25b.

8. In Yanping prefecture, Fujian, magistrates and local notables shared bridge building in the early Ming, whereas in the mid-Ming locally funded bridges outnumbered magisterially funded bridges five to one; *Yanping fuzhi* (1526), 14.51a–54a.

9. *Huian xianzhi* (1530), 3.12b–13a. Half a century later, another Huian native, Guo Zaoqing, makes the same connection between foreign trade and infrastructural investment in Quanzhou more generally in *Ming jingshi wenbian*, 26.11b.

10. Quoted in Boxer, *South China in the Sixteenth Century*, p. lvii, n. 5; p. 7.

11. Brook, "Edifying Knowledge," pp. 112–14.

12. *Wuhu xianzhi* (1919), 44.6b. The library was constructed in 1500.

13. See Brook, *Geographical Sources of Ming-Qing History*, pp. 50–51, on the dating of institutional and topographical gazetteers.

14. Zhuang Weifeng et al., *Zhongguo difangzhi lianhe mulu*, p. 463.

15. Atwell, "International Bullion Flows," p. 76.

16. *Wuhu xianzhi* (1919), 26.1a, 57.2b. The imagery is repeated for the flood of 1608: "Boats passed over dry land, and river fish swam into the markets."

17. *Huguang tujing zhishu* (1522), 2: *wen*: 20a.

18. *Nanchang fuzhi* (1588), 3.29a, quoting the Hongzhi-era prefectural gazetteer; the distance from Wuhu is taken from *TSL*, p. 47.

19. Qiu Jun, "Jiangyou min qian Jing Hu yi" [On Jiangxi people migrating into Huguang], anthologized in *Ming jingshi wenbian*, 72.9a.

20. *Ming huiyao*, p. 943.

21. Ping-ti Ho concluded that the 1542 figure seriously undercounts the actual population and proposed that population grew between 1393 and 1542 by 73 percent, an annual growth rate of 0.34 percent, which was the rate of growth in the five northern provinces; Ho, *Studies on the Population of China*, p. 263. If we apply this rate to my higher estimate of 75 million for 1393, China's population in the mid-sixteenth century was approaching 130 million. The actual total may have been somewhat less, due to natural disasters in east and northeast China in the 1530s and 1540s.

22. Ye Chunji, *Huian zhengshu* (1573, 1672), 3.1b, 5.9b, 22a, 6.10a.

23. *Linju xianzhi* (1552), 1.5b–6a.

24. Gu Yingtai, *Mingshi jishi benmo*, *juan* 38, quoted in Fu Yiling, *Ming-Qing fengjian tudi suoyouzhi lungang*, p. 110.

25. Ping-ti Ho, *Studies on the Population of China*, pp. 172–75.

26. This is mentioned in the biography of an official assigned to Huguang in 1532, in *Qiongshan xianzhi* (1917), 24.21b.

27. Chün-fang Yü, *The Renewal of Buddhism in China*, p. 149; *Da Ming huidian*, pp. 2272, 2273.

28. *TJL*, 25.25b.

29. *Ming huiyao*, pp. 947–48.

30. E.g., *Mianyang zhi* (1531), 9.18a; *Lushan xianzhi* (1552), 2.15b; *Qiongzhou fuzhi* (1619), 9b.91a.

31. *Daming fuzhi* (1506), 3.20b–27b.

32. *Jintan xianzhi* (1921), 1.3b, quoting from a Zhengde-era gazetteer.

33. *Xuzhou zhi* (1540), 6.36b.

34. The *Supplement* can be found in many catalogs of ministry and school libraries in the sixteenth century: e.g., *Nanjing hubu zhi* (1550), *yinyong shumu*, 1b; *Yanping fuzhi* (1526), 12.8a; *Huian xianzhi* (1530), 9.10b; *Hejian fuzhi* (1540), 28.58b; *Ruijin xianzhi* (1542), 3.13a; *Cili xianzhi* (1574), 11.14b.

35. Qiu Jun, *Daxue yanyi bu*, 25.1b–28b; Qiu's economic thought is discussed briefly in Pierre-Étienne Will and R. Bin Wong, *Nourish the People*, pp. 11–13.

36. Qiu Jun, *Daxue yanyi bu*, 28.6b.

37. Ibid., 25.13b.

38. Ibid., 25.16b.

39. Ibid., 25.19b.

40. Cf. Mote, "The Ch'eng-hua and Hung-chih Reigns," p. 355. In their brief biography of Qiu Jun, Wu Jihua and Ray Huang puzzle over why so few of the recommendations in the *Supplement to "Expositions on the Great Learning"* were made policy once he was appointed to the Grand Secretariat in 1491; *DMB*, p. 250.

41. Pan Huang, "Fu jigu shu," anthologized in *Ming jingshi wenbian* 197:24a–25b.

42. See *Huian xianzhi* (1530), 8.5a; also *Hengzhou fuzhi* (1536), 4.7a–8a; *Changde fuzhi* (1538), 4.16a, 25a.

43. Preparedness granaries existed in only two of Jiujiang's five counties, one of them founded as recently as 1523; *Jiujiang fuzhi* (1527), 8.17b–19b. Huian county had two preparedness granaries dating from 1391, but neither was stocking grain in the 1520s; *Huian xianzhi* (1530), 8.5a.

44. Yu Ruwei, *Huangzheng yaolan* (1589), 4.68a.

45. E.g., *Lushan xianzhi* (1552), 4.19b–22a.

46. *Lushan xianzhi* (1552), 10.2b–4a.

47. Wang Wenlu, "Yu Changsong Wei hou shu" [Letter to Master Wei of Changsong], in his *Bailing xueshan*, 2.11b.

48. *Haiyan xianzhi* (1876), 13.5a.

49. *Wuxi Jinkui xianzhi* (1881), 31.9a.

50. E.g., *Tongxiang xianzhi* (1887), 20.5a.

51. *Shang tianzhu jiangsi zhi* (1897), 1.9a–b.

52. *Tianzhu shanzhi* (1875), 12.5b. The same source also attributes to Buddhist influence the good conduct of Shandong troops stationed outside Hangzhou to protect the area from attack in 1559 (8.64a). Not all Hangzhou monasteries were so fortunate, e.g., *Shengguo sizhi* (1881), 12b.

53. *Hejian fuzhi* (1540), 10.16b–17a.

54. Morris Rossabi, "The Tea and Horse Trade," p. 152.

55. Zheng Lihua, *Mingdai zhongqi wenxue*, p. 177, quoting Lu Shen.

56. *TLT*, p. 356.

57. *Ming shi*, p. 5451; Ray Huang, "Fiscal Administration during the Ming Dynasty," pp. 74–75.

58. An exception to both courses was the official appointed to oversee the levy of commercial taxes in Beijing in 1556. When he discovered that his predecessor had collected 2,000 taels over annual customary receipts and pocketed the take, he decided to continue collecting at the higher rate but turn the 2,000 taels over to the state. He adopted the same practice when posted to the same job in Yangzhou, where he collected 1,000 taels above quota and forwarded that amount to the Ministry of Revenue; *Yanshan xianzhi* (1868), 14.41b–42a.

59. *Hanyang fuzhi* (1546), 3.36a–37a.

60. *TSL*, p. 204; *TLT*, p. 373. The shop and stall tax was not completely repealed, and early-Qing magistrates continued to agitate against it as a penalty on the poor; see Huang Liu-hung, *A Complete Book Concerning Happiness and Benevolence*, p. 215.

61. *Quanzhou fuzhi* (1763), 15.28a.

62. *Mianyang zhi* (1531), 7.8b.

63. *Songjiang fuzhi* (1630), 39.1a; the route is described in *TSL*, p. 11.

64. *Huian xianzhi* (1530), 4.1b, 3a.

65. *Shanghai xianzhi* (1524), 1.11a.

66. *Guangzhou zhi* (1660), 12.50b.

67. *Shaowu fuzhi* (1543), 2.44a.

68. *Guangshan xianzhi* (1556), 1.29b–30; see also 4.3b.

69. *Shaowu fuzhi* (19543), 2.45b.

70. *Jiujiang fuzhi* (1527), 1.19b.

71. Marmé, "Heaven on Earth," p. 34.

72. *Zhenze xianzhi* (1746), *juan* 25, quoted in Fan Shuzhi, "Mingdai Zhejiang shizhen fenbu yu jiegou," p. 186.

73. Nishijima, "The Formation of the Early Chinese Cotton Industry."

74. E.g., in Henan county, cotton was introduced by inmigrants early in the sixteenth century to meet tax burdens: "Since the Hongzhi era, migrants are the majority. They grow cotton and fiber-bearing beans between the fields, and most rely on this to pay their labor service"; *Guangshan xianzhi* (1556), 1.29a.

75. *Songjiang fuzhi* (1512), 4.11b, quoted in Nishijima, "The Formation of the Early Chinese Cotton Industry," p. 55.

76. Rawski, *Agricultural Change and the Peasant Economy*, pp. 47, 56.

77. *Chongde xianzhi* (1611), *juan* 2, quoted in Chen Xuewen, *Zhongguo fengjian wanqi de shangpin jingji*, pp. 14, 16–17. For a similar story of dumping silkworms when the supply of mulberry leaves could not meet demand, see *Tongxiang xianzhi* (1886), 20b. 2a.

78. *Guangdong tongzhi* (1561), quoted in *Qiongshan xianzhi* (1917), 2.16b. The provincial gazetteer was edited by Huang Zuo (1490–1566).

79. *Hejian fuzhi* (1540), 7.3b–4a.

80. Shen Qi, *Wujiang shuikao zengyi* (1734), 5.13a–b, quoting Zhu Gun (js. 1502).

81. *Xuanfu zhenzhi* (1561), *juan* 20, prefacing this description with "in earlier years;" quoted in Zhang Zhengming and Xue Huilin, *Ming-Qing Jinshang ziliao xuanbian*, p. 61.

82. E.g., Zhu Guozhen, *Yongchuang xiaopin, juan* 17, quoted in Zhang Zhengming and Xue Huilin, *Ming-Qing Jinshang ziliao xuanbian*, p. 116.

83. *Mianyang zhi* (1531), 6.12a.

84. *Wujiang zhi* (1488), 5.26b; *Wujiang xianzhi* (1561), 1.10b; *Shanghai zhi* (1504), 1.4b; *Shanghai xianzhi* (1524), 1.10b. For similar claims of unwillingness to undertake long-distance travel recorded in other pre-Jiajing gazetteers from South Zhili, see *Jiangnan tongzhi* (1736), 19.3a–5a.

85. Quoted from an entry in the *Veritable Records*, dated 10 May 1524, in So, *Japanese Piracy in Ming China*, p. 65.

86. *Da Ming huidian* 164.24a–b, 167.5b. I am grateful to Sun Daigang for these references.

87. Such an impersonation is described in the Veritable Records for 1471, cited in Xu Shiduan, *Ming shilu leizuan: funü shiliao juan*, p. 746.

88. *Longxi xianzhi* (1535), 8.36a. The burning of Zheng He's charts is mentioned in Ray Huang, *China: A Macro History*, p. 156; the minister was Liu Daxia (1437–1516).

89. Regarding charts in circulation, "manuscript rutters" are mentioned in Martín da Rada's 1575 account of China (Boxer, *South China in the Sixteenth Century*, p. 294). China's first printed rutter of 1537, *Duhai fangcheng* [The route for crossing the ocean], was based in part on a Zheng He text but also includes the northern coastal route up to Liaodong. The compiler, an idiosyncratic scholar named Wu Pu, was an associate of the powerful merchant-official Lin Xiyuan (ca. 1480–ca. 1560) whose defiance of the Jiajing maritime ban—and whose wealth—were legendary. Gu Yanwu included the *Duhai fangcheng* compass bearings to Japan in *TJL*, 34.59a–60b. This rutter continued to be used and modified by Fujian navigators beyond the mid-Ming. A handwritten copy acquired by a Jesuit was presented to Archbishop Laud in 1639 and deposited in the Bodleian Library at Oxford (Tian Rukang, "*Duhai fangcheng*," pp. 302–304). Tian Rukang notes for the purpose of comparison that the first printed European rutter appeared in the first decade of the sixteenth century.

90. Zhang Xie, *Dongxi yang kao*, p. 131.

91. Anthony Reid, *Southeast Asia in the Age of Commerce*, vol. 2, pp. 4–5, 12. Adshead, *China in World History*, p. 199, paints a rather different picture of severe decline for Chinese merchants after the 1430s and the Zheng He expeditions. He says that it is "hard to resist the conclusion" that those very expeditions were responsible for "killing, or at least forcing into smaller dimension, the private enterprise on which it was based," an interpretation I do not share. He does note, however, that Bengali and Persian silks were outcompeting Chinese silks in the Indian Ocean, which in turn weakened Chinese merchants' position in the spice trade.

92. *Longxi xianzhi* (1535), 1.26b.

93. Zhang Xie, *Dongxi yang kao*, p. 67.

94. Reid, *Southeast Asia in the Age of Commerce*, vol. 2, pp. 9–10.

95. Quoted from an entry in the *Veritable Records* dated 4 September 1525, in So, *Japanese Piracy in Ming China*, p. 45.

96. Geiss, "The Chia-ching Reign," p. 495.

97. Matsuura Akira, "Mindai koki no enkai kōun."

98. The connection between piracy and famine is made in So, *Japanese Piracy in Ming China*, pp. 48–49. So also links the resolution of the piracy problem to the reform of China's fiscal system at midcentury (p. 155). For an overview of piracy in the Jiajing era, see Geiss, "The Chia-ching Reign," pp. 490–505.

99. *Shanxi tongzhi* (1682), 26.2b–3a.

100. *Guangshan xianzhi* (1556), 1.30a.

101. *Qiongshan xianzhi* (1917), 2.17a, quoting the provincial gazetteer of 1561; *Huizhou fuzhi* (1542), 4.21a.

102. Yang Wenjie, *Dongcheng jiyu* (1897), 2.59a; Zhou Kefu, *Jin'gang chiyan ji* (1799), 2.12b.

103. Zurndorfer, *Change and Continuity*, pp. 126–27.

104. *TJL*, 9.62b.

105. David, *Chinese Connoisseurship*, p. 10.

106. Zurndorfer, *Change and Continuity*, pp. 49–50.

107. Wang Zhenzhong, "Ming-Qing shiqi Huishang shehui xingxiang," pp. 81–84.

108. Zurndorfer, *Change and Continuity*, p. 100; Zurndorfer notes the case of another Huizhou merchant who formed cordial relationships with officials in order to better his son's position. See also Ye Xianen, "Shilun Huizhou shangren ziben de xingcheng yu fazhan," on the dependence of Huizhou merchants on officials for protection and privileges. The growing integration of merchant and gentry circles is discussed in Zheng Lihua, *Mingdai zhongqi wenxue*, pp. 168–75; see also pp. 136–50 on the increasingly positive image of merchants in mid-Ming literature.

109. *Yangzhou fuzhi* (1733), 10.10a, quoting Wang Yu (js. 1451).

110. Zurndorfer, *Change and Continuity*, pp. 52, 96–97.

111. *Guangdong tongzhi* (1561), quoted in *Qiongshan xianzhi* (1917), 2.17a. The compilation of the provincial gazetteer was completed in 1558.

112. Yu Jiaxi, *Siku tiyao bianzheng*, p. 1,342, in reference to the 1470 republication of a Song text.

113. Lu Rong, *Shuyuan zaji*, pp. 128–29.

114. Lai Xinxia, ed., *Zhongguo gudai tushu shiye shi*, p. 288.

115. The production of paper in the Ming is discussed in Tsien, *Science and Civilisation in China*, pp. 49–53, 59–61. As of 1597, the town of Shitang in Jiangxi had thirty paper mills employing fifty to sixty thousand workers to produce paper from locally grown bamboo. Xu Hongzu in 1636 noted that some villages in western Jiangxi produced nothing but (usually coarse) paper; Xu Hongzu, *Xu Xiake youji*, pp. 126, 138.

116. *Jianyang xianzhi* (1553), *juan* 3, quoted in Lai Xinxia, *Zhongguo gudai tushu shiye shi*, p. 288.

117. The route from Nanjing to Jianyang is given in *TLT*, pp. 404–405. Regarding the Chongan route in the Song, see Su Jilang, *Tang-Song shidai Minnan Quanzhou shidi lungao*, pp. 167–69. An increase in traffic on the route in the mid-Ming led to the founding of four new post houses in Jianyang county in the last quarter of the fifteenth century and another four during the first three decades of the sixteenth, as listed in *Jianyang xianzhi* (1553), 4.10a–12a.

118. *Huian xianzhi* (1530), 9.10a. The comment may not be Zhang's own, for it is repeated verbatim thirty-four years later in a Hunan county gazetteer, *Cili xianzhi* (1574), 11.14a.

119. Meskill, *Ch'oe Pu's Diary*, p. 155.

120. Carlo Ginzburg, *The Cheese and the Worms*, p. 59.

121. Zheng Tinghu, *Qiongzhi gao* (ca. 1560), quoted in *Qiongzhou fuzhi* (1619), 3.88b.

122. Qiu's record of building this library is included in *Qiongzhou fuzhi* (1619), 11.26b, and reprinted in *Qiongshan xianzhi* (1917), 14.37a–40a. On the building of libraries in county Confucian schools in the mid-Ming, see Brook, "Edifying Knowledge."

123. Wu Han, *Jiang Zhe cangshujia shilüe*, pp. 10, 22, 145, 155, 176, 229, 232.

124. Ibid., pp. 112, 160. The name appears first to have been used in the Song dynasty; see, e.g., *Huguang tujing zhishu* (1522), 6.62a, regarding a Wanjuan Lou built at the turn of the eleventh century. For a mid-sixteenth-century reflection on the term Wanjuan Lou as potentially contradictory to the spirit of Confucian self-cultivation, see Li Kaixian, *Li Kaixian ji*, pp. 658–59.

125. *Hejian fuzhi* (1540), 7.15b–16a.

126. *Huian xianzhi* (1530), 4.3a.

127. *Huian xianzhi* (1530), 4.1b; *Ming shi*, p. 5,295. Ye Chunji, *Huian zhengshu* (1573), 9.19b, noted that well-sweeps were used in the southeastern region of Huian county where drought was a constant problem.

128. *Longxi xianzhi* (1535), 1.15b.

129. *Gushi xianzhi* (1659), 3.15a. The passage from *The Book of Changes* may be found on p. 331 of the Wilhelm and Baynes translation.

130. *Huian xianzhi* (1530), 5.7b–9a. Other compilers also related local products to those listed in *The Tributes of Emperor Yu*, e.g., *Hejian fuzhi* (1540), 7.5a.

131. *TLT*, pp. 370–71.

132. *Shexian zhi* (1609), 6.5b–10a.

133. Regarding the aestheticization of gardens in the mid-Ming, see Clunas, *Fruitful Sites*, pp. 39–44, 56–57. Clunas argues that the gentry authors who wrote about gardens engaged in the "'enclaving' of fruit as a commodity discussed as if it were withdrawn from the market-place."

134. *Huian xianzhi* (1530), 12.10b–23b. On Zhang's disputes with Wang Shouren and Nie Bao, see *Huian xianzhi* (1730), 23.5b–6a.

135. *Huian xianzhi* (1530), 12.24a.

136. Gentry formation was slower in the interior and north China,

where a county gentry began to take form only starting about the middle of the sixteenth century. See, e.g., Brook, *Praying for Power*, pp. 236–37, 287.

137. *Gushi xianzhi* (1659), 10.31a–b.

138. *Daming fuzhi* (1506), 1.21a–b.

139. *Nanchang fuzhi* (1588), 3.29b, quoting the Hongzhi-era county gazetteer.

140. *Lushan xianzhi* (1552), 1.38b.

141. Ping-ti Ho, *Studies on the Population of China*, p. 73; Yu Yingshi, *Shi yu Zhongguo wenhua*, p. 528.

142. Zhang Haipeng and Wang Tingyuan, *Ming-Qing Huishang ziliao xuanbian*, pp. 440, 439.

143. *Shaowu fuzhi* (1543), 2.43a.

144. Quoted in *Huguang tujing zhishu* (1522), 4.7a.

145. *Shaowu fuzhi* (1543), 2.43b–44a, translating the figurative *jin* (gold) as silver.

146. The examples that follow are from South Zhili and Fujian, but sixteenth-century authors in other regions also name Zhengde (or sometimes late Hongzhi or early Jiajing) as the point of turning away from "ancient" styles: e.g., in Shandong, *Wucheng xianzhi* (1549), 1.7b; in Shanxi, *Shanxi tongzhi* (1682), 66.31a; in Henan, *Guangshan xianzhi* (1556), 1.29a; and in Zhejiang, *Ningbo fuzhi* (1560), 4.32a. See also Li Yue, *Jianwen zaji* (1610), 5.68a, referring to Huzhou.

147. E.g., Yu Jideng, *Diangu jiwen*, p. 300, quoted in Brook, *Praying for Power*, pp. 312–13.

148. Quoted in Zurndorfer, *Change and Continuity*, pp. 113–14.

149. Li Yue, *Jianwen zaji*, 5.68a.

150. Quoted in Zurndorfer, *Change and Continuity*, pp. 114–15; see also Meskill, *Gentlemanly Interests and Wealth*, p. 128.

151. *Shaowu fuzhi* (1543), 2.45b–46a.

152. *Huian xianzhi* (1530), 2.9b, 4.2a, 3b. The region suffered from droughts beginning in 1512, the seventh year of the Zhengde era; *Zhongguo jin wubai nian hanlao fenbu tuji*, p. 27. Zhang Yue's comment about "harsh exaction" replacing "administration" at the beginning of the Zhengde era suggests that he was criticizing Liang Gang, who was appointed county magistrate in 1506 and who ran the county administration for the first half-decade of the Zhengde era. Liang's biography in his home gazetteer reports that he went on to a vice-prefectural posting in Guangxi, with no indication that his magistracy in Huian was found wanting; *Shunde xianzhi* (1853), 10.17d. Concerning Zhang Yue's own career under the Zhengde emperor, see *Ming shi*, p. 5,295.

153. So, *Japanese Piracy in Ming China*, pp. 42–43.

154. *Chongwusuo chengzhi* (1542, 1987), pp. 39–40. I am grateful to Michael Szonyi for providing me with a copy of this gazetteer.

155. For the rise of lineage formation in mid-Ming Huizhou, see Keith Hazelton, "Patrilines and the Development of Localized Lineages."

156. The conflicts to which adoption could give rise are explored in Ann Waltner, *Getting an Heir*.

157. A contemporary gazetteer in north China similarly blames the gentry for "the destruction of etiquette"; *Hejian fuzhi* (1540), 9.10b.

158. The same complaint about funerals is made in *Changshu xianzhi* (1539), 4.21a, though the decline of propriety is dated earlier to the new wealth in Jiangnan of the Chenghua era. Another Fujian gazetteer, *Anxi xianzhi* (1552), 1.15b, blames the lavishness of funerals for driving the poor to the practice of cremation, which was an unfilial destruction of the body given by one's parents.

159. Quoted in Lien-sheng Yang, *Studies in Chinese Institutional History*, p. 73. More recently, Lu Ji's views have been more closely analyzed in Lin Liyue, "Lu Ji chongshe sixiang zaitan." I am grateful to Kwok-yiu Wong for this reference.

SUMMER: THE LAST CENTURY (1550–1644)

1. Gu Yanwu claimed that in late-Ming Suzhou nine out of ten cultivators were tenants; *Rizhi lu jishi*, 10.18a.

2. *Ming jingshi wenbian*, 488.25b.

3. Royal Ontario Museum 921.31.30.

4. *Wulin fanzhi* (1780), 4.25b.

5. Lu Rong, *Shuyuan zaji*, p. 123.

6. Gu Yanwu, *Rizhi lu jishi*, 11.39a.

7. *Yunju shengshui sizhi* (1773), 2.13b.

8. Huo Tao, *Wenmin gong quanji*, 4a.30b–32b.

9. Li Yue, *Jianwen zaji*, 11.43a. One of the targeted monasteries found patrons to replace its bell in 1612; the copper-to-tin ratio of roughly six to one I take from Li Yue's account of the casting of this bell.

10. *Tianzhu shanzhi* (1875), 2.8a. A replacement bell cast in 1595 consumed over 6,000 catties of copper.

11. *Songjiang fuzhi* (1630), 53.39a, 58.49b. A 600-catty Buddha was relatively light by the standards of the time. By way of comparison, an eighteenth-century Japanese bronze Buddha owned by the Victoria and Albert Museum (and now on permanent loan to a Chinese temple in Birmington) standing 5.5 meters high weighs 1,300 kilograms. Verity Wilson provided me with this Buddha's vital statistics.

12. *Wuhu xianzhi* (1919), 41.4a. Zhang Tao was distressed at the growing enthusiasm among the gentry for Buddhist devotions, though he declines to scourge the Sheh elite for it in his gazetteer. Contrary to the example of Yuanzhao Monastery, Buddhist patronage was not as much a fashion among Huizhou merchants as it was among the gentry who dominated counties elsewhere; Brook, *Praying for Power*, pp. 218–20. Zhang did complain about Buddhism in Sheh, but only with respect to the practice of marriage among local monks, who took women who were called "vegetarian wives" (*zhaipo*); *Shexian zhi* (1609), 7:siguan:11b–12a. According to the 1500 gazetteer of Zhang's home prefecture of Huangzhou, Buddhism and Confucianism were not regarded as incompatible, for

"cultivated people take pleasure in being Confucian scholars but do not therefore disdain Buddhism;" *Huangzhou fuzhi* (1500), 1.17a. This attitude may have changed by Zhang Tao's time.

13. Peng Xinwei, *Zhongguo huobi shi,* pp. 44b ff.
14. *Da Ming huidian,* 167.5b.
15. Li Le, *Jianwen zaji,* 11.44a.
16. Taga Akigorō, *Sōfu no kenkyū,* pp. 604–608, translated in Ebrey, *Chinese Civilization and Society,* pp. 161–66, correcting Miu to Miao.
17. *Kuaiji xianzhi* (1575), quoted in So, *Japanese Piracy in Ming Times,* p. 123.
18. *Fuzhou fuzhi* (1613), 26.4a; Xie Zhaozhe, *Wuza zu,* 4.34a; Dong Qichang, ed., *Shenmiao liuzhong zoushu huiyao,* 6.20b; all quoted in Ping-ti Ho, *Studies on the Population of China,* pp. 261–62.
19. Ibid., p. 264.
20. Li Le, *Jianwen zaji,* 3.135b. Yao was nursing Li Le's granddaughter; Li stresses that neither he nor the women of his family drove her to suicide.
21. E.g., *Gushi xianzhi* (1659), 10.42b. I have yet to discover a late-Ming magistrate who did more than exhort the people not to kill their infants. The limited Southern Song practice of setting up a granary to provide child-support payments to the indigent, called a Child-Rearing Granary (*juzi cang*), was not taken up in the Ming to my knowledge; for an example of such a granary, see *Chongan xianzhi* (1670), 3.30b.
22. E.g., "Recently, many newborn girls are not raised, and among the wealthy there are [families] that have been drowning their girls for several generations"; *Dehua xianzhi* (1697), 2.9a–b.
23. Xu Shiduan, *Ming shilu leizuan: funü shiliao juan,* p. 1,071.
24. *Shizhong shanzhi* (1996), p. 85.
25. *Tongxiang xianzhi* (1887), 20:xiangyi:6a, 8b–9a; *Wuxi Jinkui xianzhi* (1881), 31.11b; *Jinan fuzhi* (1840), 20.18b. The 1641 epidemic is surveyed in Helen Dunstan, "The Late Ming Epidemics," pp. 29–35. For climatic conditions in this period, see *Zhongguo jin wubai nian hanlao fenbu tuji,* pp. 78–92.
26. Yu Xiangdou, *Wanyong zhengzong,* 1.1b–16b. This was not the first almanac Yu published: the smaller *Santai tongshu zhengzong* [Complete source of all texts from Yu Santai] came out the previous year; see Ruitenbeek, *Carpentry and Building,* p. 42.
27. Wu Han, *Jiang Zhe cangshujia shilüe,* p. 32.
28. *Baoding fuzhi* (1607), 40.26b.
29. Yu Jiaxi, *Siku tiyao bianzheng,* p. 1,534, concerning Ming interpretations of the work of the Song author Zheng Sixiao.
30. Song Yingxing, *Tiangong kaiwu,* pp. 3–4; Sun and Sun, *T'ien-kung K'ai-wu,* p. xiv. On Tu Shaokui, see Pan Jixing, *Song Yingxing pingzhuan,* pp. 190–98, 239.
31. Gallagher, *China in the Sixteenth Century,* p. 21.
32. Hu Yinglin, *Jingji huitong, juan* 4, quoted in Ōki Yasashi, "Min-

matsu Kōnan ni okeru shuppan," p. 31. For what is still a good overview in English of the development of commercial publishing in the Ming, see K. T. Wu, "Ming Printing and Printers."

33. Xie Zhaozhe, *Wu zazu,* 13.21b. In Sheh county, the Huang family of Qiucun became nationally known for the quality of their engraving; see Zhang Haipeng and Wang Tingyuan, eds., *Ming-Qing Huishang ziliao xuanbian,* pp. 206–207.

34. For some libraries on this scale, see Wu Han, *Jiang Zhe cangshujia shilüe,* pp. 8, 11, 16, 20, 34, 40, 54, 59, 66, 120, 121, 126, 138, 140, 205.

35. Ibid., pp. 33, 46, 56, 159.

36. Du Halde, *General History,* vol. 3, p. 63.

37. Wu Han, *Jiang Zhe cangshujia shilüe,* p. 131.

38. *DMB,* p. 1,271.

39. Wang Wenlu, whose library of ten thousand *juan* burned down in 1565, was one of the first to publish his own writings serially. By 1555 he had published fifty titles, of which he was the author of twelve; he gave them all a collectanea title, *Qiuling xueshan* [The mountain of learning], in imitation of the prototypical Song collectanea, *Baichuan xuehai* [The sea of learning from a hundred streams]. By 1584, Wang had added another fifty titles to his retitled *Bailing xueshan* [The mountain of learning from a hundred peaks], many of which again were his own works (*DMB,* p. 1,450).

40. Cited in Brook, "Censorship in Eighteenth-Century China," p. 188.

41. Xie Guozhen, *Ming-Qing zhi ji dangshe yundong kao,* p. 120.

42. Gu Yanwu, *Rizhi lu jishi,* 18.31b.

43. Cited in Ray Huang, "Fiscal Administration during the Ming Dynasty," p. 81.

44. Yin Yungong, *Zhongguo Mingdai xinwen chuanbo shi,* pp. 131–37.

45. *Dehua xianzhi* (1697), 2.8a.

46. Yu Shenxing, *Gushan bizhu, juan* 11, cited (along with the subsequent references) in Yin Yungong, *Zhongguo Mingdai xinwen chuanbo shi,* pp. 113 ff.

47. Of the transport offices shut down in the late Ming, most were closed between 1567 and 1582; *Da Ming huidian,* 147.1a–14a.

48. Shen Dingping, "Mingdai yidi de shezhi," p. 79, argues that post houses existed in name only after the mid-Ming, but evidence in local gazetteers goes against this generalization. The postal service continued to operate, albeit under constrained circumstances.

49. Gu Yanwu, *Rizhi lu jishi,* 12.18b; the text following this comment is translated in part in Lien-sheng Yang, "Ming Local Administration," p. 20.

50. Referred to in Wang Shimin (1592–1680), *Zishu* (Self-Account), translated in Wu, *The Confucian's Progress,* p. 254. Wang says that he was laughed at when he punctiliously followed the new rules and covered some of his travel expenses himself.

51. Su Tongbing, *Mingdai yidi zhidu,* pp. 436–52.

52. E.g., during a flood in Yangzhou prefecture in the late 1620s,

"bandits rose in swarms and the road running [through Xinghua county] from Gaoyou subprefecture to Yancheng county was cut. [The Xinghua magistrate] Zhao Long led the local militia and captured thirty-seven including the leader"; *Yangzhou fuzhi* (1733), 27.47a.

53. Gu Yanwu argued that the Ming should have revived the Han practice of spacing courier stations every 30 *li*. "People of ancient times established numerous courier stations so as to travel quickly and without ruining the horses," he pointed out, "whereas people of later periods amalgamated them over time in order to save money. Now there is only one station every 70 or 80 *li*, causing the horses to collapse and the officers to take off"; Zhao Lisheng, *Rizhi lu daodu*, p. 109.

54. *TSL*, pp. 204, 232–34.

55. Jianyue Duti, *Yimeng manyan*, p. 12. The larger phenomenon of Yunnanese influence on late-Ming Buddhism is the subject of Chen Yuan, *Mingji Dian-Qian fojiao kao*.

56. Xu Hongzu, *Xu Xiake youji*, p. 99.

57. Ibid., pp. 674–75; Zhou Ningxia et al., "*Xu Xiake youji* yuanshi chaoben," p. 177. Details of Xu's return journey are given in the biography by Chen Hanhui in Xu Hongzu, *Xu Xiake youji*, p. 1,189; distances are estimated from *TSL*, pp. 2, 31, 70–71, 198–99. Xu's place in the world of Chinese letters is explored in Li Chi, *The Travel Diaries of Hsü Hsia-k'o*.

58. *TSL*, p. 167.

59. Zhang Kaiquan, *Huian fengtu zhi*, p. 11, refers to this practice as "an old custom in the villages."

60. *TSL*, pp. 233, 235.

61. *TLT*, p. 373.

62. Xu Hongzu notes that local administrations made do with poor maps. When visiting the prefectural yamen of Guangxi prefecture, Yunnan, in 1638, he looked at the prefectural map on the wall and discovered it bore neither placenames nor borders; *Xu Xiake youji*, p. 687.

63. Brook, "Guides for Vexed Travelers," pp. 32–33.

64. Though published in 1570, Huang Bian's route book relied on courier route data that date to the mid- rather than the late Ming. To give one example, he identifies two courier stations in Taihe county, Jiangxi, on the second route in his book as though both were still in operation, yet they were amalgamated into one in 1534 (*TSL*, p. 11). The amalgamation is mentioned by Yang Zhengtai, editor of the modern edition (*TSL*), on p. 14.

65. Huang Bian, *Yitong lucheng tuji* (1570), author's preface; this preface is not included in Yang Zhengtai's 1992 edition.

66. The one hundred-route book in a version entitled *Tianxia shuilu tuyin* [Illustrated guide to the routes of the realm] has recently been reprinted under the editorship of Yang Zhengtai (*TLT*). It has appeared under a variety of titles. The copy in the National Archives in Tokyo was printed by a commercial publisher in Jianyang, Fujian, which suggests that the book may have circulated in an earlier form.

67. Hu Zhi (1517–85), *Kunxue ji* [A record of learning through difficulties], translated in Pei-yi Wu, *The Confucian's Progress*, p. 245.

68. Yuan Hongdao, *Yuan Hongdao ji jianjiao,* vol. 1, p. 164.

69. *Ayu wang shanzhi* (1619), 4.30a, in a text by the gazetteer's editor, Guo Zizhang.

70. The cult of craving or obsession in the late Ming is discussed in Zeitlin, "The Petrified Heart"; it bears noting that this concept was established in elite culture prior to the Ming, as Wang Lü's comments in Liscomb, *Learning from Mount Hua,* pp. 70–71, indicate. An obsession for garden stones is mentioned in *Songjiang fuzhi* (1630), 46.58a. By 1599, Yuan Hongdao was willing to characterize "craving of the heart for wealth" as a universal condition of humanity; *Yuan Hongdao ji jianjiao,* p. 817.

71. Chen Hanhui, "Xu Xiake muzhi zhiming" [Tomb epitaph of Xu Hongzu], in Xu Hongzu, *Xu Xiake youji,* p. 1,184.

72. A gazetteer editor who could claim that local women "do not climb mountains and visit monasteries and do not form vegetarian associations and conduct prayers" was a rare and happy man; see *Dehua xianzhi* (1697), 2.9a In most places, though, they did all these things, as Li Yue observes of women who flocked to Buddhist sites in his native county of Tongxiang; *Jianwen zaji,* 5.74a. The reference to excusing crones comes from *Wo shi* (1668), *juan* 24.

73. Translated in Dudbridge, "Women Pilgrims to T'ai Shan," pp. 51–52.

74. From a stele in Shuiquan, quoted in Chen Qi, ed., *Gansu gonglu jiaotong shi,* p. 126.

75. Song Yingxing, *Tiangong kaiwu,* pp. 2, 232; Sun and Sun, *T'ienkung K'ai-wu,* pp. xiii, 171.

76. Huc, *A Journey through the Chinese Empire,* vol. 2, pp. 80–81.

77. Luo Hongxian, *Nian'an wenji,* 8.40b, from an essay of 1541.

78. Zhuang's letters from Beijing are published in Japanese translation in Hamashima, "Minmatsu Kōnan kyōshin no gutaisō," pp. 174–82.

79. King, "The Family Letters of Xu Guangqi," pp. 9–12, 21, 23, 27.

80. Shi Shi, "Cong Mingdai kaishi de minyou," p. 21.

81. Ma Junchang et al., *Beijing youshi,* pp. 23–24. The later generic term for private mail couriers, "letter bureau" (*xinju*), is not attested before the eighteenth century.

82. *Chidu xinyu guangbian* [Model letters, further (third) collection], quoted in Ellen Widmer, "The Epistolary World of Female Talent," p. 9.

83. Deng Hanyi, ed., *Shi guan* (1672), *fanli* [editor's notes], 3b; Xu Shumin and Qian Yue, eds., *Zhongxiang ci* (1689), *fanli,* 2a. I am grateful to Dorothy Ko for sharing these references with me; they are cited in her *Teachers of the Inner Chambers,* p. 63. The six provinces are Shaanxi, Sichuan, Hubei, Shandong, Fujian, and Zhejiang.

84. *Yangzhou fuzhi* (1733), 32.12a.

85. Li Le, *Jianwen zaji,* 2.89a–b.

86. E.g., *Guangzhou zhi* (1660), 9.17a, regarding a magistrate calling on "rich commoners" in the 1570s; also *Yangzhou fuzhi* (1733), 32.10b, regarding a magistrate's response to a famine in 1595.

87. Fuzheng, *Hanshan dashi nianpu shuzhu*, p. 62.
88. Hamashima, "The Organization of Water Control," p. 79.
89. Brook, "The Merchant Network," p. 197.
90. Xu Hongzu, *Xu Xiake youji*, p. 100; Xu encountered the boats at Tonglu county. In south China, the movement of rice was similarly from west to east: Fujian imported grain from Guangdong, and Guangdong in turn imported an even greater volume of grain from Guangxi further west; *Guangxi hangyun shi*, p. 56.
91. *Jingzhou zhi* (1612), 3.38b.
92. Yin Yungong, *Zhongguo Mingdai xinwen chuanbo shi*, pp. 182–83.
93. Xu Hongzu, *Xu Xiake youji*, p. 158, referring to Yongxin county.
94. Zhang Haipeng and Wang Tingyuan, *Ming-Qing Huishang ziliao xuanbian*, p. 195.
95. Wu Chengming, "Lun Qingdai qianqi woguo guonei shichang," pp. 102–103.
96. E.g., *TJL*, 9.9b, cited in Brook, "The Spread of Rice Cultivation," p. 688.
97. *Jiading xianzhi* (1605), juan 15, quoted in Chen Xuewen, *Zhongguo fengjian wanqi de shangpin jingji*, p. 149.
98. Wang Zhideng, *Ke Yue zhilüe* [Brief account of my journey through Zhejiang], reprinted in Wang Ying, ed., *Mingren riji suibi xuan*, p. 143.
99. Xu Dunqiu, *Jingsuo biji* [Jottings of Master Jingsuo], reprinted in Chen Xuewen, *Zhongguo fengjian wanqi de shangpin jingji*, p. 320.
100. *Haiyan xian tujing* (1624), juan 4, quoted in Fan Shuzhi, "Mingdai Zhejiang shizhen fenbu yu jiegou," p. 186.
101. Xu Hongzu, *Xu Xiake youji*, p. 100.
102. King, "The Family Letters of Xu Guangqi," p. 14. The distance from Shanghai to Huzhou is calculated from *TLT*, pp. 378, 384, 386.
103. Fu Yiling, "Mingdai jingji shi shang de Shandong yu Henan."
104. *Songjiang fuzhi* (1630), 6.10b, quoted in Nishijima, "The Formation of the Early Chinese Cotton Industry," p. 49.
105. Brook, "The Merchant Network," p. 199.
106. *Hangzhou fuzhi* (1579), 19.8b–9a, quoted in So, *Japanese Piracy in Ming Times*, p. 129, translation revised.
107. Fu Yiling, *Mingdai Jiangnan shimin jingji shitan*, p. 87. For an account of late-Ming Suzhou, see Marmé, "Heaven on Earth."
108. Zhu Guozhen, *Yongchuang xiaopin*.
109. *Jiading xianzhi* (1605), juan 6, quoted in Chen Xuewen, *Zhongguo fengjian wanqi de shangpin jingji*, p. 154.
110. A casual reference by Song Yingxing suggests that working at night by the light of an oil lamp was as common among weavers as it was among students; Sun and Sun, *T'ien-kung K'ai-wu*, p. 215.
111. E.g., Nishijima Sadao, "The Formation of the Early Chinese Cotton Industry," pp. 63, 64, 66, 69, argues against the putting-out interpretation. Fu Yiling, *Ming-Qing shehui jingji shi lunwen ji*, p. 227, argues the other side.

112. E.g., Fu Yiling, *Ming-Qing shehui jingji shi lunwen ji*, p. 227.

113. For example, the cotton merchants in the Songjiang town of Puxie were able to monopolize the market there. Since rural weavers had no other outlet for their cloth, the merchants could discount the purchase price by 20 percent: *Jiading xianzhi* (1881), *juan* 29, quoted in Fu Yiling, *Ming-Qing shehui jingji shi lunwen ji*, p. 233.

114. Tanaka Masatoshi, "Rural Handicraft in Jiangnan," p. 85; also pp. 90, 93. For a different interpretation of the Suzhou textile trade, see Marmé, "Heaven on Earth."

115. E.g., *Anxi xianzhi* (1552), 1.15b.

116. Ye Chunji, *Huian zhengshu* (1573, 1672), 1.3b, 4.10a, 9.19a–b. Chen Keng, "Ming-Qing Fujian nongcun shitan," offers a more positive assessment of the extent of commercialization in rural Fujian, though he acknowledges that the marketing system was underdeveloped and that commodities were limited in quantity.

117. Fernand Braudel, *Capitalism and Material Life*, p. 24.

118. Li Le, *Jianwen zaji*, 4.39a.

119. *Qiongzhou fuzhi* (1619), 3.90a–b.

120. Sun and Sun, *T'ien-kung K'ai-wu*, pp. 43–66. Note that even the silk-reeling machine is operated by a man.

121. Bray, "Le travail féminin dans la China impériale," esp. pp. 809–14.

122. Fan Lian, *Yunjian jumu chao*, quoted in Meskill, *Gentlemanly Interests and Wealth*, p. 150.

123. Li Le, *Jianwen zaji*, 5.60b; Prefect Zhao Ying was a native of Shaanxi and may have been conservatively disposed for that reason.

124. Ibid., 5.74a.

125. *Huang Ming tiaofa shilei zuan* [Commentaries on criminal law in the Ming dynasty by legal category], *juan* 22, quoted in Chen Baoliang, *Zhongguo liumang shi*, p. 157.

126. Wang Shixing, *Guangzhi yi*, p. 66.

127. Huang Liuhong, *Fuhui quanshu*, 29.15b.

128. Zhang Xie, *Dongxi yang kao*, pp. 131–32; Lin Renchuan, *Ming-mo Qingchu siren haishang maoyi*, p. 149; So, *Japanese Piracy in Ming Times*, p. 154. In coordination with the governor's initiative, Zhangzhou officials moved to have Moon Harbor elevated to county status, where a full tax office could be installed to capture greater revenue from maritime trade; *Haicheng xianzhi* (1762), 21.3b–4a. I am grateful to Sun Daigang for this last reference.

129. Atwell, "International Bullion Flows," pp. 69–75.

130. Quoted in Schurz, *The Manila Galleon*, pp. 73–74.

131. See, e.g., the account of trade goods in Manila written in 1663 by the Jesuit Colín; ibid., p. 50.

132. Lin Renchuan, *Mingmo Qingchu siren haishang maoyi*, p. 224.

133. Chuimei Ho, "The Ceramic Trade in Asia," p. 39.

134. The inhibiting effect of weak domestic demand on Jingdezhen is argued in Tsing Yuan, "The Porcelain Industry at Ching-te-chen." On the

use of foreign models for export ware, see Jörg, "Chinese Porcelain for the Dutch," p. 186.

135. Lin Renchuan, *Mingmo Qingchu siren haishang maoyi,* pp. 267–69, provides sixteenth-century allegations of tenfold profit on the China-Japan trade.

136. Boxer, *The Great Ship from Amacon,* pp. 179–81; Lin Renchuan, *Mingmo Qingchu siren haishang maoyi,* pp. 270–71, working also from European records.

137. As estimated for South Zhili merchants in the Wanli era by Zhang Han; see Brook, "The Merchant Network," p. 197.

138. Sun and Sun, *T'ien-kung K'ai-wu,* p. 247.

139. Bontekoe, *Memorable Description,* p. 117.

140. Atwell, "International Bullion Flows," argues that silver imports fell at the end of the Ming, destabilizing an economy that had become dependent on foreign silver and contributing to the collapse of the dynasty. Goldstone, "East and West in the Seventeenth Century," doubts the impact of the silver trade on the collapse of the Ming. Von Glahn, "Myth and Reality of China's Seventeenth Century Monetary Crisis," doubts any argument that relies on the single factor of money supply. He argues that the importation of silver was less significant than domestic demand, and that in any case Japanese sources compensated for the decline in imports from European and American sources; the price of silver rose in the seventeenth century due to a falling demand for goods, not declining silver stocks.

141. Ye Chunji, *Huian zhengshu* (1573, 1672), 9.20a.

142. Cynthia Brokaw, *The Ledgers of Merit and Demerit,* p. 102.

143. See Brook, *Praying for Power,* p. 162, on some of the costs involved in monastic patronage.

144. Joanna Handlin Smith, "Gardens in Ch'i Piao-chia's Social World," pp. 74–77. Handlin Smith also discusses issues of value and morality in her "Benevolent Societies."

145. Xu Guangqi, *Nongzheng quanshu,* vol. 1, p. 237 (this passage was brought to my attention by Pierre-Étienne Will); see also the editor's notes by Chen Zilong, p. 1.

146. *Sichuan zongzhi* (1581), *juan* 21, quoted in Zhang Zhengming and Xue Huilin, *Ming-Qing Jinshang ziliao xuanbian,* p. 79.

147. Following the ranking of Fu Yiling, *Ming-Qing shidai shangren ji shangye ziben,* p. 161.

148. On the spread of Jiangxi merchants from the mid-Ming forward, see Fu Yiling, *Ming-Qing shehui jingji shi lunwen ji,* pp. 187–97.

149. *Jiading xianzhi* (1605), *juan* 1 and 6, quoted in Chen Xuewen, *Zhongguo fengjian wanqi de shangpin jingji,* pp. 153–54.

150. Liu Tong, *Dijing jingwu lüe,* p. 167.

151. Zhang Han, *Songchuang mengyu,* p. 87, translated in Brook, "The Merchant Network," p. 208.

152. Zhu Guozhen, *Yongchuang xiaopin,* p. 61.

153. *Qiongzhou fuzhi* (1619), 4.97b, 99b–100a, 104a. The compiler

reports that some provincial officials wanted to incorporate the tax as a permanent item into the Single Whip.

154. *Quanzhou fuzhi* (1612), 6.76b, citing the opposition of "gentry of the old families" to the Single Whip reforms because the new system failed to tax merchant wealth as fully as it taxed landed wealth.

155. Brook, "Family Continuity and Cultural Hegemony," p. 40.

156. Zhang Han, *Songchuang mengyu*, p. 119, translated in Brook, "The Merchant Network," p. 173.

157. Wang Daokun, *Taihan ji*, 53.11a, quoted in Ho, *The Ladder of Success*, p. 73.

158. Li Jinde, *Keshang yilan xingmi*, p. 311.

159. "He who goes out in the evening gains nothing, whereas he who rises early will succeed" (ibid., p. 325).

160. Ibid., p. 293.

161. Brook, "The Merchant Network," p. 201.

162. Li Jinde, *Keshang yilan xingmi*, p. 290.

163. E.g., Li Le, *Jianwen zaji*, 2.60a–b. I have not been able to discover what exactly the "cloud" style looked like; it would appear to involve the sumptuous use of silk gauze as decoration.

164. *Yangzhou fuzhi* (1733), 10.2a–b.

165. Zhang Han, "Baigong ji," *Songchuang mengyu*, p. 79. This passage differently translated is also cited in Clunas, *Superfluous Things*, p. 145.

166. Ye Mengzhu, *Yueshi bian*, p. 178.

167. Xu Shiduan, *Ming shilu leizuan: funü shiliao juan*, p. 1,068.

168. Li Rihua, *Weishui xuan riji*, 3.3b–40a (book dealer, 30b; art dealer, 36a).

169. Cited in Clunas, "Some Literary Evidence for Gold and Silver Vessels," p. 86. He Liangjun's library ran to forty thousand *juan*; *Songjiang fuzhi* (1630), 46.54a.

170. Clunas, *Superfluous Things*, p. 13.

171. Quoted in Clunas, "Connoisseurs and Aficionados," p. 151.

172. Liu Tong, *Dijing jingwu lüe*, pp. 162, 163. The term *shangjian* is examined by Clunas in *Superfluous Things*, p. 86, and "Connoisseurs and Aficionados," p. 153.

173. Liu Tong, *Dijing jingwu lüe*, p. 163.

174. Zhang Dai, *Yehang chuan*, p. 499; Zhang Dai, *Taoan mengyi*, pp. 9–10, 18, 47, quoted in part in Clunas, *Superfluous Things*, pp. 61–62. Regarding Zhu Bishan, see Clunas, "Some Literary Evidence for Gold and Silver Vessels"; regarding Lu Zigang, see Clunas, "Ming Jade Carvers and their Customers."

175. Liu Tong, *Dijing jingwu lüe*, pp. 165–66.

176. Wang Shizhen cited in Clunas, *Superfluous Things*, p. 61; Gu Yanwu cited in Johnson, *Cities of Jiangnan*, p. 85.

177. Clunas, *Superfluous Things*, pp. 61–63.

178. Dong Qichang, *Yunxuan qingbi lu*, p. 25.

179. Zhang Dai, *Taoan mengyi*, p. 66.

180. Kang-i Sun Chang, *The Late Ming Poet Ch'en Tzu-lung*, pp. 11–12.

181. The life of Liu Shi is summarized in Chang, *The Late Ming Poet Ch'en Tzu-lung*. For a complete account, see Chen Yinque, *Liu Rushi biezhuan*.

182. E.g., painter Yang Wencong (1596–1646) and Ma Jiao, poet and painter Wu Weiye (1609–71) and Bian Sai, poet Mao Xiang (1611–93) and Dong Bai (1625–51), author Hou Fangyu (1618–55) and Li Xiangjun.

183. Cf. Martin Huang, *Literati Self-Re/Presentation*, pp. 82–84.

184. The connection between love and dynastic loyalty is outlined in Chang, *The Late Ming Poet Ch'en Tzu-lung*, pp. 16–18, although she accepts the claims of the lovers too much at face value.

185. This argument is presented by Dorothy Ko, *Teachers of the Inner Chambers*; regarding the marginal position of courtesans relative to other women, see pp. 281–82. The extent to which the freedoms of elite women affected the practices of women at large has been questioned in Kathryn Bernhardt, "A Ming-Qing Transition in Chinese Women's History?"

186. Chen Hongmo, *Zhishi yuwen*, p. 53; the censorious author says he resisted this sort of entertainment and was laughed at for being so straight-laced.

187. D'Elia, *Fonti Ricciane*, vol. 1, p. 98. The reference from customary law comes from the writer Langxian, quoted in Volpp, "The Discourse on Male Marriage," p. 115. Meijer, "Homosexual Offenses in Ch'ing Law," observes that same-sex coupling was not criminalized until the Manchus inserted this prohibition into *The Qing Code*. On Ricci's concerns about homosexuality, see Jonathan Spence, *The Memory Palace of Matteo Ricci*, pp. 220–29.

188. Volpp, "The Discourse on Male Marriage," p. 116. Despite Xie's rejoinder, Fujian was less hostile to homoeroticism than other parts of China (Michael Szonyi, personal communication). On the localization of homosexuality to Fujian and its possible connection to piracy, see Vivien Ng, "Homosexuality and the State," pp. 85–86.

189. Li Le, *Jianwen zaji*, 10.11a. The magistrate's provincial superior, Geng Dingxiang, fired him for making the purchase. See also 8.51b regarding "boy singers."

190. This assertion is not entirely accurate, for some writers used love between males to depict harmonious love, contrasting it with the antagonism that tends to color erotic scenes between men and women; McMahon, "Eroticism in Late Ming, Early Qing Fiction," p. 235.

191. Zhang Dai, *Langhuan wenji*, p. 129.

192. Zhang Dai's accounts of Hangzhou quoted in this section are from *Taoan mengyi*, pp. 20, 29, 34, 48, 67–68, 72, 77–80.

193. Li Le, *Jianwen zaji*, 8.41a–b.

194. *Hangzhou fuzhi* (1922), 84.31a, quoting the 1687 gazetteer of Renhe county.

FALL: THE LORD OF SILVER (1642–1644)

1. *Huangpi xianzhi* (1871), 1.19b–20a, 28a.

2. The account that follows is drawn from Ding Yaokang, *Chujie jilüe* (1982), pp. 150–57. On the history of Zhucheng county in the late Ming, see Brook, *Praying for Power,* ch. 7; concerning Ding Yaokang, see pp. 244–47.

3. Lynn Struve, *Voices from the Ming-Qing Cataclysm,* p. 56.

4. From a provincial censorial report of 4 February 1645, in *Qing shilu Shangdong shiliao xuan,* vol. 1, p. 6.

5. The account that follows is taken from Li Tingsheng's diary as translated in Li Xiaosheng et al., "Li Tingsheng's *A Record of Hardship.*"

6. *Xinzheng xianzhi* (1693), 4.96a (epidemic), 100a (Li Zicheng).

7. For another instance of a student "using a farmer-merchant cover," see Struve, *Voices from the Ming-Qing Cataclysm,* p. 23.

8. *Handan xianzhi* (1756), 1.15a.

9. Gu Yanwu, *Rizhi lu jishi,* 12.21b–22a.

10. Gu is not the only seventeenth-century writer to invoke it; see, e.g., *Songjiang fuzhi* (1819), 55.10a, in which the scholarly brother of a 1615 *juren* is praised for passing the latter half of his eighty-five years "without directing his feet to town."

11. Gu Yanwu, *Rizhi lu jishi,* 12.22a–b.

12. Not even Wang Shimin, an earnest official who recalled being laughed at for keeping to the letter of travel regulations in the Chongzhen era, made do with such a tiny retinue; Pei-yi Wu, *The Confucian's Progress,* p. 254.

13. For a selection of texts similar to those of Ding Yaokang and Li Tingsheng, see Struve, *Voices from the Ming-Qing Cataclysm.*

14. The good speed at which one could travel overland made a difference to others during the dynastic transition. A retired official in Sichuan covered 230 kilometers on horseback in one night in 1642 in a desperate attempt to save his mother and brother from the other great late-Ming rebel leader Zhang Xianzhong (ca. 1605–47); *Yangzhou fuzhi* (1733), 27.49b. Such speed seems unimaginable for the early Ming, though it was standard for emergency dispatches in the Qing, according to the rates given in *Hubei sheng yizhan sizhi chengtu lishu xianxing shike qingce* (1802), 1.5, cited in Jerome Chen, *The Highlanders of Central China,* p. 8.

15. Li Le, *Jianwen zaji,* 8.71a. Li's gazetteer, *Wuqing zhenzhi,* survives only in a rare copy in the Shanghai Library; I have not seen it.

16. Ibid., 2.75a–b.

17. Mi Chü Wiens, "Lord and Peasant," p. 16, in the context of explaining the dissolution of bondservice in the seventeenth century.

18. *Jiangling xianzhi* (1794), 32.10b–11a.

19. E.g., *Fuzhou fuzhi* (1613), 25.15a.

20. Li Yue, *Jianwen zaji,* 3.123a.

21. The term is used by Xu Hongzu to refer to the longtime family servant Second Son Wang, who accompanied him on some of his journeys; *Xu Xiake youji,* p. 100.

22. Li Le, *Jianwen zaji*, 3.12a–b.

23. Ibid., 2.80b.

24. *Shexian zhi* (1609), 3.9a. It bears noting that Li Le elsewhere pinpoints 1556 as the turning point in the relationship between teachers and students; *Jianwen zaji*, 3.107b.

25. Li Le, *Jianwen zaji*, 3.112b.

26. Ibid., 8.46b.

27. Local scholars in Huangpi organized a "study association" (*xuehui*) in the 1580s and invited, among others, a local associate of such prominent figures as Jiao Hong, Geng Dingxiang, and Luo Hongxian to lecture; *Huangpi xianzhi* (1871), 8.6b.

28. Ibid., 8.8a.

29. Ibid., 1.25b.

Bibliography

ABBREVIATIONS

CHC   Cambridge History of China
JAS   Journal of Asian Studies
LIC   Late Imperial China

SOURCES

Abru, Hafiz. *A Persian Embassy to China.* Translated by K. M. Maitra. Reprint edited by L. Carrington Goodrich. New York: Paragon, 1970.

Adshead, S. A. M. *China in World History.* 2nd ed. London: Macmillan, 1995.

André, Jean-Marie, and Marie-Françoise Baslez. *Voyager dans l'antiquité.* Paris: Fayard, 1993.

Atwell, William. "International Bullion Flows and the Chinese Economy circa 1530–1650." *Past and Present* 95 (1982), pp. 68–90.

———. "Notes on Silver, Foreign Trade, and the Late Ming Economy." *Ch'ing-shih wen-t'i* 3:8 (1977), pp. 1–33.

———. "Some Observations on the 'Seventeenth-Century Crisis' in China and Japan." *JAS* 45:2 (February 1986), pp. 223–44.

Bernhardt, Kathryn. "A Ming-Qing Transition in Chinese Women's History?: The Perspective from Law." In *Remapping China: Fissures in Historical Terrain,* edited by Gail Hershatter et al., pp. 42–58. Stanford: Stanford University Press, 1996.

Bontekoe, William Ysbrantsz. *Memorable Description of the East Indian Voyage, 1618–25.* Translated by C. B. Bodde-Hodgkinson and Pieter Geyl. First published in Dutch, 1646. Reprint, London: George Routledge and Sons, 1929.

Book of Changes. Translated by Richard Wilhelm and into English by Carl Baynes. Princeton: Princeton University Press, 1967.

Boxer, C. R., ed. *South China in the Sixteenth Century, Being the Narratives of Galeote Pereira, Fr. Gaspar da Cruz, Fr. Martín de Rada.* London: Hakluyt Society, 1953.

———. *The Great Ship from Amacon: Annals of Macao and the Old Japan Trade.* Lisbon: Centro de Estudos Históricos Ultramarinos, 1959.

Braudel, Fernand. *Capitalism and Material Life, 1400–1800.* London: Weidenfeld and Nicolson, 1973.

Bray, Francesca. "Le travail féminin dans la China impériale." *Annales: Histoire, Sciences Sociales,* 1994, no. 4 (July–August), pp. 783–816.

Britnell, Richard. *The Commercialisation of English Society, 1000–1500.* Cambridge: Cambridge University Press, 1993.

Brokaw, Cynthia. *The Ledgers of Merit and Demerit: Social Change and Moral Order in Late Imperial China.* Princeton: Princeton University Press, 1991.

Brook, Timothy. "Censorship in Eighteenth-Century China: A View from the Book Trade." *Canadian Journal of History* 23:2 (August 1988), pp. 177–96.

———. "Edifying Knowledge: The Building of School Libraries in the Mid-Ming." *LIC* 17:1 (June 1996), pp. 93–119.

———. "Family Continuity and Cultural Hegemony: The Gentry of Ningbo, 1368–1911." In *Chinese Local Elites and Patterns of Dominance,* edited by Joseph Esherick and Mary Rankin, pp. 27–50. Berkeley and Los Angeles: University of California Press, 1990.

———. *Geographical Sources of Ming-Qing History.* Ann Arbor: Center for Chinese Studies, University of Michigan, 1988.

———. "Guides for Vexed Travelers: Route Books in the Ming and Qing." *Ch'ing-shih wen-t'i* 4:5 (June 1981), pp. 32–76.

———. "Mapping Knowledge in the Sixteenth Century: The Gazetteer Cartography of Ye Chunji." *East Asian Library Journal* 7:2 (winter 1994), pp. 5–32.

———. "The Merchant Network in Sixteenth Century Ming China: A Discussion and Translation of Chang Han's 'On Merchants.'" *Journal of the Economic and Social History of the Orient* 24:2 (May 1981), pp. 165–214.

———. *Praying for Power: Buddhism and the Formation of Gentry Society in Late-Ming China.* Cambridge: Council on East Asian Studies, Harvard University, 1993.

———. "The Spatial Structure of Ming Local Administration." *LIC* 6:1 (June 1985), pp. 1–55.

———. "The Spread of Rice Cultivation and Rice Technology into the Hebei Region in the Ming and Qing." In *Explorations in the History of Science and Technology in China,* edited by Li Guohao et al., pp. 659–90. Shanghai: Shanghai Classics Publishing House, 1982.

———. "Weber, Mencius, and the History of Capitalism in China." *Asian Perspective* 19:1 (1995), pp. 79–97.

Cai Taibin. *Mingdai caohe zhi chengzhi yu guanli* [The maintenance and operation of the Grand Canal in the Ming dynasty]. Taibei: Shangwu Yinshuguan, 1992.

Canfield, Susan. "Bridge Construction and Repair in the Ming and Ch'ing." *Papers on China* (Harvard University), no. 24 (1971), pp. 19–40.

Cartier, Michel. *Une réforme locale en Chine au XVIe siècle: Hai Rui à Chun'an 1558–1562.* Paris: Mouton, 1973.

Chang, Kang-i Sun. *The Late Ming Poet Ch'en Tzu-lung: Crises of Love and Loyalism.* New Haven: Yale University Press, 1991.

Chen Baoliang. *Zhongguo liumang shi* [A history of vagabonds in China]. Beijing: Zhongguo Shehui Kexue Chubanshe, 1993.

Chen Hongmo. *Zhishi yuwen* [Sundry things I have heard about governing the realm]. 1521. Reprint, Beijing: Zhonghua Shuju, 1985.

Chen, Jerome. *The Highlanders of Central China: A History, 1895–1937.* Armonk: M. E. Sharpe, 1992.

Chen Jian. *Huang Ming congxin lu* [Record of official activism in the Ming dynasty]. Edited from 1555 edition by Shen Guoyuan. 1620.

Chen Keng. "Ming-Qing shiqi Fujian nongcun shichang shilun" [A preliminary study of rural markets in Fujian in the Ming-Qing period]. *Zhongguo shehui jingji shi yanjiu*, 1986, no. 4, pp. 52–60.

Chen Qi, ed. *Gansu gonglu jiaotong shi* [History of road communications in Gansu province]. Vol. 1. Beijing: Renmin Jiaotong Chubanshe, 1987.

Chen Xuewen. *Zhongguo fengjian wanqi de shangpin jingji* [The commodity economy of late feudal China]. Changsha: Hunan Renmin Chubanshe, 1989.

Chen Yinque. *Liu Rushi biezhuan* [Biography of Liu Shi]. Shanghai: Shanghai Guji Chubanshe, 1980.

Chen Yuan. *Mingji Dian-Qian fojiao kao* [A study of Buddhism in Yunnan and Guizhou in the late Ming]. 1940. Reprint, Beijing: Zhonghua Shuju, 1962.

Clunas, Craig. "Connoisseurs and Aficionados: The Real and the Fake in Ming China (1368–1644)." In *Why Fakes Matter: Essays on Problems of Authenticity*, edited by Mark Jones, pp. 151–56. London: British Museum Press, 1992.

——. *Fruitful Sites: Garden Culture in Ming Dynasty China.* London: Reaction Books; Durham: Duke University Press, 1996.

——. "Ming Jade Carvers and their Customers." *Transactions of the Oriental Ceramic Society* 50 (1985–86), pp. 69–85.

——. "Some Literary Evidence for Gold and Silver Vessels in the Ming Period (1368–1644)." In *Pots and Pans: A Colloquium on Precious Metals and Ceramics* (Oxford Studies in Islamic Art, no. 3), edited by Michael Vickers and Julian Raby, pp. 83–87. Oxford: Oxford University Press, 1987.

——. *Superfluous Things: Material Culture and Social Status in Early Modern China.* Cambridge, England: Polity Press, 1991.

Da Ming huidian [The collected statutes of the Ming dynasty]. 1588. Reprint, Taibei: Dongnan Shubaoshe, 1963.

Danyizi, ed. *Tianxia lucheng tuyin* [Illustrated guide to routes of the realm]. Early-Qing edition of *Shishang yaolan*, 1626. Modern reprint edited by Yang Zhengtai and printed together with Huang Bian, *Tianxia shuilu lucheng*. Taiyuan: Shanxi Renmin Chubanshe, 1992.

David, Percival, trans. and ed. *Chinese Connoisseurship: The Ko Ku Yao Lun, the Essential Criteria of Antiquities*. London: Faber and Faber, 1971.

D'Elia, Pasquale, ed. *Fonti Ricciane*. 3 vols. Roma: La Libraria dello Stato, 1942–47.

Deng Hanyi, ed. *Shi guan* [Perspectives on poetry]. 1672.

Des Forges, Roger. See Li Xiaosheng et al.

Ding Yaokang. *Chujie jilüe* [A brief record of my escape from calamity]. 1656. Reprinted in *Mingshi ziliao congkan*, no. 2, pp. 135–66. Yangzhou: Jiangsu Renmin Chubanshe, 1982.

Dong Qichang. *Rongtai ji* [Writings from Roomy Terrace]. 1630.

———. *Yunxuan qingbi lu* [Notes on pure esoterica from Split-Bamboo Studio]. Reprint, Shanghai: Shangwu Yinshuguan, 1937.

Dreyer, Edward. *Early Ming China: A Political History, 1355–1435*. Stanford: Stanford University Press, 1982.

du Halde, Jean Baptiste. *The General History of China*. 3 vols. London: John Watts, 1741.

Dudbridge, Glen. "Women Pilgrims to T'ai Shan: Some Pages from a Seventeenth-Century Novel." In *Pilgrims and Sacred Sites in China*, edited by Susan Naquin and Chün-fang Yü, pp. 39–64. Berkeley and Los Angeles: University of California Press, 1992.

Dunstan, Helen. "The Late Ming Epidemic: A Preliminary Survey." *Ch'ing-shih wen-t'i* 3:3 (November 1975), pp. 1–59.

Ebrey, Patricia, ed. *Chinese Civilization and Society: A Sourcebook*. New York: Free Press, 1981.

Elvin, Mark. *The Pattern of the Chinese Past*. Stanford: Stanford University Press, 1973.

Fan Shuzhi. "Mingdai Zhejiang shizhen fenbu yu jiegou" [The distribution and structure of Zhejiang towns in the Ming dynasty]. *Lishi dili* 5 (1987), pp. 185–99.

Fang, Jun. "The *Gazetteer of the Nanjing Ministry of Rites*: The Record of an Auxiliary Capital Department in the Ming Dynasty." *The East Asian Library Journal* 7:1 (spring 1994), pp. 73–97.

Farmer, Edward. *Zhu Yuanzhang and Early Ming Legislation: The Reordering of Chinese Society Following the Era of Mongol Rule*. Leiden: E. J. Brill, 1995.

Feng Menglong. *Xingshi hengyan* [Lasting words to awaken the world]. Reprint, Hong Kong: Zhonghua Shuju, 1978.

Franke, Wolfgang. *An Introduction to the Sources of Ming History*. Kuala Lumpur: University of Malaya Press, 1968.

Fu Yiling. *Mingdai Jiangnan shimin jingji shitan* [Explorations in the urban economy of Jiangnan in the Ming dynasty]. Shanghai: Shanghai Renmin Chubanshe, 1957.

———. "Mingdai jingji shi shang de Shandong yu Henan" [Shandong and Henan in the economic history of the Ming dynasty]. *Shehui kexue zhanxian*, 1984, no. 3, pp. 119–27.

———. *Ming-Qing fengjian tudi suoyouzhi lungang* [Outline of the feudal landownership system of the Ming and Qing]. Shanghai: Renmin Chubanshe, 1992.

————. *Ming-Qing shehui jingji shi lunwen ji* [Essays on the socioeconomic history of the Ming and Qing]. Beijing: Renmin Chubanshe, 1982.

Fuzheng. *Hanshan dashi nianpu shuzhu* [Annotated chronological biography of Master Hanshan]. Reprint, Taibei: Zhenmeishan Chubanshe, 1967.

Gallagher, Louis, ed. and trans. *China in the Sixteenth Century: The Journals of Matthew Ricci, 1583–1610.* New York: Random House, 1967.

Gazagnadou, Didier. *La poste à relais.* Paris: Editions Kiné, 1994.

Geiss, James. "The Chia-ching Reign." *CHC,* vol. 7, pp. 440–510. Cambridge: Cambridge University Press, 1988.

Ginzburg, Carlo. *The Cheese and the Worms: The Cosmos of a Sixteenth-Century Miller.* Baltimore: Johns Hopkins University Press, 1980.

Goldstone, Jack. "East and West in the Seventeenth Century: Political Crises in Stuart England, Ottoman Turkey, and Ming China." *Comparative Studies in Society and History* 30 (1988), pp. 103–42.

Goodrich, L. Carrington, and Chaoying Fang, eds. *Dictionary of Ming Biography.* 2 vols. New York: Columbia University Press, 1976.

Gu Yanwu. *Rizhi lu jishi* [Record of knowledge gained day by day, with commentaries]. 1834. Reprint, Shanghai: Shanghai Guji Chubanshe, 1984.

————. *Tianxia junguo libing shu* [Strengths and weaknesses of the various regions of the realm]. 1662. Reprint, Kyoto: Chūbun Shuppansha, 1975.

Gu Ying. "Mingdai yubeicang jiliang wenti chutan" [Preliminary study of the question of preparedness granary storage in the Ming dynasty]. *Shixue jikan,* 1993, no. 1, pp. 20–26.

Guangxi hangyun shi [A history of transport in Guangxi]. Beijing: Renmin Jiaotong Chubanshe, 1991.

Hamashima Atsutoshi. "Minmatsu Kōnan kyōshin no gutaisō" [A concrete image of the gentry of late-Ming Jiangnan]. In *Minmatsu Shinsho ki no kenkyū* [Studies in the late-Ming, early-Qing period], edited by Iwai Shigeki and Taniguchi Kikuo, pp. 165 ff. Kyoto: Kyōto Daigaku Jimbun Kagaku Kenkyūjo, 1991.

————. "The Organization of Water Control in the Kiangnan Delta in the Ming Period." *Acta Asiatica* 38 (1980), pp. 69–92.

Handlin, Joanna. "Benevolent Societies: The Reshaping of Charity in the Late Ming and Early Qing." *JAS* 46:2 (May 1987), pp. 309–37.

Handlin Smith, Joanna. "Gardens in Ch'i Piao-chia's Social World: Wealth and Values in Late-Ming Kiangnan." *JAS* 51:1 (February 1992), pp. 55–81.

Hansen, Valerie. *Negotiating Daily Life in Traditional China: How Ordinary People Used Contracts, 600–1400.* New Haven: Yale University Press, 1995.

Hazelton, Keith. "Patrilines and the Development of Localized Lineages: The Wu of Hsiu-ning City, Hui-chou, to 1528." In *Kinship Organization in Late Imperial China,* edited by Patricia Buckley Ebrey and James L. Watson, pp. 137–69. Berkeley and Los Angeles: University of California Press, 1986.

Ho, Chuimei. "The Ceramic Trade in Asia, 1602–82." In *Japanese In-*

dustrialization and the Asian Economy, edited by A. J. H. Latham and Heita Kawakatsu, pp. 35-70. London: Routledge, 1994.

Ho, Ping-ti. *The Ladder of Success in Traditional China: Aspects of Social Mobility, 1368-1911.* New York: Columbia University Press, 1962.

———. *Studies on the Population of China.* Cambridge: Harvard University Press, 1959.

Hoshi Ayao. *Min Shin jidai kōtsū shi no kenkyū* [Studies on the history of transportation in the Ming-Qing period]. Tokyo: Yamakawa Shuppansha, 1971.

———. *The Ming Grain Tribute System.* Translated by Mark Elvin. Ann Arbor: Center for Chinese Studies, University of Michigan, 1969.

Huang Bian. *Tianxia shuilu lucheng* [Water and land routes of the realm]. 1635 edition of *Yitong lucheng tuji* [Comprehensive illustrated route book], 1570. Modern reprint edited by Yang Zhengtai and printed together with Danyizi, *Tianxia lucheng tuyin.* Taiyuan: Shanxi Renmin Chubanshe, 1992.

Huang Liuhong. *Fuhui quanshu* [A complete book concerning happiness and benevolence]. 1699.

Huang Liu-hung. *A Complete Book Concerning Happiness and Benevolence.* Translated by Djang Chu. Tucson: University of Arizona Press, 1984.

Huang, Martin W. *Literati and Self-Re/Presentation: Autobiographical Sensibility in the Eighteenth-Century Chinese Novel.* Stanford: Stanford University Press, 1995.

Huang Miantang. *Ming shi guanjian* [Observations on Ming history]. Jinan: Qi Lu Shushe, 1985.

Huang Ming zhishu [Regulatory handbooks of the Ming dynasty]. Edited by Zhang Lu. 1579. Reprint, Tokyo: Koten Kenkyūkai, 1967. 2 vols.

Huang, Ray. *China: A Macro History.* Armonk: M. E. Sharpe, 1990.

———. *1587, A Year of No Significance.* New Haven: Yale University Press, 1981.

———. "Fiscal Administration during the Ming Dynasty." In *Chinese Government in Ming Times: Seven Studies,* edited by Charles Hucker, pp. 73-128. New York: Columbia University Press, 1969.

———. *Taxation and Governmental Finance in Sixteenth-Century Ming China.* Cambridge: Cambridge University Press, 1974.

Huc, Évariste-Régis. *A Journey through the Chinese Empire.* New York: Harper and Brothers, 1855.

Huo Tao. *Wenmin gong quanji* [Complete writings of Master Huo Wenmin]. 1576.

Jiang Zanchu. *Nanjing shihua* [An informal history of Nanjing]. Nanjing: Jiangsu Renmin Chubanshe, 1980.

Jianyue Duti. *Yimeng manyan* [Rambling words about this one dream]. Kangxi era. Reprint, Putian: Guanghua Monastery, ca. 1987.

Johnson, Linda Cooke, ed. *Cities of Jiangnan in Late Imperial China* Albany: State University of New York Press, 1993.

Jörg, Christiaan. "Chinese Porcelain for the Dutch in the Seventeenth Century: Trading Networks and Private Enterprise." In *The Porcelains of Jingdezhen*, edited by Rosemary Scott, pp. 183–205. London: David Percival Foundation, 1993.

King, Gail. "The Family Letters of Xu Guangqi." *Ming Studies* 31 (spring 1991), pp. 1–41.

Ko, Dorothy. *Teachers of the Inner Chambers: Women and Culture in Seventeenth-Century China.* Stanford: Stanford University Press, 1994.

Lai Xinxia, ed. *Zhongguo gudai tushu shiye shi* [History of library enterprises in ancient China]. Zhongguo Wenhuashi Congshu series. Shanghai: Shanghai Renmin Chubanshe, 1990.

Langlois, John. "The Hung-wu Reign, 1368–1398." *CHC*, vol. 7, pp. 107–181. Cambridge: Cambridge University Press, 1988.

Li Chi. *The Travel Diaries of Hsü Hsia-k'o.* Hong Kong: Chinese University of Hong Kong Press, 1974.

Li Jinde. *Keshang yilan xingmi* [Bringing traveling merchants to their senses at a glance]. 1635. Modern reprint edited by Yang Zhengtai and printed with Huang Bian, *Tianxia shuilu lucheng*. Taiyuan: Shanxi Renmin Chubanshe, 1992.

Li Kaixian. *Li Kaixian ji* [Collected writings of Li Kaixian]. 3 vols. Beijing: Zhonghua Shuju, 1959.

Li Rihua. *Weishui xuan riji* [Diary from the Water-Tasting Gallery]. Jiaye Tang edition, 1923.

Li Xian, ed. *Da Ming yitong zhi* [Unity gazetteer of the Great Ming dynasty]. 1461.

Li Xiaosheng, Wei Qianzhi, and Roger Des Forges. "Li Tingsheng's *A Record of Hardship*: A Recently Discovered Manuscript Reflecting Literati Life in North Henan at the End of the Ming, 1642–44." *LIC* 15:2 (December 1994), pp. 85–122.

Li Le. *Jianwen zaji* [Miscellaneous notes on things seen and heard]. 1601, with two supplementary chapters, 1610. Reprint of 1632 edition, Shanghai: Shanghai Guji Chubanshe, 1986.

Liang Fangzhong, ed. *Zhongguo lidai hukou, tiandi, tianfu tongji* [Chinese historical statistics on population, land, and taxes]. Shanghai: Renmin Chubanshe, 1980.

Lin Liyue. "Lu Ji chongshe sixiang zaitan" [A further discussion of Lu Ji's praise of lavishness]. *Xin shixue* 5:1 (1994), pp. 131–53.

Lin Renchuan. *Mingmo Qingchu siren haishang maoyi* [Private maritime trade in the late Ming and early Qing]. Shanghai: Huadong Shifan Daxue Chubanshe, 1987.

Liscomb, Katherine. *Learning from Mount Hua: A Chinese Physician's Illustrated Travel Record and Painting Theory.* Cambridge: Cambridge University Press, 1993.

Liu Tong. *Dijing jingwu lüe* [Sights of the imperial capital]. 1635. Reprint, Beijing: Beijing Guji Chubanshe, 1980.

Lu Rong. *Shuyuan zaji* [Miscellaneous records from Bean Garden]. 1494. Reprint, Beijing: Zhonghua Shuju, 1985.

Luo Hongxian. *Nian'an wenji* [Collected writings of Luo Hongxian]. Siku Quanshu Zhenben edition. Reprint, Taibei: Shangwu Yinshuguan, 1974.

Ma Junchang et al. *Beijing youshi* [History of mail in Beijing]. Beijing: Beijing Chubanshe, 1987.

Marmé, Michael. "Heaven on Earth: The Rise of Suzhou, 1127–1550." In *Cities of Jiangnan in Late Imperial China,* edited by Linda Cooke Johnson, pp. 17–45. Albany: State University of New York Press, 1993.

Matsuura Akira. "Mindai koki no enkai kōun" [Coastal boat traffic in the late Ming]. *Shakai keizai shigaku* 54:3 (1988), pp. 86–102.

McMahon, Keith. "Eroticism in Late Ming, Early Qing Fiction: The Beauteous Realm and the Sexual Battlefield." *T'oung Pao* 73 (1987), pp. 221–64.

Medley, Margaret. "Organization and Production at Jingdezhen in the Sixteenth Century." In *The Porcelains of Jingdezhen,* edited by Rosemary Scott, pp. 69–82. London: David Percival Foundation, 1993.

Meijer, M. J. "Homosexual Offenses in Ch'ing Law." In *Asian Homosexuality,* edited by Wayne R. Dynes and Stephen Donaldson. New York: Garland, 1992.

Meskill, John, ed. and trans. *Ch'oe Pu's Diary: A Record of Drifting Across the Sea.* Tucson: University of Arizona Press, 1965.

———. *Gentlemanly Interests and Wealth on the Yangtze Delta.* Ann Arbor: Association for Asian Studies, 1994.

Mills, J. V. G., trans. *Ma Huan, Ying-yai Sheng-lan: "The Overall Survey of the Ocean's Shores" [1433].* Cambridge: Cambridge University Press, 1970.

Ming huiyao [Essential documents of the Ming dynasty]. Edited by Long Wenbin. 1887. Reprint, Beijing: Zhonghua Shuju, 1956.

Ming jingshi wenbian [Statecraft documents of the Ming dynasty]. Reprint, Beijing: Zhonghua Shuju, 1962.

Ming lü jijie fuli [The Ming code, with collected explanations and substatutes appended]. Reprint, Taibei: Chengwen Chubanshe, 1969.

Ming-Qing Huizhou shehui jingji ziliao congbian [Compendium of materials on socioeconomic history from Huizhou in the Ming-Qing period]. 2 vols. Beijing: Zhongguo Shehui Kexue Chubanshe, 1988, 1990.

Ming shi [The standard history of the Ming dynasty]. Edited by Zhang Tingyu. 1735. Reprint, Beijing: Zhonghua Shuju, 1974.

Ming shilu [Veritable records of the Ming dynasty]. Nanjing, 1940.

Mote, Frederick. "The Ch'eng-hua and Hung-chih Reigns, 1465–1505." *CHC,* vol. 7, pp. 343–402. Cambridge: Cambridge University Press, 1988.

———. "Chinese Society under Mongol Rule, 1215–1368." *CHC,* vol. 6, pp. 616–64. Cambridge: Cambridge University Press, 1994.

Needham, Joseph. *Science and Civilisation in China,* vol. 4, pt. 3: *Civil Engineering and Nautics.* Cambridge: Cambridge University Press, 1971.

Ng, Vivian W. "Homosexuality and the State in Late Imperial China." In *Hidden from History: Reclaiming the Gay and Lesbian Past,* edited by Martin Duberman et al., pp. 76–89. New York: NAL Books, 1989.

Niida Noboru. *Chūgoku hōseishi kenkyū: tochi hō, torihiki hō* [Studies in

Chinese legal history: land law, property law]. Tokyo: Tōkyō Daigaku Shuppankai, 1962.

Nimick, Thomas G. "The County, the Magistrate, and the Yamen in Late Ming China." Ph.D. diss., Princeton University, 1993.

Nishijima Sadao. "The Formation of the Early Chinese Cotton Industry." In *State and Society in China: Japanese Perspectives on Ming-Qing Social and Economic History*, edited by Linda Grove and Christian Daniels, pp. 17–77. Tokyo: University of Tokyo Press, 1984.

Ōki Yasashi. "Minmatsu Kōnan ni okeru shuppan bunka no kenkyū" [Studies on the publishing culture in Jiangnan in the late Ming]. *Hiroshima Daigaku bungakubu kiyō* 50, special issue no. 1 (1991).

Pan Jixing. *Song Yingxing pingzhuan* [Critical biography of Song Yingxing]. Nanjing: Nanjing Daxue Chubanshe, 1990.

Peng Xinwei. *Zhongguo huobi shi* [A history of Chinese currency], vol. 1. Shanghai: Qunlian Chubanshe, 1954.

Peterson, Willard. *Bitter Gourd: Fang I-chih and the Impetus for Intellectual Change*. New Haven: Yale University Press, 1979.

Qing shilu Shandong shiliao xuan [Selections of historical materials relating to Shandong from the Qing Veritable Records]. 3 vols. Jinan: Qi Lu Shushe, 1984.

Qiu Jun. *Daxue yanyi bu* [Supplement to "Expositions on the Great Learning"]. 1506. Reprint of Siku Quanshu edition, Taibei: Shangwu Yinshuguan, 1971.

Qiu Shusen and Wang Ting. "Yuandai hukou wenti chuyi" [Preliminary views on the question of population in the Yuan dynasty]. *Yuanshi luncong* [Essays on Yuan history] 2 (1983), pp. 111–24.

Rawski, Evelyn Sakakida. *Agricultural Change and the Peasant Economy of South China*. Cambridge: Harvard University Press, 1972.

Reid, Anthony. *Southeast Asia in the Age of Commerce, 1450–1680*. Vol. 2: *Expansion and Crisis*. New Haven: Yale University Press, 1993.

Ricci, Matteo. *See* D'Elia, Pasquale.

Rossabi, Morris. "The Tea and Horse Trade with Inner Asia during the Ming." *Journal of Asian History* 4:2 (1970), pp. 136–68.

Ruitenbeek, Klaas. *Carpentry and Building in Late Imperial China: A Study of the Fifteenth-Century Carpenter's Manual "Lu Ban Jing."* Leiden: E. J. Brill, 1993.

Sato, Masahiko. *Chinese Ceramics: A Short History*. Tokyo: Weatherhill, 1981.

Schurz, William. *The Manila Galleon*. 1939. Reprint, New York: Dutton, 1959.

Scott, Rosemary, ed. *The Porcelains of Jingdezhen*. London: Percival David Foundation of Chinese Art, 1993.

Seybolt, Peter. *Throwing the Emperor from His Horse: Portrait of a Village Leader in China, 1923–1995*. Boulder: Westview Press, 1996.

Shen Dingping. "Mingdai yidi de shezhi, guanxia he zuoyong" [The setting up, administration, and uses of the Ming courier and postal services].

Wenshi zhishi [Knowledge in the humanities], 1984, no. 3, pp. 78–82.

Shen Qi. *Wujiang shuikao zengyi* [A study of the waterways of Wujiang, expanded edition]. Edited by Huang Xiangxi. 1734. Original edition compiled in the third quarter of the sixteenth century.

Shi Shi. "Cong Mingdai kaishi de minyou" [The beginning of private mail service in the Ming dynasty]. *Jiyou* [Philately], 1963, nos. 10–11, p. 21.

Shiba Yoshinobu. *Commerce and Society in Sung China*. Translated by Mark Elvin. Ann Arbor: Center for Chinese Studies, 1970. Edited translation of *Sōdai shōgyōshi kenkyū* (Tokyo: Kazama Shobō, 1968).

———. "Ningpo and Its Hinterland." In *The City in Late Imperial China*, edited by G. William Skinner, pp. 391–439. Stanford: Stanford University Press, 1977.

Shigeta Atsushi, "The Origins and Structure of Gentry Rule." In *State and Society in China: Japanese Perspectives on Ming-Qing Social and Economic History*, edited by Linda Grove and Christian Daniels, pp. 335–85. Tokyo: University of Tokyo Press, 1984.

So, Kwan-wai. *Japanese Piracy in Ming China during the Sixteenth Century*. Michigan State University Press, 1975.

Song Yingxing. *Tiangong kaiwu* [The exploitation of the works of nature]. 1637. Reprint, Shanghai: Shanghai Guji Chubanshe, 1992.

Spence, Jonathan. *The Memory Palace of Matteo Ricci*. Harmondsworth: Penguin, 1985.

Struve, Lynn. *Voices from the Ming-Qing Cataclysm: China in Tiger's Jaws*. New Haven: Yale University Press, 1993.

Su Gengsheng. "Mingchu de shangzheng yu shangshui" [Early-Ming policies toward merchants and commercial taxes]. Reprinted in *Mingshi yanjiu luncong*, vol. 2, edited by Wu Zhihe, pp. 427–48. Taibei: Dali Chubanshe, 1985.

Su Jilang. *Tang-Song shidai Minnan Quanzhou shidi lungao* [An account of the historical geography of Quanzhou in southern Fujian in the Tang-Song period]. Taibei: Shangwu Yinshuguan, 1991.

Su Tongbing. *Mingdai yidi zhidu* [The courier system of the Ming dynasty]. Taibei: Zhonghua Congshu Bianshen Weiyuanhui, 1969.

Sun, E-tu Zen and Shiou-chuan Sun, tr. *T'ien-kung K'ai-wu: Chinese Technology in the Seventeenth Century*. University Park: Pennsylvania State University Press, 1966.

Taga Akigorō. *Sōfu no kenkyū* [Studies in lineage genealogies]. Tokyo: Tōyō Bunko, 1960.

Tanaka Masatoshi. "Popular Uprisings, Rent Resistance, and Bondservant Rebellions in the Late Ming." In *State and Society in China: Japanese Perspectives on Ming-Qing Social and Economic History*, edited by Linda Grove and Christian Daniels, pp. 165–214. Tokyo: University of Tokyo Press, 1984.

———. "Rural Handicraft in Jiangnan in the Sixteenth and Seventeenth Centuries." In *State and Society in China: Japanese Perspectives on Ming-Qing Social and Economic History*, pp. 79–100.

Terada Takanobu. *Shanxi shangren zhi yanjiu* [Studies on the merchants of Shanxi]. Translated by Zhang Zhengming et al. Taiyuan: Shanxi Renmin Chubanshe, 1986. Translation of *Sansai shōnin no kenkyū* (Tokyo: Tōyōshi Kenkyūkai, 1972).

Tian Rukang. "*Duhai fangcheng*: Zhongguo di yiben keyin de shuilu pu" [The first printed Chinese rutter, *The Route for Crossing the Sea*]. In *Explorations in the History of Science and Technology in China*, edited by Li Guohao et al., pp. 301–308. Shanghai: Shanghai Classics Publishing House, 1982.

Tong, James. *Disorder under Heaven: Collective Violence in the Ming Dynasty*. Stanford: Stanford University Press, 1991.

Tsien, Tsuen-hsuin. *Science and Civilisation in China*, vol. 5, pt. 1: *Paper and Printing*. Edited by Joseph Needham. Cambridge: Cambridge University Press, 1985.

Tsurumi Naohiro. "Rural Control in the Ming Dynasty." In *State and Society in China: Japanese Perspectives on Ming-Qing Social and Economic History*, edited by Linda Grove and Christian Daniels, pp. 245–77. Tokyo: University of Tokyo Press, 1984.

Twitchett, Denis, and Tilemann Grimm. "The Cheng-t'ung, Ching-t'ai, and T'ien-shun Reigns." *CHC*, vol. 7, pp. 305–42. Cambridge: Cambridge University Press, 1988.

Volpp, Sophie. "The Discourse on Male Marriage: Li Yu's 'A Male Mencius' Mother.'" *positions* 2:1 (spring 1994), pp. 113–32.

Von Glahn, Richard. "Myth and Reality of China's Seventeenth Century Monetary Crisis." *Journal of Economic History* 56:2 (June 1996), pp. 429–54.

Wakeman, Frederic. *The Great Enterprise: The Manchu Reconstruction of Imperial Order in Seventeenth-Century China*. 2 vols. Berkeley and Los Angeles: University of California Press, 1985.

Waltner, Ann. *Getting an Heir: Adoption and the Construction of Kinship in Late Imperial China*. Honolulu: University of Hawaii Press, 1990.

Wang Shixing. *Guangzhi yi* [Further deliberations on my record of extensive records]. Reprint, Beijing: Xinhua Shudian, 1981.

Wang Wenlu. *Bailing xueshan* [The mountain of learning from a hundred peaks]. 1584. Reprint, Shanghai: Shangwu Yinshuguan, 1938.

Wang Xiaochuan, ed. *Yuan Ming Qing sandai jinhui xiaoshuo xiqu shiliao* [Materials on the suppression of fiction and drama in the three dynasties of Yuan, Ming, and Qing]. Beijing: Zuojia Chubanshe, 1958.

Wang Xingya. "Mingchu qian Shanxi min dao Henan kaoshu" [A study of the relocation of Shanxi residents to Henan in the early Ming]. *Shixue yuekan*, 1984, no. 4, pp. 36–44.

Wang Zhenzhong. "Ming-Qing shiqi Huishang shehui xingxiang de wenhua toushi" [A cultural elucidation of the social image of Huizhou merchants in the Ming-Qing period]. *Fudan xuebao*, 1993, no. 6, pp. 80–84, 96.

Wang Zhideng. *Ke Yue zhilüe* [Brief account of my journey through Zhejiang]. Reprinted in Wang Ying, ed., *Mingren riji suibi xuan* [Selections from Ming diaries and jottings], pp. 141–52. Shanghai: Nanqiang Shuju, 1935.

Wanli dichao [Wanli-era excerpts from the Beijing Gazette]. Taibei: Taiwan Guoli Tushuguan, 1963.

Wei Qingyuan. *Mingdai huangce zhidu* [The Yellow Register system of the Ming dynasty]. Beijing: Zhonghua Shuju, 1961.

Widmer, Ellen. "The Epistolary World of Female Talent in Seventeenth-Century China." *LIC* 10:2 (December 1989), pp. 1–43.

Wiens, Mi Chü. "Lord and Peasant: The Sixteenth to the Eighteenth Century." *Modern China* 6:1 (1980), pp. 3–39.

Will, Pierre-Étienne, and R. Bin Wong. *Nourish the People: The State Civilian Granary System in China, 1650–1850.* Ann Arbor: Center for Chinese Studies, University of Michigan, 1991.

Wu Chengming. "Lun Qingdai qianqi woguo guonei shichang" [The domestic market in China in the early Qing dynasty]. *Lishi yanjiu*, 1983, no. 1, pp. 96–106.

Wu Han. *Jiang Zhe cangshujia shilüe* [Brief history of book-collectors from Jiangsu and Zhejiang]. Reprint, Beijing: Zhonghua Shuju, 1981.

Wu Jihua. *Mingdai haiyun ji yunhe de yanjiu* [Studies on maritime transport and the Grand Canal in the Ming dynasty]. Taibei: Zhongyang Yanjiuyuan Lishi Yuyan Yanjiusuo, 1961.

Wu, K. T. "Ming Printing and Printers." *Harvard Journal of Asiatic Studies* 7:3 (1943), pp. 203–60.

Wu, Pei-yi. *The Confucian's Progress: Autobiographical Writings in Traditional China.* Princeton: Princeton University Press, 1990.

Xiancheng Ruhai. *Canxue zhijin* [Knowing the fords on the way to knowledge]. 1827. Reprint, Hangzhou, 1876.

Xie Guozhen. *Ming-Qing zhi ji dangshe yundong kao* [Studies on the movement to form political factions and literary societies during the Ming-Qing transition]. Reprint, Beijing: Zhonghua Shuju, 1982.

Xie Zhaozhe. *Wu zazu* [Five offerings of miscellany]. 1608.

Xu Dunqiu. *Jingsuo biji* [Jottings of Master Jingsuo]. Reprinted in Chen Xuewen, *Zhongguo fengjian wanqi de shangpin jingji,* pp. 318–21. Changsha: Hunan Renmin Chubanshe, 1989.

Xu Guangqi. *Nongzheng quanshu* [Complete handbook of agricultural administration]. 1643. Reprint, 2 vols. Shanghai: Shanghai Guji Chubanshe, 1979.

———. *Xu Guangqi ji* [Collected writings of Xu Guangqi]. Edited by Liang Jiamian. Shanghai: Shanghai Renmin Chubanshe, 1984.

Xu Hongzu. *Xu Xiake youji* [The travel diaries of Xu Hongzu]. 3 vols. Shanghai: Shanghai Guji Chubanshe, 1980.

Xu Shiduan, ed. *Ming shilu leizuan: funü shiliao juan* [Thematic selections from the Ming Veritable Records: Volume of historical materials on women]. Wuhan: Wuhan Chubanshe, 1995.

Xu Shumin and Qian Yue, eds. *Zhongxiang ci* [Song lyrics of the fragrant crowd]. 1689.

Xue Zongzheng. "Mingdai yanshang de lishi yanbian" [Historical development of Ming salt merchants]. *Zhongguo shi yanjiu*, 1980, no. 2, pp. 27–37.

Yang Guozhen. *Ming-Qing tudi qiyue wenshu yanjiu* [Studies on land contract documents of the Ming and Qing]. Beijing: Renmin Chubanshe, 1988.

Yang, Lien-sheng. "Ming Local Administration." In *Chinese Government in Ming Times: Seven Studies,* edited by Charles Hucker, pp. 1–21. New York: Columbia University Press, 1969.

———. *Studies in Chinese Institutional History.* Cambridge: Harvard University Press, 1961.

Yang Wenjie. *Dongcheng jiyu* [Various notes on east Hangzhou]. Reprint, Hangzhou, 1897.

Yang Zhengtai. "Ming-Qing Linqing de shengshuai yu dili tiaojian de bianhua" [The rise and fall of Linqing in relation to changes in geographical conditions in the Ming and Qing]. *Lishi dili* 3 (1983), pp. 115–20.

Ye Chunji. *Huian zhengshu* [Administrative handbook of Huian county]. Preface dated 1573. Reprinted in the author's *Shidong wenji* [Collected writings from the Stone Grotto], 1672.

Ye Mengzhu. *Yueshi bian* [Notes on crossing an era]. Kangxi era, first published 1935. Reprint, Shanghai: Shanghai Guji Chubanshe, 1981.

Ye Sheng. *Shuidong riji* [Diary from east of the river]. Reprint of Siku Quanshu edition, Beijing: Zhonghua Shuju, 1980.

Ye Xianen. "Shilun Huizhou shangren ziben de xingcheng yu fazhan" [On the formation and development of Huizhou merchant capital]. *Zhongguo shi yanjiu*, 1980, no. 3, pp. 104–18.

Yin Junke. "Mingdai Beijing jiaoqu cunluo de fazhan" [Development of villages in the Beijing region in the Ming period]. *Lishi dili* 3 (1983), pp. 121–30.

Yin Yungong. *Zhongguo Mingdai xinwen chuanbo shi* [History of news dissemination in China in the Ming dynasty]. Chongqing: Chongqing Chubanshe, 1990.

Yu Jiaxi. *Siku tiyao bianzheng* [Analytical studies on the "Outline of the Four Treasuries"]. In *Siku quanshu zongmu* [General catalog of the Complete Books in the Four Treasuries], vols. 9–10. Reprint, Taibei: Yiwen Yinshuguan, 1969.

Yu Jideng. *Diangu jiwen* [Hearsay notes on statutory precedents]. 1601 Reprint, Beijing: Zhonghua Shuju, 1981.

Yu Ruwei. *Huangzheng yaolan* [A conspectus of famine administration]. 1589.

Yu Xiangdou, ed. *Wanyong zhengzong* [The correct source for a myriad practical uses]. 1599.

Yu Yingshi. *Shi yu Zhongguo wenhua* [The gentry and Chinese culture]. Shanghai: Shanghai Renmin Chubanshe, 1989.

Yü, Chün-fang. *The Renewal of Buddhism in China: Chu-hung and the Late Ming Synthesis.* New York: Columbia University Press, 1981.

Yuan Hongdao. *Yuan Hongdao ji jianjiao* [The works of Yuan Hongdao with basic annotations]. 2 vols. Beijing: Zhongguo Gudian Wenxue Chubanshe, 1981.

Yuan, Tsing. "The Porcelain Industry at Ching-te-chen, 1550–1700." *Ming Studies* 6 (spring 1978), pp. 45–53.

Zeitlin, Judith. "The Petrified Heart: Obsession in Chinese Literature, Art, and Medicine." *LIC* 12:1 (June 1991), pp. 1–26.

Zhang Dai. *Langhuan wenji* [Collected writings from Langhuan Retreat]. 1877. Reprint, Taibei: Danjiang Shuju, 1956.

———. *Taoan mengyi* [Dream recollections from Tao's hermitage]. Shanghai: Zazhi Gongsi, 1936.

———. *Yehang chuan* [Night ferry]. Hangzhou: Zhejiang Guji Chubanshe, 1987.

Zhang Haipeng and Wang Tingyuan, eds. *Ming-Qing Huishang ziliao xuanbian* [Selected materials on Huizhou merchants of the Ming and Qing]. Hefei: Huangshan Shushe, 1985.

Zhang Han. *Songchuang mengyu* [Dream discourses at the pine window]. Preface dated 1593. Reprinted together with Chen Hongmo, *Zhishi yuwen* and *Jishi jiwen*. Beijing: Zhonghua Shuju, 1985.

Zhang Kaiquan. *Huian fengtu zhi* [Monograph on local customs of Huian county]. Taibei: Yongxin Yinshuaju, 1963.

Zhang Lu, ed. *Huang Ming zhishu* [Regulatory texts of the Ming dynasty]. 1579. Reprint, Tokyo: Koten Kenyukai, 1967.

Zhang Sun, ed. *Gu hanghai tu kaoshi* [Ancient maritime map with annotations]. Beijing: Haiyang Chubanshe, 1980.

Zhang Xie. *Dongxi yang kao* [Notes on the eastern and western maritime regions]. 1617. Reprint, Beijing: Zhonghua Shuju, 1981.

Zhang Zhengming and Xue Huilin, eds. *Ming-Qing Jinshang ziliao xuanbian* [Selected materials on Shanxi merchants in the Ming and Qing]. Taiyuan, n.d.

Zhao Lisheng, ed. *Rizhi lu daodu* [A reader for "Record of Knowledge Gained Day by Day"]. Chengdu: Ba Shu Shushe, 1992.

Zheng Hesheng and Zheng Yijun, eds. *Zheng He xia xiyang ziliao huibian* [A collecton of materials on Zheng He's maritime voyages to the west]. 2 vols. Jinan: Qi Lu Shushe, 1980, 1983.

Zheng Lihua. *Mingdai zhongqi wenxue yanjin yu chengshi xingtai* [The evolution of literature and urban formation in the mid-Ming]. Shanghai: Fudan Daxue Chubanshe, 1995.

Zheng Xiao. *Jin yan* [Comments on the present]. 1566. Reprint, Beijing: Zhonghua Shuju, 1984.

Zhongguo jin wubai nian hanlao fenbu tuji [Atlas of the distribution of drought and flood in China over the past five hundred years]. Beijing: Ditu Chubanshe, 1981.

Zhou Chen. "Yu xingzai hubu zhugong shu" [Letter to officials in the Ministry of Finance]. *Zhaodai jingji yan*, 2.10b–14a. Reprinted in *Lingnan yishu* [Surviving writings from Guangdong], vol. 37, n.p., 1850.

Zhou Kefu. *Jin'gang chiyan ji* [Verifications of the Diamond Sutra]. 1799.

Zhou Ningxia, Wu Yingshou, and Chu Shaotang. "*Xu Xiake youji* yuanshi

chaoben de faxian yu tantao" [Discovery and examination of the origi-
nal manuscript of the travel diaries of Xu Hongzu]. *Zhonghua wenshi
luncong* [Essays in Chinese culture] 12 (1979), pp. 155–88.
Zhu Fengji. *Mumin xinjian* [New mirror for shepherding the people]. 1404.
Japanese reprint, n.p., 1852.
Zhu Guozhen. *Yongchuang xiaopin* [Minor essays from the portable
kiosk]. 1622. Reprint, Beijing: Zhonghua Shuju, 1959.
Zhu Tingli. *Yanzheng zhi* [Monograph on the salt administration]. 1529.
Zhu Yuanzhang. *Ming taizu ji* [The writings of the founding Ming emperor].
Edited by Hu Shi'e. Hefei: Huangshan Shushe, 1991.
Zhu Yunming. *Ye ji* [Notes of an outsider]. 1511. Reprinted in Lidai Xiao-
shi series, Shanghai: Shangwu Yinshuguan, 1940.
Zhuang Weifeng, Zhu Shijia, and Feng Baolin, eds. *Zhongguo difangzhi
lianhe mulu* [Union catalog of Chinese local gazetteers]. Beijing: Zhong-
hua Shuju, 1985.
Zurndorfer, Harriet. *Change and Continuity in Chinese Local History: The
Development of Hui-chou Prefecture, 800 to 1800.* Leiden: E. J. Brill,
1989.

GAZETTEERS

Anxi xianzhi [Gazetteer of Anxi county]. 1552.
Ayu wang shanzhi [Gazetteer of King Asoka Mountain]. 1619.
Baoding fuzhi [Gazetteer of Baoding prefecture]. 1607.
Changde fuzhi [Gazetteer of Changde prefecture]. 1538.
Changshu xianzhi [Gazetteer of Changshu county]. 1539.
Changyuan xianzhi [Gazetteer of Changyuan county]. 1554.
Chaozhou fuzhi [Gazetteer of Chaozhou prefecture]. 1547.
Chongan xianzhi [Gazetteer of Chongan county]. 1670.
Chongwusuo chengzhi [Gazetteer of Chongwusuo citadel]. 1542, with later
revisions. Reprinted with *Huian zhengshu*, Fuzhou: Fujian Renmin Chu-
banshe, 1987.
Cili xianzhi [Gazetteer of Cili county]. 1574.
Daming fuzhi [Gazetteer of Daming prefecture]. 1506.
Dehua xianzhi [Gazetteer of Dehua county]. 1697.
Funing zhouzhi [Gazetteer of Funing subprefecture]. 1593.
Fuzhou fuzhi [Gazetteer of Fuzhou prefecture (Fujian)]. 1613.
Fuzhou fuzhi [Gazetteer of Fuzhou prefecture (Fujian)]. 1754.
Fuzhou fuzhi [Gazetteer of Fuzhou prefecture (Jiangxi)]. 1876.
Ganzhou fuzhi [Gazetteer of Ganzhou prefecture]. 1536.
Guangshan xianzhi [Gazetteer of Guangshan county]. 1556.
Guangxin fuzhi [Gazetteer of Guangxin prefecture]. 1873.
Guangzhou zhi [Gazetteer of Guangzhou subprefecture]. 1660.
Gushi xianzhi [Gazetteer of Gushi county]. 1659.
Gutian xianzhi [Gazetteer of Gutian county]. 1606.
Haicheng xianzhi [Gazetteer of Haicheng county]. 1762.
Haiyan xianzhi [Gazetteer of Haiyan county]. 1876.

Handan xianzhi [Gazetteer of Handan county]. 1756.
Hangzhou fuzhi [Gazetteer of Hangzhou prefecture]. 1546.
Hanyang fuzhi [Gazetteer of Hanyang prefecture]. 1546.
Hejian fuzhi [Gazetteer of Hejian prefecture]. 1540.
Hengyue zhi [Gazetteer of Heng Mountain]. 1612.
Hengzhou fuzhi [Gazetteer of Hengzhou prefecture]. 1536.
Hongwu jingcheng tuzhi [Illustrated gazetteer of the capital (Nanjing) in
    the Hongwu era]. 1393. Reprint, n.p., 1928.
Huangpi xianzhi [Gazetteer of Huangpi county]. 1871.
Huangzhou fuzhi [Gazetteer of Huangzhou prefecture]. 1500.
Huguang tujing zhishu [Illustrated gazetteer of Huguang province]. 1522.
Huian xianzhi [Gazetteer of Huian county]. 1530, with additional material
    to 1547.
Huian xianzhi [Gazetteer of Huian county]. 1566.
Huian xianzhi [Gazetteer of Huian county]. 1730.
Huizhou fuzhi [Gazetteer of Huizhou prefecture (Guangdong)]. 1542.
Jiangling xianzhi [Gazetteer of Jiangling county]. 1794.
Jiangnan tongzhi [Gazetteer of Jiangnan province]. 1736.
Jianyang xianzhi [Gazetteer of Jianyang county]. 1553.
Jinan fuzhi [Gazetteer of Jinan prefecture]. 1840.
Jingzhou zhi [Gazetteer of Jingzhou subprefecture]. 1612.
Jinling fancha zhi [Gazetteer of the Buddhist monasteries of Nanjing]. 1607.
Jintan xianzhi [Gazetteer of Jintan county]. 1921.
Jiujiang fuzhi [Gazetteer of Jiujiang prefecture]. 1527.
Lanyang xianzhi [Gazetteer of Lanyang county]. 1545.
Leizhou fuzhi [Gazetteer of Leizhou prefecture]. 1614.
Linju xianzhi [Gazetteer of Linju county]. 1552.
Longxi xianzhi [Gazetteer of Longxi county]. 1535.
Lushan xianzhi [Gazetteer of Lushan county]. 1552.
Mianyang zhi [Gazetteer of Mianyang prefecture]. 1531.
Nanchang fuzhi [Gazetteer of Nanchang prefecture]. 1588.
Nanchang xianzhi [Gazetteer of Nanchang county]. 1935.
Nanjing hubu zhi [Gazetteer of the Nanjing Ministry of Revenue]. 1550.
Ningbo fuzhi [Gazetteer of Ningbo prefecture]. 1560.
Ningguo fuzhi [Gazetteer of Ningguo prefecture]. 1919.
Qiongshan xianzhi [Gazetteer of Qiongshan county]. 1917.
Qiongzhou fuzhi [Gazetteer of Qiongzhou prefecture]. 1619.
Quanzhou fuzhi [Gazetteer of Quanzhou prefecture]. 1612.
Quanzhou fuzhi [Gazetteer of Quanzhou prefecture]. 1763.
Raozhou fuzhi [Gazetteer of Raozhou prefecture]. 1873.
Ruijin xianzhi [Gazetteer of Ruijin county]. 1542.
Shang tianzhu jiangsi zhi [Gazetteer of Upper Tianzhu Monastery]. 1646.
    Reprint, Hangzhou, 1897.
Shanghai xianzhi [Gazetteer of Shanghai county]. 1524.
Shanghai zhi [Gazetteer of Shanghai county]. 1504.
Shanxi tongzhi [Gazetteer of Shanxi province]. 1682.
Shaowu fuzhi [Gazetteer of Shaowu prefecture]. 1543.

Shaoxing fuzhi [Gazetteer of Shaoxing prefecture]. 1792.

Shengguo sizhi [Gazetteer of Shengguo monastery]. 1662. Reprint, n.p., 1881.

Shexian zhi [Gazetteer of Sheh county]. 1609.

Shexian zhi [Gazetteer of Sheh county]. 1771.

Shizhong shanzhi [Gazetteer of Shizhong mountain]. 1883. Reprint, Nanchang: Jiangxi Renmin Chubanshe, 1996.

Shunde xianzhi [Gazetteer of Shunde county]. 1853.

Songjiang fuzhi [Gazetteer of Songjiang prefecture]. 58-*juan* edition. 1630.

Songjiang fuzhi [Gazetteer of Songjiang prefecture]. 1819.

Taiping fuzhi [Gazetteer of Taiping prefecture]. 1903.

Tianjin fuzhi [Gazetteer of Tianjin prefecture]. 1899.

Tianzhu shanzhi [Gazetteer of the Tianzhu monasteries]. 1875.

Tongxiang xianzhi [Gazetteer of Tongxiang county]. 1887.

Wo shi [Gazetteer of Quwo county]. 1668.

Weishi xianzhi [Gazetteer of Weishi county]. 1548.

Wucheng xianzhi [Gazetteer of Wucheng county]. 1549.

Wuhu xianzhi [Gazetteer of Wuhu county]. 1919.

Wujiang xianzhi [Gazetteer of Wujiang county]. 1561.

Wujiang zhi [Gazetteer of Wujiang county]. 1488.

Wulin fanzhi [Gazetteer of Hangzhou monasteries]. 1615. Reprint, n.p., 1780.

Wuxi Jinkui xianzhi [Gazetteer of Wuxi and Jinkui counties]. 1840. Reprint, n.p., 1881.

Xinxiang xianzhi [Gazetteer of Xinxiang county]. 1506.

Xinzheng xianzhi [Gazetteer of Xinzheng county]. 1693.

Xuzhou zhi [Gazetteer of Xuzhou subprefecture]. 1540.

Yangzhou fuzhi [Gazetteer of Yangzhou prefecture]. 1733.

Yanping fuzhi [Gazetteer of Yanping prefecture]. 1526.

Yanshan xianzhi [Gazetteer of Yanshan county]. 1868.

Yongfeng xianzhi [Gazetteer of Yongfeng county]. 1544.

Yunju shengshui sizhi [Gazetteer of Yunju-Shengshui Monastery]. 1773.

Glossary and Index

Calendar, 63
Cannibalism, 104–5
Cao Zhao 曹昭 (fl. 1388), 76–79
Capitalism, 198–201
Carriages, 50–51, 67, 185, 186
Carters, 176, 246–47
Carts, 52, 90, 118, 174, 182, 241, 247
Catamites, 232–33
Censors, 51, 82, 104, 109, 170–71, 222
Census, 27–30, 94, 95, 162. See also
   Lijia; Taxation
Chenghua 成化: emperor (r. 1465–1487),
   97; era (1465–1487), 121, 225
Chen Longzheng 陳龍正 (1585–1656),
   209–10
Chen Yao 陳堯 (js. 1533), 220–22
Chen Zilong 陳子龍 (1608–47), 210, 230
Childbirth, 99
Ch'oe Pu 崔溥 (1454–1504), 15, 40,
   43–51, 75, 131
Chongwusuo, 147–48
Chongzhen 崇禎: emperor (r. 1628–44),
   163, 173, 222, 239
City God Temple, 211, 236, 239
Classic of Filial Piety (Xiao jing 孝經), 61
Classics Workshop (*Jing chang*), 129
Cloisonné (*jingtai lan* 景泰藍), 78
Clothing, 103, 113, 159–60; female, 184;
   lavish, 144, 149, 220–22; northern, 51;
   regulations, 30–31, 70, 219, 269n30,
   273n102; rural, 125; urban, 43. *See
   also* Fashion
Clunas, Craig, 78, 224, 226
Collectanea (*congshu* 叢書), 170
Columbus, Christopher, 124
Combs, 227
Commerce, 69, 101–23; commercial
   agents, 10, 119, 173, 189, 210,
   211; commercial carriers, 174;
   commercialization, 143, 197, 264n13;
   commercial networks, 9, 48, 71, 74,
   117, 144, 190, 210, 262; commercial
   tax (*shangshui*), xx, 10, 54, 69, 107–
   11; commercial transportation, xx,
   10, 34, 44, 48, 67, 90, 107, 208;
   commercial wealth, 93, 128, 259; and
   connoisseurship, 134–39; and culture,
   124–38; and the gentry, 211–15, 247–
   50, 261–62; and knowledge 129–34;
   and mobility, 28; and production, 198–
   201; social effects of, 9–11, 87, 147,
   160, 177; and the state, 69–70, 94; and
   transportation, 56, 66; and women,
   201–4. *See also* Confucianism;
   Markets; Trade
Commodities, 66, 69, 73–75, 79, 102,
   108, 114, 158, 160–61, 233

Communication, 10, 11, 30–57, 65, 94,
   171–73, 201, 264n13
*Comprehensive Gazetteer of the Ming
   Dynasty (Da Ming yitong zhi* 大明一
   統志), 129, 174, 179–80
*Comprehensive Illustrated Route Book
   (Yitong lucheng tuji),* 180
Concubines, 62, 107, 222, 234
Confucianism, 69, 90, 100, 102, 124–25,
   140–43, 151–52, 168, 170, 250;
   Confucian classics, 57, 39, 43, 62–65,
   71, 90–91, 103, 249; disdain for
   commerce, 71–72, 104, 134, 201; and
   money, 208–10; morality, 95, 213–18,
   232, 250–51; norms, 233
Connoisseurship (*shangjian* 賞鑒), 134–
   39, 218–37
Consumption, 102, 113, 144, 160, 192,
   194, 199, 201, 224; and production,
   190–204
Contracts, 58–62, 67
Convents, 157
Copper, 50, 68, 107, 112, 119, 160, 206,
   207, 209, 240; shortage, 154–58. *See
   also* Bronze
*Correct Source for a Myriad Practical
   Uses (Wanyong zhengzong* 萬用正宗),
   163–67, 214
Corvée labor, 7, 23, 28, 34, 64, 84; and
   commercialization, 48, 89, 207;
   commuted to cash payment, 81, 88,
   93–94
Cotton: clothing, 159, 220; crop, 113,
   192, 194–97; fabric, 114–16, 197,
   205; merchants dealing in, 179, 211;
   production, 195–99, 202; as tax item,
   xx
Counterfeit money, 63
Courier service (*yichuan* 驛傳), 10, 34,
   35, 37–40, 43–45, 50, 93–94, 176,
   186, 188; conveyance by, 34–51;
   routes, 38–39, 43–44, 48; soldiers,
   173; stations, 35–38, 39, 44, 48–49,
   88, 118, 173
Courtesans, 229–31
Court record (*chaobao* 朝報), 34
Cross-dressing, 247–50, 257
Culture, 11, 124–38, 139, 154, 237,
   264n13; high, 78, 144, 218–37, 250;
   local, 5, 73; popular, 58; public,
   150
Customs duties, 49, 70, 108

da Cruz, Gaspar, 44
Daoism: 8, 19, 57, 96, 156, 157, 192,
   193, 209, 250; as social model, 8, 19
de Morga, Antonio, 205–6

Compositor: Asco Trade Typesetting Limited
Text: 10/13 Sabon
Display: Sabon